MULTIPLE BARRIERS

The Multilevel Governance of Homelessness in Canada

Despite decades of efforts to combat homelessness, many people continue to experience it in Canada's major cities. There are a number of barriers that prevent effective responses to homelessness, including a lack of agreement on the fundamental question: what is homelessness?

In *Multiple Barriers*, Alison Smith explores the forces that shape intergovernmental and multilevel governance dynamics to help better understand why, despite the best efforts of community and advocacy groups, homelessness remains as persistent as ever. Drawing on nearly 100 interviews with key actors in Vancouver, Calgary, Toronto, and Montreal, as well as extensive participant observation, Smith argues that institutional differences across cities interact with ideas regarding homelessness to contribute to very different models of governance. *Multiple Barriers* shows that the genuine involvement of locally based service providers, with the development of policy, are necessary for an effective, equitable, and enduring solution to the homelessness crisis in Canada.

(Studies in Comparative Political Economy and Public Policy)

ALISON SMITH is an assistant professor of Political Science at the University of Toronto Mississauga.

Studies in Comparative Political Economy and Public Policy

For a list of books published in the series, see page 367.

MULTIPLE BARRIERS

The Multilevel Governance of Homelessness in Canada

Alison Smith

UNIVERSITY OF TORONTO PRESS
Toronto Buffalo London

© University of Toronto Press 2022
Toronto Buffalo London
utorontopress.com
Printed and bound by CPI Group (UK) Ltd, Croydon, CR0 4YY

ISBN 978-1-4875-4242-9 (cloth)   ISBN 978-1-4875-4244-3 (EPUB)
ISBN 978-1-4875-4243-6 (paper)   ISBN 978-1-4875-4245-0 (PDF)

Library and Archives Canada Cataloguing in Publication

Title: Multiple barriers : the multilevel governance of homelessness in
    Canada / Alison Smith.
Names: Smith, Alison (Professor of political science), author.
Series: Studies in comparative political economy and public policy.
Description: Series statement: Studies in comparative political economy
Identifiers: Canadiana (print) 20220175195 | Canadiana (ebook) 20220175314 |
    ISBN 9781487542436 (softcover) | ISBN 9781487542429 (hardcover) |
    ISBN 9781487542443 (EPUB) | ISBN 9781487542450 (PDF)
Subjects: LCSH: Homelessness – Government policy – Canada. |
    LCSH: Homeless persons – Government policy – Canada. |
    LCSH: Homeless persons – Services for – Government policy – Canada.
Classification: LCC HV4509.S65 2022 | DDC 362.5/920971–dc23

We wish to acknowledge the land on which the University of Toronto Press
operates. This land is the traditional territory of the Wendat, the Anishnaabeg,
the Haudenosaunee, the Métis, and the Mississaugas of the Credit First Nation.

University of Toronto Press acknowledges the financial support of the Government
of Canada, the Canada Council for the Arts, and the Ontario Arts Council, an
agency of the Government of Ontario, for its publishing activities.

Canada Council   **Conseil des Arts**
for the Arts   **du Canada**

ONTARIO ARTS COUNCIL
CONSEIL DES ARTS DE L'ONTARIO
an Ontario government agency
un organisme du gouvernement de l'Ontario

Funded by the   Financé par le
Government   gouvernement
of Canada   du Canada

Contents

Acknowledgments

This book took me a long time to write, spanning two parental leaves and two years (and counting) of a global pandemic. On bad days, what I understood to be my slow progress was frustrating and led me to doubt myself, this project, or both. Looking back, however, this time was necessary, for it allowed me to reflect carefully on the story I am trying to tell, to move things around, put things together, and make connections I didn't see during the first (or second or third) edit. Sometimes this reflection was in front me, on my computer screen, sometimes it came to me while I was walking circles around the block trying to get a baby to sleep. This work has been a privilege, and I have so many to thank.

My first thank you is to the people who participated in this research. Though the primary research was conducted before the pandemic, service providers have long been facing a housing crisis. When starting my fieldwork, I had assumed that many interview requests would go unanswered, so I sent out more than I thought I could handle. This often resulted in a scheduling pickle, because nearly everyone responded with some version of "happy to help." Service providers and those working with them have been underfunded, underappreciated, and overworked, yet they made time in their day to talk to me. Running around cities to meet them was an absolute honour and my favourite part of this research by a long shot. I thank them for their time, their stories, their reflections, their contributions, and their efforts to create a fairer and more equitable place.

Most of the empirical research for this book was conducted while I was a PhD student at l'Université de Montréal, under the supervision of Alain Noël. I sometimes think he is the only person who could have supervised me and this project. I first walked into his office in 2011, eager to tell what I thought was a story about urban governance. He responded, with equal enthusiasm, that provincial variation would be fascinating to track. Over the course of edits, rewrites, and restructures, I have realized that we were both partly right – this isn't just a story about urban governance, nor is it a story just about federalism; it is both. He was patient and supportive, intervening when I needed him to but giving me the space I needed as well. His influence extends not only through this book from the first to the last page, but to how I teach and continue to research. *Merci.*

Other faculty members at UdeM shaped this work directly, including Laurence Bherer and Denis Saint-Martin, from early conversations to final questions at my thesis defence. My thesis external examiner, Keith Banting, challenged me to think about what this could be as a book. Other profs at UdeM supported and challenged my understanding of this project; they included Christine Rothmayr-Allison, Richard Nadeau, and Éric Bélanger (at McGill), as well as André Blais, Jean-François Godbout, Vincent Arel-Bundock, Martin Papillon, Jane Jenson, and Eric Latimer (at McGill).

My classmates at UdeM saw this project when it was just a thesis proposal, asking me questions, telling me when things didn't make sense, and (finally) instructing me to call them "grandes villes" instead of "grosses villes." *Merci à* Joanie Thibault-Couture, Jean-Philippe Gauvin, Alexandre Blanchet, Alejandro Angel-Tapias, Benoît Morissette, Kaisa Vuoristo, Martin Beddeleem, and Daniel Marcelino. Thanks also to Chris Cooper, Sule Tomkinson, Mireille Paquet, Ludovic Rheault (with whom I have co-taught POL2100 at U of T!), and Maroine Bendaoud for conversations and questions. Though not directly related to this project, I have nevertheless learned a whole lot over the past few years through collaborations related to urban governance, multilevel governance, and homelessness with Zac Spicer, Carey Doberstein, Jack Lucas, Zack Taylor, Martin Horak, Neil Bradford, and Tari Ajadi; and Debra Thompson's book about ideas and institutions, *The Schematic State*, was a scholarly and intellectual roadmap for this work.

After a year of parental leave, I started my current position at the University of Toronto Mississauga. At UTM, I have been able to work alongside and with some of the best scholars and finest people, who have supported me throughout the process of writing this book and in navigating years as a junior scholar with a young family. I have been privileged to be part of an outstanding junior cohort at UTM, which includes Emily Nacol, Alexander Reisenbichler, Noel Anderson, Shivaji Mukherjee, Sarah Hughes, Naomi Adiv, Randy Besco, Martha Balaguera, Nadège Compaoré (a Pearson second year!), Arturo Chang, and Spyro Kotsovilis. Erin Tolley reached out to me before I even started my position and has consistently pulled up a chair for me, including at her own kitchen table for our writing groups. She has been the best mentor I could have asked for and I can't believe how lucky I was to have landed in her department for a few years; for the fritters, advice, and truth, I am grateful. Chairs Ronnie Beiner, Ed Schatz, and Andrea Olive have supported this project in many ways, from words of encouragement to funding dollars. Various meetings with junior faculty, especially Martha Balaguera, Nadège Compaoré, and Andrew McDougall, as well as Raul Pacheco-Vega, have helped me clarify some important pieces of this work. Thank you to research assistants Anna Kopec and James Ankers for such outstanding and varied help with this; Yasmine Gill, Fatima Sajid, Isra Wasim, and Farah Rana for informed, lively class discussions that helped me keep this book in perspective; and Arianne Padillo for consistently excellent RA support. My gratitude also goes to students I have taught in POL2100, who have directly or indirectly shaped my thinking and understanding of this project and how it fits in the subfield: Andreea Musulan, Marcus Closen, James Ankers, Joseph Dattilo, Alex Pekic, Etienne Cardin-Trudeau, Thomas Bergeron, Megan DeVries, Vanita Claire, Ashley Splawinski, Marc-Antoine Rancourt, Riley Yesno, Hayley Russell, Alison Anderson, and Sam Henderson.

The first time I co-taught POL2100, U of T's core Canadian politics seminar for PhD students, it was with Chris Cochrane. I'm thankful that he was my co-instructor that year, as he made every effort to make my load lighter, to fact-check, and to help me translate feedback or reviews. I have also co-taught with Robert Schertzer. He has a big heart and no ego and has shown up for me every time I have asked him to (which has been a lot, considering our very similar research perspectives). They have become valued friends and mentors. I also thank other mentors for interventions – specific, requested, and unexpected – including Jonathan Malloy, Peter Loewen, and Robert Campbell. I knew the first time that I met Amanda Bittner, when she reviewed my CV on a CPSA break at UBC, that she was that hard to find, big sister, special kind of mentor, and I'm so grateful for her texts, advice, and friendship.

Daniel Quinlan has a stellar reputation as an editor, yet he fully exceeded all of my expectations throughout the process of working on this book. Working with me over the course of the pandemic can't have been easy, but he was endlessly flexible and used every opportunity to take pressure off me, all while never letting me doubt that he believed in me and this project. Thanks also to managing editor Christine Robertson, to copy editor Matthew Kudelka (thanks also for the secret goulash ingredient!), as well as to Siusan Moffat for an impeccable index.

Thank you to the many people who hosted me during fieldwork or while I was working away on this project: Solanna, Dan, Fahreen,

Auntie Marilynn and Uncle Alan, Joy and Peter, Ritu, Pam, Stacey and Graham, and Aunt Sue. Heather and Robert have done more than host; they have welcomed me into their home as family. And thank you to Thomas Kerr and Tim Richter, who provided an institutional home for me while I was doing research in Vancouver and Calgary respectively.

Thank you to two anonymous reviewers who undoubtedly helped make this book a much, much better one. Transforming this from a thesis into a book and responding to those reviews was challenging, and at one point I had to phone a couple of experts. Rianne Mahon and Daniel Béland so graciously made the trip to Toronto to spend a day with me in a book workshop. Daniel Béland explained how to write a strong conclusion, not just for my book but for future work. Using gifs and talking with his hands, he insisted that a conclusion should go BOOM, and then explained exactly how to make it so. I pass his advice along every chance I get. Early in the workshop, Rianne Mahon leaned forward, put her hands on the table, looked me in the eye, and told me to tell my own story. It was as much of a push as it was permission to believe in myself, something I needed to hear, and I thank her so sincerely for that. The purpose of the workshop was to work through my reviews, but, good mentors that they are, they used it for much more than that, so their influence will continue well beyond the pages of this book.

I was part way through a serious reorganizing edit of this book when the pandemic hit (as I write this, it has been two years ago to the day). Daycares closed but universities stayed open, and I wasn't sure how that was going to work. Like I often do when I need help, I texted Erin Tolley. She sent me a link to what was at first affectionately called "Amanda Bittner's writing group," now the SMASH lab collective. This group has met on Zoom through various lockdowns and has continued to meet and write even during periodic reopenings. We have laughed, cried, raged, supported, advised, "just" listened, grieved, celebrated, comforted, commiserated, strategized, woop-wooped, and uplifted. (We also write.) They have been a gift, and words will never allow me to fully express to them my gratitude. They are Amanda Almond, Victor Asal, Julia Azari, Salil Benegal, Amanda Bittner, Daria Boltokova, Yolande Bouka, Christine Bricker, Leonore Camarena, Erin Cassesse, Alana Cattapan, Gina Comeau, Nyron Crawford, Melody Crowder-Meyer, María Martín de Almagro, Jennifer Decerff, Nana aba Duncan, Megan Gaucher, Roxana Gutierrez-Romero, Carmen Jacqueline Ho, Cat Jones, Elizabeth Juhasz, Veronica Kitchen, Sharon Lauricella, Jamie Levine Daniel, Sarah Martin, Heather Millar, Lama Mourad, Lori Lee Oates, Neema Opiyo, Mireille Paquet, Raul Pacheco-Vega, Kate Perry, Luxana Reynaga-Ornelas, Joelle Rodway, Lara Rusch, Beth Schwartz,

Jenn Selby, Heather Smith, Tabbey Sindani, Mara Sidney, Elizabeth Strom, Marcela Suarez, Carole Therrien, Lahoma Thomas, Erin Tolley, Bertha Vallejo, Nadia Verrelli, and Christiana Zenner.

Childcare is always important for working parents, even more so during a pandemic. Ruth-Anne Baldry was heaven-sent. Heather and Robert have filled large childcare gaps during transitions, closures, busy days, and what may have seemed to be an endless number of "book pushes." Planned and sometimes impromptu "games with Bubbe" have added up and made a big difference in allowing me to get this done. My big brother Adam has been cheering me on for as long as I've been alive and has now turned much of that attention to his nephews. He has been the most wonderful uncle; when he visits, he dotes on my boys, tidies, and does the dishes. During the pandemic, he has had lunch with my boys on FaceTime every single week, giving them something to look forward to and affording me a little extra time to write (or nap).

Over coffee and a treat in the Byward Market in Ottawa in 2010, I told my mom that I wanted to do a PhD but also that I thought I couldn't do it. She told me I was wrong, and she was right. My mom and dad taught me to love to read, to ask questions, and to finish things (even if they take a long time). I likely would not have set out on this journey if they hadn't believed in me. During the pandemic, when we have been apart for unbearable lengths of time (them in BC, us in Ontario), my parents have spent time *almost every single day* of the past two years reading, colouring, and playing chess/uno/checkers/golf with their grandsons on the iPad. This has kept their bond with my boys strong while allowing me some extra time to write (or nap!). Before the pandemic, they stepped up in a big way, my mom especially, coming to visit and creating space for me to work away on edits and filling my freezer with pre-made meals and treats.

Insofar as this book has a dedication, it is to the people who participated in the research and those working with them. This book might well not even exist, however, were it not for Xander. The only word that can describe his relationship to me is partner. He has read and reviewed every possible version of this, from a tiny baby research proposal for a PhD application, to a research design, to a thesis, to various versions of this book. He has always loved and never doubted me. He has created and held space for me, supported my career, and been the best possible dad I could ever have imagined. I don't think I could have done any of it without him, nor would I have wanted to.

My beautiful boys, Bo and Leo, have made me laugh and filled me with love every day of their lives. I love everything about them, and

I always will. Watching them learn, their joy in getting up after falling, and their persistent insistence on figuring things out have been a
reminder that learning is hard but also a delightful, wonderful thing.
They are beautiful little researchers who show me how to do my job
well, looking at things from every possible side and answering each
answer with another why. They have contributed to this project directly
by keeping things in very proper perspective, whether that's in terms
of a bad writing day or in terms of the injustice of the fact that so many
people are without housing. This book took such a long time in part because of my beautiful little boys, and for that I can't thank them enough.

MULTIPLE BARRIERS

1 Introduction

Nowadays, people don't seem to be shocked that children, pregnant women, seniors are homeless. But it certainly was very shocking for us [in the 1990s]. A clear sign that something was happening. Not just more alcoholics. There was something going on in the housing system causing this catastrophic failure and more and more people were out there.

Toronto advocate Michael Shapcott (personal interview, 2014)

The reality for the Indigenous population in Canada is that the government of Canada at all levels, federal and provincial particularly, worked very hard for many generations to render Indigenous peoples landless. The result was that Indigenous people were moved from place to place, or forced to relocate, or had their rights, their entitlement to stay in a particular area taken away from them or interfered with ...

There's no question that the impoverishment of Indigenous people was a forced impoverishment. This was created impoverishment by the Government of Canada.

Murray Sinclair (personal interview, 2018)

When the COVID-19 pandemic hit in March 2020, the instruction from public health officials was to stay home. This assumes, of course, that everyone has a home. That is far from the reality in Canada, where tens of thousands of people are unhoused or underhoused. The global health crisis collided with the Canadian housing crisis, and homeless encampments developed across the country. These encampments would appear to be related to COVID-19, and in a very direct way they were; for example, emergency shelters decreased their capacity in order to enforce social distancing to limit the transmission of the respiratory virus, meaning people were forced outdoors. But the reality is that the pandemic exposed what was already known, turning a largely hidden, or ignored, reality of homelessness into a highly visible one in public spaces and parks.

The housing system in Canada consistently fails to provide a safe and adequate home for everyone, instead forcing people to live in insecure environments – in emergency shelters, overcrowded spaces, or inadequate or unsafe housing. The pandemic was a shock to a system that was already inadequate, and the profound housing insecurity in which some of the most vulnerable people in Canada live is nothing new. Indeed, activists and advocates have long warned that our emergency shelter system is vulnerable to an infectious respiratory virus (Crowe 2019; Leung et al. 2008). They begged and pleaded with governments to implement housing-based solutions to homelessness, to no avail. Weaknesses and fault lines were known. Under the pressure of a global pandemic, the system burst apart. Understanding why a country as rich, and as cold, as Canada has failed to protect people from homelessness is an important motivation of this book. It is not inevitable that tens of thousands of people do not have homes. Rather, it is the result of colonialism, of action and inaction, and of decades of decisions about policies and priorities. Homelessness is political.

It is difficult to know exactly how many people experience homelessness in Canada. Figures vary widely depending on the definition of homelessness that is used, and any estimate is almost certainly an underestimate. While challenging to measure, a widely cited study by researchers at the Canadian Observatory on Homelessness estimates that between 30,000 and 35,000 people are homeless on any given night in Canada and that 235,000 people are homeless over the course of one given year. This is in addition to upwards of 50,000 people per year who are said to experience hidden homelessness, including those who lack permanent housing of their own but find shelter by couch-surfing with friends or acquaintances, or live in overcrowded or otherwise unsafe environments (Gaetz et al. 2016). A 2020 poll reinforced the finding that homelessness is a relatively widespread experience, with 5 per cent of respondents indicating that they had experienced homelessness themselves and 10 per cent saying they have a family member who has experienced homelessness (CAEH 2020c). This suggests that 1.5 million Canadians have been homeless at some point in their life. More and more seniors and children are counted among the homeless population; Indigenous people, racialized people, and queer youth are overrepresented among the homeless population (ESDC 2017), revealing deep and wide inequities in social protection. This is a tremendous failure of the welfare state.

The Canadian Alliance to End Homelessness (CAEH) estimates that it would cost $44 billion over ten years to end homelessness in Canada (Gaetz et al. 2014). Much of this would be for investments in affordable housing and supports. Housing and social services, including various forms of health care and income support, have been woefully underfunded in Canada, leaving vulnerable people unable to access the services they require to find and maintain adequate housing. Calls for increased funding are justified, for expanded services are sorely needed. Systemic and structural reforms – including to child welfare, drug policy, health, and policing – are needed just as urgently so that homelessness is prevented in the first place. But ending homelessness is not just a spending problem: efforts to combat homelessness must also be coordinated. This book endorses the call for increased funding and system reforms as necessary measures in fighting and preventing homelessness. But it also assumes that homelessness is a complex problem and requires the involvement of a multiplicity of actors. Its primary purpose, therefore, is to identify why groups and governments do or do not become involved in the fight against homelessness in the first place, and why they do or do not work together in their efforts. Funding matters. But so does governance.

Governance Matters

Studies have shown that governance dynamics – who does what and with whom – directly affect the quality of the social protection produced by the Canadian welfare state. Keith Banting's work has demonstrated that the intergovernmental mix that characterizes the governance of different social policies matters to the social protection that is produced and how that protection evolves over time (Banting 1990, 2012, 2020). Banting has found that policies under shared governance arrangements (such as pensions and health care, which involve federal and provincial governments) tend to be more stable and resistant to retrenchment because such changes require intergovernmental agreement (Banting 2012). Policies governed by one actor, such as social assistance, however, are more vulnerable to change and retrenchment because a single government can act on its own without needing the consent of another. These governance dynamics help explain what many see as a baffling contradiction of the Canadian welfare state, which is that health care has remained universal whereas other areas of social protection, including housing and social assistance, have become much more targeted and less generous.

With respect to homelessness, Canadian and international scholars have also found that governance matters to the effectiveness of policy solutions. Examining cities in Canada, the United States, and Europe, using a variety of methods ranging from participant observation to statistical analysis, these studies are uniform in their conclusion that governance matters. Carey Doberstein (2016) studied networks created to implement the federal National Homelessness Initiative/Homelessness Partnering Strategy in Vancouver, Calgary, and Toronto and found that inclusive and institutionalized governance networks design more innovative solutions than ones that are not. In Vancouver, local homelessness governance networks meet regularly, bringing together a wide-ranging membership that includes representatives from civil society, Indigenous communities, and the local bureaucracy. This inclusive and institutionalized network allows actors to bring their expertise and different perspectives into conversation frequently, resulting in innovative and coordinated action. In Toronto, by contrast, the city has long dominated the homelessness policy field, historically seeking little input from civil society actors. In part due to the lack of inclusive and institutionalized governance, the city's response to homelessness was stagnant for years. In a similar study of the local governance of homelessness in Amsterdam, Copenhagen, and Glasgow, Nienke Boesveldt finds that "heterogeneous" governance networks lead to more effective policy outputs, such as improved quality of housing and emergency shelter services, and that "centralized" systems tend to be more efficient. She concludes emphatically that "governance really does matter" (Boesveldt 2015, 179).

Christopher Leo and Martine August draw similar conclusions regarding the importance of governance dynamics. In their study of the early operations of the federal National Homelessness Initiative in Winnipeg, they found that local leaders were not involved in setting the community objectives for NHI funding. The exclusion of Winnipeg-based voices meant that the NHI was not responsive to the fact that homelessness in Winnipeg is different than it is in other cities. They conclude that the NHI precluded "the types of solutions that will actually work to alleviate homelessness in Winnipeg" (Leo and August 2006, 1). They go on to note that local interests and expertise must be considered more closely all throughout the policy-making process if national policy is to be more responsive to local needs.

Governance dynamics are found to be of similar significance to homelessness policy in the United States. David Lee and Michael McGuire conclude that intergovernmental alignment – from the local to the national level – leads to improved homelessness program outcomes: "county governments aligned with federal and state governments are likely to provide more permanent housing properties than county governments not aligned" (D. Lee and McGuire 2017, 640). They continue, "the federal homelessness program has a larger impact on the chronic homelessness population ... when county governments have direct, official intergovernmental alignment than in county governments not aligned in this way" (640–2). Also in the US context, Charley Willison (2021) asks what shapes the involvement of municipal governments in homelessness governance. She contends that the decentralization of responsibility for homelessness and a lack of coordination among policy actors (service providers, economic elites, municipal governments, and states) results in increased policy opportunities for private-sector actors. Where governance dynamics privilege private-sector actors over service providers and homeless people, policy responses tend to criminalize homelessness. In contrast, when policy actions are coordinated and less decentralized, municipalities are more likely to adopt evidence-based approaches to homelessness.[1]

These studies of the local, intergovernmental and multilevel governance of homelessness make clear that governance matters. But they leave unexplored the pressing questions of what shapes the governance networks that have emerged and why they are so different. Local governance dynamics clearly impact homelessness policy innovation, effectiveness, and efficiency, and intergovernmental alignment has been shown to lead to greater reductions in chronic homelessness. It is because governance is clearly so important that this book takes a necessary step back to ask *what shapes these governance networks in the first place*. What factors influence the development of homelessness governance networks? Why do some actors with ample authority and resources sit on the sidelines while others with no authority and scant resources take the lead? Why do some actors work together whereas others do not? Why are some governance arrangements more inclusive than others? The remainder of this book considers these questions, evaluating two decades of action and inaction in Vancouver, Calgary, Toronto, and Montreal from 2000 to 2020.

Overview of Cases

As this section will explain, the governance of homelessness varies considerably in big cities across Canada. This book considers why these homelessness governance networks have developed and continue to evolve so differently across Canada, specifically in Vancouver, Calgary,

Toronto, and Montreal. I ask why some governance networks are centralized while others are more fragmented. Where networks are fragmented, I ask whether actors collaborate, and if not, why? If they do not collaborate, do they coordinate? Where they are centralized, I ask about the roles played by other actors: Are they included by the centralizing agency? If yes, how? If not, why? What role do Indigenous-led services and organizations play in homelessness governance? What role do people who are or who have been homeless play in homelessness governance? Are they meaningfully involved in policy development? Deep case studies and cross-case comparisons provide valuable insights into what forces shape governance. In identifying what motivates the formation of these governance networks and their evolution, I hope this book will help strengthen the governance of homelessness in large Canadian cities and reinforce social protection for those who find themselves without a home of their own.

Vancouver

Homelessness governance in Vancouver is fragmented and includes deep divisions not just between but also within sectors. Six actors or networks are involved in homelessness governance: the province; the city; the StreetoHome Foundation; two regional networks – the Regional Steering Committee on Homelessness and the Aboriginal Steering Committee on Homelessness – which were set up to steward federal homelessness funding in 1999; and, though they do not have a specific plan on homelessness, third-sector groups are also deeply involved in homelessness governance.

Actors coordinate with one another relatively well, with certain exceptions. British Columbia has long been one of the most interventionist and innovative provinces in Canada when it comes to housing policy, and it plays a leading role in homelessness governance in Vancouver. After the federal government stopped funding new social housing in the 1990s, the province of BC continued to invest in the development of new units.[2] Except for five years in the early 2000s, BC has continually committed to funding new housing developments, most of which are now for people experiencing homelessness. In 2006, the responsibility for homelessness was transferred from the Ministry of Social Development to BC Housing, allowing for a direct link between housing and homelessness in provincial policy. The City of Vancouver has also been involved in homelessness governance for decades, though it has done so without official jurisdiction. Following a series of plans that depended extensively on senior government funding in the early 2000s (and were undermined by a lack of said funding), left-of-centre mayor Gregor Robertson, elected in 2008, made the bold promise to end street homelessness by 2015 and, importantly, to do so using city powers as much as possible. This promise was ultimately not kept; even so, the city invested significantly in homelessness services, and for years the fight against homelessness was the city's top priority.

The StreetoHome Foundation, a non-governmental group with strong ties to the private sector, emerged at the same time that Robertson was implementing his plan to end street homelessness. The StreetoHome Foundation, which resulted from right-of-centre Mayor Sam Sullivan's *Project Civil City*, was intended to increase the participation of private-sector actors in homelessness governance. It developed a ten-year plan to end homelessness (2010–20), which, though it did not meet its goal, contributed to the creation of partnerships with the province and municipal governments to develop new supportive housing throughout the city. Third-sector groups do not have a formal policy or plan on homelessness, but they are deeply involved in advocacy at all levels. They also participate directly in policy development and implementation, particularly at the local level (and especially when their political allies are in control of City Council). Finally, two regional networks, one Indigenous and one non-Indigenous, are involved in the governance of homelessness in Vancouver, specifically in the administration of federal funding. These two regional groups are well organized, meet frequently, and coordinate closely.

There are power struggles among various actors in Vancouver, notably with respect to who should lead in the fight, yet there is also a high degree of coordination and collaboration among them. For example, a 2003 plan developed by the Regional Steering Committee on Homelessness directly influenced both the StreetoHome Plan (2010) and two 2005 City of Vancouver plans. The two regional networks coordinate consistently, and the province and city collaborate on projects to develop housing for people experiencing homelessness, with both partners bringing valuable resources and expertise to the policy-making table. And while there are tensions between the city and the province in terms of blame and credit, officials at both levels nevertheless insist on the importance of working together and describe their relations in family terms. The province has also been very willing to work with the federal government on housing and homelessness projects. Local actors involved in homelessness governance coordinate their efforts formally and informally, even when they are advancing slightly different goals. Some deeper divisions exist, however, notably within the third sector and within the political party representing the political left, which can destabilize governance dynamics, resulting in decreased influence and involvement of those actors. At times, influential groups have been at odds with one another, pulling in different directions, a dynamic that is unfortunate but not unique to Vancouver.

Montreal

The governance of homelessness is similarly fragmented in Montreal, where the province, the city, two local third sector networks, and two regional networks are involved (one to implement the provincial plan and one to implement the federal NHI/HPS; unlike other cities, there is no "Indigenous community" network to oversee federal homelessness funding specifically for Indigenous people in Montreal, as I will discuss below). Some groups coordinate and collaborate fully, but others – especially locally – do not. The province has taken a leadership role for decades. In 1999, provincial officials insisted on jointly governing, with their federal counterparts, federal NHI/HPS funding that everywhere else in the country flows directly to the local level. The province also adopted a plan on homelessness in 2010, a homelessness policy in 2014 (including an updated definition), and a second plan on homelessness in 2015. The plans are led by the Minister of Health – an interesting contrast with BC Housing's leadership in BC. Quebec's involvement and actions are informed by extensive community consultation and involvement; even so, provincial documents make clear the view that the province of Quebec is the main actor responsible for homelessness.

In Quebec, third-sector groups have an institutionalized role in policy-making, meaning they have access to the policy-making process in a number of venues and channels; they therefore play an important role in homelessness governance. Homelessness service providers organized in the 1970s to create the RAPSIM (the Réseau d'aide aux personnes seules et itinérantes de Montréal), an organization that represents homeless people as well as service providers. The RAPSIM is frequently identified by the city and the province as a main partner in the fight against homelessness. The RAPSIM does not have a plan *per se* but does have an approach to ending homelessness that it has long promoted: social housing with community supports. More recently, the MMFIM (Mouvement pour mettre fin à l'itinérance à Montréal) has been created, a group that has strong ties to Canadian networks, including the Canadian Alliance to End Homelessness. The MMFIM advances a different approach to homelessness than the RAPSIM – Housing First – and developed a plan to end homelessness in Montreal in 2015. The two groups overlap considerably in terms of their membership – even in terms of their founding members – yet they advance different visions of homelessness, propose different solutions to it, and do not coordinate formally.

The City of Montreal has been involved in homelessness governance since at least the 1980s, when city officials developed a definition of homelessness that was subsequently adopted by the province. That definition remained in effect until the provincial policy on homelessness was introduced in 2014. City officials have been guided by a liaison committee on homelessness since the 1990s, which is comprised of service provider representatives and advocates, and they have relied on that committee to inform their actions and decisions related to homelessness. The committee wrote a draft plan on homelessness for the city in 2007; it was not immediately adopted, but it informed the city's first official plan on homelessness in 2010. In this early municipal plan, the city was narrowly involved in homelessness governance, stressing that its limited powers prevented it from doing more; rather, the city looked to the province for leadership. This changed in 2013 with the election of Mayor Denis Coderre, who saw a greater role for the City of Montreal in the fight against homelessness and in urban governance more generally. Accordingly, he sought to increase the city's powers through negotiations with the province. The 2014 city plan on homelessness introduced under Mayor Coderre broke from provincial plans and priorities and sought to expand the city's powers so that it could assume more of a leadership role in homelessness. Valérie Plante, who replaced Coderre as mayor in 2017 (and defeated him again in 2021), was critical of many of Coderre's policies; Mayor Plante has nevertheless maintained significant continuity with the 2014 plan, but is also seeking to align the city's work with future provincial plans.

A regional group is responsible for developing an action plan for Montreal for federal NHI/HPS funding. When the federal government imposed requirements on this funding in 2014, stipulating that 65 per cent of the funding in big cities must go to Housing First programs (a development reviewed more fully in chapter 3), some local groups objected and demanded that the co-governing province object. The federal government would not change these terms, and the province agreed to them. Following this decision, however, a second regional plan was developed to implement the province's homelessness plan, which specifically did *not* prioritize Housing First. These two plans were overseen by the same person, allowing for coordination and information-sharing between them despite their different objectives, resulting in a rich array of services available at the regional level. Unlike in big cities outside of Quebec, there is no Indigenous network in Montreal to oversee the implementation of federal National Homelessness Initiative/Homelessness Partnering Strategy funding for Indigenous people, perhaps a result of the colonial division of powers between federal and provincial governments that give the federal government authority for Indigenous people and their lands (Section 91(24)). The province is not involved in the administration of this funding, and Indigenous groups apply directly to the federal government (though they can also apply to the non-Indigenous regional network).

Calgary

These fragmented models of governance can be contrasted with Calgary, where a single organization, the Calgary Homeless Foundation (CHF), dominates the homelessness policy space, though the province and an Indigenous network have come to play an influential role over time as well. The CHF was founded in the late 1990s by a small group of business leaders primarily from the oil and gas sector. From a small organization with five employees in the late 1990s, it has grown into a large foundation with dozens of employees. By 2008 it was overseeing tens of millions of dollars per year in funding, and was tasked with implementing a ten-year plan to end homelessness in Calgary. The CHF administers provincial and federal homelessness funding, including dollars that are designated for Indigenous communities by the federal NHI/HPS. Most service providers in the city have aligned with the CHF and its vision. Where there have been disagreements, agencies have tended to be either marginalized or eventually won over by the CHF. The Aboriginal Standing Committee on Housing and Homelessness (ASCHH), the community advisory board for the federal NHI/HPS, developed what was at the time the only plan to end Indigenous homelessness in Canada in 2012; this plan was developed following frustration and disappointment that Indigenous voices were not more fully included in the CHF's plan to end homelessness. During the early 2000s, the relationship between the ASCHH and the CHF was difficult and characterized by distrust; this relationship has started to improve, however, as the CHF has become more inclusive and less dominant in Calgary.

The municipal government has had little involvement in homelessness governance, though in the 1990s the City of Calgary was one of the first cities in Canada to begin regularly conducting homeless counts. Yet even this responsibility was transferred to the CHF in 2008, and the city now plays a supporting role in the CHF's efforts. Of the municipal governments considered here, it is the least involved in the issue. The heavy-hitting business leaders who positioned the CHF to become the lead actor in the fight against homelessness were instrumental in getting the municipal government and even the provincial government to support the plan and invest in it. Working with allies in other cities across Alberta, business leaders convinced the province to develop its own ten-year plan on homelessness, in close collaboration with what was being done at the local level, an example of local business leaders uploading social policy and driving the provincial agenda. The province has thus gone from a laggard in the 1990s and early 2000s to a leader in Canada: it was the first province to adopt a ten-year plan to end homelessness and has developed extensive coordination between agencies and departments. That said, the ten-year plans to end homelessness in Calgary and Alberta did not succeed. Key actors identify the lack of investment in affordable housing and a lack of systemic reforms as the main reasons for this. Under the leadership of the NDP and Rachel Notley, the province committed to developing a provincial housing strategy for the first time since the 1990s, but that commitment has waned significantly under Jason Kenney's United Conservative Party.

Toronto

One actor dominates the governance of homelessness in Toronto as well: the municipal government. Having been given the responsibility for housing and homelessness through provincial devolution in the 1990s, Toronto is the only municipality under study here to have official jurisdiction for the administration and funding of housing and homelessness. In addition to formal jurisdiction, the city also has density bonusing powers and was recently given inclusionary zoning powers by the province, meaning it is institutionally the strongest municipality in this study. The City of Toronto guarded its housing and homelessness powers jealously for many years, leaving little space for third-sector, private-sector, or Indigenous-led groups to contribute expertise to the policy-making process. That has changed recently: city officials have opened the door to more collaboration with third-sector groups, particularly the Toronto Alliance to End Homelessness (TAEH). The province is involved in homelessness governance through funding transfers to the City of Toronto and by stewarding the housing system. In this capacity, the province's involvement has evolved over time, peaking in the mid-2010s, when provincial officials committed to ending homelessness in Ontario. That commitment has faded under Doug Ford's Progressive Conservative government.

As noted, the city has long governed homelessness with little formal involvement of private or third-sector groups. It is somewhat surprising that the city's strong private sector and its passionate third sector have *not* been more institutionally involved in homelessness governance in the past, though not all movements seek formal involvement (Withers 2021). The Toronto Disaster Relief Committee, lacking a formal or institutionalized relationship with the city through the 1990s and early 2000s, was at key moments able to influence not only Toronto's responses to homelessness but federal ones as well. The TDRC disbanded in 2012; following this, province-wide groups such as the Ontario Coalition Against Poverty (OCAP) and, very recently, the Encampment Support Network (ESN) pressured the municipal government to act, sometimes with important success (Withers 2021). But there was no Toronto-specific advocacy group that filled the gap created when the TDRC disbanded until 2015, when the Toronto Alliance to End Homelessness (TAEH) formed with the explicit purpose of engaging with the city. This has led to the creation of a venue for the co-governance of federal homelessness funding, though this is not without controversy (Withers 2021). The city also controls non-Indigenous federal NHI/HPS funding. Federal NHI/HPS funding for Indigenous communities is governed separately by an Indigenous advisory board and administered by the Aboriginal Labour Force Development Agency. There is increasing collaboration between the Indigenous HPS network, the non-Indigenous one (TAEH), and the city, but this is recent. In Toronto, therefore, significant power is concentrated in the city, and its institutional strength has increased recently with the addition of inclusionary zoning powers to its policy toolbox. Despite this increase in institutional strength, the city has also become more open to third-sector involvement.

Argument

The objective of this book is to more fully map and explain these very different power and governance dynamics. For more than two decades, service providers, outreach workers, Indigenous-led organizations, and others have worked ingeniously to turn shoestring budgets and inadequate resources into – with no hint of exaggeration – life-saving solutions to homelessness. Abandoned by senior governments on the front lines of what advocates have long called a crisis, they have supported thousands of people who have been left with nowhere to go but the streets. If the welfare state is a safety net, the federal and many provincial governments have made cuts to it, wide and deep. Primarily local groups have done their very best to patch the safety net back together; to continue the analogy, lacking adequate financial resources they have done so in the classic Canadian fashion of repair with duct tape. Despite

their efforts, the number of people experiencing homelessness continues to grow as more people fall into homelessness year after year. This
book seeks to understand why, from a governance perspective, that is
the case. Doing so will shed light on why progress in the fight against
homelessness has been so difficult. Theoretically, this will contribute to
our understanding of the drivers of multilevel governance in complex
policy areas and to our ability to assess the state of social protection in
the context of a federal, but also highly urbanized, welfare state.

I begin this book with the assumption, supported by the literature,
that governance matters. The purpose of this book, then, is to explain
why different patterns of governance have emerged in Vancouver, Calgary, Toronto, and Montreal and to consider what consequences this
may have for social protection in Canada. As I will show, the causes of
homelessness are complex and can be traced to the actions and inactions
of various levels of government and sectors of society. It follows, then,
that homelessness governance and the production of social protection
for people who are homeless require the involvement of all these groups
and sectors. To make this even more challenging, it requires not just the
involvement but the collaboration, or at least coordination, of multiple
groups. In the pages that follow, I consider as many as seven distinct
groups of actors[3]: the federal government; provincial governments;
municipal governments; third-sector actors; private-sector actors; and
two regional or otherwise local networks set up to administer federal
NHI/HPS funding, one for Indigenous-led groups (referred to as Aboriginal Communities and more recently as Indigenous Communities)
and one for the general population (referred to as Designated Communities, though this network also funds Indigenous-led services)[4].

To explain different governance dynamics, I consider these actors as
they relate to two dimensions of multilevel governance. The first is their
involvement in various parts of the policy-making process (advocacy,
policy development, funding, and implementation [Horak 2012]). I also
consider who is perceived to be the leader or – as we see in a number
of cases – how many different actors view themselves as the leader. The
second dimension of multilevel governance is the *interactions* among
and within the different groups of actors. In cases of relatively centralized governance (Calgary and Toronto), I ask whether the governance
dynamic is inclusive of other actors, notably third-sector, private-sector,
and Indigenous-led groups and networks. In fragmented cases where a
number of actors are involved (Vancouver and Montreal), I ask whether
they coordinate with one another, collaborate, or work at cross-purposes, and I explain why. To do this, I develop an innovative framework that combines insights from research on multilevel governance

in Canada with a growing body of research that considers ideational processes in social policy development.

I insist on the importance of *ideas*, but I also draw attention to ways in which actors were constrained or enabled by *resources* and *institutions*. Involvement may be easier when financial resources are abundant and may be more difficult when they are constrained. Furthermore, resources are not just financial, though financial resources are particularly important for certain actors, notably governments and the private sector. Resources of other kinds – such as expertise and political connections – are of tremendous value in complex place-based policy-making, and they often drive the involvement of local actors in particular. Literature on multilevel governance also stresses the importance of institutions, particularly the importance of policy jurisdiction (Horak 2012). If a government has jurisdiction over housing and homelessness, its involvement is much more likely; likewise, local governments with no formal jurisdiction over housing but that nevertheless have important related powers – such as density bonusing and inclusionary zoning – are more likely to be involved. Non-governmental actors are more likely to be involved in policy governance when there are *institutionalized* venues or other avenues for involvement that allow for relationship-building, the exchange of information, and a recognition of their value as partners. Absent an institutionalized role, these groups seek to use key relationships with sympathetic insiders or with their own personal connections to push their ideas into policy-making discussions.

A consideration of institutions and resources goes a long way toward allowing us to understand multilevel governance dynamics. The City of Toronto, for example, is responsible for housing policy; it is therefore unsurprising that its involvement in the governance of homelessness is comparatively high. Similarly, the private sector in Calgary, which led the charge in the fight against homelessness, has extensive resources and personal relationships with powerful elected officials that have facilitated its deep involvement. Yet focusing just on institutions and resources leaves important questions unanswered. For example, why did the province of Alberta remain uninvolved in housing and homelessness policy for so long, despite its clear jurisdiction over the issue and abundant financial resources? Why has the wealthy private sector in Toronto not been more involved in homelessness governance? Why did the City of Vancouver, with few material resources and no formal jurisdiction, take on such a leadership role? And why are there multiple, locally based advocacy organizations in the same city in some cases? To answer these questions, I turn to an important body of literature that points to the role of ideas in shaping behaviour, which in this case translates into governance dynamics. An important contribution of this book is that while institutions and resources matter, ideas are often even more powerful in shaping governance dynamics.

Three kinds of ideas complete the explanation of what shapes multilevel governance dynamics. The first idea relates to social protection. Ideas regarding whose role it is to produce social protection for those experiencing homelessness differ across cities and sectors (Jenson 2013). These ideas matter for all actors and include ideas regarding their *own* role in the production of social protection as well as ideas about the role of *other* actors (i.e., which actor should or should not lead). Interacting with this idea in some instances are ideas regarding federalism, which can have implications for an actor's understanding of the responsibility to produce social protection as it relates to the division of powers between federal and provincial governments.

The second idea that shapes governance dynamics occurs at the local level; ideas regarding the "conceptualization" of the city's role matter (Horak 2012). If local officials conceptualize the city's role as that of a comprehensive government with wide-ranging responsibilities, rather than simply a service provider or policy implementer, the city is much more likely to be involved in homelessness governance. The third idea that shapes governance dynamics relates to the definition of homelessness. As I will discuss in chapter 2, there has been significant evolution in how homelessness is understood by policy-makers, moving from definitions focused on individual causes to those that blame systemic and structural factors (interacting with individual-level factors) as well as colonialism. Legitimate disagreements exist as to whether homelessness is primarily about housing; about housing *and* community; or according to an Indigenous definition (Thistle 2017), a more holistic definition that encompasses relationships with land, ancestors, and traditions (definitions are reviewed thoroughly in chapter 2). Ideas regarding the nature of homelessness can, in some instances, drive the involvement of actors in homelessness governance, but this kind of idea more often structures the interactions of actors. Where there is agreement on the definition of homelessness, groups are more likely to work together. Disagreements on the nature of homelessness are by no means fatal to overall efforts to fight homelessness, but they can lead to fragmentation. The pages that follow include examples of disagreements over the nature of homelessness that have led to instability, but there are also examples of productive, coordinated disagreements.

Interacting with ideas, local institutions can facilitate collaboration or can drive a wedge between disagreeing groups. In other words, institutions may facilitate the coordination of ideational disagreements, but a different institutional landscape may turn a seemingly small disagreement into a significant one. Following the work of Béland and Waddan (2015), this book concludes that ideas in interaction with institutions shape governance dynamics. Interacting with institutions, I contend that ideas influence governance networks through environmental and cognitive mechanisms (Jenson 2010). In some instances, ideas become particularly powerful and turn into "coalition magnets" (Béland and Cox 2016). When an idea becomes a coalition magnet, it attracts individuals or groups to work together in a coalition, including people with sometimes widely divergent political beliefs. Ambiguous ideas, which mean different things to different people, are particularly powerful magnets. Just as magnets can attract, they can also repel; similarly, the magnetism of ideas can pull people together but can also push them apart. Ambiguous ideas can be powerful in building diverse networks, but they can also lead to fragmentation or instability. All ideas can become coalition magnets, but I find that ideas related to the understanding of homelessness are particularly powerful and can lead to the creation of a strong governance network or, conversely, can force groups apart. As I will demonstrate, a key, but by no means insurmountable, barrier to the development of effective responses to homelessness is that there are so many different ways to define homelessness.

Agency

Failures of the welfare state that produce homelessness have led some to use the words *unhoused* or *underhoused*. These latter terms draw attention not to the characteristics or presumed deficiencies of people who are without housing, but rather to the systems and structures that force them into that situation.[5] But that does not mean they are passive and need to be governed[6]. People who are or who have been homeless are what Caroline Andrew calls "the knowers" (2003). Lived expert and former coordinator at a small service for homeless men in Montreal Star Gale writes, "I am often asked 'how can I/we help the homeless?' The best answer is, 'I'm not sure, let's ask them!'" Gale says this is essential because of their deep knowledge of homelessness, though she notes that it is usually untapped in policymaking because of stereotypes and stigma that devalue this form of expertise. She writes, "There are new initiatives in Canada that show great promise, such as Housing First, but the expertise needed to expand, advance, and assess the efficacy of these initiatives resides in a population so heavily stigmatized by the public and institutions that serve them that they are essentially excluded from participation. These experts are people with lived experience, individuals who identify as being under-housed or homeless" (Gale 2015).

Governance is about power. To study governance dynamics is therefore to study who has power; those who have not historically had power risk being overlooked. To the extent that homeless people are excluded from the formal analysis of this book, it is because they have historically been excluded from the development of policies that determine their fate. This is deeply problematic; it is they who have the most direct experience and expertise regarding the system and policy failures that create homelessness. Expertise is a resource, and the lived experience of unhoused people's lived experience is too valuable to ignore (Kopec 2022). As Gale concludes: "Transition from life in crisis on the streets to secure housing for this subpopulation has proven notoriously difficult. Therefore, it is imperative that those who have made that transition or are in the process of navigating it can provide input into what service provision and housing supports worked for them. It's not simply helping; it is about working with" (Gale 2015). This book finds, as Gale noted, that the expertise of homeless people is often overlooked or excluded; an important conclusion is that the equity, justice, and efficacy of homelessness policies and programs requires the inclusion of lived expertise.

Contributions

Compared to other disciplines, political science has produced comparatively little research on homelessness. Chronic homelessness is a relatively new policy problem, but nevertheless it has been widely studied in a range of fields, including medicine, psychology, psychiatry, and to a lesser extent social work, sociology, and geography (Smith and Kopec 2021). Acknowledging the expertise in this rich body of literature, I look at efforts to respond to homelessness through the classic political science lens: power. For that is what governance is ultimately about: Who has power? How is that power deployed? Who does not have power and why? Understanding that service providers, Indigenous-led groups and communities, and homeless people have unparalleled expertise and experience designing and delivering life-saving solutions, as well as a profound understanding of the primary causes of homelessness, this book pays particular attention to their role. This is the value of a political science perspective on homelessness governance – to place homelessness in a political context. This means calling homelessness what it is: the result of government actions and inactions.

With that in mind, this book makes several contributions to theories of governance and social protection. It is the first comparative study of the multilevel governance of homelessness in Canada. This approach allows us to look deep into and across cases to more clearly understand what forces are shaping governance dynamics, including why different actors are involved and what shapes their interactions. In doing so, it also presents a comprehensive history of homelessness plans and policies in four cities since 2000, considering as many as seven groups of actors. This extensive history is valuable for understanding contemporary challenges and providing a record of government actions and the stories behind key moments and decisions.

A second contribution of this book is to expose the central and powerful role that ideas play in the development and evolution of multilevel governance dynamics. In this regard, I uncover the different, sometimes political, ways in which homelessness is understood across the country. An important theoretical contribution, this emphasis on ideas (interacting with institutions) allows us to better understand multilevel governance dynamics, but also why progress in the fight against homelessness has been so difficult. Far from undermining the life-saving work being done by those on the ground, an ideas and institutions lens allows us to understand why, despite thousands of people transitioning out of homelessness every year, people continue to experience homelessness.

I also contribute to ideational theories, specifically regarding the mechanisms by which ideas influence governance dynamics. Across the four cases, I find that ideas have been used to build powerful coalitions. One of most powerful ideas in this process has been about ending homelessness; as I demonstrate, part of the power of this idea is its ambiguity, which enables people to bring different understandings to their collaborative work fighting homelessness. In addition to confirming what ideational theory and analysis has found – that ambiguous ideas can attract sometimes conflicting groups and individuals to work together – I add to this theory: like magnets, ideas attract but can also repel. Different understandings of homelessness have, in some instances, driven groups apart, resulting in fragmentation in governance dynamics. In cases where ambiguous ideas have attracted groups or individuals that are motivated by fundamentally different understandings of homelessness, coalitions can be unstable or can even collapse. As a result, part of what makes ideas so powerful and magnetic – their ambiguity – also makes those ideas volatile.

This book is also in conversation with literature on federalism and the welfare state. Studies of social policy governance in Canada have tended to look at federal and provincial actions (Banting 2012; Béland and Daigneault 2015; Boychuk 1998; Boychuk 2008; Noël 2002, 2015; Wallner 2010, 2014). Canadian scholars have long examined the consequences of the fact that the Canadian welfare state is federal (Banting

1990; Noël 2001; Rose 1980), even asking whether "federal welfare state" is a contradiction in terms (Banting 2006). Federalism implies the coexistence of difference, but the welfare state requires some degree of equality or similarity in social protection. Considerable energy has thus been spent understanding how federalism and social protection interact (Noël 1999; Wallner 2010, 2014). Federalism has been and will remain a central force in the production of social protection. But studies of social protection are incomplete when they do not also consider the roles of local and non-governmental groups.

A starting assumption of this book is that civil society groups, private-sector actors, Indigenous-led organizations, and municipalities are centrally involved in producing social protection. This look at social protection from the bottom up sheds new light on welfare state governance by bringing these local actors into full view alongside senior governments (Michener, SoRelle, and Thurston 2022). Studying the Canadian welfare state from the bottom up thus reveals a further complicating, but deeply enriching, characteristic of the welfare state: it is federal, but it is also urbanized, meaning differences within provinces can be as significant as those between provinces. In this sense, I contribute to a growing body of literature stressing the important role that municipal governments are playing in Canadian governance (Good 2009), and respond to the call from federalism scholars to include local, non-governmental and Indigenous-led groups in theories of complex policy making (Paquet and Schertzer 2021).

On that note, I find that Indigenous-led groups face additional barriers to involvement in homelessness governance, including constant devaluing and exclusion of Indigenous knowledge and expertise. Indigenous communities also face additional *burdens* to involvement and ultimately implementing solutions, such as over-policing (though all homeless people are generally over-policed [Bellot and Sylvestre 2017]), and racist assumptions that Indigenous-led groups are unable to manage funding. Yet Indigenous-led organizations are best-placed to understand the complexities of homelessness for Indigenous people, and they are consistently effective in their work despite a lack of resources and exclusion. In this context, some Indigenous-led service providers have adopted a resurgence approach to producing social protection and ending homelessness (Corntassel 2012). While homelessness governance requires coordination and collaboration, it also sometimes requires governments to get out of the way and let the knowers do their work with the resources that are required to do so.

Studies in Canada and internationally have been ambivalent as to the place of housing policy in the welfare state. Housing has often been viewed – in theory and in policy – as an economic good or infrastructure (Hulchanski 2002; Pomeroy and Falvo 2013). Yet as we will see, housing is a primary means of protecting people against the risk of becoming homeless; indeed, it is central to the prevention of a host of other risks and unlocks the potential for improving one's quality of life through employment, education, safety, and good health. Housing is central to the welfare state, and though this study does not specifically study housing as carefully as homelessness, it makes a strong case that housing policy should be brought directly into the study of the provision of social protection.

This book also contributes to a small but growing body of political science research on homelessness governance. First, it provides important background and context to Carey Doberstein's groundbreaking book *Building a Collaborative Advantage*, which is about the local governance of the federal Homelessness Partnering Strategy. Doberstein writes that governance matters to the quality of efforts to fight homelessness and makes recommendations in light of his findings about the importance of institutionalized and inclusive networks. This book takes a step back, examining the forces that shape governance networks in the first place, including what barriers might exist that prevent inclusive governance. Furthermore, Doberstein concedes that the local actions considered in his study are not, and can never be, sufficient in the fight against homelessness: federal and provincial governments must also step to the plate. This book considers not only local networks but also the involvement and interactions of municipal, provincial, and federal actors, situating local actors within the full picture. No single actor, level, or sector can solve homelessness on its own; they must work together.

The challenge of producing social protection for people experiencing homelessness is also its strength; it requires a broad, inclusive, multilevel, multisector governance network. The title of this book, *Multiple Barriers*, is a reference to the fact that there are institutional and ideational barriers to the development of this kind of network. Historically, multiple barriers has referred to people who are homeless. In this individualized understanding that dominated in the 1990s and 2000s, people experiencing homelessness were viewed as having "barriers" to housing – drug use, mental illness, disability, unemployment, and so on. Over time, as I demonstrate in this book, dominant understandings of homelessness have changed, and barriers to housing are today less often understood as existing within individuals. Rather, they are increasingly understood to be located in systems and structures, and include discrimination, systemic poverty, colonialism, and a lack of safe, adequate, and affordable housing. The title of this book is a nod to this history and should be a constant reminder of the importance of the definition of homelessness.

Book Overview

The next chapter of this book introduces the reader to homelessness in Canada, beginning with a historical overview of the definitions of homelessness used by service providers and policy-makers. In the empirical chapters that follow, when I speak of "ideas regarding the nature of the problem/homelessness," I am referring to the definition of homelessness. As I will illustrate, the dominant understandings of homelessness have been shifting focus away from individual causes and toward more structural and systemic ones. Yet differences in how homelessness is understood persist to this day, with some definitions focusing exclusively on housing, some insisting on the equal importance of community and inclusion, and others drawing on Indigenous worldviews and knowledge to draw attention to the importance of a more holistic understanding of emplacement. I lay out, briefly, the history of homelessness in Canada, identifying some of the policy causes of homelessness. This will inform readers about some common misconceptions around why people experience homelessness as well as illustrate how all three levels of government and various sectors of society bear some responsibility for the rise in homelessness that began in the 1980s. It follows that they are all required partners in efforts to combat it.

The third chapter develops the book's theoretical framework by bridging research on multilevel governance with ideational analysis of the governance of the welfare state. I also outline this project's research design, including case selection and research methods. The fourth chapter is the first of the book's five empirical chapters. I begin with the federal government, tracing its involvement in homelessness governance from 1999 until the National Housing Strategy was introduced in 2017. For nearly twenty years, the federal government's involvement in homelessness governance was timid and short-term, prioritizing individual-level solutions. I argue that this was because of prevailing ideas at the time regarding the nature of homelessness, notably a narrow, individualized definition of homelessness. In other words, homelessness was not understood to be a structural problem. In addition to the federal government, I present the more recent history of the Canadian Alliance to End Homelessness (CAEH), a powerful advocacy group that has become the most influential non-governmental actor on the national level in the development of homelessness policy.

The four chapters that then follow offer detailed case studies of the urban multilevel governance of homelessness, including the involvement of different actors and their interactions in Vancouver, Calgary, Toronto, and Montreal. Each chapter follows the same logic and structure and reconstructs history, actor by actor, though each also takes a slightly different form. For example, the provincial story is long in some cases, short in others. In some instances, I consider the operation of the federal homelessness program on its own; in others, I consider it alongside another actor and explain why. In each of these city-based chapters, I first consider the provincial government, focusing on its involvement in homelessness but also including the relevant history of its housing policy. I then consider local actors, including the municipal government, third-sector groups, private-sector actors, and groups created by the federal government's National Homelessness Initiative in the late 1990s and early 2000s, which includes an Indigenous network (bureaucratically referred to as "Aboriginal communities") in all cities except Montreal[7] as well as a non-Indigenous network (bureaucratically referred to as "designated communities"). While reconstructing the involvement of each of the actors and their interactions, I highlight the importance and interactions of resources, ideas, and institutions in driving governance dynamics, drawing on evidence from interviews, archives, extensive document review, and participant observation. In the final chapter, I return to the book's main contributions, explaining more fully the implications of this work.

The story that emerges reveals both the challenges and successes of multilevel policy-making in one of Canada's most complicated policy areas. One of the main messages to emerge from the following pages is that the social safety net is indeed frayed across the country, but that actors not traditionally associated with welfare production, notably third-sector groups, Indigenous-led organizations, and municipalities, are using their resources and skills to fill the gaps, plug the holes, and mend the net as best as they can. With deep respect to those involved in service provision and those who are or have been unhoused, I hope that this book will help explain why, from a political perspective, homelessness continues at such intolerable levels.

2 Homelessness

What is homelessness? People who are homeless, of course, do not have a home. But that raises a deeply personal question: What is a home? The definition is important, and the preoccupation with it is not purely academic. From a political perspective, the definition of homelessness determines who is prioritized for housing and support services, how resources are allocated and distributed, and how long services are made available. A definition is also necessary for us to consistently measure how homelessness changes over time and understand why those changes happen. Furthermore, given the targeted nature of housing policy in many provinces, the definition of homelessness may determine how many units of housing governments are willing to commit to funding in the first place. Some object to efforts to define homelessness or to prioritize certain "types" of homelessness, and their concerns are valid. From a political perspective, however, the definition of homelessness is essential to understanding governance and power dynamics in the production of social protection.

This chapter is not an exhaustive account of homelessness in Canada, but rather an exploration of its definition and what we know about its history from a political perspective. I begin with an overview of the different ways homelessness is defined and understood and how definitions have evolved over time, focusing on Canada but looking internationally for context. When I talk about ideas regarding the nature of homelessness, I am referring to the definition of homelessness. This chapter also shows that chronic, long-term homelessness is a new problem of Canadian public policy, but other forms have a longer history. To do this, I highlight what is known about the causes of homelessness, including public policy changes and their interactions with "individual"-level risk factors. I also stress the colonial causes of homelessness especially for the Indigenous population,[1] which predate Confederation.

After presenting this history, I describe the contemporary realities of homelessness in Canada, while keeping in mind a central message of this book, which is that ending homelessness is so difficult to do because there are many answers to the question: What is homelessness?

Homelessness Definitions

> Adding the suffix "-ness" turns the adjective *homeless* into an abstract concept. As such, it allows readers and listeners to imagine whatever they want. It tosses all sorts of problems into one handy term. We thus have the ongoing problem of defining what homeless-*ness* is and isn't. There is no single correct definition, given the different mix of problems that goes into the hodgepodge of issues, and depending on who is using the term. (Hulchanski 2009, 4)

According to the European Federation of National Organizations Working with the Homeless (FEANTSA[2]), there are three aspects to a home: an adequate physical domain, a social domain, and a legal domain (FEANTSA 2011). The absence of even one domain would lead someone to experience homelessness. Australia's Bureau of Statistics similarly emphasizes three domains in its definition of homelessness, which overlap with FEANTSA's: adequacy of the dwelling; security of tenure in the dwelling; and control of and access to space for social relations (Australian Bureau of Statistics 2012). As with FEANTA's definition, a person in Australia is considered homeless if they lack any of these domains. Thus, someone who does not have a lease or a private social space would be considered homeless. This may surprise a person who has lived in a rooming house for years (if, in a legal sense, only ever month to month) and who may not identify as homeless. Similarly, a person living in overcrowded housing or who is couch-surfing (living or sleeping at the home of family and/or friends for short periods of time) would also be considered, according to this definition, to be homeless. According to the European and Australian definitions, homeless is therefore more than just roofless or bedless.

Quebec is the only province that has developed its own definition of homelessness, and it appears to be the first government in Canada to do so. That province has played a more active role in social policy than other provinces since the 1960s, guarding its social policy powers jealously and exercising them comparatively rigorously (Banting 1990; Noël 2002). Housing and homelessness are not exceptions to this. In 1987, a committee on homelessness in Montreal defined homelessness as "a person with no fixed address, stable, safe and decent[3] housing for the next 60 days, an extremely low income, adversely discriminated against in access to services, with problems of mental health, alcohol and drug abuse or social disorganization, and not a member of any stable group" (Comité des sans-abri 1987, 2). This definition was also adopted by the province and remained in effect until 2014. It is simultaneously narrow and broad; it is narrow because it associates homelessness with individual causes such as substance abuse or illness. It is also broad, however, in that it identifies poverty as a cause, specifies that housing should be safe and adequate, and notes the importance of community integration.

Efforts to define homelessness at the national level in Canada, formally at least, began in the 1990s. Early definitions pointed to individual causes, implying that homelessness is experienced because of personal failings, deficiencies, or bad choices. In response to growing numbers of people experiencing homelessness, a report published by the Library of Parliament noted the importance of defining homelessness but also stressed the difficulty doing so. The report identified three forms of homelessness – chronic, cyclical, and temporary – but only defined chronic homelessness. People who experienced that form of homelessness were said to be "people who live on the periphery of society and who often face problems of drug or alcohol abuse or mental illness" (Begin et al. 1999, 8). That same year, the federal government's response to homelessness, the National Homelessness Initiative, was introduced. Like the Library of Canada report, the definition adopted was extremely narrow, and related exclusively to the lack of housing: "in the context of the NHI, homelessness is defined as living on the street or in temporary shelters" (HRDC 2003, 1).

The 1999 Library of Canada report also noted that Indigenous people experience homelessness for different reasons, but consistent with the individual-level focus of the above definition, it also focused on individual deficiencies: "Research has shown that the Aboriginal population is characterized, among other things, by lower educational attainment and income levels, higher unemployment and poverty levels, a larger proportion of single-parent families, and generally poorer housing. These factors are major contributors to Aboriginal homelessness, although others (such as drug and alcohol abuse and mental illness) are often cited" (8). As I will explain below, these early definitions of homelessness are informed by stereotypes and, for the Indigenous population, racism and a lack of historical context.

These definitions have evolved. Importantly, they have moved away from focusing exclusively on individual-level factors and have come to understand homelessness as the result not just of individual-level barriers but also of systemic and structural failures. Drawing on input from experts, advocates, and service providers across the country, the Canadian Homelessness Research Network (CHRN) proposed a new definition of homelessness in 2012. This definition marked an important evolution in the understanding of homelessness, thanks in large part to a community-driven (but by no means unanimous) process. Homelessness was defined as "the situation of an individual or family who does not have a stable address or residence; the living situation of an individual or family who does not have stable, permanent, appropriate housing, or the immediate prospect, means and ability of acquiring it." It went on to note: "[Homelessness] is the result of systemic or societal barriers, a lack of affordable and appropriate housing, the individual/household's financial, mental, cognitive, behavioural or physical challenges, and/or racism and discrimination" (CHRN 2012). This national definition identified not just personal deficiencies but also broader forces, such as racism and the lack of affordable housing, that also contribute to homelessness. Consistent with past federal definitions of homelessness, this definition is housing based. While many Canadian plans to end homelessness were developed before this definition was adopted (notably those in Alberta and BC), the CHRN definition has been used in many plans developed since 2012, including in Ontario, and was adopted nearly word for word by the federal government in 2019.

A new definition was also developed in Quebec in 2014 following extensive consultation with community groups across the province: "Homelessness refers to a process of social disaffiliation and a situation of social rupture that manifests in a person's difficulty maintaining a stable, safe, adequate, and decent home as a result of the unavailability of housing or of his or her inability to maintain it and, at the same time, by a person's difficulty maintaining functional, stable and safe relations in the community. It is explained by a combination of social and individual factors" (Gouvernement du Québec 2014, 30; author's translation). Here, we see an enduring difference between the Québécois and Canadian definitions: the Canadian definition considers homelessness to be the lack of housing. According to Quebec's definition, however, the solution to homelessness involves *more* than just access to and maintenance of housing: it involves community integration and relations as well. But we also see a similar evolution, compared with the Canadian definition, in that this new Québécois definition focuses less on individual features and places more emphasis on broader forces.

The updated definition of homelessness does not specifically mention Indigenous homelessness, though Quebec's policy on homelessness identifies different causes of homelessness among Indigenous communities; "a lack of housing, poverty, physical health problems, mental illness, addiction, family violence, transience, marginalization of an individual in his/her community and gaps in the accessibility and continuum of social and health services. Some of these causes are closely linked to experiences by children and their parents in residential schools" (Gouvernement du Québec 2014, 24; author's translation). Interesting, considering the evolution away from individual-level causes in the broader definition, this understanding of causes of homelessness among Indigenous populations is still very individualized. To the extent that it is related to colonialism, it is only with respect to residential "schools" and not historic processes of displacement from land or contemporary practices of child welfare agencies.

Indigenous people continue to be overrepresented among the homeless population (BCNPHA and Thomson 2017; Kauppi et al. 2017; Latimer et al. 2015; Schiff and Turner 2014; SPARC BC 2011). To fully consider colonialism, genocide (National Inquiry into Missing and Murdered Indigenous Women and Girls 2019; TRC 2015), residential "schools," forced impoverishment and displacement, and to incorporate Indigenous traditions and ways of knowing, an Indigenous definition of homelessness was recently developed by Métis-Cree scholar and lived expert Jesse Thistle. Thistle recalls that the origins of the Indigenous definition were in the Canadian definition of homelessness developed in 2014: "[They] framed it around being unhoused, and there's a range of unhoused conditions. And I was like, 'this is not articulating my experience as an Indigenous person with prior [homelessness] experience'... I said, 'we need to fully articulate it to direct dollars, interest, funding and resources to Indigenous service providers. And how we need to do that is we need to articulate what the problem is. [But] we don't even know what the problem is because no one's defined it'" (qtd in Hyslop 2017).

To this end, Thistle[4] worked on the development of an Indigenous definition of homelessness in consultation with Indigenous elders, lived experts, and service providers. Informed by this knowledge, he explains that an Indigenous perspective on homelessness is less concerned with a physical place or structure than the definitions referenced above. Homelessness is conceptualized not just as the lack of legal or social space but rather as resulting from prolonged and ongoing colonization and a separation from "All My Relations": "Indigenous worldviews conceptualize home more deeply as a web of relationships and responsibilities involving connection to human kinship networks; relationships with animals, plants, spirits and elements; relationships with the Earth, lands, waters and territories; and connection to traditional stories, songs, teachings, names and ancestors" (Thistle 2017, 14). He continues: "The Indigenous concept of home, then, is a holistic metaphysical understanding of emplacement, rather than a built environment" (15). Rather than placing responsibility at the individual level, Thistle writes, "Indigenous homelessness is best understood as the outcome of historically constructed and ongoing settler colonization and racism that have displaced and dispossessed First Nations, Métis and Inuit Peoples from their traditional governance systems and laws, territories, histories, worldviews, ancestors and stories" (6).

Recall that, defined by federal officials in 1999, Indigenous homelessness was understood to be the result of personal failings and deficiencies; one reason Indigenous people were said to experience homelessness was low levels of educational attainment. This was written a mere three years after the last government run residential "school" in Canada had closed. The notion that Indigenous people experience homelessness because of a lack of education is astonishing, harmful gaslighting of Indigenous communities by the federal government. Indeed, in an interview for this book, Murray Sinclair explained: "[The federal government] established what they called 'schools' in terms of residential schools, but the schools were not about education, the schools were about cultural genocide. And so, the reality is that the Indigenous population, for many generations until very recently, was largely uneducated or poorly educated and did not receive the educational benefits that the rest of the population was entitled to." He continued: "In fact, if you look at the Indian Act, there was a provision that said if you went to university and you got a university degree, that you would be disenfranchised from your status" (personal interview, Murray Sinclair 2019). The emphasis in Thistle's definition of homelessness on structural, systemic, and colonial causes of homelessness is a significant departure from the individualizing definitions of the past (and arguably Quebec's modern understanding), and leads logically to different solutions.

As noted above, the Canadian government released its official definition of homelessness in 2019 following a report by an Advisory Committee on Homelessness. The definition is almost exactly the same as the CHRN's 2012 definition.[5] While the *Reaching Home* definition does not use the Indigenous definition of homelessness developed by Jesse Thistle, it acknowledges the importance of an Indigenous perspective on homelessness, and defines Indigenous homelessness separately: "Indigenous homelessness refers to Indigenous peoples who are in the state of having no home due to colonization, trauma and/ or whose social, cultural, economic and political conditions place them in poverty" (ESDC 2019b). This recognition that colonialism is a cause of homelessness is a change from past perspectives and points to an awareness that responses and solutions must address this cause, though recognition is not enough and the definition makes no mention of the holistic, metaphysical understanding of place that is so central to Thistle's definition (and, by implication, to solutions that would need to flow from it). Early NHS documents note that this definition may evolve as the program is implemented.

Beyond the specific definition of homelessness, efforts have been made to define other dimensions of homelessness in Canada as well. This includes what it means to end homelessness and what it means to prevent homelessness. With respect to ending homelessness, the Canadian Alliance to End Homelessness (CAEH) and the Canadian Observatory on Homelessness in collaboration with Alina Turner, Tom Albanese, and Kyle Pakeman distinguish between "absolute zero" and "functional zero" (Turner, Albanese, and Pakeman 2017). Absolute zero refers to the situation in a community in which no one ever experiences homelessness and there is therefore no need for emergency shelters; they explain "[absolute zero] is simply not realistic in practice. People may find themselves homeless, at least temporarily. We need a meaningful and useful definition of 'ending homelessness' that recognizes that reality, while pushing us towards an ideal situation" (3). Functional zero, by contrast, describes a situation in which "there are enough services, housing and shelter beds for everyone who needs them. Further, the experience of homelessness is brief and system intervention results in successful resolution and few returns" (3). While functional zero and absolute zero are analytically distinct, the authors insist they are not binary; functional zero constitutes progress toward what some may see as the ultimate goal of absolute zero.[6]

There is also increasing attention to defining what it means to prevent homelessness (though of course advocates have argued for decades that the solution to homelessness requires a strong prevention strategy [Crowe 2019]). In a Canadian Observatory on Homelessness report that defines prevention, Stephen Gaetz and Erin Dej insist on their support Housing First as an intervention to end homelessness,[7] but also stress that waiting until someone falls into crisis is not the most effective, or just, response. Quoting Peter Jacobson, who works in the homeless-serving system in Australia, they give examples from other sectors to illustrate the importance of prevention: "If we want to stop people dying on roads, we invest money in seatbelts, not in the emergency department" (qtd in Gaetz and Dej 2017). A similar logic, Gaetz and Dej imply, should apply to responses to homelessness. Because of the number of systems and institutions implicated in the production and prevention of homelessness, Gaetz and Dej insist that prevention work must be done not just by the homeless-serving system but by a host of other institutions and systems as well. They are correct to challenge the assumption that people working in the homeless-serving system are the ones responsible for ending homelessness, an assumption that "has also allowed us to avoid addressing the large scale structural drivers of homelessness, many of which are the domain and responsibility of other sectors (health, justice, child protection, housing, education, etc) and/or other parts of government" (40).

The authors define homelessness prevention as "policies, and interventions that reduce the likelihood that someone will experience homelessness. It also means providing those who have been homeless with the necessary resources and supports to stabilize their housing, enhance *integration and social inclusion*, and ultimately reduce the risk of the recurrence of homelessness" (35, emphasis added). Consistent with the more recent definitions of homelessness, this definition of homelessness prevention makes clear that individual-level solutions (and even individual-level interventions like preventing eviction) are not enough to prevent homelessness in a meaningful way. It also brings together important elements from the national and Québécois definition; homelessness prevention requires both housing and inclusion.[8] To be clear, this is not a government document, but rather a report by academics. But these academics are influential – Gaetz sat on the National Advisory Committee on Homelessness, and has been involved in the dissemination of Housing First practices around Canada and indeed around the world. Governments have proven willing to listen to and even follow the advice of researchers, Gaetz included. This recent evolution in the understanding of homelessness, which includes a focus on inclusion as well as housing, and the focus on the need to prevent and what it will take to respond meaningfully to it, is significant and broadens the understanding of homelessness and solutions to it.

Typologies

To operationalize definitions and guide implementation, definitions of homelessness are often accompanied by typologies. One kind of typology spells out a spectrum of housing insecurity that ranges from people who experience absolute or chronic homelessness (people who sleep outside, for example, or have been homeless for over one year) to those who are at risk of experiencing homelessness (those who are paying more than 30 per cent of their income for rent or are living in substandard housing, for example). This clearly relates to housing-focused definitions of homelessness. The CHRN definition from 2012 includes four types of homelessness: unsheltered, including people sleeping on streets or in tents; emergency sheltered, including people sleeping in emergency homeless shelters (and including shelters for those fleeing family violence); provisionally accommodated, which includes individuals who are in insecure or untenured housing; and at risk of homelessness. This typology closely mirrors FEANTA's typology, which similarly distinguishes between street and sheltered homelessness (Smith 2015).

Thistle also identifies what he calls dimensions of Indigenous homelessness to accompany the Indigenous definition of homelessness. Some of the twelve dimensions overlap with the CHRN typology: nowhere-to-go homelessness, for example, which Thistle defines as "a complete lack of access to stable shelter, housing, accommodation, shelter services or relationships" (2017, 12), is similar to unsheltered homelessness from the CHRN typology. Other dimensions, however, are more specific to the Indigenous population, such as "historic displacement homelessness" and "contemporary geographic separation homelessness" (2017, 13–14). Thistle insists that dimensions of homelessness can be layered and experienced at the same time, which means that solutions to homelessness must take into consideration different types of homelessness someone may be experiencing simultaneously.

Another way of understanding the different forms homelessness can take is in terms of its duration, or chronicity. Most jurisdictions in Canada, including Quebec, differentiate between chronic homelessness, episodic homelessness, and transitional homelessness. Chronic homelessness is the longest of these types, usually referring to people who have been homeless for longer than six months or one year. Episodic homelessness is experienced by people who have been in and out of different forms of insecure housing several times over the course of one year, usually for short periods of time. Transitional homelessness, the most common type of homelessness (Aubry et al. 2013; Rabinovitch, Pauly, and Zhao 2016), is experienced by people who have a single, limited period of homelessness; homelessness is resolved relatively quickly, usually through access to affordable housing.

Studies of shelters in Ontario and Victoria have found that the vast majority of people who use an emergency homeless shelter over the course of one year do so for a short period of time.[9] In a study of a sample of emergency shelters Ontario, Tim Aubry and colleagues found that approximately 85 per cent of people using those facilities over the course of one year experienced one brief episode of homelessness (Aubry et al. 2013). These people temporarily have nowhere to go, so they spend a brief amount of time in an emergency shelter; they quickly find somewhere to live and never again experience homelessness. When third-sector groups or governments aim to "end homelessness," they are usually not talking about this kind of transitional homelessness, understanding that there will always be a need for short-term, emergency support (Turner, Albanese, and Pakeman 2017). A further 3 to 11 per cent of people staying in shelters experienced "episodic homelessness," meaning they had experienced several episodes of homelessness for relatively short periods of time. That study concludes that only a very small minority of people staying in shelters, 2 to 4 per cent, experience chronic or "long stay" homelessness.

In a similar study of shelter use patterns in six emergency shelters in Victoria, BC, between 2010 and 2014, Rabinovitch and colleagues (2016) identified similar patterns. Interestingly, they found a similar breakdown in terms of percentage of the homeless population experiencing long-term, episodic, and transitional homelessness,[10] though their study revealed that the average length of time spent homeless for each of these groups was much shorter in Victoria than in Ontario. Temporarily homeless individuals experienced homelessness for an average of 17 days (compared to 30 in Ontario); episodically homeless individuals experienced homelessness for an average of 31 days (compared to 180 in Ontario); and chronically homeless individuals experienced homelessness for an average of 471 days (compared to 710 in Ontario). Groups seeking to raise awareness of homelessness often use the image of an iceberg to send the message that what we see on the streets is a mere fraction of the broader homeless population, which is often much more hidden than we realize.

These different typologies – regarding housing stability and chronicity in particular – can interact, as will be seen in the chapters that follow. For years, the City of Vancouver prioritized chronically homeless, unsheltered individuals. The federal government prioritized sheltered and unsheltered chronic forms of homelessness through its National Homelessness Initiative/Homelessness Partnering Strategy. *Reaching Home*, the federal government's current response to homelessness, prioritizes all forms of chronic homelessness, including individuals who are unsheltered, emergency sheltered, *and* provisionally housed. In important ways, this represents a substantial broadening of the definition of homelessness.

This review of definitions and typologies may seem academic or overly technical, and classification or types of homelessness are fully rejected by some groups. Explaining the perspective of OCAP, Withers writes that "OCAP, on the other hand, rejects these classifications and organizes around homeless issues and homeless people – those without homes … For OCAP, homelessness is a social rather than a statistical question" (Withers 2021, 12–13). They continue, "official definitions flatten the diversity within homelessness and erase the uniqueness of what is going on" (13). Yet Withers also notes the importance of definitions to understanding government action and considers the broadening of Ontario's definition of homelessness in 2017 to be an important success of OCAP advocacy. Understanding definitions and typologies is essential to understanding the politics of homelessness and its governance. As the empirical chapters will make clear, while differences between types of homelessness may seem small or insignificant, when integrated into policies, even these small differences can become of great consequence.

The definition of homelessness continues to evolve, and disagreements endure. Some are easily reconciled, others less so. A senior federal bureaucrat involved in *Reaching Home* explained with great frustration how challenging policy-making can be when there are competing definitions of homelessness:

> The National Housing Strategy advisory committee came up with four definitions. So, a definition of homelessness and a definition of Indigenous homelessness. We've already heard from certain groups that they see that as a First Nations definition, not an Inuit or Métis definition. The advisory committee also wanted a separate definition for women's homelessness, because they felt the other two didn't encompass that. And then we had a definition for youth homelessness. I finally had to say "come on people, four definitions? And then what? The Inuit and the Métis and then what, the Métis woman? The young Métis woman? What am I doing here guys? How do I explain that to the public? No. no. That doesn't help me prioritize what I need to do." (personal interview 2018)

One of the strongest barriers to ending homelessness is the difficulty defining it. To be sure, the homelessness sector is drastically underresourced and has suffered from inadequate funding and short or uncertain timelines for decades. The federal government's investment in homelessness was for decades only ever on a one- to three-year basis, which was scandalously unfair to service providers. An important finding of this book is that the confluence of limited resources and uncoordinated ideational disagreements on definitions can be devastating to efforts to combat homelessness. In the following chapters, I show how in locales where there are definitional disagreements between key actors, the governance network tends to be more fragmented. This is not necessarily a problem, however, as disagreements can be productive, leading to an enriched and diverse service sector, but only when coordinated. If not, disagreements can threaten to undermine the work being done to meaningfully reduce homelessness by setting service providers at cross-purposes, fighting for limited funding and fragmenting governance arrangements. All of this can lead to the ultimate consequence of homeless people getting lost in the system and more people falling through the cracks.

Causes of Homelessness

There has long been extreme poverty in Canada. Indeed, even in the country's early years, some people were so poor they had no permanent, safe, adequate housing of their own. The Old Brewery Mission, the largest emergency shelter in Montreal, opened its doors in 1890. For well over one hundred years, some individuals have found themselves so poor and excluded from society that they have relied on emergency shelters like the Old Brewery Mission for a bed and basic services like food, often called "three hots and a cot" (Ranasinghe 2017).[11] Yet it is common to hear advocates and experts call homelessness a new problem (Hulchanski 2009).

Three decades ago, Fallis and Murray suggested in *Housing the Homeless and the Poor* that "a cynic – or a person with a strong historical sense – might well ask if homelessness is just the 1980s' word for poverty" (1990, 12). Answering their own rhetorical question, they insist that "things are not the same; things are qualitatively different" (12). David Hulchanski agrees: "While it is true that all societies through history tend to have some people who are homeless – without a home – we have not always had the set of social problems we associate with the word *homelessness*" (Hulchanski 2009). Debates may surround its definition, but there is a general consensus among advocates and researchers that in its chronic, long-term form, homelessness *is* new (Crowe 2007; Gaetz 2010; Hughes 2012; Hulchanski 2009; Layton 2008; RAPSIM 2012).

So, what happened? While formal definitions have evolved over time, scholars and activists have identified structural, systemic, and what are called individual factors or circumstances alongside ongoing colonialism that have caused (and continue to cause) homelessness. Internationally recognized Canadian homelessness expert Stephen Gaetz does not mince words when attributing responsibility for the rise in homelessness in Canada to the federal[12] and provincial[13] governments: "Beginning in the 1980s and accelerating through the 1990s, a transformation began to take place. Global and domestic changes in the economy (trade liberalization, deindustrialization), coupled with profound changes in government social and housing policies had *a direct impact* on the growth of poverty and began to lead to growing numbers of people winding up on the streets or in emergency shelters because they lacked access to safe, affordable housing" (Gaetz 2010, 22, emphasis added). He adds that "the dismantling of Canada's national housing strategy had the most profound impact on homelessness" (22), though he points to the decision to cut social transfers to provinces as also contributing. This reduced social spending transfer, enacted unilaterally by the federal government in the 1990s, led many provinces to cut their own social policies – notably social assistance incomes and their own investments in housing[14] – owing to a lack of resources to continue offering services of the same quality and to the same extent as in the past. For many scholars and activists, homelessness is political, and the responsibility for the increase in homelessness rests squarely on the shoulders of federal and provincial governments who retrenched and restructured the welfare state (Gaetz 2010; Hulchanski 2009; Layton 2008).

Throughout the late 1990s and early 2000s, senior levels of government made cuts to the social safety net, going so far as to remove sections of it entirely, notably social housing. A few years after the cuts, some senior governments responded to rising numbers of people experiencing homelessness. When they did, it was with narrowly defined, short-term, underfunded programs such as the federal National Homelessness Initiative (covered more fully in chapter 4). Even federal government reviews of its own program concluded that it failed to meet the needs of people experiencing homelessness, largely because it was not designed (in funding or timeline) to address root causes of the problem: a lack of affordable housing and intensive social supports (HRDC 2008, 2009; see chapter 4). Where provinces became involved, it was similarly through emergency measures, such as funding emergency shelters on a per person or per bed basis, a funding model that some say led to the entrenchment and institutionalization of homelessness (Dej 2020; Hughes 2012; Hughes, ed., 2018). These responses were insufficient to end or prevent homelessness. Failure to respond to a new risk – policy drift – combined with direct cuts tore at the social fabric. Welfare restructuring and retrenchment cut holes in the safety net, and lack of action to address rising and transforming social risks put further pressure on the net, tearing those holes even bigger.

The federal and provincial governments created gaps in social protection, allowing the most vulnerable to fall all the way through to the streets. But these governments were not alone in contributing to the rise in homelessness – municipalities played a role as well. Former City of Vancouver councillor and subsequent federal NDP House Leader Libby Davies explains that decisions made by Vancouver City Council to prioritize development projects in the 1990s led to an explosion of unaffordable condominium developments in the downtown core: "The biggest change at city hall was [former Mayor Gordon Campbell's] love of zoning changes that conferred massive densities in massive developments that benefited the development industry with millions of dollars in profits" (Davies 2019, 57). These expensive housing options, directed at a market where little and then no affordable or social housing was being built, led to the decimation of affordable housing options for those unable to afford a condo or market rental housing. Similar dynamics can be seen in cities across the country (Bendaoud 2016). Predictably, the private sector, seeking profits and lacking incentives or subsidies from any level of government to make affordable housing developments more appealing, has failed to develop deeply affordable housing. Coupled with a collapse of senior government investment, zoning and local land use planning decisions have meant that large urban centres have become increasingly unaffordable.

Perhaps most controversially, some social service providers see the third sector as contributing to the rise in homelessness as well. Experienced advocates and service providers Matthew Pearce in Montreal and John Rook in Calgary, among others, maintain that service providers have contributed to the problem, though they note that they have done so with nothing but good intentions. Rook explains: "I believe that the problems shelters have created are actually bigger than the ones we are trying to solve" (2018, 165). Matthew Pearce agrees: "Shelters allowed homelessness to become more than a difficult period in one's life – they allowed it to become normalized as a lifestyle ... It took courage for shelter Boards of Directors and staff to admit their institutions were part of the problem, not the solution" (Pearce 2018, 89–90). Some service sector leaders insist that managing homelessness through emergency responses is an obstacle to ending it.

Though Pearce does not directly blame the federal government, he does note that "services rendered to the homeless by community organizations in Montreal came about by evolution and not careful or strategic planning" (91–2). The system evolved haphazardly, resulting in people getting lost or even trapped. Gaetz agrees with this assessment that the homeless serving sector grew on a largely uncoordinated basis. In the context of a frayed welfare state in the 1990s and 2000s, more people fell into homelessness; this increase in the number of people in need of emergency assistance caught local services, notably the limited and uncoordinated emergency shelter system that existed in the 1990s, unprepared. Gaetz explains what that meant for people seeking emergency supports: "The number of people who wound up living on the streets and in parks in communities across Canada (including families, women and youth) began to grow quite dramatically, putting pressure on the homelessness infrastructure that was largely set up to serve single adult men. The homelessness infrastructure was not sufficient to respond to this rapid growth in numbers, nor designed to effectively respond to the needs of specific sub-populations such as youth, women and ethno-racial minorities (particularly Aboriginal persons)" (Gaetz 2010, 23; see also Hulchanski 2009; Layton 2008). The system has been in crisis from the beginning and has evolved in that context.

While also appreciating the need for emergency shelters, Erin Dej is similarly critical of what she calls the Homelessness Industrial Complex (Dej 2020). She notes that emergency shelters inadvertently contribute to the exclusion of already vulnerable people by individualizing responses to homelessness (primarily in the form of mental health care). The failure of senior governments to step up with meaningful structural and systemic changes has meant that existing solutions to homelessness address symptoms that present at the individual level as opposed to root causes, which are more structural and systemic. Though she does not review Quebec-based services or the Quebec definition (her book is a thoughtful study of two Ottawa-based emergency shelters), Dej is clear that the solution to homelessness must involve some form of community inclusion or integration. This directly informs her understanding of why shelters and other services in some cases contribute to the reproduction of homelessness: because they reinforce exclusion. As we will see, shelters are controversial among service providers, advocates, and politicians (to say nothing of the NIMBYism among neighbourhood associations), though opponents of this view insist that shelters connect people to services and provide the community and connection that is so desperately sought. It is no exaggeration to say that in the context of unaffordable housing and repeated structural and systemic failures, shelters quite literally save lives, and even the most critical voices recognize that there will long be a need for emergency shelter of some sort in the Canadian safety net.

The subject of mental health and deinstitutionalization is inescapable when discussing causes of homelessness, though it is treated with caution and nuance in the literature and by advocates as well. A national study titled *Homelessness in Canada* was conducted in 1987 (the UN's International Year of Shelter for the Homeless), as deinstitutionalization was under way in provinces across the country. Deinstitutionalization was the process whereby institutions for individuals with mental illness were shut down in the 1980s and 1990s. This was done by all accounts with good intentions, so as to allow more independent, community-based living, but the social and health supports to promote community-based living were not made available. The 1987 report found that 20 per cent of shelter users were at the time or had previously been psychiatric patients (Canadian Council on Social Development 1987). The authors of the report insisted on the importance of supports, cautioning that failure to provide them to people who had formerly lived in those institutions "will only increase the social and monetary costs" to the system, presumably resulting from the increased use of emergency services (Canadian Council on Social Development 1987). This is exactly what happened when the supports that were promised did not follow; indeed, front-line service providers around during this period note that the work of shelters shifted following deinstitutionalization, with one explaining that after deinstitutionalization, shelters became "de facto mental health institutions" (qtd in Ranasinghe 2017, 19).

There is a tendency in academic studies and policy reports to consider mental illness an individual-level factor because it presents at the individual level, but it is important to remember this history and that *government decisions* led to thousands of Canadians being abandoned without the supports they needed, and that they had been promised; people were entering a context of scant social supports and increasingly unaffordable or inaccessible housing. Furthermore, as the head of Aboriginal services at the Centre for Addiction and Mental Health Peter Menzies notes, "individual level" factors such as mental illness and homelessness must, for Indigenous people, be placed in historic context of colonialism and government-led assimilation efforts, including residential "schools" and child welfare practices, that resulted in intergenerational trauma. Menzies writes that "rather than pathologizing the individual, as is often done, I would argue that [individual indicators] should be viewed as resulting from a historical process" (Menzies 2010, 75).

Hulchanski and colleagues note that in this context of inadequate supports, untreated mental illness can cause homelessness, but they add that the arrow points both ways: homelessness can also lead to a deterioration in mental health. They stress that "it is important to note that not all people with mental illness are homeless, and not all people who are homeless report a mental illness" (Hulchanski et al. 2009, 1–2; see also Preston et al. 2009). This last point is important, for the centrality of mental illness to a government's or community group's definition of homelessness is key to understanding the definition of homelessness that is motivating its actions. If a definition insists that mental illness is a key cause of homelessness, this tells us that the definition is likely quite narrow.

The history and causes of homelessness among Indigenous populations are also different. While there are certainly similarities in terms of how changes to the welfare state have led to increased exposure to new and old social risks, ongoing colonization is a powerful force as well. Recall that Thistle places Indigenous homelessness at the end of a very long but also ongoing history of colonialism (Thistle 2017, 6). Murray Sinclair, chair of the Indian Residential Schools Truth and Reconciliation Commission, insists that homelessness among Indigenous people is a by-product of deeper efforts at dispossession on the part of the Canadian state that began before Confederation.[15] "The government of Canada at all levels, federal and provincial particularly, worked hard for many generations to render Indigenous people landless … Indigenous people were often moved from place to place or forced to relocate or had their rights, their entitlement to stay in a particular area, taken away from them. As a result, there's a multigenerational experience of moving from place to place and not being connected to a particular spot or residential area" (personal interview, Sinclair 2018).

Sinclair is clear: "There's no question that the impoverishment of Indigenous people was a forced impoverishment. This was a created impoverishment by the government of Canada" (personal interview, Sinclair 2018). Indigenous people were displaced and dispossessed of their lands. In addition, Indigenous social, political, and governance practices were outlawed for decades; important systems of wealth redistribution were outlawed during the potlatch ban, for example (Lafferty 2020; Wilson-Raybould 2019). And while banning these practices, governments forced Indigenous people into at best underfunded and at worst genocidal programs and institutions. Mohawk elder and scholar Marlene Brant Castellano explains that this reality of colonialism is complex and includes "shocks of epidemics, displacement from lands, depleted food supply, suppression of ceremonies and language, and the loss of children to residential schools and child welfare agencies" (2010, 8–9).

Former NDP Member of Parliament for Nunavut Mumilaaq Qaqqaq powerfully challenges the notion that colonialism is confined to the past; one of the ways this can be seen is with respect to housing access in the North. In a study of housing conditions in remote communities in Nunavut, Qaqqaq writes: "In the history of colonialism and forced relocation there were many changes, including moving from tents and iglus to wooden structures. I saw many homes with furnace ventilation covered that shouldn't have been, people not turning on their bathroom fans after the shower is used. Not knowing these kinds of things is not the fault of Inuit. Inuit were forced from their homes and way of life into communities and continued to be forced into situation[s] that are incredibly difficult to get out of, to this day" (Qaqqaq 2021, 40). She also writes about a child who was removed from their home and placed in foster care because the home was too mouldy to be considered safe. Qaqqaq asks, "Can we say that colonization is no longer alive if we continue to see Inuit children forced into the foster care system?" (18). Colonialism is not just history when these Indigenous services are systematically underfunded and in need of reform (Blackstock 2015; Trocmé, Knoke, and Blackstock 2004; APTN Nation to Nation 2018).

Qaqqaq does not attempt to put a price tag on the status quo or on repairs, insisting instead that "the damage caused by this neglect is beyond measure" (2021, 3). She does, however, insist that funding is the immediate solution: "Money for remediation and new units is the only solution. It is clear that the Nunavut Housing Corporation is underfunded ... The fault for Nunavut's housing concerns lies squarely with the Federal Government that needs to do more to support the NHC and every organization in Nunavut, with greater funding, and by listening to local solutions" (3).

These, then, are some of the causes of rising homelessness in Canada: cuts to housing programs and social spending, local planning decisions, deinstitutionalization, and colonialism. Myra Piat and colleagues consider how these macro forces play out on the individual level, and identify common pathways into homelessness on the implicit assumption that affordable housing and supports are not available or extremely limited (Piat et al. 2015). While there are some identifiable and common pathways into homelessness, especially its chronic variant, it is also clear that different groups of people face different risk factors. Violence, specifically intimate partner violence, is the most frequently cited cause of homelessness for women (Beattie and Hutchins 2014; Goodhand 2017). Queer and trans individuals also report violence, as well as family rejection (meaning that this population is particularly overrepresented among *youth* who are homeless) and system failures such as unsupported transitions out of foster care (Abramovich and Shelton 2017).

People living in rural and northern communities often cite unemployment or problems accessing social assistance as main causes of homelessness (Kauppi et al. 2017; Schiff and Turner 2014). When seniors experience homelessness for the first time, it tends to be due to poverty or a lack of safe, affordable housing (Grenier et al. 2016). All of

these risk factors play out at the individual level; in a context of housing unaffordability, ongoing racism and colonialism, transphobia and
homophobia, violence, and inaccessible or unaffordable health care,
they can make individuals more vulnerable to the experience of homelessness. Comparisons with other jurisdictions where the social safety
net is more robust (Benjaminsen and Andrade 2014; Benjaminsen, Dyb,
and O'Sullivan 2009), reinforce the conclusion that it is in a context of
limited affordable housing, inadequate social supports, and ongoing
colonialism that homelessness continues to be so widespread.

Who Experiences Homelessness?

Welfare state cuts, ambivalent responses by senior governments to new
social risks, and Canada's colonial history and present led to changes
in the homeless population. With governments slow to respond to their
needs, the increasingly diverse homeless population, already vulnerable and marginalized, had nowhere to turn and ended up on the streets
or in emergency homeless shelters that were poorly suited and adapted
to their needs. *More* people find themselves without housing today than
in the past. Long-term, comparable information on homelessness in
Canada to support this observation is hard to find; indeed, even just going back to the 1990s, systematic information is non-existent. While we
cannot create a simple chart illustrating the rise in homelessness across
Canada since the 1990s, we can patch together substantial evidence to
document that increase. Advocates and activists who have long been
involved on the front lines of the fight against homelessness stress
that they started to see more people experiencing homelessness in the
late 1980s and 1990s (Christensen 2017; Crowe 2019; Goodhand 2017;
Ranasinghe 2017; personal interviews). Corroborating these accounts
are a number of data sources that, when put together, show a clear increase in homelessness across Canada. Bearing in mind the preceding
discussion of definitions, it is important to note that these studies often consider people using the homeless shelter system and, in the case
of point-in-time counts, people living rough on the streets, and usually
do not capture people who are housing insecure, living in inadequate,
inappropriate, or overcrowded environments. And they are usually motivated by a housing-specific definition of homelessness. With that in
mind, we can still see a stark increase in the number of people experiencing homelessness and in chronic homelessness in particular.

One of the earliest studies of homelessness in Canada was conducted
in 1987, the UN's International Year of Shelter for the Homeless. In
that year, Canadian researchers found 472 shelter facilities across the

country with capacity for 13,797 people per night. Of those facilities, 274 (with a nightly capacity of 4,703) were for women fleeing violence and 198 shelters (with a nightly capacity of 9,094) were for the broader homeless population, including men, youth, and women not experiencing violence.[16] Thirty years later, the National Shelter Study (NSS) showed significant changes from 1987 (ESDC 2017). In 2017, the NSS identified more than 400 emergency shelters in Canada with a nightly capacity of 15,000 beds. Care should always be taken when comparing numbers, however, and two important caveats should be noted. First, violence-against-women shelters were *not* included in the 2017 NSS study but *were* included in the 1987 study. According to Statistics Canada, in 2016 there were an additional 455 violence-against-women shelters in the country, with 6,749 beds. When added to the NSS results, the total number of shelter beds in Canada in 2017 was closer to 22,000, compared to a total shelter capacity of a little less than 14,000 in 1987. The second important caveat is that the occupancy rate of the emergency shelter system has steadily increased, from 70 per cent in 1987 to 80 per cent by 2005 and 91 per cent in 2016 (ESDC 2017).[17] This means that while there were around 9,800 shelter beds in use in 1987, the number had more than doubled by 2016, to over 20,000. Even relative to increases in the overall Canadian population, this is significant growth.

Studies have also considered changes with respect to the chronicity of homelessness as a portion of the overall homeless population. These have shown a clear increase in the number of people experiencing chronic homelessness, though they remain a very small portion of the overall homeless population. The National Shelter Study found that while there was a drop in the number of *people* experiencing homelessness from 2005 to 2016, there were more *shelter beds* in the system and *occupancy rates* had gone up. This indicates that there was a marked increase in the chronicity of homelessness between 2005 and 2016; that is, more shelter beds were needed to accommodate a smaller number of people using the system annually because people were staying in the shelter system for longer than they had in the past.

Another attempt to understand homelessness, particularly chronic homelessness, has been through point-in-time counts, a methodology used in Canada and around the world to generate a "snapshot" image of how many people are homeless on one single night. Long-running annual counts in Vancouver and Calgary have shown there was an increase in the number of people experiencing chronic homelessness from the late 1990s to the mid-2000s (CHF 2008; City of Vancouver 2011), though again, care must always be taken when comparing numbers over time. Point-in-time homeless counts are widely recognized as accurately representing chronic homelessness; however, they under-represent other forms of homelessness (such as transitional or hidden) (Smith 2015). Though they ask slightly different questions over a different period of time, NSS surveys tell the same story as PiT counts: the number of people experiencing chronic homelessness has been increasing in Canada over the past twenty years.

In addition to this increase in the number of people experiencing homelessness and the number of people experiencing chronic homelessness, there have been changes since the 1990s in terms of who experiences homelessness. Researchers, advocates, and activists agree that in the past, homelessness tended to be experienced mostly by white men. In the 1990s, this started to change: chronic homelessness began to affect other groups, including women, racialized people, youth, and children (Crowe 2019; ESDC 2017; RAPSIM 2012; personal interviews). Changes to the homeless population continue today: a troubling trend identified recently has been a 58 per cent increase in the number of seniors experiencing homelessness for the first time over the 2005–14 period (ESDC 2017).[18] This confirms what many researchers have long argued – that the population of people experiencing homelessness is aging in tandem with the Canadian population as a whole (Burns, Sussman, and Bourgeois-Guérin 2018). At the same time, service providers and policy-makers have found that more trans people are experiencing homelessness and that this group is particularly vulnerable, requiring specialized and safe spaces. Big cities such as Toronto have started to respond accordingly, but the need to develop new approaches remains pressing (Abramovich and Lawless 2016).

Also, more children under the age of fourteen needed access to emergency shelters in 2014 than in 2005. Given that numerous governments at all levels have prioritized reducing childhood poverty, this is an outrageous failure of social protection. The National Shelter Study indicates that more than 6,000 children annually use the emergency shelter system, though this number is most certainly higher as it does not include children staying in violence-against-women shelters. The same study finds that across the country, 30 per cent of people staying in shelters are Indigenous, a massive overrepresentation relative to the general population: "the rate of shelter use is 10 times higher for Indigenous peoples than for non-Indigenous peoples" (ESDC 2017, 7). It is difficult to know how this has changed over time, given that federal attempts to understand homelessness across the country did not begin asking about Indigenous identity until 2014.

A widely respected homelessness advocate recalled seeing changes to the homeless population in Toronto right before their eyes. They reflected on their work prior to the 1980s: "I was a good advocate. I was out on evenings and weekends. I never, ever, ever, ever saw children homeless. I never saw seniors homeless" (personal interview 2014). They noted that this changed quickly: "beginning in the 1980s, as the cuts started to happen, there was a changing face of homelessness in Toronto. More women, more families ... senior citizens." In the past, those who required emergency services tended to be adult males, white, middle-aged, and unable to work; today a much more diverse population experiences homelessness (see Davies 2019; Goodhand 2017; Hughes 2015, 2018; Ranasinghe 2017; RAPSIM 2012). Today, people who are able to work experience homelessness. Indeed, people who *are* working are homeless (Calgary Drop-In 2007). Women, seniors, racialized people, and children all experience homelessness today (ESDC 2017; Goering et al. 2014; Latimer et al. 2015; Turner Strategies 2018). This has not always happened. This is new.

Place-Based Policy

Finally, we know that homelessness is place-based, meaning it varies from city to city and even from neighbourhood to neighbourhood (RAPSIM 2016). Those who are homeless in small cities, suburbs, or rural environments tend to be less visible: "rural homelessness [is] a 'hidden phenomenon' characterized by families and individuals doubling up and couch-surfing, or living in makeshift housing" (Schiff, Schiff, and Turner 2016, 76). This is in part due to a lack of emergency services in small towns and rural environments; a study of homelessness in rural Ontario noted "that in villages and small towns right across rural and northern Ontario, there are few coordinated institutional mechanisms in place that provide emergency services for those who experience homelessness" (Kauppi et al. 2017). Also, there can be a lack of rental housing in rural areas and small cities, and a lack of public transit means that people without cars are isolated from what services do exist.

Absent senior government support, small communities can have a harder time responding to the needs of homeless people. Kading and Walmsley explain that "[small cities] are obliged to rely more heavily on the largesse and the good will of federal and provincial governments in order to make substantive inroads in addressing homelessness. This dependence introduces a highly unpredictable variable into the planning process in small cities, no matter how committed the local government may be to addressing the long-term needs of the homeless population" (Kading and Walmsley 2018). For these reasons, individuals may experience more hidden types of homelessness, or they may move to larger cities where there are more services, as well as more jobs and opportunities. Homelessness and housing adequacy are in many ways more of a challenge in the North, where housing materials are more expensive as well as more difficult to access and where colonialism remains a dominant and present force (though colonialism remains present in the South as well). Accompanied by pictures, Qaqqaq's housing report highlights the health hazards associated with living in mouldy housing as well as the interpersonal stress that severely run-down and overcrowded housing environments place on families and children. Colonialism has interacted with place to bring about a uniquely profound housing crisis in Nunavut and across the North.

Homelessness is increasingly experienced across the country and in different kinds of spaces (urban, suburban, rural). Future research should continue to explore the governance dynamics of homelessness and how housing crises present themselves in different types of spaces. In this book, however, I consider the responses to homelessness in Canada's largest cities, where comparatively large numbers of people are homeless (ESDC 2017). Studies of service availability in the GTA illustrate how concentrated supports and services are in the downtown core. While social housing providers are scattered throughout the urban and suburban areas of Toronto, services specifically for homeless people – such as drop-in centres and shelters – are decidedly downtown (City of Toronto 2013). Furthermore, the 2018 Shelter Capacity report found that while 59 per cent of Canada's emergency shelters are in cities of over 300,000, 81 per cent of shelter beds are in big cities; in other words, shelters in big cities are larger than in small cities: "the average number of beds per shelter is 18 in small communities versus 55 in large communities" (ESDC 2019a). The concentration of homelessness services and needs underscores Bradford's important observation: "urban centres … are the places where today's most complex problems concentrate" (Bradford 2005). A primary motivation of this book is to understand how actors are responding to these localized needs.

Conclusion

Across Canada today, people who are pregnant are homeless. Babies are born into homelessness and children are raised homeless. The elderly fall into homelessness, and people die while experiencing homelessness. A Canadian shelter recently tweeted a request for donations of soothers because there were more babies in their homeless shelter than expected. Not too long ago, it would have been shocking to hear that an emergency shelter anticipated babies in its care; today, an unexpectedly large number of homeless babies hardly merits remark. This has not always been the case. It is the case now because of government decisions across multiple decades, including changes to the welfare state (both cuts to important programs and a failure of governments to respond to new social risks), local land-use planning and development decisions, and intentionally created landlessness and impoverishment of Indigenous people. No single actor or decision is responsible for the current situation; rather, the causes are persistent colonialism and systemic failures in our past and in our present. The causes involve multiple actors, so the solutions must be multiple as well. This makes the development of effective policy difficult, because it necessitates the involvement of so many groups. Further complicating the challenges we face are persistent disagreements about what homelessness *is*. The next chapter builds a framework to understand efforts to fight homelessness, a framework that centrally considers the definition of homelessness.

3 Governance Matters

Who governs? Who should govern? These empirical and normative questions are at the heart of the discipline of political science.

(Skogstad 2003, 955)

This book employs a distinctly place-based lens to study the multilevel governance of homelessness in four large urban centres. This lens, of course, does not negate the importance of the provinces and the federal government. All orders of government and sectors of civil society have a hand in producing social protection for those experiencing homelessness. Yet in studies of Canadian social policy, the local dimension of social policy governance has received considerably less attention than senior orders of government, a regrettable oversight that has limited our understanding of social protection. And while the urban governance literature is rich and highlights the innovations (as well as the constraints) of local actors, studies of complex and localized social policy problems are incomplete when they do not fully consider the actions of senior governments. A place-based approach to multilevel governance allows for a careful consideration of all these actors, from hyper-local to federal.

A central axiom of this study is that governance matters. Our theoretical task, then, is to understand the forces that structure governance dynamics. Drawing on insights from studies of the welfare state as well as multilevel governance, this book develops a novel framework for theorizing the involvement and interactions of various governmental and non-governmental actors in the multilevel governance of one of this country's most complex policy areas: homelessness. The following section reviews what we know about the governance of the welfare state and the producers of social protection in Canada. I then build a theoretical framework to map and explain the varying dynamics of homelessness governance across Canada, a framework that can be used for other complex policies as well. In doing so, I pay careful attention to institutions, resources, and ideas. Finally, I turn to the research design, carefully explaining the case selection and research methodology.

Who Governs the Welfare State?

Federal and provincial governments have a central role in welfare state governance or, as I also refer to it in this book, in the production of social protection[1]. The postwar expansion of the Canadian welfare state was largely a federal and provincial exercise. Senior governments, often led by the federal government, developed and expanded income security programs such as pensions and unemployment insurance; they also created a system of universal health care in the two decades following the Second World War (Banting 2005; Rice and Prince 2013). Despite early federal government leadership in welfare state development, provinces have come to be seen by some as the main producers of social protection in Canada, given their important jurisdictional responsibilities for health care, education, and social assistance (Rice and Prince 2013). James Rice and Michael Prince argue that social policy has become provincialized, writing that "in most matters of social policy, Canadian citizens are increasingly provincial citizens … In turn, it is from provincial governments that Canadians seem increasingly to expect policy responses" (299).

While the provinces have authority over substantial areas of the welfare state, the federal government maintains an inescapable role in welfare state governance as a primary funder, in part because its revenue-raising power exceeds what is needed to exercise its policy authorities, a reality referred to as the fiscal imbalance (Noël 2008). In addition to providing pensions outside of Quebec and employment insurance, the federal government transfers funding to the provinces to ensure that a similar level of social services can be offered across the country. These social transfers and equalization payments are political in nature and frequently generate disagreements among governments and regions (Lecours and Béland 2010).

Federal and provincial governments are central to welfare state governance, but so too is the practice of federalism in Canada, or the distribution of responsibilities between federal and provincial governments and the nature of the interactions between them. Official transfers of responsibility between orders of government are rare because they require constitutional amendment;[2] yet federalism as a practice has nevertheless evolved greatly since Confederation in 1867, and the interactions between federal and provincial governments have been characterized at times as cooperative and at times as conflictual. Periods of conflict between federal and provincial governments have in many ways been "a struggle for control over the welfare state" (Banting 2005, 16). According to Rose, housing policy in particular was a main battleground in constitutional conflicts during the 1970s (Rose 1980, 16). In part because of their constitutional status as holders of jurisdiction over so many social policies, and in part because of existential constitutional battles in the 1980s and 1990s, research into the production of social protection in Canada has focused strongly on the role of senior governments, either on their own or working together. This includes studies of health care (Boychuk 2008), education (Wallner 2010, 2014), income security and social assistance (Banting 1987, 2005; Banting and Myles 2013; Béland and Daigneault 2015; G. Boychuk 1998; Noël 2015), pensions (Babich and Béland 2009; Béland 2006; Béland and Waddan 2014), and poverty reduction (Larocque 2011; Larocque and Noël 2014; Noël 2002).

As the study of the history of federalism in Canada makes clear, federalism has been and continues to be a disputed arrangement, both in theory and in practice (Rocher 2009; Rocher and Fafard 2013). Federalism is viewed as hierarchical by some (with the federal government at the top) but as horizontal by others (with the federal and provincial governments being equals) (Noël 2001). Alain Noël has stressed conflict as opposed to collaboration in the history of Canadian federalism, coining the term "federalism with a footnote" to draw attention to the fact that so-called collaborative agreements involving the federal and provincial governments frequently do not include Quebec as a signatory (Noël 2000). This was the case with the Social Union Framework Agreement (SUFA), an agreement for social policy provision in Canada that was signed in 1999 by the federal government and all provinces and territories, except Quebec, as noted in an endnote. Studies of federalism and social policy governance are thus often accompanied by explicit or implicit assumptions regarding which senior level of government *should* do what in the production of social protection. Debates surrounding centralizing power in the federal government versus decentralizing power to the provinces (Noël 1999; Rice and Prince 2013), the fiscal imbalance between federal and provincial governments (Lecours and Béland 2010; Noël 2001, 2009), and the highly contested spending power (Choudhry, Sossin, and Gaudreault-DesBiens 2006; Noël 2001; Rice and Prince 2013) are thus often at the heart of the literature on the Canadian welfare state.

Federal and provincial governments are central actors in welfare state governance and thus are primary producers of social protection in Canada. Jane Jenson's work highlights the central role of these governments, and she too pays attention to the changing relationships between them in her work on the evolving governance – or "social architecture" as she calls it – of the welfare state (Jenson 2013). Informed by the traditions of feminist and critical political economy, however, Jenson observes that markets, families, and voluntary associations are also producers of social protection, alongside governments. Women's unpaid labour, for example, has historically been built into the very foundation of the welfare state, as women have been assumed to be caregivers for children and others requiring care. In this way, families (often seen through heteronormative gender roles of a male breadwinner and a stay-at-home wife) have produced social protection and have formed an important part of Canada's social architecture. Voluntary associations such as foodbanks and emergency shelters have been the very last line of defence against social risks (including poverty, food insecurity, and homelessness), many with funding cobbled together from private donations and small government grants. The private sector plays an important role in the social architecture of the welfare state as well, in that some social protections are afforded only to those attached to the labour market (employment insurance, for example) and, for our purposes, through its central role in the provision of housing.

Indigenous people and communities are often absent from studies of welfare state governance. They are often assumed to be care receivers or service users, but have not always been viewed as producers of social protection either on their own or in partnership with other actors. This ignores the tremendous capacity in Indigenous communities and the history of Indigenous governance and social practices. Recognizing the role Indigenous people play in the production of social protection, as well as the expertise and knowledge held by Indigenous-led organizations and communities, the pages that follow consider Indigenous actors to be important, necessary actors in the production of social protection in addition to the governments and non-governmental actors identified earlier. This is at times as partners and collaborators, but also using resurgent practices on their own. All levels of government (federal, provincial, and municipal) as well as civil society actors (third-sector and private-sector actors) and Indigenous-led organizations and communities have some role to play in protecting people in Canada against social risks such as poverty, unemployment, or illness.

Welfare state governance is not static, but evolves over time. In other words, the distribution of responsibility among actors producing social protection has changed over time. Further, it varies from policy to policy as well. The 1960s and 1970s are sometimes seen as the golden age of the welfare state, largely because this was a time when *both* senior orders of government were developing and expanding social programs, including a national housing program. While the welfare state certainly was expanding, critical and feminist political economists have questioned how "golden" this era really was, arguing that "large numbers of minorities and women, especially those who were not engaged in full-time employment, were excluded from the full benefits of the welfare state … Thus the welfare state itself helped sustain and reinforce structural inequalities" (McKeen and Porter 2003, 115). Stephen McBride similarly notes that the early Canadian welfare state was "a gendered and racialized one" (McBride 2019, 153). And, of course, during this period, Indigenous people were facing aggressive colonization on a number of fronts, including the suppression and outlawing of their traditions and systems of governance, and children were being forced to attend residential "schools" or were removed from their homes and placed in underresourced child welfare systems. Indeed, this Golden Era coincided with the Sixties Scoop.[3] Both perspectives hold true: in certain respects (such as access to affordable housing and social assistance incomes), social protection was at its high-water mark in Canadian history, yet the social protection offered by the Keynesian welfare state was not always just and did not extend to everyone equitably.

Keynesianism came under attack in the 1980s, in Canada as in the rest of the world. This was a political and ideological process (McBride 2019; McKeen and Porter 2003), with debates raging within the Liberal Party regarding the role the federal government should play in the production of social protection: Keynesians argued for increased government involvement, while members on the more neoliberal side of the party envisioned a smaller role for government. Neoliberal monetarists would ultimately come to control the Liberal Party, with the result that the federal government – led through these decades by either the Progressive Conservatives or the newly neoliberal Liberal Party – backed away from substantial areas of social protection in the 1980s and 1990s, including housing. The distribution of responsibility among producers of social protection was changing, with the federal government playing a smaller role than it had in the past.

In addition to directly cutting its own social spending, the federal government unilaterally changed its system for transferring funds to the provinces for social programs, substantially reducing the amount of that funding. Prior to the mid-1990s, the federal government offered provinces essentially limitless cost-shared dollars for social policies through the Canada Assistance Plan; the catch was that conditions were imposed on these funds, such as what this funding could be spent on (conditions to which the provinces had long objected). The replacement model, introduced abruptly in 1996, was the Canada Health and

Social Transfer (CHST). The CHST removed federal conditions (a long-time provincial demand) but also transferred less money. Faced with reduced funding, many provinces shrank their involvement in the production of social protection, making sweeping cuts to social spending, including cutting social assistance by as much as 20 per cent. Furthermore, eight of the ten[4] entirely eliminated their investments in future social housing developments. Interestingly, throughout this process of welfare state change, universal health care was largely untouched (Graefe 2018; see also Banting 2020; Boychuk 2008).

Social protection further decreased as a result of the inability or unwillingness (or both) of senior governments to respond to changing demographics; this produced new social risks against which Canadians were left unprotected. Some of the most important demographic changes were declining birth rates; increasing divorce rates; growing numbers of single-parent (mostly female-led) families; the rapid entrance of women into the workforce and, if they had children, a need for childcare; an aging population; and an increase in both Indigenous people and immigrants among the urban population (Jenson 2004; see also Banting and Thompson 2021). The failure to respond to new social risks – called "drift" in social policy literature to refer to government inaction in the face of new or changed social risks (Hacker 2004; Hacker and Pierson 2010) – combined with decisions to cut and retrench led to significant gaps in coverage against new social risks such as working poverty, the need for childcare for women (sometimes single mothers) who needed or decided to work, food insecurity, and chronic homelessness. Banting and Thompson (2021) have further noted how the failure to respond to changing demographics particularly in terms of increasing racial diversity has led to persistent racial inequality.

Keith Banting and John Myles look back on decades of changes to the welfare state and conclude that "retrenchment has mattered but inaction has mattered more. A critical part of the story has been the quiet indifference to new social risks and rising inequality" (Banting and Myles 2013, 426). As a result of political decisions to cut and retrench the welfare state, and political inaction in the face of new and exacerbated risks, senior governments were playing a smaller role in the provision of social protection in the 1990s than they had in the post-war past, leaving markets, families, and voluntary associations to fill the gaps and pick up the slack. Rice and Prince explain that in the wake of welfare state changes, "social safety nets are now badly frayed and closer to the ground" (Rice and Prince 2013, 137).

These foundational changes to Canada's social architecture produced a restructured and rescaled welfare state. *Restructuring* refers to the shift in responsibility for producing social protection from governments to non-governmental actors; it is conceptualized as an "outward" or horizontal shift of power (Mahon 2007, 56). This includes a shift in power from governments to the private sector, families, and voluntary associations. McKeen and Porter note that following welfare state changes there was "an increase in the numbers of other organizations of civil society, such as food banks, that are attempting to fill the needs of those who fall between the cracks" (2003, 116) as these groups worked to produce the protection against risks that governments now ignored or abandoned. As Rice and Prince agree, "the consequences of this retrenchment of public programs, and of parallel changes to the market economy, have been emergency shelters, food banks, and soup kitchens" (Rice and Prince 2013, 135).

Rescaling is a shift of responsibility "downward" (Mahon 2007, 56) and involves an offloading of responsibilities from senior to local governments or to local groups, often without a corresponding transfer of funding. This can be done in one of two ways. The first is a deliberate transfer of authority, as was the case with housing policy in Ontario, which was officially transferred to local governments in the 1990s. But it can also be done less directly, as Graham, Phillips, and Maslove explain: "The second type of downloading occurs when the provincial or federal government simply abandons a service or activity area. The assumption is that if a real need exists, someone will fill the void" (Graham, Phillips, and Maslove 1998, 174). The "someone" who fills the void, they write, is often a municipal government. In the Canadian context, downloading responsibility without the accompanying funding is especially problematic because municipalities are so limited in their policy autonomy and financial capacity (Smith and Spicer 2018), meaning they are ill-equipped to respond to social needs.

These changes to the welfare state's architecture and governance have resulted in fundamental changes in the production of social protection, three of which are important here. First, policy change and policy drift have exacerbated old social risks (such as poverty) and created new ones (chronic homelessness), placing considerable stress on the welfare state. One has to fall farther before encountering the safety net, a net that is itself thin and full of holes through which one can easily fall further. However, these changes to the welfare state also created opportunities for a new way of producing social protection. Thus, the second consequence of the restructured and rescaled welfare state was that it created new actors, and empowered existing ones, in the production of social protection. These actors, primarily locally based and are on the front lines of the welfare state, have the knowledge, expertise, and tolerance for risk required to develop effective and innovative social protection. Municipal governments,

Indigenous-led organizations and communities, and civil society actors, forced to meet needs no one else was meeting, opened their toolboxes (and often looked outside those toolboxes) in search of creative ways to respond to social needs, not just through advocacy but also through policy and program efforts. To be clear, emergency measures are a far cry from the structural responses needed to respond effectively to social risks, as many foodbank and emergency shelter managers themselves would say. Yet through this front-line work responding to the most basic needs of shelter and food, these groups have developed extensive expertise and capacity, proving that they are necessary partners in the development and implementation of effective and equitable solutions to complex problems (including homelessness). This is even more the case because complex policies like homelessness manifest themselves in highly localized ways, meaning they require local expertise even more urgently.

Finally, while it may not have been the intention of senior governments, retrenchment and restructuring created new, local spaces for social policy experimentation and innovation. While they often had neither the jurisdictional authority nor the financial resources to fully occupy this vacant policy space, local groups innovated at the local or even neighbourhood level, designing emergency responses, such as foodbanks and emergency shelters, and experimenting with ways to produce social protection against new social risks through sophisticated responses to local problems (Andrew 2003; Mahon 2007; Rice and Prince 2013). In the context of this rescaled and restructured welfare state, Rianne Mahon illustrates how the local level became a space for experimenting with new approaches to childcare in Toronto. Gaps in social protection were created by government inaction in the face of a growing need for childcare for single-parent households or those with two working parents, gaps that "offered feminists opportunities to challenge federal policy at the provincial and local level" (Mahon 2007, 55). Working together in Toronto, local actors designed a universal childcare system, one that contrasted with the targeted, residual nature of provincial and federal approaches to the welfare state. Caroline Andrew has also argued that the local level is an important space for policy experimentation; she has documented how the direct involvement of women in policy processes can create a safer city, offering as an example Montreal's "Between Two Stops," which enables women to ask bus drivers to stop between two official stops so they do not have to walk far alone at night (Andrew 2003). This local space has allowed for the sort of innovation, experimentation, and risk-taking that is not possible at the larger provincial or national scale.

The rescaled and restructured welfare state created new risks, many of which, including homelessness, were concentrated in urban centres;

but it also empowered new actors in the policy-making process, including municipal governments and locally based private and third-sector groups; and it opened up new, local venues for policy-making and service delivery. In other words, though the changes made by senior governments in a "neoliberal moment" tore at the fabric of the social safety net by scaling back government provision of social protection (Banting and Myles 2013), welfare state restructuring also made way for a new, place-based approach to policy-making that has afforded a vital role for local actors to produce social protection alongside senior governments.

Explaining the Governance of Homelessness: Involvement and Interactions

In an area of policy as complex as homelessness, government and non-governmental actors all have a role to play in the production of social protection. Indeed, they need each other: local groups (including municipalities and third-sector and private-sector groups) and Indigenous leaders are the "knowers," as Caroline Andrew would say, of needs and solutions (Andrew 2003). But they do not have the resources or authority (or both) to develop long-term solutions. The opposite can reasonably be said for senior governments: they have the capacity, including jurisdiction and financial resources, but may lack place-based knowledge. Homelessness governance therefore requires the involvement and interaction of a multitude of actors. Looking across the country, we see that a number of governmental and non-governmental actors are involved in homelessness governance and have formed very different governance networks. The objective now is to map and theorize these governance arrangements, paying particular attention to the involvement of various actors and their interactions.

The literature on multilevel governance in Canada is useful here. For Christopher Leo and Martine August, multilevel governance is "the commonplace attempt to ensure that national government policies are formulated and implemented with sufficient flexibility to ensure their appropriateness to the very different conditions in different communities. Elsewhere we have referred to this condition, where it is achieved, as deep federalism" (Leo and August 2009). Leo and a variety of collaborators, including August, have explored deep federalism in thirteen case studies across Canada, operating with the assumption that deep federalism refers to national policy that is sensitive to local contexts.

Multilevel governance need not to be national in scope, however; Charles Conteh conceptualizes multilevel governance as both "inter-jurisdictional (involving several levels of government) and inter-organizational (involving policy engagement between state and non-state actors)" (Conteh 2013, 32), and he considers several regional, rather than national, initiatives across the country. Similarly, Martin Horak defines multilevel governance as "a mode of policymaking that involves complex interactions among multiple levels of government and social forces" (Horak 2012, 339). The study of multilevel governance in Canada has thus paid attention to two dimensions: the *involvement* of actors, or the extent to which they participate in various stages of the policy-making process, including agenda-setting, policy-development, funding, and implementation; and their *interactions*, referring to the nature of the relationship between the actors and the extent to which their actions are collaborative or coordinated (Horak 2012).

Scholarship on multilevel governance has made clear that there is extensive variety in its form and shape across the country. Looking back on thirteen case studies of multilevel governance, Leo and August conclude that "the pattern, in other words, is that there is no pattern" (Leo and August 2009, 57). They continue: "Circumstances alter cases. Indeed, if there is any point at all to multilevel governance, it is that circumstances must alter cases, that we can achieve better governance by treating each policy and each community as a discrete, individual set of circumstances, not entirely the same as any other" (57). Leading place-based policy scholar Neil Bradford identifies three types of multilevel governance: federal–provincial/territorial agreements with municipal involvement; direct federal–municipal/community programming; and federal–provincial–municipal policy adaptation (Bradford 2018). And within each of these models, great variety is possible with respect to the degree of involvement of each actor, which actor is leading, and the dynamics between them. Reviewing the results of Robert Young's flagship study of multilevel governance in Canada, the Fields of Governance series, Horak agrees, noting the diverse forms of multilevel governance: "one of the most striking aspects of multilevel governance in Canada's big cities is the tremendous variety of forms that it takes" (2012, 340).

The framework developed below follows these scholars in assuming that multilevel governance considers both the involvement and interactions of different actors and that variety in form is the rule rather than the exception. Thus, I consider the involvement and interactions of federal, provincial, and municipal governments, the private sector, and the third sector,[5] as well as Indigenous leaders. There is a rich tradition of Indigenous governance and Indigenous resurgence that centres Indigenous systems of governance in the context of the settler colonial Canadian state (Ladner 2003, 2005; Corntassel 2012; Voth 2020; Coulthard 2015; Simpson 2021). Within the specific literature on multilevel governance, however, with certain exceptions primarily relating to intergovernmental relations (Abele and Prince 2006; Alcantara 2018; Papillon 2009), Indigenous leaders and communities are rarely included in their own right as policy-making actors. Another important exception to this is *Urban Aboriginal Policy Making in Canadian Municipalities* (Peters 2012), which is part of the Fields of Governance series. The primary interest of the contributors is "Aboriginal policy" in urban centres, in which Indigenous groups are assumed to be important participants. In the conclusion, series leader Robert Young makes the case for increased autonomy for Indigenous groups in the development of Aboriginal policy: "if so, policy will improve" (Young 2012). Indigenous groups are not, however, included as actors in the broader series, which includes other areas of policy including infrastructure, immigrant settlement, federal property, image building, and emergency planning.

In the following chapters, it will become clear that Indigenous-led networks and organizations (working on their own or in collaboration with other networks, sectors or governments) have a central role to play in policy areas outside of urban Indigenous policy, including in the fight against homelessness in Canada. Indigenous-led organizations are therefore considered key producers of social protection. Finally, I do not assume that policies must be national in scope. Indeed, I consider only one national program: the National Homelessness Initiative/Homelessness Partnering Strategy. Other initiatives that form an integral part of the homelessness landscape are provincial, regional, and local in scope, and must also be included in the analysis. As will become clear, some of the most innovative and exciting ideas originate at the local level.

The framework developed below structures actors and their involvement and interactions primarily through the lenses of ideas and institutions, while acknowledging the importance of different kinds of resources as well. To explain the first dimension of multilevel governance – the *involvement* of actors – Horak stresses the importance of institutions. Perhaps most obviously, jurisdiction is central to understanding why one level of government is (or is not) involved in a policy field: "if a single level of government has primary authority in a policy field, it usually plays a central role in policy development, and is often involved in implementation as well" (Horak 2012, 349). Other policy-specific institutional features structure municipal government involvement (or non-involvement) as well. With respect to homelessness, these are housing-related powers: density bonusing and inclusionary zoning powers. Density bonusing allows cities to increase the allowable number of units in new private housing developments (by allowing for smaller units or more floors, for example) in exchange for public amenities, such as affordable housing, parks, libraries, or public art (Moore 2013, 1). Because of differences in local housing markets, density bonusing is a more meaningful power in some study cities than in others.

Inclusionary zoning allows cities to mandate that developers provide the city either with affordable housing units, with land that can be used for future affordable housing developments, or with a cash contribution to an affordable housing fund (Mah 2009, 25). In cases where land is provided to the city, the city can use it as leverage to encourage others (usually not-for-profits or provincial governments) to partner in an affordable housing development. As with density bonusing, the strength of this power depends on the context, including the availability of land and how negotiations between private developers and the city unfold. This power must be granted to local governments by provincial governments. Though important, these powers are often criticized because they depend on private-sector development and result in few units of social or affordable housing relative to the number of market units that are produced (Davies 2019).

Though institutions are important, a striking conclusion arising from studies of multilevel governance is that "the distribution of resources plays an equally – *and sometimes more* – important role [than jurisdiction] in shaping multi-level governance systems" (Horak 2012, 349; emphasis added). Horak's understanding of resources is broad, including not just financial resources but also locally specific knowledge and expertise. This holistic understanding of resources characterizes many place-based studies of policy, where local knowledge and expertise is understood to be key to responding effectively to wickedly complex policy problems (Andrew 2003; Bradford 2014). Given the place-based nature of this analysis and the variety of forms homelessness takes across the country, and even within a single city, this understanding of resources as including knowledge and expertise is maintained in this book.

The second dimension of multilevel governance is the *interactions* of actors, which are particularly important in complex areas of policy where power is fragmented among a number of actors. Challenges to the development of collaborative governance in fragmented contexts are not insurmountable, and here, the literature points to the importance of institutionalization:

> Since multilevel coordination often takes a great deal of time, the potential for a change in agenda at any one level of government presents a significant threat to the achievement of multilevel policy objectives. This

threat can, however, be mitigated if multilevel governance becomes institutionalized. In other words, if the sharing of resources and authority among agents is regularized through the establishment of a formal agreement or the development of a multilevel governing agency or body. (Horak 2012, 363)

Bradford also notes the importance of regular interactions, which build trust. He adds that informal interactions among actors can develop trust but like Horak, he also concludes that institutionalization, which allows for regular interactions among policy-making actors, is required (Bradford 2018).

From studies of multilevel governance, it is clear that resources and institutions, in their various forms, structure the involvement and interactions of actors. Yet a focus on institutions and resources leaves unanswered important questions, such as why actors with substantial resources were not, at various points in history, involved in homelessness governance. This is the case with Toronto's resource-rich private sector, and also for the Government of Alberta, which had both jurisdiction for housing and financial resources to invest throughout the early 2000s and yet did not. It also leaves unanswered the question of why, in a situation where resources and institutions did not change, actors increased (or decreased) their involvement in the governance of homelessness, as was the case in Montreal in 2013. Furthermore, why did third-sector actors overcome significant institutional barriers to govern collaboratively in Toronto? To understand these seeming contradictions, we turn to the literature on welfare state governance and the importance of ideas.

There is a rich tradition of research on the role of ideas in political processes (Thompson 2016), including in studies of welfare state governance in Canada (Béland 2005; Béland and Cox 2016; Haddow 2015; Jenson 2010, 2013; McKeen and Porter 2003; Banting and Thompson 2021). And if we look closely, we see that ideas hold explanatory potential in existing studies of multilevel governance, as I will explain below. Given what we know about the role of ideas in structuring welfare state governance, and this opening to a role for ideas in studies of multilevel governance, this present study considers them centrally. Horak concluded that resources may be more important than jurisdiction in the development of multilevel governance arrangements; an important conclusion of this book is that ideas may be more powerful than both.

Ideas are defined as "historically constructed beliefs and perceptions of both individuals and collective actors" (Béland 2019, 4). Béland and Cox explain that they "are the products of cognition. They are produced in our minds and are connected to the material world only via our interpretations of our surroundings" (Béland and Cox 2010, 3), continuing to note that they "posit connections between things and between people in the world" (3). Ideas are therefore understood to be causal forces that shape the behaviour of political actors and the outcomes of political processes (Béland and Cox 2010). Ideational theory seeks to explain the ways in which ideas shape outcomes: "ideational theory posits a causal effect of the content of actors cognitions on their choices" (Jacobs 2014, 43). This approach is particularly useful for studies of political coalitions and governance networks because of the power of ideas to attract individuals or groups to work together, as will be explained below (Béland and Cox 2010, 2016). Three kinds of ideas structure multilevel governance arrangements: ideas regarding the responsibility to produce social protection, which can interact with ideas regarding federalism; conceptualizations of the role of local government; and ideas regarding the nature of homelessness, or the definition of homelessness. While these three kinds of ideas can be seen across the two dimensions of multilevel governance (involvement and interactions), I find that the first two tend to structure involvement and the third tends more often to structure interactions.

The first idea is regarding the responsibility to produce social protection. Jane Jenson explains its significance: "changing ideas about individual and collective responsibility, as well as the respective role of market, families, voluntary associations and states have driven the recent redesign of Canadian social architecture" (Jenson 2013, 47). For our purposes, this means considering which level of government or sector of society key actors believe is responsible for producing social protection against the risk of homelessness. Importantly, this involves not only actors' ideas about their *own* role in producing social protection but also their ideas about the role *other* actors should (or should not) play. Rice and Prince give an example of this: looking back to the period of welfare state retrenchment, they write, "governments that want to dismantle their welfare state must believe that the private sector, families, or local communities can provide social supports more effectively than states" (Rice and Prince 2013, 116).

In some instances, these ideas are coloured by related ideas about federalism, which include disagreeing as well as evolving understandings of which senior level of government is and should be responsible for the production of social protection. These ideas have been particularly important forces with regard to federal and provincial involvement, but in some instances we also see these ideas influencing local actors. In studies of the Canadian welfare state, these ideas have been well-documented:

"Interpretations of the constitutional division of powers, recognition of national identities, and the ways to accommodate difference and diversity are notions that have been extensively debated and have shifted over time. Such ideas have shaped the politics of redistribution" (Jenson 2013, 47). A province that views federalism as an arrangement between equal federal and provincial governments and jealously guards its jurisdiction may *increase* its involvement in a certain field, motivated by ideas concerning a strong provincial role (and small federal role) in the production of social protection. A province that understands federalism differently and believes that key areas of social policy are, or can be, shared or perhaps even primarily belong to the federal government, may accordingly *minimize* its involvement in governance.

The second kind of idea that structures multilevel governance relates specifically to local governments. Horak points to the importance of ideas in his discussion of factors that drive local governments' involvement in multilevel governance, stressing "the importance of conceptions of local government held by local political leaders" (Horak 2012, 351). When city councillors and local officials in the government bureaucracy view their city as a mere implementer or "policy-taker" (Horak and Young 2012), local governments tend to be less involved in multilevel governance. In contrast, Horak finds that a "'comprehensive' conception of local government … calls for municipal leadership in seeking solutions to emerging local problems of all kinds and encourages local politicians to deepen their involvement in multilevel governance" (Horak 2012, 351). In other words, local officials who believe that their government has a bigger role to play than just fixing potholes or picking up the garbage are more likely to increase their involvement in multilevel governance. For local governments, then, in addition to ideas regarding the responsibility to produce social protection, conceptualization of the local government is the second ideational factor that structures their involvement in homelessness governance.

The third kind of idea relates to the nature of the problem, or, as Jenson explains, "the ways in which political actors interpret problems and identify solutions" (Jenson 2013, 46). When it comes to homelessness, as the previous chapter explained, this is primarily operationalized as the definition of homelessness. In some cases I find that a very specific idea about homelessness has motivated involvement or structured interactions – for example, that ending homelessness will save money. I find that ideas regarding the nature of homelessness tend to structure the interactions of groups; that said, ideas regarding the nature of homelessness also shape actor involvement. If actors define homelessness narrowly, for example, they may conclude that it is not their responsibility (or they may alternatively conclude that it *is*); if homelessness is defined more broadly, however, actors may increase their involvement because the broad definition has shaped their understanding of their greater responsibility to produce social protection. These ideas are powerful, and even small differences can have significant implications for the governance of homelessness by leading to the development of competing groups and even different plans to fight homelessness.

Ideational analysis requires that researchers find evidence that ideas shape political outcomes; in the case at hand, that means finding evidence that ideas have shaped the involvement and interactions of actors in governance networks. Alan Jacobs writes that ideational theory and analysis present a number of challenges to empirical study, most notably because ideas are difficult to observe. It can also be a challenge to separate ideas from material interests, which makes the independent study of the effects of ideas even more difficult. To guide researchers in empirical ideational research, Jacobs suggests that ideational theory must therefore do three things: "seek evidence that: (1) decision-makers possessed particular cognitions ... (2) those cognitions shaped their choices ... and (3) those cognitions were not simply reducible to material features of the circumstances of choice" (Jacobs 2014, 45).

Jacobs argues that process-tracing, which includes searching for evidence of causal mechanisms, is an appropriate method for ideational analysis (Jacobs 2014; see also Béland 2019). Establishing causality – that ideas shaped the networks – thus requires the identification of mechanisms by which this happens. Causal mechanisms allow researchers to look inside the "black box of causation" (Trampusch and Palier 2016). In other words, mechanisms identify the "nuts, bolts, cogs and wheels that move a process forward" (Campbell 2004, 64). Drawing again from the welfare state literature, I argue that ideas influence governance and coalition-building through environmental and cognitive mechanisms. Environmental mechanisms "work to expand the political space for discussions of alternatives" (Jenson 2010, 68); cognitive mechanisms occur when "perceptions of policy challenges shift and possible solutions were reinterpreted" (71). In the pages that follow, we can see cognitive mechanisms at work when ideas, particularly ambiguous ones, become what Béland and Cox (2016) call a "coalition magnet." An idea becomes a coalition magnet when it appeals "to a diversity of individuals and groups, and [is] used strategically by policy entrepreneurs ... to frame interests, mobilize supporters and build coalitions" (Béland and Cox 2016, 429). Ambiguous or polysemic ideas, which can mean different things to different people, can be particularly powerful coalition magnets, for they attract actors who hold what might otherwise be diverging, perhaps even opposed, ideologies and beliefs (Jenson 2010; Palier 2005). Furthermore, an idea's "valence," which "refers to the attractiveness of an idea" (Béland and Cox 2016, 432), is also important. Ambiguous ideas with high positive valence are more likely to transform into powerful coalition magnets and shape the construction of political coalitions.

Establishing that an idea has transformed into a coalition magnet requires that three mechanisms be identified: first, "the ideas are effectively manipulated by policy entrepreneurs" (Béland and Cox 2016, 429), often resulting in a redefinition or new understanding of a problem. Second, the idea must be "embraced or promoted by key actors in the policy process" (429). Third and finally, an idea becomes a coalition magnet when it brings together individuals or groups of individuals who might otherwise disagree on policy or politics. In the pages that follow, we will find that it is ideas regarding the nature of homelessness that are most likely to transform into coalition magnets; moreover, even more specific ideas related to the definition of homelessness often do this work. Magnetic ideas are powerful because they can pull wide-ranging groups together; yet they can also push groups apart with just as much force, an idea left unexplored by Béland and Cox and an innovative contribution of this book to ideational theory. This has happened in some cities, where groups that disagree on the nature of homelessness sometimes work separately or even at cross-purposes.

Studies of complex policy problems cannot and should not examine ideas and institutions in isolation. A similar ideational disagreement can result in fragmentation in one environment, but productive coordination in another. Therefore, a careful consideration of the interactions of ideas and institutions offers significant leverage and explanatory power when it comes to complex problems and governance networks. Béland and Waddan write that "both ideational and institutional analyses have clear analytical value on their own terms but, under many circumstances, it is the combination of the two perspectives that allows for a full understanding" (Béland and Waddan 2015, 176). Turning our attention to the *interaction* of ideas and institutions, this study's findings repeatedly reinforce Béland and Cox's conclusion that "institutional factors can constrain the production and dissemination of ideas" (Béland and Cox 2010, 16). I also find ample evidence to support findings from other work, that institutions can also bolster ideas (Béland and Waddan 2015).

Resources also matter, and this analysis considers how different forms of resources bolster or constrain the power of ideas as well. But ideas help governments and other groups decide what to *do* with their resources (Hay 2011). It is certainly true that governments go through periods of fiscal restraint and times when they have more money to spend. Yet in either case, governments must decide what to do with their resources and whether to exercise or even exceed their authority; for this reason, the pages that follow take a constructivist approach to the understanding of resources and how they are deployed. The three ideas reviewed here allow actors to make decisions regarding what to do with their resources and institutions. Without assuming that resources and institutions necessarily pose barriers, or necessarily reinforce ideas, this work considers how ideas interact with, and are affected by, institutions. In tracing ideas held by key actors in each sector, and combining this with institutional insights drawn from studies of multilevel governance and a consideration of different kinds of resources, the framework will allow us to explain how the multilevel governance of homelessness is differently shaped in Vancouver, Calgary, Toronto, and Montreal.

Research Design and Methods

The four cities under study here have been selected because of their similarities. Vancouver, Calgary, Toronto, and Montreal are Canada's largest urban centres in their respective provinces, and according to the best available comparable data (i.e., the nationally coordinated point-in-time homeless count conducted in 2018), they have the largest numbers of people experiencing homelessness of all cities in their provinces. Table 3.1 reviews the results of recent efforts to understanding how many people are homeless. Because of population differences between the four cities, the table does not allow us to make direct numerical comparisons; it does, however, show trends *within* cities, though changes to methodologies and the fact that Calgary conducted counts during different parts of the year for periods of time mean that even within-city comparisons should be made with caution. Homelessness in Vancouver has risen steadily since the early 2000s, whereas homelessness in Calgary rose quickly during the early 2000s but then reversed (though this is in part due to a change in methodology, introduced in the early 2000s, which resulted in services that had previously been excluded from the count being included). In Toronto, the number of people experiencing homelessness dropped in the mid-2000s only to rise again in 2013, and then dramatically so in 2018. The stark rise in people experiencing homelessness in Toronto in 2018 was in part due to the large number of refugees and asylum-seekers in Toronto at that time. Montreal has the fewest available data, at least when it comes to point-in-time counts; what is available shows considerable stability between 2015 and 2018.

Table 3.1. Results of homeless counts: Vancouver, Calgary, Toronto, and Montreal

	Vancouver	Calgary[a]	Toronto	Montreal
2004		2,397		
2005	1,364			
2006		3,157	5,052	
2007				
2008	1,576	3,601		
2009			4,467	
2010	1,751			
2011	1,581			
2012	1,602	3,190		
2013	1,600		4,969	
2014	1,803	3,533		
2015	1,746			3,016
2016	1,847	3,430		
2017	2,138			
2018	2,181	2,911	8,715[b]	3,149
2019	2,223			

[a] Calgary began homeless counts in 1992. The results of those early counts are: 1992: 447; 1994: 461; 1996: 615; 1998: 988 (CHF 2012).
[b] The 2018 homeless count in Toronto identified a large number of people in the emergency shelter system who had crossed the border irregularly and were seeking asylum. This sudden increase in asylum-seekers was unusual and in part related to global events (Paquet and Schertzer 2020).
Sources: Vancouver counts – see Singh 2021; Calgary counts – see Calgary Homeless Foundation 2018; Toronto counts – see City of Toronto 2018; Montreal counts – see Latimer et al 2018.

Using population data from Statistics Canada, table 3.2 allows us to begin comparing cases by considering the number of people who experience homelessness relative to the city's general population. This presentation is intended to demonstrate how the lived experience of homelessness varies in cities across the country; it should not, however, obscure the fact that these numbers represent people. Counts in 2018 were coordinated, meaning they took place at the same time of year and used the same methodology, including the CHRN's definition of homelessness, which relates homelessness exclusively to the lack of adequate, affordable housing. Comparisons before 2018 should be approached with some caution, for the counts used different methodologies; in addition, those counts took place at different times of the year, which perhaps affected the results (see Smith 2015).[6]

Bearing in mind methodological differences before 2018, table 3.2 reveals that more people experience homelessness in Vancouver and Calgary than in Toronto and Montreal. When placed in an international

Table 3.2. Homeless population per capita

	Vancouver	Calgary	Toronto	Montreal
2004		1 in 410		
2005	1 in 424			
2006		1 in 288	1 in 495	
2007				
2008	1 in 367	1 in 213		
2009			1 in 560	
2010	1 in 330			
2011	1 in 382			
2012	1 in 377	1 in 344		
2013	1 in 377		1 in 585	
2014	1 in 335	1 in 310		
2015	1 in 346			1 in 565
2016	1 in 342	1 in 361		
2017	1 in 296			
2018	1 in 290	1 in 426	1 in 313	1 in 541
2019	1 in 284			

context, however, it becomes clear that these Canadian cities are peers in terms of the scale of the challenge they are facing. New York City, for example, has a population of almost 9 million, and it is estimated that between 70,000 and 80,000 people there experience homelessness – that is, a staggering 1 in 125 people (Blint-Welsh 2019). The reality for Los Angeles is even worse; that city has an estimated 36,000 homeless people – a ratio of 1 in 110 (*The Guardian* 2019).

The four Canadian cities are also comparable in terms of the local housing market, though Montreal is notably more affordable than other cities, especially since 2005. Using Statistics Canada data, figure 3.1 compares the average cost of a one-bedroom apartment in the four cities. While Calgary fluctuates more than other cities and Montreal is noticeably more affordable, the cost of a one-bedroom apartment has been increasing steadily in all four cities. And while Montreal is much more affordable, it will become clear below that even an affordable one-bedroom apartment in Montreal is unaffordable for an individual on social assistance (the income support received by many individuals experiencing homelessness; see Prince 2015).

Vacancy rates are used to assess how much private rental housing is available in a given city. When vacancy rates are low, rents tend to increase, as the supply of housing cannot meet the demand for it. Also, it can be more difficult for a person experiencing homelessness to find

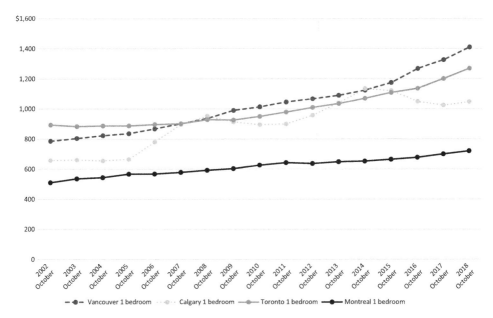

Figure 3.1. Average rent, one-bedroom apartment. Information from the CMHC Rental Market Survey

somewhere to rent when vacancy is low, in no small part because of discrimination and racism (Alini 2017; Johnson 2019; Newman-Bremang and Ebrahim 2021; Springer 2021). Vacancy rates have consistently been low in Vancouver and have, over time, become lower in Toronto. We again see instability in Calgary, where vacancy rates fluctuated between very low in 2006 to much more reasonable in the mid-2010s. Montreal is more stable, with rates generally remaining at or above 3 per cent.

One final relevant point of comparison between the cities is their respective social assistance incomes. Social assistance is provided provincially and is often seen as the safety net of last resort (Prince 2015). Rates for "single people considered employable" are well below the poverty line in all cities, and the rates in the four cities under study converged somewhere between $8,000 and $9,500 per year in 2010 (see figure 3.3). Montreal's housing market is more affordable, but social assistance incomes are not lower than what they are in other cities.

Yet the average one-bedroom apartment in Montreal in 2018 cost $721/month, or $8,652/year, unaffordable for someone with $9,000 per year in social assistance income. So while housing is more affordable in Montreal, it is clear that market housing in that city remains well out of

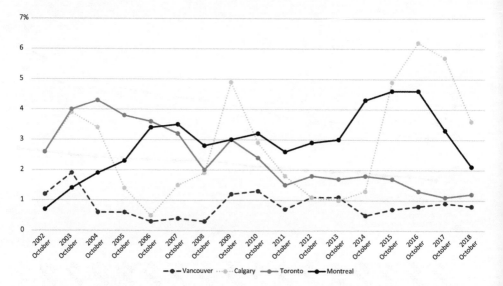

Figure 3.2. Vacancy rates, one-bedroom apartments. Information from the CMHC Rental Market Survey

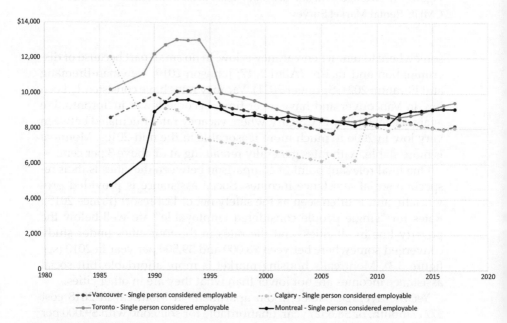

Figure 3.3. Single-person social assistance. Information taken from Tweddle and Aldrige 2019

reach of an individual on social assistance. All four cities, then, share a similar scale of homelessness and a private housing market that is unable to meet the housing needs of that population. All four face similar challenges of homelessness, housing unaffordability, and chronic poverty. The housing crunch is noticeably less acute in Montreal; even so, considering the comparability of its homeless population and the rich tradition of inclusive and interventionist policy-making there, the benefits of including that city far outweigh the costs of excluding it from the analysis on the basis of that difference. It is, however, important to bear in mind differences in context when making claims and comparisons.

Following the comparative historical institutionalist tradition, this book explains why different governance approaches have emerged in Vancouver, Calgary, Toronto, and Montreal in response to such a similar policy challenge. Comparative historical institutionalism is suited to "how" and "why" questions in social science research that seek to explain divergent outcomes – in this case, why such strikingly different multilevel governance networks have emerged over the past two decades in each city. Comparative historical institutionalist studies share three important elements: "a concern with causal analysis, an emphasis on processes over time, and the use of systemic and contextualized comparison" (Mahoney and Rueschemeyer 2003, 10). Process-tracing techniques are useful to these ends. George and Bennett write that "process tracing provides a common middle ground for historians interested in historical explanation and political scientists and other social scientists who are sensitive to the complexities of historical events but are more interested in theorizing about categories of cases as well as explaining individual cases" (George and Bennett 2005, 223). Furthermore, process-tracing "takes 'time seriously' and considers it as part of the causal explanation, hence relies on detailed tracing of processes" (Trampusch and Palier 2016, 438), allowing for a careful consideration of the timing and sequence of decisions and actions.

Process-tracing can be used deductively, to test hypotheses and refine theories (Beach and Petersen 2013), but it is also useful for building theories because it allows for extensive within-case analysis. It further allows for systemic and contextualized comparison, both by highlighting differences between cases and by allowing for intensive within-case analysis, thus making room for a deep exploration of causal mechanisms as they play out over time. As noted earlier, process-tracing is also a useful method for ideational analysis; it "represents an especially powerful empirical approach for distinguishing between ideational and material effects" (Jacobs 2014, 41). The present study does not put forward a strict cause-and-effect theory of multilevel governance; it does, however, use process tracing to identify compelling causal inferences regarding the role of ideas, resources, and institutions in the development of governance networks. While there is a trade-off in small-N studies – notably a limited generalizability of the conclusions – comparative historical institutionalism is nevertheless seen as a "bargain" approach (Mahoney and Rueschemeyer 2003, 13) because of its numerous advantages. Most notably, the detailed understanding it provides for each case allows for comparisons that are highly contextualized.

Evidence was collected using a variety of qualitative methods. Between 2014 and 2018, I conducted nearly 100 semi-structured interviews in English and French with governmental and non-governmental actors involved in the governance of homelessness in Vancouver, Calgary, Toronto, and Montreal. Interviews included (but were not limited to) elected officials and bureaucrats at the municipal, provincial, and federal levels; activists; police officers;[7] service providers; Indigenous leaders; and private sector representatives. I identified participants in part through primary document research. I also asked interviewees to identify any other key actors with whom I should speak, a method called "snowballing" (Denzin and Lincoln 2005).[8]

The purpose of these semi-structured interviews was to trace the development of the homelessness governance networks and to identify the role of ideas in that process. I asked all interviewees several identical questions, notably regarding their role in the fight against homelessness, whom they work with in their efforts, and what they perceived as the causes of homelessness and solutions to homelessness. However, a semi-structured approach allows for flexibility, which was important given the different perspectives that were being considered, in that "the interviewers are allowed freedom to digress; that is, the interviewed are permitted (in fact, expected) to probe far beyond the answers to their prepared standardized questions" (Berg 2011, 95); interviews inevitably became more focused on the person's particular experience, allowing for more of a conversation than an interrogation (Fujii 2017). This approach to the interviews allowed me to inquire about an actor's understanding of the nature of homelessness in a natural and open way. Instead of asking "What is your definition of homelessness?," I asked more general questions about the nature of homelessness, notably its causes and solutions. This allowed actors to answer organically – to draw on their experiences, examples, and ideas instead of trying to remember specific government or academic definitions of homelessness. This question generated insightful and passionate responses.

Recognizing that memories may fade and that actors may seek to shape the history they were involved in, I triangulated in three ways.

First, without revealing identities, I asked actors to respond to what others had told me in interviews, to see if they agreed with that person's interpretation. Sometimes, this revealed factual inaccuracies; other times, it revealed legitimate disagreements, often regarding the nature of homelessness or the responsibility to produce social protection. In addition, I had a number of informal meetings with journalists, academics, and activists to test ideas and evidence that had been presented to me during the interviews. I also triangulated through archival research. By reviewing hundreds of primary documents, such as annual reports, policies, plans, and newspaper articles, I was able to place the interviews in a broader context and test what one person said against another data source. I also used books and secondary sources to check factual details.

The final method I used to triangulate was participant observation in a number of environments. Participant observation has been called "an omnibus field strategy" (Patton 2002, 265), for it allows the researcher to gather information in various formal and informal ways. Denzin writes that participant observation "simultaneously combines document analysis, interviewing of respondents and informants, direct participation and observation, and introspection" (Denzin 1978, 183). Though I was not, at the time, conducting participant observation, an early exposure to the realities of homelessness in Canada and to the importance of governance was in 2008, when I volunteered in a low-barrier emergency shelter in Vancouver's Downtown Eastside. This shelter, First United, was a newly opened Homelessness Emergency Action Team (HEAT) shelter, part of then-mayor Gregor Robertson's plan to end street homelessness. Engaging with people living or working in the shelter exposed me to the evolving power dynamics in Vancouver, where Robertson was seen as a new and leading actor in the fight against homelessness. This experience also underscored the importance of the definition of homelessness for those experiencing homelessness and working in the sector and illustrated how even small differences in definitions can have significant implications for service provision and the production of social protection.

I was able to use the participant observation method in Montreal, where a new actor – the Mouvement pour mettre fin à l'itinérance à Montréal (MMFIM) – had begun to form and gain influence as I started my fieldwork in 2013. After interviewing a number of members of the network, I was invited to their meetings to present my research. With the permission of the new movement's leadership, I began to observe most network meetings; I took notes during the meetings, and during breaks I had informal conversations with members of the movement and asked questions regarding homelessness in Montreal. As my role became more than participatory (I was lead researcher for Montreal's first homeless count, which was led by the MMFIM, as well as a researcher for the MMFIM's plan to end homelessness), I was invited on calls with national leadership, including the Homeless Hub and the Canadian Alliance to End Homelessness, and was involved in a number of communications discussing the movement and its place within Montreal's policy community. I also attended a number of meetings with City of Montreal officials to discuss homelessness, notably regarding the 2015 point-in-time homeless count and future planned counts. All of this provided crucial insight into the actions of key public-policy actors and how those actors fit with respect to one another. Finally, I have regularly attended National Canadian Alliance to End Homelessness conferences since 2013, attending panels relating to homelessness governance and research, talking with people during breaks, and listening as attentively to keynote announcements as to reactions from the crowd.

As I have explained, homelessness is political, and in environments where there are disagreements over the nature of homelessness and solutions to it, becoming involved in the system that serves people experiencing homelessness is of tremendous value, both for scholarship and for social citizenship. Participant observation has contributed to the empirical rigour of this study by providing direct insights into policy-making, governance dynamics, and relationships between key groups and actors. But this involvement risks alienating groups as well. Though I was involved with the MMFIM in Montreal, I was able to speak with many individuals involved with or allied with the city's other important local network, the RAPSIM; I also extensively reviewed RAPSIM documents to ensure that I understood their perspective and role. I recognize that the MMFIM adopts a particular definition of homelessness – one that is housing-focused – and my involvement might suggest an implicit agreement or adoption of that particular definition. However, I also have direct experience volunteering with a group that has adopted a broader and very different definition: First United Church in East Vancouver (reviewed in chapter 5). These experiences have informed my empirical scholarship and the conclusions I draw regarding the importance of the definition of homelessness. Involvement in a sector that is at times divided and political may give the appearance of a lack of objectivity; yet my experiences were in a variety of environments that adopted very different perspectives. While I was a participant, it was with a wide range of actors. As a white woman who has never been unhoused, I recognize that these experiences do not replace or even approximate lived expertise and knowledge. They were, however, essential to my own understanding of power dynamics and the political nature of efforts to produce social protection.

The following pages do not pretend to contain policy solutions to homelessness; those solutions are best developed by those on the ground and, perhaps most urgently, by those with lived experience with homelessness. Nor is the objective to create a unifying and universal theory of multilevel governance. Leo and August warned long ago against such an effort: "anyone who believes that a theory of governance can be applied, like a recipe for goulash, to the production of a predictable and satisfying outcome in every individual circumstance greatly underestimates the subtlety and complexity of policy making and implementation" (Leo and August 2009, 507). I make no claim to have discovered a magic recipe; that said, an understanding of the forces that structure governance dynamics can shed light on what makes governance networks more or less successful and how those lessons can be applied elsewhere. In other words, the specifics of the recipe will vary from place to place and from policy to policy, just as a goulash will vary from kitchen to kitchen, but theories of multilevel governance can point us toward some key ingredients. It is to this task that we now turn.

4 Federal Government

The federal government has an important role to play in homelessness governance, but it has not always lived up to its responsibilities. The first section of this chapter reviews federal involvement in homelessness governance, beginning in 1999, the year the National Homelessness Initiative (NHI) was launched. The NHI was a federal program that partnered with local groups to develop emergency responses to homelessness, though the program operated differently in Quebec, where the province has been involved since the beginning. This federal involvement came only a few years after it made significant cuts to social spending, which included eliminating investments in new social housing developments, cuts that are widely said to have contributed directly to a rise in homelessness across the country (Gaetz 2010). The NHI was renamed the HPS (Homelessness Partnering Strategy) in 2007. For the first fifteen years after 1999, it was renewed continually, but only for one- to three-year periods, and local groups were given significant discretion regarding how to use the funding. Then, in 2014, the federal government extended the program for five years while also requiring that 65 per cent of the funding received by big cities be spent on Housing First programs.

In 2017 the federal government introduced a ten-year National Housing Strategy (NHS) and made the fight against homelessness a core part of it. In so doing, it linked homelessness directly with housing for the first time. The NHS increased investments in Reaching Home (the new version of the HPS, which began in 2019); made funding available for ten years; allowed that funding to be spent on a wide variety of interventions, including temporary and permanent housing; and was coupled with significant investments in new housing developments, portable rent allowances, and investments to improve, protect, and renovate existing housing stock. When COVID-19 hit, the federal government responded by increasing funding for the homeless-serving system, enabling that funding to be used more flexibly, and launching a new rapid housing initiative to allow for quick development of new housing.

The evolving federal involvement in homelessness did not result from a change in institutions or resources; rather, it was powerfully driven by ideas, especially regarding the nature of homelessness. Though the NHI/HPS has been renewed continuously since 1999, the federal government's involvement in homelessness governance was minimal for nearly twenty years, reflecting its understanding of homelessness as an emergency and as a largely individual and short-term problem as opposed to a structural one. This narrow definition of homelessness also shaped the federal government's interactions with other actors, notably its direct relationships with local groups; provincial governments were left out of NHI/HPS governance, with the exception of Quebec. The provinces have authority over important structures such as health, housing, and income support; they were not included in federal homelessness initiatives for two decades because homelessness was not understood to be a structural problem. The federal government's understanding of homelessness has since evolved, away from individual-level causes toward more systemic and structural ones, and includes an acknowledgment of the colonial roots of homelessness for Indigenous people. As a result, its involvement has increased and its interactions with other groups have changed as well: more, longer-term funding has been made available; interactions with provincial governments have increased; and homelessness and housing are linked.

The second section of this chapter reviews the CAEH's involvement in homelessness governance. The Canadian Alliance to End Homelessness emerged on the national scene in 2012 with two principal objectives: to support communities in their fight against homelessness; and to steer the federal government toward particular solutions to homelessness, such as Housing First (explained below). The CAEH uses various strategies to influence and participate in policy, including holding well-attended annual national conferences to allow for regular interactions among policy-makers and stakeholders, conducting email campaigns and engaging in sophisticated and targeted lobbying. In mid-2021, the CAEH launched a national non-partisan campaign called Vote Housing. Aimed at all parties during 2021 federal election, the CAEH worked closely with allies and community groups across the country to make housing a ballot box issue, with the ultimate goal of using the pandemic recovery as an opportunity to fix the housing affordability crisis and end homelessness once and for all.

The CAEH's involvement in homelessness governance has been driven largely by its understanding of homelessness, and to the extent that its involvement and interactions with other groups have changed, it has been as a result of the evolution of this idea. As with the federal government, there has been considerable evolution in how key officials with the CAEH understand homelessness – there has been a shift in thinking away from individual causes toward an understanding that structures and systems are central. Partly because of the influence of the CAEH on the national level, we see ideational convergence on the national level when it comes to how homelessness is understood. Drawing on primary sources, interviews with key actors, and several years attending and observing CAEH annual conferences, this chapter traces and explains the involvement of these national actors in homelessness.

The Federal Role in Homelessness

The federal government's role in homelessness governance can be broken into three periods: 1999–2014, when its involvement was minimal and it granted considerable discretion to the local level; 2014–19, years in which its involvement remained minimal, but it limited the control previously exercised at the local level, particularly in big cities; and post-2019, which has seen the federal government taking a more interventionist and collaborative leadership role. The first era of the federal government's involvement in homelessness began in 1999, following intense advocacy efforts by groups across the country, particularly in Toronto (Crowe 2019; Layton 2008; S. Scott 2012). This involvement came on the heels of a series of high-impact decisions by Progressive Conservative and Liberal federal governments to cut investments in housing, transfer the administration of existing housing units to the provinces, and cut social funding transfer payments to the provinces (which in turn often made cuts to their own housing expenditures and social assistance) (see Gaetz 2010).

While Canada was not historically a leader in housing policy by any stretch, the federal government, working together with and sometimes in competition with the provinces, had consistently built social housing since the end of the Second World War, at times up to 25,000 units per year (Hulchanski et al. 2009). This all came to an abrupt end in the mid-1990s when the federal government announced that it would no longer fund social housing developments. Jeanne Wolfe writes that "it was never imagined that a system that had taken 50 years to build-up could be dismantled so rapidly" (Wolfe 1998, 131). Yet it was. The cuts to housing developments and transfer of housing administration to the provinces, eight out of ten of which also cut their housing policies, have generally been seen as a turning point in the history of homelessness in Canada (Gaetz 2010), given that the number of people experiencing homelessness began to rise across the country in the 1990s and 2000s.

By the late 1990s, "there was widespread agreement that homelessness had reached intolerable proportions, especially in Canadian cities" (Leo 2006, 501). Several events contributed to this crisis situation. These included the tragic and preventable deaths of three homeless men – Eugene Upper, Irwin Anderson, and Mirsalah-Aldin Kompani – on the streets of Toronto during the winter of 1996. This led to changes in local responses to homelessness and drove advocates to put more pressure on senior governments to engage (Crowe 2018). And in 1998, influential Toronto activists on the Toronto Disaster Relief Committee, including then Toronto city councillor Jack Layton, worked with big city mayors across the country to declare homelessness a disaster (Layton 2008). Toronto Mayor Mel Lastman was an unlikely leader in this effort (see chapter 7). Led by Lastman, big city mayors across the country agreed to declare homelessness a national disaster. While this declaration by big city mayors did not unlock any emergency funding – which such announcements sometimes do – it drew the media's attention and fuelled a wave of advocacy for more effective responses to meet the needs of the growing number of people who found themselves without housing (Suttor 2016).

Local groups responded to the homelessness crisis as well as they could, and together with advocates they pressured the federal government for solutions. Advocacy was taking place on the streets, but concerted efforts were taking place behind closed doors as well, including in then Prime Minister Jean Chrétien's office. A City of Toronto bureaucrat recalled efforts to get the federal government engaged: "[Anne] Golden, with myself and others, went and met with social policy advisers in the Prime Minister's Office. These connections were happening behind the scene[s]" (personal interview 2014). Another City of Toronto actor recalled stressing the urgency of the situation during a meeting with the Prime Minister's Office: "We said, 'You have got to do something'" (personal interview 2014). In response to these increasing pressures from advocates and sympathetic insiders in the PMO (Klodawsky and Evans 2014), the federal government appointed a Minister Responsible for Homelessness, the late Claudette Bradshaw, in the late 1990s.

In 1998, Minister Bradshaw embarked on a cross-country tour to learn more about homelessness. This tour would inform her understanding of homelessness and shape the involvement of the federal government and its interactions with other actors for decades to come. As noted earlier, advocates across the country were declaring that homelessness had reached crisis levels, thus defining the problem in emergency terms. Christopher Leo writes that "by the time the federal government took note of the problem, it was defined, in the public mind as well as in the minds of government officials, as an urban crisis requiring an emergency response" (Leo 2006, 501). Fran Klodawsky and Leonore Evans note that out of this context came an important decision regarding the program design: "The tour convinced Bradshaw of ... a focus on the 'absolute homeless,' those living on the streets and in the emergency shelters, and thus on homelessness in the country's largest cities" (Klodawsky and Evans 2014, 86).

It is no exaggeration to say that homelessness had become a life-or-death situation in many big cities, and not just in the cold of the winter months; the heat of the summer can be deadly as well (Withers 2021). Those living on the streets were at risk, and indeed some had died. The anger generated by those deaths led some advocates to push for an immediate response to the emergency of homelessness. But it also – inadvertently perhaps, for advocates also sought housing-based solutions – allowed the federal government to overlook the structural and political causes of homelessness and to bypass deeper reforms to the housing system and the broader social safety net. Guided by assumptions that homelessness was an individual-level emergency, the National Homelessness Initiative developed by the federal government prioritized relief for people experiencing chronic homelessness, most of whom were living on the streets or in emergency shelters. This led to the expansion and improvement of that emergency system, especially shelters. The long-term hope, of course, was for people to find housing of their own, but the program's initial impulse was to respond to the crisis as it had been defined, by finding ways for the local homeless-serving system to better meet emergency needs and prevent future deaths.

For many advocates who espoused a more structural definition, it was clear early on that the federal government's homelessness initiative would be separate from housing initiatives and, indeed, that the federal government would continue to limit its involvement in the development of social or affordable housing. This absence of housing in the federal response to homelessness infuriated advocates to no end, who believed homelessness resulted from cuts to housing policy in the first place. Michael Shapcott, a Toronto-based advocate with the TDRC at the time, recalls frustrating interactions with Bradshaw as she was on the cross-country tour:

> The fiction they kept promoting was that homelessness had nothing to do with housing. That it was the result of personal pathology, people became homeless because they are alcoholics, they are crazy ... [Federal officials]

said "We are not going to provide any funding for housing because there is no credible research that demonstrates that a lack of housing causes homelessness." It was an astonishing position to take. Minister Bradshaw went across the country to these big community forums. I went to almost half of them myself … She was a smart person, she knew a lot better. I would say "What are you going to do about housing?" and she would say "Oh Michael, you know that housing has nothing to do with homelessness." And of course, everyone in the room would go "Oh that is so stupid!!!" (personal interview 2014)

Informed by this narrow, individualized, emergency-based definition, the governance structure of the NHI would bypass provinces outside of Quebec and instead involve local actors in the development of solutions. Meeting with service providers and advocates, Bradshaw came to appreciate the expertise of local groups, and she committed to designing a federal homelessness response that would allow them "a lead role in planning, deciding on and administering any funds that would be made available" (Klodawsky and Evans 2014, 86). This federal-level recognition of the value of local expertise is significant, and the strong involvement of local groups in the planning process is one of the reasons the NHI is sometimes seen as an early example of place-based policy-making (Bradford 2014). But it also let the provinces, and broader structural reform, off the hook.

In other words, ideas about the nature of homelessness shaped ideas about the responsibility to produce social protection: homelessness was not understood to be a structural problem requiring the social policy might of the provinces, but rather as a problem requiring urgent alleviation and thus only the expertise and comparatively limited capacity of local service providers. Because it understood homelessness narrowly and in emergency terms, the federal government concluded that only emergency solutions to homelessness were required, solutions that could be developed on a short-term basis by local groups aided with federal funding. This understanding and the direct federal–local relationship would remain standard for nearly two decades.

Following her consultations across the country, Bradshaw introduced the National Homelessness Initiative, a cautious short-term homelessness-fighting program focused mainly on individual-level interventions. The Supporting Communities Partnership Initiative (SCPI), an important component of the NHI, was effectively a transfer of $305 million over three years to community-driven efforts to alleviate or prevent homelessness. Most of this funding was for the ten largest cities in the country, with a small portion going to smaller communities.

Through the NHI, each community was allocated a specific amount of funding. While communities had control over the development of plans, this approach to homelessness established the federal government as the system's "metagovernor" (Bradford 2014; Doberstein 2016), with the power to change funding requirements or amounts, governance dynamics, and, crucially, to define the problem. While communities had significant discretion, limits to their activities were implicit in terms of the time communities had to accomplish their projects (three years) and the small amount of funding each community was allocated. In other words, not nearly enough time or money was made available for the structural changes many advocates insisted were needed to respond effectively to the needs of people experiencing homelessness.

Separate streams of funding were available for what at the time were called "Aboriginal communities" and for youth homelessness; each stream received $59 million in funding over three years. The original program required funding for "Aboriginal communities" to be administered through Aboriginal Human Resources Development Agreements, meaning any emergency responses to homelessness were required to also have a focus on employment. This imposed an additional burden on communities seeking to respond to the immediate needs of Indigenous homeless people. By 2001, changes were made so that "Aboriginal community" funding was not required to involve an employment dimension, but the first three years of NHI funding for Indigenous groups were largely unspent because of this disastrous governance arrangement imposed by the federal government (20 per cent of available funding for Aboriginal communities was spent in three years, compared to 85 per cent of funding for designated communities [HRDC 2003]).

Large communities that received federal NHI funding were (and still are) required to develop community plans for homelessness and were (and still are) required to cost-match the federal government's contributions. Plans are created by a Community Advisory Board, a locally developed governance council comprised of experts, advocates, and service providers from the community. Once approved, community plans on homelessness are implemented in one of two ways. The first is through the Community Entity model, whereby federal funding is transferred to an existing agency (such as the United Way) or municipality (in the case of the City of Toronto and many other Ontario municipalities). The Community Entity issues a call for proposals for projects that align with the Community Plan, selects the programs to be funded, and oversees implementation. The second model of implementation is the Shared Delivery model, a model chosen by Vancouver for ten years as well as by other mid-sized cities such as Winnipeg. In this model, the Community Advisory Board teams up with a federal bureaucrat to jointly choose projects to be funded. The federal government plays a supporting role but generally follows the advice of the advisory board as closely as possible (Doberstein 2016). The federal government is responsible, alongside the local board, for distributing the funding and monitoring local progress.

While this main pool of NHI funding can be used for programs for Indigenous people experiencing homelessness, the NHI continues to have a separate stream of funding for "Aboriginal Communities" (changed in 2017 to "Indigenous Communities"). Indigenous groups are not required to develop community plans in order to access funding, though some do, and they are not required to cost-match. For overseeing and distributing federal funding, a Community Entity is the only option for Indigenous communities, though in Quebec, Indigenous groups interface directly with the federal government when applying for funding from the Indigenous homelessness stream. Implicit in this separate funding stream and governance structure is the idea that Indigenous people experience homelessness differently and for distinct reasons and that Indigenous groups are best-placed to understand that experience and develop appropriate solutions. This appreciation of the expertise of Indigenous-led groups is significant, yet the resources needed to implement meaningful solutions, a longer (and more predictable) timeline, and partnerships (where appropriate) were all lacking. Furthermore, local and Indigenous-led groups were not involved in a crucial step of the program's design: defining what homelessness is.

To further complicate matters, control of and access to federal funding has been governed differently in Quebec from the beginning.[1] The NHI/HPS bypassed nine of the ten provinces, whereas the Province of Quebec is deeply involved in NHI/HPS operations. Community plan development in Quebec is done by community groups, but decisions as to which programs will be funded are made by a bilateral committee comprised of provincial and federal officials rather than by a community-based agency as is the case in other provinces. This gives the program an intergovernmental flavour in Quebec, as opposed to one of co-governance with community groups; the influence of ideas about federalism is pervasive (see chapter 8 for more details on NHI/HPS operations in Quebec).

The NHI rolled out in 1999 in most Canadian cities, but it took until 2001 for Indigenous communities to see the funding and for the province and federal government to reach a Canada–Quebec agreement regarding the program's operations in Quebec. The Canada–Quebec agreement has been consistently renegotiated and re-signed each time the federal program funding has been reapproved. Early on, relations between the different parties, including local third-sector actors, were difficult (personal interviews). Over time, however, plan development and implementation has become routine. Interestingly, the operations of the NHI/HPS in Quebec today stand as one of the longest and likely most successful examples of multilevel governance, precisely because the province demanded a seat at the table.

In a discussion about how the HPS operates in Quebec, a federal bureaucrat interviewed for this book paused for a moment to reflect on the practice of federalism over the course of the NHI/HPS: "I just want to say I find it really strange that the other provinces don't argue for the Quebec model. The previous government really offered that asymmetrical federalism to everybody, and no one else took it up. And I always think that's kind of funny … [Provinces] can come to me and say 'I want to negotiate the Quebec model' and I would have to say 'Okay, great'" (personal interview 2018). The actor continued to express disbelief that Quebec is the only province that pushes back: "I always just find it funny that no one really fights for the Quebec model. Occasionally they might ask for more and we go 'no' and they are just like 'okay.' Why wouldn't they be more vocal?" This is indeed interesting, and likely reflects one of two things: either provinces are not jealous of this area of jurisdiction, or perhaps provincial officials do not see homelessness as structural and therefore requiring their involvement.

The first NHI ran from late 1999 to 2003 and was then renewed for another three years, from 2003 to 2006, and again for one year from 2006 to 2007; all of these renewals were under Liberal governments. After being elected in 2006, the federal Conservative government maintained a strikingly similar degree of involvement in homelessness governance. They changed the name of the NHI to the Homelessness Partnering Strategy (HPS) and extended it for two years from 2007 to 2009 with similar levels of funding as in the past ($134.8 million per year). The governance dynamics, which afforded extensive discretion to the local level, also remained the same, as did the cost-matching requirements, leading many to suggest that the name change was simply a rebranding exercise (Klodawsky and Evans 2014; personal interviews). The HPS included a more focused effort on homelessness prevention; it also prioritized "a shift from emergency to longer-term solutions" (ESDC 2014, 35), though this was not accompanied by increased funding or an extended time frame, nor was it linked with housing policy, which would have been required to prevent homelessness or implement longer-term solutions in any meaningful way.

It is worth pausing here, technically in the middle of the first era (1999–2014), to review what was known at the time about the NHI/HPS operations. Reviews of the first ten years of the NHI/HPS identified several strengths and weaknesses. In its early years, the NHI led to the opening of a number of homeless shelters across the country, including homeless shelters specifically for Indigenous people, and early evaluations showed that the program was effective at meeting some short-term needs of the homeless population (Webster 2007). An early program review also noted increased capacity for fighting homelessness across the country. Indigenous communities, however, did not develop capacity as quickly as non-Indigenous networks largely as a result of institutional roadblocks imposed early on by the federal government (HRDC 2003).

A key strength of the program was the discretion it afforded local-level actors: "the greatest value of the HPS lies in its direct support to communities' local capacity to address homelessness and its encouraging of a collaborative approach to setting priorities, identifying needs and gaps in services and programming, and allocating funding" (ESDC 2014, 23). This model of devolving authority to local groups was also looked on positively by people interviewed for this book. One of them stressed that "in the bad old days, the government would just tell communities what to do. And they didn't always know what was best for Red Deer or Montreal or St John's. [The NHI/HPS] approach was actually quite brilliant: let the local communities set the priorities" (personal interview 2014).

However, program reviews also highlighted important limitations of the NHI/HPS. A significant one related to funding levels, which were wholly insufficient to comprehensively meet the needs of the homeless population. Also, community groups were critical of the time lines they faced; recall that the program was renewed continuously but never for more than three years – an insurmountable barrier to long-term planning (HRDC 2003; 2008). A 2003 review of the NHI found that "spending on emergency services was disproportionately high relative to their ranking on community priority lists ... Projects addressing emergency needs (such as soup kitchens) were relatively easy to implement once funding had been allocated, compared to services meeting more long-term needs (such as mental health or employment supports)" (HRDC 2003, 23). Some groups even prioritized projects that could be completed within that time frame, as opposed to projects that best met local needs. Important to note here is the evidence of a profound and enduring disagreement in terms of the *nature* of homelessness: federal government officials viewed it as an individual-level, short-term problem that was only in need of emergency solutions. Community and other on-the-ground groups disagreed; they understood it to be structural, requiring increased funding to be made available and over a longer period of time – crucially, for investments in housing.

Moreover, some saw the NHI as designed with only a small number of big cities in mind. According to Leo and August, the NHI was unable to meet local needs in Winnipeg, where homelessness takes a different form than it does in larger urban centres: "The mandate of the [NHI], however, was written to address the problems of such centres as Toronto and Vancouver, growth magnets with hot housing markets. The conditions of funding proved too narrow for slow-growth Winnipeg, precluding the types of solutions that are more likely actually to alleviate homelessness there" (Leo and August 2006, 2). Leo and August note that the NHI had been developed to support communities with high numbers of people living in absolute homelessness on the streets, and that its design had not considered different environments, like Winnipeg, where "housing is likely to be priced so low that, in older neighbourhoods, it does not pay to maintain it. With housing that is decaying but affordable, street people may be less in evidence" (Leo and August 2006, 5).

Given the differences in local housing markets, Leo and August argued that Winnipeggers were more likely to experience relative rather than absolute homelessness; that is, comparatively few people are unhoused but more are likely to be drastically underhoused. The types of interventions required to improve their situation, many of which were directly related to housing (as opposed to emergency shelters), had been precluded in NHI/HPS programming because of how it defined homelessness. That narrow definition meant that "no concrete provisions [were] offered to move the homeless into secure tenure. In practice, the program *institutionalizes homelessness* rather than seeking strategies for moving as many as possible out of those woeful circumstances" (Leo and August 2006, 9; emphasis added). James Hughes, who ran the Old Brewery Mission in Montreal from 2004 to 2008 and returned to that position in late 2020, agrees with this analysis, noting that in its early days "the [NHI/HPS] continued to focus principally on building the sector's capacity *to sustain individuals suffering through homelessness,* rather than on preventing homelessness in the first place" (Hughes 2012, 5; emphasis added).

Despite criticisms revealed during the government's own program review, NHI/HPS governance, time lines, funding, and definitions remained relatively unchanged for fifteen years. The tide started to turn, albeit slowly, in 2008, when the recently elected federal Conservative government announced an extension of the HPS to 2011, as well as an investment of $110 million over five years in a research project related to homelessness (2008–13). Specifically, the federal government funded a large, randomized controlled study of Housing First, an emerging and promising homelessness intervention. The federal government established research teams in Vancouver, Winnipeg, Toronto, Montreal, and Moncton to study the effectiveness of Housing First. Titled the At Home/Chez Soi project, this research would directly inform the federal government's understanding of homelessness and would prove highly influential in structuring its future involvement in the policy field.

Housing First is typically targeted at people who experience chronic homelessness. While some community groups in Canada have for years espoused the core tenets of Housing First (Lupick 2017a; Withers 2021), the idea is often credited to Sam Tsemberis, a Canadian psychologist who tested the model in New York City and showed its effectiveness not only as a solution to homelessness but as a cost-saving measure as well. Housing First is in many ways a change from traditional approaches to homelessness, which required homeless people to be sober and in otherwise stable health (especially with respect to mental health) before being accepted into permanent housing. These requirements were, according to Tsemberis, significant barriers preventing people from exiting homelessness, particularly people who experience chronic homelessness.

Housing First flips the order of operations, putting housing at the beginning rather than the end of a person's transition out of homelessness. In Housing First programs, individuals are immediately given access to permanent housing and are offered social supports in that environment. Besides making a strong social justice statement that individuals have the right to immediately access housing, the Housing First model claims that this approach is less expensive than the previous model, especially over the long term. Because of the need for readily accessible and low-barrier housing, Housing First programs typically use private-market housing instead of social housing; there can be requirements for accessing social housing, such as sobriety, and there are often long wait lists as well. Private-sector housing can be accessed more quickly, especially if community groups already have relationships with private landlords, though problems can still exist in private-market housing, including for drug users (Housing First espouses harm reduction principles; see Withers 2021). Dependence on private-sector rental housing means that the units are often scattered throughout the city, including in suburbs; the model of housing is therefore sometimes called "scatter site," which results in previously unhoused people living throughout the city, as opposed to in "congregate" settings, in which previously unhoused people live in the same building. This can be an attractive feature of Housing First for someone who wants to move to a different neighbourhood. The reality of housing markets in urban contexts across Canada, however, is that choices are very limited. International studies show that Housing First is most effective in environments where social and affordable housing is more readily available (Henley 2019).

The federal government put the claims about long-term success and cost savings associated with Housing First to a literal test.[2] For the At Home/Chez Soi project, 2,148 homeless people were recruited from Moncton, Montreal, Toronto, Winnipeg, and Vancouver to participate in the study. They were divided into two groups, with around half of the participants (1,158) receiving the "treatment," a Housing First intervention. The others were in a control group; for them, nothing changed, and they navigated the homeless system as they had before. Besides being divided into control and treatment groups, participants were also evaluated according to their "support needs": very high, high, and moderate. Participants from both treatment and control groups took part in extensive and regular follow-up interviews over the course of the study so that researchers could track their housing stability as well as a host of other factors, such as interactions with police, use of emergency medical services, and quality of life.

At the end of the study, the researchers came out strongly in support of Housing First as an effective and potentially cost-saving approach to homelessness: "Housing First can be effectively implemented in Canadian cities of different size and different ethnoracial and cultural composition ... Housing First rapidly ends homelessness" (Goering et al. 2014, 1). The research team carefully detailed the costs and associated savings of Housing First (HF): "Over the two-year period after participants entered the study, every $10 invested in HF services results in an average savings of $9.60 for high needs and $3.42 for moderate needs participants" (1). A small minority, 10 per cent of participants, were considered to have very high support needs, and for this group, cost savings were significant: "every $10 invested in HF services resulted in an average savings of $21.72" (1).

The At Home/Chez Soi study provided powerful evidence that Housing First was an effective and cost-saving measure for ending homelessness, particularly chronic homelessness. There was some controversy, of course, including over the experimental method used. Furthermore, the question of who would fund the housing and continued social supports for people involved in the study after the end of the study period was an important concern. In many cases, provinces or municipal governments had to step in to continue funding these supports once the federal study (and the funding it made available so as to test Housing First) ended.

These findings directly informed the federal government's decision to renew the HPS in 2014 for five years, the longest funding period in the program's history.[3] However, the renewed HPS contained much more direction for community groups from the federal government than it had before, another example of increased funding transfers made available but with conditions attached. Up until 2014, communities had been afforded autonomy to design local homelessness plans according to their needs (within the obvious strictures of time and funding); after that year, however, the HPS stipulated that large cities must dedicate 65 per cent of their HPS funding to Housing First programs (this requirement did not extend to "Aboriginal communities").

This orientation to Housing First and focus on more targeted interventions was also a response to earlier critiques that the NHI/HPS led not to a decrease in homelessness but rather, in the words of Leo and August (as well as Hughes), to "institutionalized" homelessness. Further, Hughes noted that after more than $1 billion in investments in homelessness since 1999, "it is difficult to conclude that homelessness was shrinking. If anything, it seemed to be growing ... In cities where homelessness counts were regularly conducted, the numbers were definitely rising" (2012, 6–7). Indeed, studies of emergency shelters during this period show an increase in the number of people experiencing chronic homelessness between 2005 and 2016. Ideas operating through environmental mechanisms created the space for the discussion of new approaches; old approaches weren't working, enabling new ideas regarding the nature of homelessness and the responsibility to produce social protect to take hold and lead to changing governance dynamics.

In the *Toronto Star*, Sam Tsemberis and Vicky Stergiopoulos, a lead investigator with At Home/Chez Soi, applauded the federal decision to prioritize Housing First: "it's no wonder the federal government supports Housing First: it is highly effective and can save money" (Tsemberis and Stergiopoulos 2014). The emphasis on cost savings is important, and offers insights into how the Conservative government understood homelessness. Claims that ending homelessness could save money needed qualification or at least specificity; researchers were always clear that Housing First would result in cost savings for only 10 per cent of the homeless population – that is, for people who experienced the most chronic form of homelessness. According to the study, Housing First would not result in cost savings when it came to people viewed as having moderate support needs, and it would break even for those with high support needs. Insisting that Housing First can save money made clear that the target of program interventions would be a very narrowly defined group of people (though advocates of Housing First are quick to insist that prioritizing people who experience the most severe form of chronic homelessness will, over time, enable the system to respond much more quickly and effectively to people experiencing shorter periods of homelessness.)

The decision to limit local discretion was not universally applauded, however. Some groups object to the prioritization or classification of any group (Withers 2021) and opposed this increasingly targeted approach to homelessness immediately (RAPSIM 2013). It was fiercely challenged in Quebec by an influential and long-standing advocacy group, the RAPSIM, which pushed for a "generalist" HPS that would allow funding to be used for a variety of projects and equally for anyone considered homeless by Quebec's broad definition (as had been the case in the past) (RAPSIM 2013c). In this conflict between Quebec actors and the federal government, we can see the importance of ideas around the understanding of homelessness, as well as challenges regarding the responsibility to produce social protection. Local actors in Quebec disagreed with the federal government's orientation toward Housing First – a disagreement arising from the very different understanding of homelessness espoused by the RAPSIM (see chapter 8) – and also disagreed with the principle of federal direction to local actors. The RAPSIM pushed the co-governing province to reject the requirements, but provincial officials eventually agreed to the federal government's Housing First orientation; implementation would be co-governed by the province and federal government, but with the federal government remaining the dominant "meta-governor."

For nearly twenty years, the NHI/HPS was a short-term and poorly funded program. The National Housing Strategy, introduced in 2017 and implemented shortly afterwards, marked a significant departure from this past and the beginning of a new era in federal involvement in homelessness. The HPS has again been renamed – Reaching Home – and has been redesigned and implemented in the context of a broader housing strategy. Funding has been increased to $2.2 billion over ten years, meaning long-term funding is finally guaranteed, a demand of local groups for two decades. And while the federal government has identified outcomes for the first time in the program's history, including substantial reductions in chronic homelessness, the requirement that 65 per cent of funding be directed toward Housing First has been removed (though the federal government remains highly supportive of

Housing First as an intervention). This reflects an effort to "keep decision making at the local level and give communities greater flexibility to address local priorities and achieve results for the most vulnerable within their communities" (ESDC 2020).

The process leading up to the adoption of the NHS and Reaching Home directives involved extensive consultations with community groups and a commitment from the very top to respond to community input. An actor involved in consultations with community groups spoke with some light-hearted frustration for the minister responsible for overseeing the development of the NHS: "We got to the end [of the consultations] and the minister, being the minister that he is, he said, 'I want you to go out to communities again and validate the report, that this is truly what they think.' I'm like, 'No. It's over. The end ... We've heard from literally thousands and thousands of people, which is huge for any topic to get that kind of response'" (personal interview 2018).

Following the adoption of the NHS, an expert advisory committee was struck to, among other tasks, recommend a definition of homelessness for adoption federally. An actor involved in NHS development explained the enthusiasm on the part of community groups for participating in that committee: "For other advisory committees they get like 100 applicants. We got over 800 applicants for our advisory committee" (personal interview 2018). The committee was inclusive and included people with lived experience, Indigenous leaders, and people from all regions of the country, including the North. And in a sense, the advisory committee was a team of rivals. Tim Richter of the CAEH and Pierre Gaudreau of the RAPSIM both sat on the committee, representing groups that have tended to be strongly at odds over homelessness program priorities and implementation, as future chapters will show. In recruiting both of them to the committee, the minister responsible for the NHS displayed an effort to develop a policy that would not alienate anyone. Looking at the details, it seems that a compromise was indeed struck: the Housing First requirement was removed from the federal homelessness program, a demand of the RAPSIM since 2014; yet at the same time, the NHS adopted the Canadian, not Québécois, definition of homelessness. It also includes a separate, but short, definition of homelessness among Indigenous people.

While the definition that was recommended and adopted is highly similar to the one created by the Canadian Homelessness Research Network, it contains several important changes. It is significant that someone who has been homeless for six months is now understood to be chronically homeless, whereas in the past most definitions assumed this time period to be one year. This is a substantial broadening of the definition of chronic homelessness and will allow more people to be prioritized. It is also significant that the definition specifies that anyone living in an unsheltered location, an emergency shelter, or staying temporarily with others for six months is considered chronically homeless. This last category, hidden homelessness, was not prioritized by the NHI/HPS, which focused on visible forms of homelessness (either on the streets or in emergency shelters). The definition has therefore broadened considerably, but has also remained consistent with the earlier definitions motivating federal government actions, which define homelessness as a lack of housing.

Interviews with key actors illustrate that there has also been a profound shift in the ideas of main actors regarding the responsibility to produce social protection and federalism, ideas that drove increased federal government involvement in 2017: "There is always debate about whether housing and homelessness are provincial jurisdiction or federal jurisdiction. The minister and this government believe it's shared jurisdiction ... The previous government saw housing and homelessness as provincial jurisdiction and they were really getting out of the game so to speak. We were supposed to be winding this program down ... so if there had not been a change in government, we would not be having this conversation because I would have a very small team and we would be working towards the end" (personal interview 2018).

The re-engagement of the federal government followed a change in the party in power in 2015, as the Liberal Party defeated the previously ruling Conservative government. There are important ideological differences between the two parties, but party ideology alone does not explain this re-engagement; recall that it was also the Liberal Party that fully dismantled the federal government's commitment to a housing program in the 1990s and initially limited involvement in homelessness as well. Evolving ideas regarding shared responsibility for housing and homelessness led to a reinvigoration of the program. The actor referenced above went on to note that key federal government officials, including ministers and the prime minister, see themselves as leaders, not just collaborative partners, in the production of social protection. Community engagement was extensive, but in terms of making decisions, the federal government would maintain the power of the pen: "You have to have close relationships with the people delivering the services. Though there are times when I say 'No, you guys are wrong' and you have to be able to stand your ground" (personal interview 2018).

Federal investment does not amount to what advocates say is required to end homelessness. Even so, motivated by ideas that homelessness is a structural problem and that the federal role in producing social protection for the homeless is one of leadership, the federal government has increased its involvement in homelessness governance and taken important steps toward allowing communities to move away from alleviation efforts in favour of enduring solutions. This includes working with provinces to create more housing options, including rent allowances and contributing funding to the development of new housing units of affordable housing. The success of these programs will depend on funding but also on the ability of all actors to stay at the table. And of course, just as Reaching Home and the NHS were being implemented, COVID-19 hit; while the country was being thrown into a lockdown and Canadians were being told to stay home, advocates pushed the government to keep the needs of people without homes front of mind. A few weeks into the lockdown, the federal government announced an additional $157.5 million for communities through Reaching Home. This funding allowed for increased flexibility for community groups to fund general health and medical services (previously ineligible expenses), cost-matching requirements were waived, and groups were allowed to fund projects outside of their immediate service boundaries to reduce the spread of COVID-19 between communities. As a part of its fall economic update, the federal government announced an additional $236.7 million for Reaching Home (CMHC 2020).

These efforts, before and during the pandemic, have involved direct relationships between the federal government and local communities, except in Quebec, where the province is also involved. Meanwhile, the federal government has also worked on bilateral agreements with the provinces to build new affordable housing, protect and renovate existing social housing, and introduce portable housing allowances to be used in private-market housing. In the context of COVID-19, the federal government introduced the Rapid Housing Initiative, a $1 billion program to create as many as 3,000 new permanent units of affordable housing. All cities under study in this book have benefited from the Rapid Housing Initiative, using that funding to purchase and make available modular housing (prefabricated housing that is quick to assemble and less expensive to build); to rent or purchase hotels to create isolation centres, shelters, or temporary housing; or to otherwise make immediate contributions to affordable housing availability (PMO 2020).

What is interesting about the Rapid Housing Initiative is that, like the NHI/HPS and Reaching Home, it involves a direct relationship between the federal government and local communities; provinces outside of Quebec have been overstepped. While the weaknesses in the housing and homeless-serving systems long predate the pandemic, the pandemic resulted in large numbers of vulnerable people needing housing immediately, either because shelters were no longer an option or because of threat of eviction. In other words, the weaknesses in the welfare state were pre-existing conditions, but the trigger for the immediate, urgent need was the pandemic. During this global public health emergency, speed of action was critical, and because of the immediate, life-and-death nature of the need, there was no time to reform systems. In a sense, bypassing provinces during the emergency stage of this response was appropriate because unhoused people faced a genuine crisis. This approach also sheds further light on how this direct federal-local approach may have been inappropriate in the past; homelessness was indeed a crisis, but the cause of the rise in homelessness across the country in the 1990s and 2000s was not an external shock creating an urgent and immediate need, but rather a failure of systems and policies.

The federal government has been consistently involved in homelessness since 1999. Funding has rarely increased and certainly has never reached the levels that advocates say are needed; nevertheless, federal bureaucrats point out with some pride that the program was never eliminated or even cut (personal interview 2014). That the funding did not change even during times of economic decline is a testament to the importance of ideas over resources. Until 2014, the federal role in homelessness was minimal, reflecting its emergency and individualized understanding of homelessness. Changes in 2014 to prioritize Housing First programs reflected some changes to the understanding of homelessness as a costly and fixable problem. The introduction in 2017 of a National Housing Strategy further underscores the importance of ideas regarding the nature of the problem and the responsibility to produce social protection; these ideas cannot be said to be purely ideological, for the changes were made by the Liberal Party, which introduced the original NHI in 1999. As I will explain below, advocacy around homelessness by key actors, importantly including the CAEH, were also instrumental in pushing ideas about homelessness, and the federal responsibility in efforts to combat it, onto the radar of key federal officials.

Canadian Alliance to End Homelessness

The CAEH emerged in Calgary in 2012. It originally focused on local action but has become increasingly influential at the national level as well. Other groups have also exercised influence on the national level, including the Toronto Disaster Relief Committee. But the CAEH has become a long-standing, powerful, national agenda-setting organization. The understanding of a small number of key officials – led by founding

CEO Tim Richter – regarding the nature of homelessness has evolved significantly since its origins, but the CAEH has been consistent in prioritizing people experiencing chronic homelessness, its support of Housing First, and on the need for local groups to coordinate their interventions. The CAEH has advanced particular solutions to homelessness, ranging from prioritizing veterans' homelessness to a National Housing Strategy, and has powerfully employed ideas to persuade others to join its efforts to end homelessness. The CAEH has done this mainly by defining (and redefining) homelessness, showing the power that understanding the problem can wield in driving the actions of governmental and non-governmental actors through multilevel governance. Its work can be divided into two short eras: 2012 to 2016, during which its actions were oriented largely toward helping community groups end homelessness; and 2016 to the present, during which CAEH leadership has advocated much more on the national level, particularly for structural and systemic changes to end homelessness.

Calgary-based but nationally focused, the CAEH is a national advocacy group boasting nearly 200 community partners across the country.[4] Its mission is to "prevent and end homelessness in Canada," and it seeks to do so by ensuring that "all Canadians have a safe, decent and affordable home with the support necessary to sustain it" (CAEH 2020b). The CAEH has always adopted a housing-based definition of homelessness, though it has evolved and expanded considerably since 2012. Former president of the Calgary Homeless Foundation (CHF) Tim Richter was the founding CEO of the CAEH; he entered the field of homelessness policy in the mid-2000s, developing Calgary's first plan to end homelessness (see chapter 6). Prior to this, he had a successful career in government relations for TransAlta, a major oil and gas company based in Calgary. His work as a lobbyist (combined with his background in political science) have provided him with important insights into how to interact effectively with governments; it also allowed him to build up a powerful network of what he calls "the unusual suspects," including private-sector actors, in the fight against homelessness (Scott 2012). Richter's skills as a lobbyist have allowed the CAEH to become highly effective in its targeted interactions with governments at all levels, but especially the federal government.

The CAEH has invested substantial energy in Canada-wide campaigns, the first of which was to support communities in the development and implementation of local ten-year plans to end homelessness. The same year the CAEH launched, it published *A Plan, Not a Dream: How to End Homelessness in Ten Years* (2012), intended to serve as a roadmap for communities across Canada to develop their own ten-year plans to end homelessness. The Canadian plan was "directly derived from a document of the same name developed by the National Alliance to End Homelessness (NAEH) in the United States" (CAEH 2012, 3). *A Plan, Not a Dream* confidently championed the idea that it is possible to end homelessness: "Everything you need to know to end homelessness is known in your communities or is available from others. There are many effective partnerships at the community level that engage government, non-profit agencies and private sector groups in innovative initiatives. And the financial resources exist" (CAEH 2012, 3). It continues: "What's missing is a practical community-based approach that shifts the focus from managing homelessness, to a system focused on ending it. We need to move from crisis responses (like shelters and soup kitchens) to solutions – permanent, appropriate, safe and affordable housing with the support necessary to sustain it" (3).

Evident in these early CAEH efforts are ideas regarding the nature of homelessness and the responsibility to produce social protection. *A Plan Not a Dream* was not about structural change; tellingly, the first "essential" item in a community's efforts to end homelessness was planning. The CAEH boldly claimed that the resources existed to end homelessness and that they simply needed to be put together in a way that would allow people to exit homelessness. For example, the plan noted that to end homelessness, people need income support, so communities should connect them to *existing* rent supplements and career-based employment services as opposed to arguing for a basic income or some other form of living wage. People leaving prisons and the child welfare system often end up homeless, so communities should *manage those exits* so that people enter housing instead of re-enter homelessness, as opposed to reforming those systems. And people need housing, so communities should work with private market landlords to help homeless people access *available* housing as opposed to creating new affordable housing, making that private sector housing affordable through rent supplements. These specific examples reveal guiding assumptions regarding the responsibility to produce social protection: governments had simultaneously done enough and not enough – they had done enough because the resources (income supports, affordable housing) existed, but not enough because they were not being managed and organized properly. The problem was more technical than structural; required, then, was someone to put it all together at the local level.

With support from the CAEH, a few Plans to End Homelessness were developed across the country,[5] and they made a number of contributions to local efforts to combat homelessness; for example, new community groups were organized, and attention was drawn to the importance of data-driven approaches. But except in Medicine Hat, Alberta, none of these plans succeeded in ending homelessness in ten years, though some plans did succeed in halting or reversing what had been a rapid increase in the number of people experiencing homelessness, as was the case in Calgary (CHF 2018). Following earnest but ultimately unsuccessful efforts to turn the CAEH plan to end homelessness into a reality across the country, and facing evidence that existing plans would not succeed, the CAEH pivoted, turning its attention to other campaigns.

A second campaign, launched in June 2015, set out to house 20,000 homeless people across the country in three years. These efforts were locally based and not funded by the CAEH, whose role was to encourage and support those efforts through training and workshops and to track the collective efforts. While much of this work would have been done otherwise, the CAEH facilitated collaboration between communities, encouraged them to orient funding to permanent solutions like Housing First, provided them with considerable support, and managed to secure $885,000 from the federal government to "scale up" its efforts (CAEH 2018). Announcing in 2018 that 21,254 individuals had been housed over the course of the campaign, the CAEH seized the momentum and launched the Built for Zero campaign, "an ambitious national change effort helping a core group of leading communities end chronic and veteran homelessness – a first step on the path to eliminating all homelessness in Canada" (CAEH 2020a).

Over the course of these campaigns, the CAEH underwent significant change, particularly in terms of how it engaged with other actors. Changes in involvement and interactions were motivated primarily by changing ideas about the nature of homelessness. The CAEH had focused on supporting local communities in its first few years, but in 2016, Richter turned more and more attention to engaging senior governments, particularly the federal government. That year, the beginning of the second era in the CAEH's involvement, Richter registered as a lobbyist for the CAEH, powerful evidence of evolving ideas regarding the responsibility to produce social protection. The private market was no longer seen as capable of meeting housing needs with only minimal government support; the federal government was now understood as having an important, perhaps central, role in the production of social protection for people experiencing homelessness. As a lobbyist, Richter sought to convince the federal government to increase its involvement in homelessness governance. He has several entries in the Canadian Registry of Lobbyists; up until 2007, of course, he had lobbied on behalf of TransAlta Corporation, so he was familiar with the process and had significant expertise communicating with governments as the lobbying record shows. In 2016, he began lobbying the federal government on behalf of the CAEH, including to provide funding for that organization, to adopt a Housing First approach to existing homelessness investments, to prioritize ending homelessness among veterans, as well as for a National Housing Strategy that would encompass a meaningful right-to-housing approach.

Since late 2016, nearly 200 communication reports (official lobbying disclosures) have been filed on behalf of Richter and the CAEH. A close look at those records points to the targeted lobbying strategy from which the CAEH benefits. Documented lobbying efforts include written and oral communications as well as "grassroots communications." Those efforts have been aimed at a wide variety of institutions and individuals, including the Senate; the Canadian Mortgage and Housing Corporation (CMHC); Finance Canada; the Prime Minister's Office; individuals closely involved in housing policy such as Toronto MP Adam Vaughan, the Minister of Veterans Affairs, the Minister of Families, Children and Social Development Ahmed Hussen; and members of all political parties except the Bloc Québécois. Richter strikes with precision, and rapidly; given the priority of ending veterans' homelessness, he was always in touch with the minister for that portfolio. The lobbying registry indicates that he communicated on behalf of the CAEH with Jody Wilson-Raybould on 15 January 2019, one day after she was named Minister of Veterans Affairs.

In tandem with efforts to prioritize ending veterans' homelessness, Richter's lobbying increasingly focused on the need for a National Housing Strategy. In a recent webinar to promote the CAEH-led campaign, Recovery for All, Richter recalled that an official in the Prime Minister's Office had told him "your advocacy made [the National Housing Strategy] happen" (Richter 2020). This comment was not just in reference to Richter, and he did not present it in the webinar as such; rather, it was in reference to the broad movement of people, many of whom were mobilized by the CAEH, who had advocated for a National Housing Strategy (though certainly groups not allied with the CAEH advocated for a NHS as well).

That movement, however, was combined with a highly sophisticated approach to lobbying and an ability to maintain good relationships; a key actor in the NHS's development said unprompted in an interview that "Tim Richter and I talk twice a week" (personal interview 2018). Richter's skill at maintaining relationships with powerful individuals in most parties is an important reason why the CAEH has become such a powerful organization, and evolving ideas regarding the structural, not individual-level, causes of homelessness have led the CAEH to engage more aggressively with the federal government. There are criticisms of this approach, including self-censoring criticism of the government and making more moderate as opposed to radical demands. But if the government's involvement is seen as key to efforts to combat homelessness, this approach has been highly effective in getting the government on board.

Changes to the rules governing the non-partisan activities that charities and non-profits, such as the CAEH, can engage in were introduced in 2018. The previous rules had restricted what non-profits could do in terms of advocacy (technically, "public policy dialogue and development activities"); now, charities can engage in unlimited activities, though they cannot support a particular party or politician. With this space opened up, the CAEH has ramped up its activities, launching national campaigns to pressure the federal government to invest in housing and to build an end to homelessness directly into its COVID-19 recovery. The Recovery for All campaign sought to ensure that the rebuilding efforts in the wake of the pandemic would include the promise to end homelessness through "bold investments in housing, homelessness and income support to end homelessness in Canada, once and for all" (CAEH 2020c). Though the campaign only lasted a few months, it is significant because of the demonstrated evolution in ideas regarding the nature of homelessness and the responsibility to produce social protection. Long gone is the assumption that governments have done enough in terms of housing affordability and income security; instead, the federal government was being called upon to commit to a major investment in new affordable housing developments and income supports.[6]

With the impending federal election in 2021, the CAEH again pivoted: Recovery for All was rolled up, or perhaps rather morphed into Vote Housing, an election-oriented campaign. Vote Housing was a national non-partisan campaign to make housing a ballot box issue. Turning his eyes again to the political system and making political demands, Richter teamed up with Zain Velji, a Calgary-based organizer with a track record for managing successful political campaigns, including for former Calgary mayor Naheed Nenshi. Vote Housing's demands were similar to those of Recovery for All; they included 300,000 units of affordable housing and 50,000 units of supportive housing over ten years. The program also emphasized urban, rural, and northern Indigenous housing, along with demanding an expansion of rental assistance as a means to reduce core housing need.[7] While the CAEH was deeply involved in the campaign, it was a collaborative effort with other networks, including the Canadian Lived Experience Leadership Network and Indigenous-led networks. Furthermore, past campaigns, including Built for Zero, had a small presence in Quebec; by contrast, Vote Housing was national in scope, with allies in Quebec and bilingual campaign materials.

Complementing its lobbying and organizing efforts, the CAEH since 2013 has run an annual conference to end homelessness, which has become an important policy-making venue. It is designed to share the mission of the CAEH, recruit partners and members, launch campaigns, make important announcements, and spread knowledge about the fight against homelessness. Beginning in 2013 in Ottawa, these conferences have become an important venue for policy-makers and community stakeholders to meet, learn, discuss, and collaborate. Over time, they have become more inclusive, though the Housing First orientation remains, as does the emphasis on learning from one another, with a focus on learning from American experiences.

Academic and housing activist Emily Paradis has examined the importance of the annual CAEH conference from a critical perspective, writing that the conferences are "discursive sites in which framings of homelessness are defined, circulated and consolidated; as sites of governance, in which policy-makers and non-governmental actors develop policy and program responses; and as sites of contestation, in which people facing homelessness claim space for oppositional perspectives" (Paradis 2016, 99). They particularly consider the 2014 conference in Vancouver,[8] a pivotal moment in the history of the conference and of the CAEH as well. A group of activists, some of whom were conference attendees, protested the conference itself and called for "a major mobilization to confront, expose, and oppose the government policies and NGO industries that manage homeless, low-income and Indigenous people without challenging or disrupting the systems and social conditions that cause homelessness and poverty" (Paradis 2014). The protest was uncomfortable, Paradis explains: "It was a surreal scene: outside in the courtyard, dozens of homeless people and allies, waving red banners and chanting; inside the glass causeway above, hundreds of conference delegates, enjoying wine and salmon skewers. And between us, a line of police and hotel security, barricading the lobby. Two groups of people working to end homelessness, one being 'protected' by armed police from the other" (Paradis 2014).

Conference attendees, some of whom were attending the conference on a lived experience scholarship paid for by the CAEH, participated in, spoke at, and organized the protest: "we were defying protocol and polite etiquette, in protesting the very meeting that we had been invited, and paid for, to attend" (Jarrett 2016). Many on the inside at the conference were sympathetic: "Participants in the event that was the target of the protest [were] actually standing alongside and in agreement with the people protesting, who had some very valid input and direction to give to the professionals filling the seats in the workshops and speaking events. This was a momentous time, and the energy filling the air that evening and for the rest of the conference was buzzing with new possibilities" (Jarrett 2016).

Protesters were eventually invited inside and continued organizing. They created space for themselves, demanded power, addressed conference attendees, and insisted on the need for their voices to be included in CAEH operations and future conferences. The protest could have been avoided had dissenting voices been included from the beginning; however, a permanent rupture between community groups and the CAEH was avoided. CAEH leadership and board members with strong credibility among community groups demonstrated openness and an ability to listen and evolve. The Lived Experience Advisory Council developed in the wake of the protest, and in 2020 a Lived Experience Leadership Network was created and became an allied network of the CAEH. It would be influential in future campaigns, including Vote Housing.

Governments use CAEH conferences not just to make announcements but also to develop policy with direct input from community groups. For example, the 2018 conference in Hamilton, held during the lead-up to the implementation of the NHS, included a round-table session led by federal officials soliciting community input in the identification of which policy outcomes should be measured and prioritized. Politicians also attend the conference, to give keynote addresses and make policy announcements as well as to listen. The annual conference is as close to an institutionalized venue as a non-governmental organization can create. Through it, the CAEH has carved out a powerful place for itself in the governance of homelessness in Canada. While the conferences are in theory inclusive – anyone who wishes can attend – significant barriers remain in terms of conference fees (upwards of $600 for people who are not presenting) and the time and funding required to travel to the conference, which is held in a different city every year. Because of these barriers, the conferences tend to be for government officials as well as executives and staff from service providers that have the resources to participate.

Though the conferences are expensive and elite, efforts have been made to create inclusive spaces at them, including gender identification on name tags, tables during meals specifically for people with lived experience, and a quiet room for those who feel anxious or uncomfortable in the conference space. People with lived experience present regularly at the conferences, engaging directly with policy-makers, and people with lived experience are on the board of the CAEH. This space was not initially offered, but once it was demanded, the leadership of the CAEH adapted and brought protesting voices in. In doing this, the CAEH turned a significant threat to its legitimacy into an ally, increasing its strength in the community. This has strengthened the CAEH and also limited threats from the outside, which Withers (2021) may consider a demobilizing tactic to undermine the effectiveness of social movements advancing a different, more radical perhaps, agenda. The CAEH is very much a mainstream organization; they do not criticize capitalism and look to governments for solutions. It is true that in winning over some of its opponents, the CAEH may have made it more difficult for a radical housing justice movement to take hold nationally.

These numerous campaigns illustrate the CAEH's adaptability, especially its ability to remain relevant following difficult early years in which the promised plans to end homelessness did not lead to the changes that had been envisioned. And while they have not secured an end to chronic homelessness, many communities – notably in Alberta, where the CAEH is most influential – have seen significant reductions in the number of people experiencing chronic homelessness. The CAEH has remained consistent over time in its prioritization of chronic homelessness; insistence on the promise of Housing First; and belief in data-driven responses to homelessness, including homeless counts as well as more coordinated and sophisticated systems of data gathering, such as By-Name lists (CAEH 2018). CAEH actors are also consistent in their belief that ending homelessness will save money. But the group's interactions with other actors have changed over its relatively brief lifespan; it is moving away from individualized understandings of the causes of and solutions to homelessness toward more structural and systemic ones. The CAEH has further broadened its understanding of homelessness through its appreciation of the different realities of homelessness for Indigenous individuals, including an acknowledgement of its colonial roots (CAEH 2020; 2021).

Housing and Homelessness: Conclusions

Resources and institutions matter to these two national actors – the federal government and the CAEH – but ideas have been the driving force behind their involvement in homelessness governance and their interactions with other actors. Having eliminated investments in affordable housing and made cuts to other parts of the welfare state in the 1990s, the federal government was slow to respond in a meaningful way as homelessness emerged as a new social risk. Where it did act, through the NHI (followed by the HPS), ideas regarding the nature of homelessness were instrumental in shaping its response. Though the program has been funded non-stop since 1999, that funding has never been permanent; investments were, until 2019, only for short periods; and they were wholly inadequate to make any meaningful contribution to the availability of affordable housing. That was by design and by definition; for decades, federal officials did not view homelessness as an outcome of political and policy decisions. It was, rather, seen as a short-term and individualized emergency.

This idea was also reflected in the NHI/HPS governance dynamics. A narrow and emergency-based understanding of homelessness helps to explain the federal government's decision to bypass the provinces – which have policy responsibility for many areas that are structurally related to homelessness such as health, social assistance, child welfare, and housing – and instead work directly with the local level. For nearly twenty years, efforts to fight homelessness were divorced from housing policy (and social policy more broadly) and bypassed provinces, reflecting the idea that homelessness is not caused by structural issues such as a lack of affordable housing or a frayed welfare state. This idea led federal officials to play a minimal role in the production of social protection. With the introduction of the National Housing Strategy in 2017, which has increased investments in homelessness programs, extended the time period of funding to ten years, directly linked homelessness with housing, and which partners with provinces in the production of housing, we see an evolving understanding that homelessness is related to housing and requires structural and systemic changes.

The CAEH has become a powerful voice representing service providers and people experiencing homelessness; since the early 2010s, it has evolved into an influential policy-making actor in its own right. It has consistently defined homelessness as the absence of housing and has insisted that chronic homelessness must be the first priority of interventions. Its understanding of the nature of chronic homelessness has broadened considerably, and that has influenced not only the solutions it proposes but also its understanding of the responsibility to produce social protection, leading to more collaborative interactions with the federal government in particular. In its early days, the CAEH encouraged local groups to use existing resources more effectively and efficiently, arguing that everything that was needed to end homelessness was already available. To the extent that changes to systems were proposed, they were minimal and around the edges. This has changed considerably: the CAEH has come to see homelessness as a more complex and systemic problem that requires new resources and sweeping systemic and structural changes, including a guaranteed minimum income and substantial new investments in housing. The CAEH has succeeded in engaging governments, and along with other groups across the country, it has recently pushed for the first National Housing Strategy in nearly thirty years. Ideas regarding the nature of homelessness and the responsibility to produce social protection have become broader and have allowed the CAEH to not just lobby and coach community groups but also to meaningfully partner with governments in shaping homelessness policy.

5 Vancouver

The governance of homelessness in Vancouver is complex and involves multiple actors. In general terms, homelessness governance in Vancouver is fragmented but, with important exceptions, coordinated. The province, the city, the private sector, and two regional networks that implement the federal homelessness program have plans on housing and homelessness, and third-sector groups are strongly committed to advocacy and direct policy participation as well. Many of these actors are deeply involved and have been for decades, creating their own plans and adopting their own approaches to homelessness. Leadership of the issue is at times contested, and some groups advance slightly different approaches, but for the most part, the actors work well together. There have at times, however, been deep disagreements between and within groups that have resulted in fragmentation, instability, and decreased influence for some.

In Vancouver, we clearly see the importance of ideas, as well as how institutions can make ideas even more powerful by facilitating the creation of coalitions but also competing groups. Ideas regarding their responsibility to produce social protection and a very particular understanding of the nature of homelessness have at times led municipal officials to take what they see as a leadership role in the fight against homelessness. The local party system has turned subtle ideational disagreements regarding the nature of homelessness into political ones. In such a context, ideas regarding the nature of homelessness become magnetic, drawing people to work together but also pushing groups apart. This has occurred not only between the private sector and the city, but also within the third sector, with some actors espousing fundamentally different definitions of homelessness. Where disagreements about the nature of homelessness are small, local groups are often able to overcome institutional obstacles and collaborate. Where they are not reconcilable, however, disagreeing groups tend to be pushed out by more powerful actors, resulting in decreased influence and periodic destabilization in the governance network.

Homelessness History in BC

Relative to other provinces, the Government of British Columbia's involvement in housing and homelessness has been innovative and interventionist since the 1970s, be it in times of centrist NDP governance or right-of-centre Liberal Party governance. The province has kept its housing powers (intentionally not downloading them to the municipal level), and, for all but a five-year period in the early 2000s, it has exercised them. Since 2006, its response to homelessness has been in the context of the province's housing plan. While its involvement at times follows what would be expected based on ideology (i.e., more interventionist under NDP governments than Liberal ones) and the availability of resources (i.e., increasing with economic prosperity and diminishing with economic decline), ideas regarding the nature of homelessness and the responsibility to produce social protection have also structured the degree of provincial involvement.

The principal body that implements the province's housing policies is BC Housing, an arm's-length public corporation established in the 1960s. In 1975 the province implemented an inclusionary housing policy, unique in Canada at the time, that encouraged mixed-income developments by allocating approximately two-thirds of units to low-income residents and the remainder to middle-income residents (BC Housing 1980).[1] By 1986, there were 52,350 units of housing in the province, produced by a variety of federal and provincial programs (BC Housing 1997). That same year, the provincial and federal governments jointly created the Non-Profit Housing Program, which involved housing constructed by the private sector, managed by the non-profit sector, and subsidized by the federal and provincial governments to make up the difference between the affordable rent that was charged to tenants and what was needed to keep the buildings financially viable. The 11,000 units produced through this program were "strictly targeted for those with low incomes" (BC Housing 1986, 3), including seniors, families, and people with disabilities. Earlier housing policy had been broader and more mixed. This was the beginning of a shifting understanding of housing need and the government's role in meeting that need.

By the early 1990s, around 70,000 units of social housing had been developed across the province (BC Housing 1994a, 3). In 1993 the federal government announced that it would no longer fund new social housing developments (BC Housing 1994a). The following year, the provincial NDP government introduced *Homes BC*, the province's own social housing policy. Ideas regarding the province's responsibility to produce social protection are evident in the introduction to that document: "Unlike the federal government, BC recognizes the importance of continuing to support housing programs that increase the permanent supply of affordable housing for British Columbians" (BC Housing 1994b, 2). Moreover, this involvement in housing would continue despite "fiscal constraints" (BC Housing 1994a, 2). Here we see how ideas regarding the government's role in producing social protection bring meaning to resources, even during periods when financial resources are limited. This willingness to spend was in line with the NDP's centre-left ideology, of course, but BC was not the only province under NDP governance when the federal government cut its housing program: at the time, Roy Romanow and Bob Rae were also NDP premiers (of Saskatchewan and Ontario respectively). Rae was defeated in mid-1995 and did not have time to develop and implement his vision for affordable housing. Romanow, on the other hand, served as premier until 2001, yet he did not develop a housing program for Saskatchewan, which suggests that other factors were at play besides left/right ideology or partisan politics.

The definition of housing need in *Homes BC* expanded somewhat so as to include low- *and* moderate-income people, as well as seniors and people who were homeless or at risk of it. *Homes BC* initially committed to creating 600 units of social housing per year (about half of what had been produced with the federal partner), but housing production consistently exceeded that target. *Homes BC* was expanded in 1999: the number of units it intended to develop was doubled to 1,200 in 1999–2000; that commitment was exceeded as the province developed more than 1,600 units. By 2001, 4,027 units of housing had been funded and completed by the province alone, with an additional 3,200 planned over the following two years (2001–3).

After ten years of NDP governance, the Liberal Party of BC was elected in 2001.[2] Of primary concern to the new right-of-centre government was the economy: "Over the last decade British Columbia's economy consistently underperformed. Of all the Canadian provinces, BC had the lowest productivity growth, the lowest growth in private-sector investment, the lowest growth in per capita gross domestic product, and one of the least competitive tax regimes in the country. BC's debt doubled from 1990 to 2001" (Government of British Columbia 2001, 9). During this period, we see clear, seemingly ideological differences in understanding what limited resources mean for government decisions;

facing public debt, Liberal premier Gordon Campbell planned to cut, not spend. To that end, in August 2001 he announced a core services review (CSR) to examine government expenditures.

Following the CSR's recommendations, significant cuts were made across most government departments. Unprecedented restrictions were added to social assistance benefits, many of which were immediately reversed as even conservative voices criticized them (Klein and Long 2003). Deep cuts were made to education, health, and, of course, housing. *Homes BC* was immediately cancelled, though previous housing commitments made by the NDP would be honoured through the Liberals' Provincial Housing Program (PHP), including for the 3,200 units of new social housing promised in the NDP's 2001 budget.[3] So while there was no provincial housing policy during this period, the province honoured past commitments, which was not the case in other provinces (notably Alberta and Ontario).

A senior actor involved with the BC government at the time explained that the economic context was important to decision-making at the time: "Provinces were dealing with debts and deficits and so what do you do? You stop doing some of what you are doing" (personal interview 2014). While this context was important, this actor noted that ideas regarding the production of social protection were also at play: "We got out of the business of social housing. It's something we did. The premier felt there were other ways to create social housing," suggesting that the private sector could play a more significant role. While the Liberal government fulfilled commitments for future housing developments made by the NDP under *Homes BC*, there were no future commitments beyond that: "The completion of these units will bring the [provincial housing] program to conclusion" (BC Housing 2003).

Interestingly, given this context, BC became the first province to sign an Affordable Housing Agreement (AHA), a cost-sharing agreement announced by the federal government in 2001. The federal government transferred $89 million to the province between 2002 and 2007 for affordable or social housing, funding that was matched by the BC government (BC Housing 2018). Looking at what this funding was used for makes clear that in the short term, the provincial commitment to invest in housing was consistent with its long-term commitment to limit its involvement in housing. One-third of this funding[4] was applied to the Provincial Housing Program (the 3,200 units previously committed to by the NDP through *Homes BC*), with the remainder going "towards supportive housing options for seniors and people with disabilities" (BC Housing 2002, 15).[5] Analysis of housing during this period indicates that much of this funding was *not* used to build new housing but rather to convert existing social housing into assisted-living housing for seniors (Klein and Copas 2010), reflecting a tightening of the province's understanding of housing need and of the government's role in producing social protection (personal interview 2014). Over the first five years of the AHA, the province's role in producing social protection was oriented toward an even more targeted population than had been the case in the past: "Among the priorities ... is the goal of building the best system of support in Canada *for persons with disabilities, those with special needs, children at risk and seniors*. This goal reinforces the government's commitment to building a strong social safety network *for the most vulnerable*" (BC Housing 2006a; emphasis added). Under the Liberal Party, social protection was being produced by the province for only the very most housing-insecure, defined narrowly as those with disabilities, children, seniors, and those at risk of homelessness. In other words, the strong, government-funded social safety net was not for everyone, only the most vulnerable.

In the mid-2000s, homelessness was becoming an increasingly visible and political issue in BC, particularly in big cities (interviews; Campbell, Boyd, and Culbert 2009; Lupick 2017a). Though advocates note that they had begun to observe increases in the number of people experiencing homelessness in Vancouver as early as the 1990s, the number of people experiencing homelessness in the city doubled between 2002 and 2006 (from 628 to 1,291) (SPARC BC 2005). In this context, and only a few years after he made the decision to cut investments in housing, Premier Campbell announced a Task Force on Homelessness, Mental Health, and Addiction in 2004. Its mandate was to come up with ways for the province to work quickly with local governments and community partners to build supportive housing for people experiencing chronic forms of homelessness.[6] The task force was concerned primarily with a narrowly defined group of homeless people and aimed "to provide better coordination of resources in communities and to develop innovative strategies to give people with addictions and mental illness the opportunity to move from temporary shelters to long-term, stable housing" (BC Ministry of Finance 2005).

A former mayor involved in the task force linked the increase in homelessness with the CSR and the cuts to social spending that followed it: "[CSR] marching orders were that almost every ministry had to slash the budget ... So you can cut 10 per cent from roads and just build fewer highways for a period of time. But in the area of social services, when you start to cut dollars when there are not enough dollars to begin with, you can see it on the street almost immediately. That's what happened" (personal interview 2014). They went on to explain their perception that the task force was as much about doing the right thing as it was about controlling the damage resulting from the CSR cuts a few years earlier: "The whole idea was that we would come up with a strategy to deal with the problem that had been created without [The Premier] sort of saying 'I created [homelessness], I am now solving it'" (personal interview 2014).

Others disagreed with this assessment. For those involved with the province at the time, the improving economic situation was important to this renewed provincial involvement, but so too were ideas about the nature of homelessness, especially chronic homelessness. A senior official noted: "I think there was a recognition that there was a real problem and a real need. And the government had turned a corner a little on some of its fiscal situation, so it was in a situation where it could choose priorities and act on them" (personal interview 2014). Resources mattered, but senior officials also insisted that changing ideas were driving the government to turn around and invest a few short years after it had cut: "[The minister] had some kind of come-to-Jesus moment when he realized that this was a real problem. It's not just 'what if you just stop drinking and doing drugs and turn your life around' kind of bullshit. And he then began to be very creative about how to create the capital to make it possible to make a significant contribution to new social housing." There was not a change in the leadership within the party; the same people – Premier Gordon Campbell, Housing Minister Rich Coleman, Attorney General Geoff Plant – were still in charge. The province was newly convinced that homelessness is structural and not individual; its reinvolvement was motivated by an understanding that with its social policy might, it had to lead.

It is particularly notable that the BC Liberals reinvested only a few years after cutting social spending and housing expenditures. This contrasts with decisions made in Alberta and Ontario (reviewed in chapters 6 and 8 respectively). In Alberta, for example, the economic situation also improved following deep cuts to social spending (as was the case in BC). But rather than use the surplus to reinvest in housing, Premier Ralph Klein sent $600 cheques to individual Albertans. Resources matter, but leaders decide what to do with those resources, and that process is shaped by ideas. Changing ideas led the BC government to deploy its resources to combat homelessness, rather than holding on to them or spending the money elsewhere. In linking homelessness with mental health and addiction, Campbell was guided by an admittedly narrow understanding of homelessness. That understanding likely led to the province's re-engagement: the province has jurisdiction over those areas of policy, which meant it could not reasonably pass the buck to another level or sector. In other words, the understanding of homelessness shaped government beliefs in provincial responsibility to produce social protection.

While its understanding of homelessness was indeed narrow, the province's actions were always linked with important systems such as housing and health. Following the task force's recommendations, in the mid-aughts the province committed itself to constructing *new* units of supportive housing through partnerships with municipalities and third-sector groups. As a senior provincial official explained it, "we went to the Union of BC Municipalities and the Premier said, 'bring us your challenges, and if you've got land or opportunities where you want to partner, we'll partner'" (personal interview 2018). The province moved quickly, explained a former mayor: "By the second or third meeting [of the Task Force], it was made very clear to us that those of us who were on board would have funds made available to us ... but the city must be able to move very fast and be a partner" (personal interview 2014). This person further noted that cities' plans needed to be "shovel ready" or they would lose out on provincial funding. In addition to constructing new housing, the province began purchasing old buildings, particularly in Vancouver's Downtown Eastside, to protect fragile and vulnerable affordable housing stock.

To formalize the partnerships, the province signed Memorandums of Understanding[7] with local governments across the province to expedite the development of new units of supportive and transitional housing, which would be specifically for people experiencing chronic homelessness. A senior provincial actor stressed repeatedly that while these were partnerships with local governments, the province was doing most of the heavy lifting in terms of policy and funding, noting that new housing was built with "90 per cent of the funding from the province. It's great to have city land, philanthropic donations, but they represent about 10 to 12 per cent of the total cost. And no operating costs" (personal interview 2014). Local governments seek credit for these developments as well, as I explain below, but the above quotation illustrates that provincial officials had a clear understanding that the production of social protection for people who experience chronic homelessness would require collaboration with the local level but provincial *leadership*.

Following the task force, the same Liberal government that had cut *Homes BC* a few years earlier tabled a new housing plan, *Housing Matters*, in 2006. Housing developed through the NDP's *Homes BC* had been targeted at vulnerable *and* low-income British Columbians; by contrast, *Housing Matters* explicitly prioritized people who were most vulnerable, again reflecting the idea that the government has an important role to play in protecting the *most vulnerable*: "Individuals or households with *special housing needs* will be given priority access to subsidized housing, and provincially-owned subsidized housing will be renovated to better meet the needs of low-income households *with special housing needs*, such as seniors with enhanced accessibility requirements" (BC Housing 2006b, 2; emphasis added). Where the housing needs of low-income people were referenced in *Housing Matters*, the government would rely heavily on the private sector and aim to facilitate "improved access to affordable rental housing." Furthermore, "portable housing allowances that can be used in the private rental market are the most economical way for the government to assist these low-income households" (BC Housing 2006b, 12). Thus, written right into the government's policy was the assumption that the private sector is the primary generator of social protection for low-income British Columbians; if necessary, the private sector would be bolstered by minimal government support in the form of rent supplements.

The number-one priority identified in *Housing Matters* was the fight against homelessness; indeed, the top three strategies were oriented toward "vulnerable populations," which by the government's definition included people who experience homelessness and Indigenous people. The policy did not include a definition of homelessness, but it made clear that programs would be tightly targeted at those with the greatest needs, that is, "individuals who are repeat users of shelters and who have multiple barriers" (BC Housing 2006b, 7). The province would also continue to renovate existing housing stock to make it more suitable for seniors needing supports, and begin buying low-income housing buildings across the province.

Housing Matters resulted in a transfer of the responsibility for emergency shelters from the Ministry of Social Development to BC Housing. A senior actor with BC Housing explained the logic: "With the addition of the shelters, you can begin to knit the housing continuum together, so people can move from outreach to shelters to Single Resident Occupant rooms to other forms of housing. So you had outreach, you had a better shelter system, then you had the province buying fifty buildings across the province, including twenty-six in Vancouver. That was a strategy to stabilize a vulnerable housing stock" (personal interview 2014). *Housing Matters* was not a comprehensive response to homelessness (which would involve other provincial ministries); nevertheless, it addressed the broad housing spectrum and spoke to the full range of housing needs, from emergency shelters to homeownership (BC Housing 2006b).[8] Homelessness was defined narrowly, but provincial actions were directly linked to housing, including the construction of new supportive housing. Indeed, the government was most involved in developing housing at the most insecure end of the spectrum. While the province was not as aggressive in terms of building housing between 2006 and 2014 as it had been in the past, there were nevertheless important increases in options across the housing spectrum.[9]

The BC Liberals would continue to govern through the 2000s and 2010s. However, the party changed leaders in 2011, with Christy Clark becoming premier, the second woman to assume that role in BC. Though it was not enough to meet the growing needs across the province and in Vancouver in particular, under Gordon Campbell's leadership the province had engaged quite intensely in the production of affordable and supportive housing, including the construction of new supportive housing buildings, renovations, and the purchase of buildings containing affordable units as a means of protecting that stock (against the potential that it might be converted into condominiums, for example). Under Christy Clark, the province was much less energetic in its involvement in housing and homelessness. Clark repeatedly stressed concerns that provincial interventions in the housing market might result in homeowners losing some of the value of their homes; in 2016, for example, Premier Clark said: "Anybody who owns a home or a condo – a house or a condo, a townhouse, or any property – doesn't want to see the value of that cut in half after they've already paid for it" (qtd in Lupick 2018). At the time, housing costs were soaring, particularly in Vancouver; in 2016, the average detached home in that city was worth $1.4 million, up 30 per cent from the previous year. Clark was also reluctant to commit to further construction of supportive housing for people experiencing homelessness. To the extent that interventions were needed, she made perfectly clear her understanding of whose responsibility she believed *that* was: "The only way to really solve this problem is to address supply, and that is 100 per cent in the ballpark, on the side of the field, for the cities. They need to step up and do their job here" (quoted in Dembicki 2017). This is an interesting and, in the Canadian context, somewhat uncommon interpretation of provincial and local powers.

She also made this view known in a letter to Vancouver mayor Gregor Robertson. In 2015, Robertson wrote letters to Premier Clark and federal Minister of Finance Bill Morneau, requesting "thousands of new housing units that are affordable for lower and middle income taxpayers." He said this could be achieved in a number of ways, including the stimulation of market rental housing in BC, increases in investments in social housing, or increased support for non-profit and co-op housing. He signed off on the letter to Clark with a handwritten note,

"Call me anytime to discuss!" (Robertson 2015). He can only have been disappointed with the response from Clark, who reiterated her concern about home values: "It's important that we consider any actions carefully to make sure we are helping first-time homebuyers get into the market while protecting the equity of existing homeowners – not just simply raising more taxes for government." And she emphasized again that housing supply was a municipal responsibility: "Beyond any new taxes to curb demand, there is also the option of increasing supply through better land-use planning" (Clark 2015). Acting on these ideas regarding the nature of housing needs (including of those experiencing homelessness) and the responsibility to produce social protection, which Clark viewed as municipal, the province decreased its involvement in homelessness governance.

Clark would eventually introduce a foreign buyer's tax of 15 per cent: "I can tell you [influential developer Peter Wall] and every other major developer in BC was mighty upset with me when we brought in a foreign tax of 15 per cent. They were mighty upset when we brought in a luxury tax on homes over $2 million" (Meralli 2017). Importantly, these actions followed the retirement of Clark's chief fundraiser, Bob Rennie, a highly influential developer in the province.[10] So Clark did introduce some measures to cool the housing market. Overall, however, her time as premier is cited by many in the province as a period when the province was less engaged in housing policy and responses to homelessness. The province did not entirely disengage, however, and investments in housing continued, though more slowly than in the past and not at the pace many advocates and local government officials would have liked. Framed as a refresh, *Housing Matters* was renewed in 2014. In its introduction, Housing Minister Rich Coleman declared that "*Housing Matters BC* remains the most progressive housing strategy in Canada" and concluded that it had been "extraordinarily successful" (BC Housing 2014b, 3). Compared to other jurisdictions, Coleman may not have been exaggerating, but this may have said more about other provinces and their lack of action; indeed, following Clark's disengagement, housing need and the number of people experiencing homelessness across the province continued to grow, especially in Vancouver.

It is interesting to note that these housing interventions were being celebrated as progressive by a party (the BC Liberals) that does not often identify with that word, further evidence that ideas driving this involvement were not strictly ideological. Also important to note is that provincial involvement in housing was supported not just by the Minister of Housing but by others in the right-of-centre government as well. As a senior official responsible for housing policy explained it, "we got pretty aggressive as we went through [housing policy], and I never had pushback from finance to say 'you can't spend that money,' because they always believed you should be integrating people with mental health, addictions, homelessness into something to stabilize them. And it actually has a positive effect on the other budgets, which would be social services, health, even policing" (personal interview 2018). Involvement in housing was admittedly seen as contributing to the broader government plan to reduce spending in other areas.

The 2014 policy renewed the commitment to providing housing supports to those with the greatest need, including seniors and people experiencing or at risk of homelessness. Like the 2006 version, it did not contain a definition of homelessness and continued the highly targeted approach to government involvement. It was also explicit about ideas regarding the responsibility to produce social protection (though its involvement was not as extensive as it had been under Campbell): "The Province is a leader and active partner, acting as a catalyst for investment in housing and services. These partnerships are founded on the notion that the development, maintenance and provision of both social and affordable market housing are enhanced through collaboration with a wide range of stakeholders" (BC Housing 2014b, 9). A senior official echoed this sentiment, making clear the leadership role the province had always played in collaboration with other groups, specifically noting the role of non-profits: "I've always believed that the government can [provide operating funds], but they can't put the heart in a building ... Our non-profits in BC do an exceptional, exceptional job of that" (personal interview 2018).

Provincial officials also said that relations with the federal government were strong, though BC officials always defended and communicated their interests: "I worked well with them all. The only thing I ever asked them: please don't do a unilateral project in British Columbia. Do it with us." This request to the federal government followed an important lesson learned from others, again reinforcing the importance of regular and open communication between ministers and senior officials and their counterparts in other provinces: "I think it was the minister from [redacted] said, 'We have a problem. The federal government came in and did a project. They built it in our province and gave it three years of funding. Then they left with the funding and we are stuck holding the bag'... So that was one of my early messages, is, 'Look, listen, if you're going to do something, do it with us. Don't do it on your own'" (personal interview 2018).

Looking back at the early 2000s, a senior official also stressed the importance of collaboration with municipal governments. Yet this person also noted that the province had intentionally maintained and exercised its housing powers instead of devolving them to the local level: "I refused to do that. I was asked that a couple of times. And I said, 'The challenge is, if you devolve it and don't have the money to send with it, it will deteriorate and just become someone else's problem'" (personal interview 2018). This insistence on provincial leadership in housing was due in part to what had been heard from people in Ontario, where housing was devolved to the local level. "[Ontario] was the early mover. So they were telling me some of the challenges they were facing. When it came time for me to answer the question, I said 'let's not do that.'" This official went on to say that senior Ontario officials would come to see housing devolution as "one of their mistakes" and noted that this example illustrates the importance of information-sharing between ministers: "That's why it's important for ministers to get together and talk about these things once or twice a year, to be able to chat about what's going on in jurisdictions and learn from one another" (personal interview 2018). Again and again, it is clear that the province of BC understands the importance of collaboration but also sees itself as a leader in efforts to fight homelessness in its most chronic form.

The province of BC had invested significantly and progressively in affordable housing over the course of nearly twenty years of Liberal governance; the NDP government, elected in 2017, promised to do even more. Under the NDP, the province has expanded its role in homelessness by defining homelessness and housing need more broadly than previous Liberal governments. This is consistent with differences in ideology, of course: the left-of-centre NDP has developed more generous and interventionist social policies than the Liberals. A few months after being elected, the NDP government released a thirty-point plan for housing affordability titled *Homes for BC*, a nod to the NDP's previous housing policy in the 1990s, *Homes BC*. In it, the NDP has pledged to invest $6.6 billion over ten years to construct 114,000 units of rental housing, including housing for the "missing middle" (three- and four-bedroom apartments for families, for example), housing for women and children fleeing violence, 1,750 units of social housing for Indigenous people, and 2,500 new supportive housing units for people experiencing homelessness. The province has also promised to introduce legislation to protect renters, and to attempt to cool the housing market by introducing a speculation tax and raising foreign buyer taxes. Housing affordability also features prominently in the province's Poverty Reduction Strategy (astonishingly, the first PRS ever adopted in the province) and reinforces the broader understanding of homelessness that is motivating provincial actions. Housing and homelessness had long been the mandate of BC Housing (recall that responsibility for shelters and interventions was transferred from the Ministry of Social Development to BC Housing in 2006). The Poverty Reduction Strategy notes that more ministries need to be involved: "Reducing homelessness is a shared mandate of the Ministers of Social Development and Poverty Reduction and Municipal Affairs and Housing" (Province of British Columbia 2019, 29). In a return to past provincial housing policies, housing need is again defined broadly, and the province's involvement has expanded considerably.

In addition to a broadly targeted housing strategy, BC introduced a rapid response to homelessness program, which allocated $291 million for the creation of 2,000 modular units across the province[11] and $75 million per year in operating costs to allow for 24/7 staff and support on-site. These units are highly targeted at people experiencing homelessness on the streets or in emergency shelters. This program was expanded by an additional $76 million in 2019, allowing for the creation of an additional 200 units of modular housing. Furthermore, the federal announcement of the National Housing Strategy led to a Canada–BC bilateral agreement, a ten-year, $990 million agreement to implement the strategy. The agreement notes that the funding will be used for BC's priorities, outlined through *Homes for BC*, and the federal priority of the Canada Community Housing Initiative. Canada and BC have also signed an agreement for the Housing Benefit, another $517 million over ten years to support 25,000 low-income, vulnerable households with a portable rent allowance that will make market rental housing affordable.

City of Vancouver (Municipal Government)

Though the province has been heavily involved in housing and homelessness and has never transferred responsibility to the local level, the City of Vancouver has long been involved in homelessness governance as well. City of Vancouver officials worked on draft plans on homelessness in the 1990s; the city began adopting and implementing those plans in 2005. The first municipal plans were introduced at a time when the province and the federal government were uninvolved in housing and minimally involved in responses to homelessness; these early plans primarily advocated for increased senior government involvement and stressed the limits on what the municipality could do to meet the needs of people experiencing homelessness. The year 2008 marked an important change: city officials, led by newly elected mayor, Gregor Robertson, increased their involvement in housing and homelessness. During this period, the city took on a leadership role and made big promises, including to end street homelessness by 2015, a promise that would not be fulfilled. Homelessness has remained an important priority for City Council, now under the leadership of progressive mayor Kennedy Stewart, but municipal officials have also gone back to calling on senior governments for more involvement and partnership.

Vancouver does not have jurisdiction for housing, but the city has long had important housing-related powers – notably density bonusing and inclusionary zoning – and these are made even more powerful by the limited availability of land and the lucrative nature of developments in the city. This has put the city in a powerful position with respect to the private sector and provincial actors when it comes to new housing developments, though critics of these powers note that excessive use of them can result in far more condominiums and unaffordable market housing overall, ultimately contributing to the problem of unaffordability (Davies 2019). Ideas have also been important in driving municipal involvement, notably regarding the responsibility to produce social protection and the nature of homelessness. These ideas take on a political nature in Vancouver because of local institutions, notably the local party system, through which seemingly small ideational differences can solidify into opposing political views. This interaction of ideas and institutions explains the fragmentation of governance at the local level in Vancouver. Fragmentation is manageable, however, with certain notable exceptions, and groups have demonstrated an ability to collaborate as the understandings of homelessness are in general easily compatible.

While homelessness is experienced throughout the city, the Downtown Eastside neighbourhood (DTES) contains one of the highest concentrations in the country of people experiencing chronic homelessness (Campbell et al. 2009; City of Vancouver 2018). Once the economic heart of the city, the community has since undergone dramatic change: the business sector left the neighbourhood decades ago; more recently, gentrification has been pushing low-income people out; the neighbourhood has also suffered from provincial and national social policy cuts as well as international changes in the drug market. In the 1990s, advocates became more and more concerned about the increase in the number of people living in shelters or on the streets and called for action to respond to the needs of those without housing (Campbell, Boyd, and Culbert 2009; personal interviews). The province remained engaged in housing policy in the 1990s, but the federal government's cuts meant that fewer social housing units were being built across the province. Though housing needs were great during this time, public health needs were even more urgent: the DTES had become the epicentre of the HIV/AIDS epidemic not just in the province (L. Campbell, Boyd, and Culbert 2009; Christopher 2012), but with the highest rate of infection in the Western world and rising overdose deaths (Lupick 2017a). In this context, a *Draft Housing Plan* for the city was presented to City Council in 1998; however, it was not adopted. A subsequent plan for housing in the DTES explains why: "Instead, the focus of attention was on addressing the impact of substance abuse and illegal activity in the area. As the Draft Housing Plan was prepared, these significant problems came to the forefront, including the HIV epidemic, high drug use and crime – issues which needed some attention before considering the Housing Plan" (City of Vancouver 2005, 3).

Phillip Owen, leader of Vancouver's centre-right Non-Partisan Association (NPA), was mayor of Vancouver during the public health crisis of HIV/AIDS transmission and overdose deaths. Responding to this crisis with effective, innovative, and unprecedented solutions was the top social priority for City Council, which worked closely with unlikely allies, including an influential network of drug users called VANDU[12] (for the full story, see Lupick 2017a, 2017b), as well as federal Liberal cabinet minister Hedy Fry and provincial NDP MLA Jenny Kwan. Together with Owen, Kwan and Fry formed a multilevel, multi-party alliance. Calling themselves "the Vancouver caucus," they created the Vancouver Agreement, which resulted in institutionalized intergovernmental cooperation for ten years in the areas of housing, economic revitalization, safety and security, and health and quality of life.[13] In part due to strong intergovernmental relations and interpersonal relationships, but more due to the innovation and risk-taking of local advocates, InSite, North American's first safe injection site, was opened in 2003. Larry Campbell, leader of the Coalition of Progressive Electors (COPE), was elected mayor of Vancouver at that point (the fight to open InSite having cost Phil Owen his political career [Lupick 2017a]), but Campbell credits Owen with having done much of the early legwork and risk-taking, without which InSite might not have been possible (Campbell, Boyd, and Culbert 2009; Lupick 2017a). InSite led to important public health changes, including declines in overdose deaths and HIV transmission (Lupick 2017a, 2017b).[14]

After the opening of InSite, City Council returned more attention to the issues of housing need and homelessness. Mayor Campbell was well aware of the housing and homelessness needs in the DTES; in his previous work as provincial coroner, he had spent considerable time and care investigating the deaths of marginalized individuals, many of whom were in the Downtown Eastside (CBC News 2005). He ran successfully for Vancouver mayor as leader of the left-wing Coalition of Progressive Voters (COPE) in 2002, at which point City Council initiated another process to develop a *Housing Plan for the DTES*, as well as a *Homelessness Action Plan* for the city more broadly.

The *Housing Plan for the DTES*, adopted by City Council in 2005, sought to protect and improve the quality of nearly 1,000 units of low-income housing and to double the amount of market housing in the DTES. Improving low-income housing in the neighbourhood would require substantial investment for renovations and, in some cases, the replacement of existing low-income housing. While the plan noted that the city had an important role to play in all of this, it was clear that the *primary* responsibility for producing social protection for the homeless did not lie with the city. Rather, "senior governments are primarily responsible for funding social and low-income housing" (City of Vancouver 2005, 9).

The *Homelessness Action Plan*, developed at the same time as the *Housing Plan for the DTES*, prioritized new social (as opposed to market) housing and targeted the entire city. The *Homelessness Action Plan* was developed with extensive community involvement. A draft of the plan was sent to 300 individuals and presented at fourteen meetings by city staff. Following these engagements, more than forty changes were made to the plan to reflect community voices. The final version of the *Homelessness Action Plan* used the same three-pronged framework as the regional plan on homelessness, developed in 2003 for federal National Homelessness Initiative (NHI) funding (reviewed below): income, housing, support. During this time, there was a high degree of coordination and alignment of agendas as well as evidence of shared ideas at the municipal and regional levels regarding the nature of homelessness. The *Homelessness Action Plan* recommended 4,000 new units of social housing over ten years for the City of Vancouver; it also contained eighty-six recommendations for all three levels of government, specifying the role to be played by each level for each recommendation. The city's role was often to coordinate actors, both governmental and non-governmental. Like the *Housing Plan for the DTES*, the *Homelessness Action Plan* advanced the idea that the responsibility for producing social protection is a shared one: "tackling homelessness is something that can only be done successfully if all sectors of the community are involved – all levels of government, business, non-profit services, and residents" (City of Vancouver 2005 4).

Also like the *Housing Plan for the DTES*, the *Homelessness Action Plan* stressed that senior governments must lead. Indeed, it went further, stressing the *limitations* specific to the municipal government and calling for senior government leadership in the production of social protection: "While homelessness is most visible at the local level, municipalities are least able to address the underlying causes ... Of all levels, municipal government is least able to pay for these solutions because of its heavy reliance on the extremely regressive property tax and limited access to revenues that are more appropriately applied to solving this problem." It continued: "These issues need to be considered well beyond municipal boundaries and should be supported by the broader range of progressive taxation available to senior governments. *These senior governments have the jurisdiction, responsibility and financial resources to deal with these problems and we should look to them to provide the resources to move the Plan ahead"* (City of Vancouver 2004, 8–9; emphasis added). City officials believed that responses to homelessness must involve a wide range of actors but also required senior government leadership; the city's involvement was limited mostly to advocacy and coordination.

Drawing on the Vancouver Agreement as evidence that intergovernmental collaboration was possible, Vancouver city officials expressed optimism that institutionalized intergovernmental collaboration in the areas of housing and homelessness was possible, albeit dependent on senior governments. The broader context of this period of time is important; recall that during the early 2000s, the provincial and federal governments were minimally involved in new housing developments. To the extent that money was being spent through the Affordable Housing Agreement,[15] much of it was being used to convert existing social housing into assisted living for seniors, and the province was openly announcing plans to end future investments in new housing developments. The municipality was leaning hard on senior governments to increase their involvement in housing policy, emphasizing that they, at the local level, could not do it alone. Ideas about the responsibility to produce social protection frustrated local actors, who were willing to play a role but believed that engagement and leadership from senior governments was needed to maximize that role.

Though the implementation of the *Housing Plan for the DTES* and the *Homelessness Action Plan* was ultimately limited by senior governments' lack of interest, the documents offer insight, not only into ideas regarding the responsibility to produce social protection, but also into local officials' understanding of homelessness at that time, ideas that remain influential to this day. The definition of homelessness in the 2005 *Homelessness Action Plan* was both broad and narrow. It was broad in the sense that homelessness was seen as including not just people living in shelters or on the streets but also those at risk of homelessness and those staying with friends or family, a category of people often considered to be *more* housing secure than those living on the streets or in shelters and thus not always prioritized. It was narrow, however – or it opened up the possibility of a narrow implementation – in its differentiation between street and sheltered homelessness. A chart on page 2 of the plan distinguished between people who were experiencing absolute homelessness and those at risk of homelessness. In that chart, under "absolute homelessness," are three categories: street homeless; in shelters; and staying with friends/family (City of Vancouver 2005, 2). This distinction between street and shelter continues: for nearly two decades, key officials with the City of Vancouver have viewed these forms of homelessness as distinct and have made decisions to prioritize street homelessness over other forms.

Vancouver officials used their housing-related powers to bolster the city's involvement. The *Housing Plan for the DTES* and the *Homelessness Action Plan* both planned to use density bonuses to create more social or affordable housing. In Vancouver, density bonusing agreements (DBAs) allow the city to increase the allowable density or height of a new private development in exchange for a public amenity given to the city. DBAs are negotiated individually, and city staff lead the process. This last point is particularly important, as Aaron Moore explains: "Vancouver's process is largely driven by city staff, and to some extent insulated from politics" (Moore 2013, 35). In other words, the fact that DBAs are negotiated by city staff gives them, and not politicians seeking re-election, more control over what the city is able to get in exchange for density. Clayton and Schwartz found a marked difference in terms of the outcomes of DBAs in Vancouver and Toronto, where the process is political and led by councillors: in Vancouver, housing makes up 48 per cent of the contributions the city is able to acquire through negotiations, whereas in Toronto, only 9 per cent of contributions involve housing (Clayton and Schwartz 2015; see also Moore 2013).

When a city is eager to use DBAs and is enthusiastic about prioritizing exchanges of density for housing, it is in a position of power and can use its institutional tools to generate resources in the form of land or actual housing units to contribute to the housing stock and the fight against homelessness. This power is even more meaningful in Vancouver because land[16] is so limited; higher and denser buildings are more profitable for developers, and the city can leverage that interest, albeit minimally. By resorting early on to its institutional strengths such as density bonusing, as well as to ideas regarding the city's partnership role in addressing homelessness, the city was able to become meaningfully involved in homelessness, though much of its involvement was dependent on other actors (the private sector and senior governments).

The *Homelessness Action Plan* and *Housing Plan for the DTES* were impeded by their reliance on senior levels of government, and they were difficult to implement and track because of the significant number of recommendations made (personal interview 2014). The plans were further limited by the political cycle: having been adopted in the summer of 2005 under Mayor Campbell, the plans were put on the backburner when Sam Sullivan, leader of the right-of-centre Non-Partisan Association Party, was elected mayor in November of that year. Guided by an informal and unscientific survey run on his official website and by a letter from local business executives concerned about extremely negative stereotypes – they characterized the problem in the city as "an urban malignancy manifested by an open drug market, rising property crime, aggressive panhandling and a visible, growing population of the homeless" (quoted in Paulsen 2006) – Sullivan launched *Project Civil City* (PCC). This municipal plan was organized around the objective of reducing street disorder by "tackling illegal and nuisance behaviour such as open drug use, aggressive panhandling and noise infractions" and "work[ing] as a community to find compassionate solutions to the root causes of poverty" (City of Vancouver 2006). Under Sullivan, the city's response to homelessness would be within this framework. That framework did not specifically define homelessness but associated it directly with negative conceptualizations of street disorder (see City of Vancouver 2006; 15).

Project Civil City committed $1 million for "enhanced civic responses" to tackle street disorder and another $300,000 for an office of Civil City Commissioner (Hume 2006), a role assumed by former Liberal Attorney General Geoff Plant. PCC aimed to reduce homelessness and street-level disorder by at least 50 per cent by 2010 and to reduce the open drug market and aggressive panhandling by 50 per cent. It would do this in part by increasing "eyes on the street," asking parking enforcement officers and garbage collectors to identify and report criminal activity (a sensational mischaracterization of what Jane Jacobs originally meant by that term [J. Jacobs 1961]). According to a senior official involved in implementing *Project Civil City*, the objective of a 50 per cent reduction in chronic homelessness was "wildly arbitrary and purely political" (personal interview 2014), giving credence to critics who claimed that the project was a mere "marketing exercise" (J. Lee 2006) that would further criminalize poverty and homelessness. David Eby, then a lawyer with the Pivot Legal Society and member of Vision Vancouver, the progressive opposition to Sullivan, lamented, "What kind of a legacy is a year or two of bylaw enforcement? ... it's not a lasting solution to the poverty issues down here" (Paulsen 2006).

Project Civil City was an easy political target, as even insiders understood. A senior official involved in the project explained competing perceptions around what it was:

> It's a hard thing to do to try to figure out what Project Civil City was really about, because almost from the moment the mayor launched this idea, he got on the wrong end of the spin cycle. It was, from the word go, criticized as an attempt to criminalize a social problem or a series of social problems. Now let me just be objective enough to say that I don't know that that was a problem for Sam [Sullivan], because Sam actually was interested in kind of both sides of the social policy. And Sam was elected as an NPA mayor, which is to say the mayor from a political party that is usually associated with the political right. So, get tough on street disorder is a very resonant political message ... We tried to change the conversation, because just trying to find more effective ways to punish people who spit on the streets is about as ineffective and boring a job as you can find. Now, it became politically convenient for Sam's opponents to hang on to that critique, and they still hang on to it today. The reality is Project Civil City was in part concerned with ensuring there was effective bylaw enforcement. But really, fundamentally, we were concerned with finding ways to deal with the causes of street disorder. (personal interview 2014)

Actions such as cleaning up graffiti, creating dumpster-free alleys, and sending out more police officers to "work the beat" in the DTES created the impression that this approach to addressing homelessness was more about image and enforcement than about the "compassion" touted by Sullivan and his allies. Yet important housing developments and renovations also were carried out on Sullivan's watch, and while many of those were at the province's initiative, Sullivan's administration was a willing and capable partner in collaborative efforts to protect vulnerable housing stock and develop new supportive housing. In December 2007, in the wake of Premier Campbell's province-wide task force on homelessness, mental health, and addiction, the City of Vancouver and BC Housing signed a Memorandum of Understanding regarding the development of supportive housing.[17] The city contributed land – a valuable contribution given its limited availability – and BC Housing paid development costs as well as operational costs for keeping the buildings safely running, with supports in place for those living there. Those units were completed by December 2015. Sullivan can be criticized for taking a heavy-handed approach to homelessness guided by a narrow understanding of the problem, but following through with the Supportive Housing Framework and partnering aggressively with the province to build thirteen new buildings for supportive housing has been a lasting legacy. PCC also led to the founding of the StreetoHome Foundation, originally designed to allow the private sector to play a larger role in the fight against homelessness and (it follows) the production of social protection. This foundation is thoroughly discussed in the following section on civil society.

Toward the end of what would be Sullivan's first and only term as mayor, a man named Darrell Mickasko died in a fire while sleeping on the streets of Vancouver. It was a cold night in January, and Mickasko and his girlfriend had been turned away from shelters in the city because they were full (*Vancouver Sun* 2008). They tried to keep warm in a makeshift shelter he had built on the sidewalk, using a camping stove for heat. The stove caused a fire, killing Mickasko and severely burning his girlfriend. This incident took place in the riding represented by Gregor Robertson, who at the time was an NDP MLA, and was, as Robertson would often recount, the reason he left provincial politics to run for mayor of Vancouver: "The horrific death of Darrell Mickasko was what catalyzed my decision to run for mayor … His death – and he's one of many who have died from homelessness in Vancouver – cannot be in vain. There are vitally important issues facing our city, but we need a Mayor who is committed to ending homelessness. My goal is to end street homelessness by 2015 in Vancouver" (Robertson 2008b). Ensuring that there would always be enough space indoors for those seeking shelter would become a crucial plank of Robertson's approach to ending homelessness.

Project Civil City was an easy target for Robertson and the progressive Vision Vancouver party. According to a senior actor in Sullivan's administration, "Gregor and the Vision crew were successful in demonizing *Project Civil City* from the beginning, and that rhetoric helped them get into office" (personal interview 2014). This stance was in part strategic, as was confirmed by a Vision Vancouver insider, who noted that there had been a backlash from a large part of the DTES community in response to *Project Civil City* (personal interview 2014). Yet Robertson was also motivated by a different understanding of homelessness, one that viewed the difference between street and shelter as being the difference between life and death. This understanding was informed by the tragic death of Mickasko but was also consistent with past ways of understanding homelessness in Vancouver. Robertson pledged to create enough space inside for people on the streets. Opening new shelters is not without controversy, and the right-of-centre Non-Partisan Association would position itself in the 2008 and future elections as against new shelters. Describing the different approaches to homelessness

taken by the two political parties, Robertson said during the 2008 election: "[NPA leader] Peter Ladner has said that he's opposed to shelters.
In effect, he's telling people who are living on the street, and who care
about homelessness, to keep waiting, to stay there living on the street
… I believe that shelters and temporary housing are part of the solution
when combined with permanent long-term housing" (Paulsen 2008b).

Upon winning the municipal election, Robertson recommitted to ending homelessness, saying that it would be his top priority: "I decided
to run for the office of mayor to end street homelessness in Vancouver.
And I'm telling you today, that hasn't changed. It is your council's single most important priority in this term of office." Again referencing
Darrell Mickasko by name, Robertson emphasized that remedying the
shortage of shelter beds would be the first step of his plan: "First, most
urgently, ensuring there are enough shelter beds so people don't have
to sleep in the streets." In the medium and long term, he pledged to
draw on the city's institutional strengths to protect affordable housing
and, finally, create new affordable housing by "leading development,
unlocking vacant stock, using zoning and tax incentives, and accelerating investment from other levels of government" (Robertson 2008a).
Driving these actions, and indeed municipal leadership, was a very
specific idea about homelessness. Robertson was convinced that street
homelessness is more dangerous than sheltered homelessness. Accordingly, he sought to first help homeless individuals by getting them off
the streets. A former Vision Vancouver city councillor confirmed that
people living on the streets were seen as distinctly vulnerable: "First we
made the pledge [to end street homelessness] in the campaign of 2008,
and we had a plan in our minds for how to do this. Starting with shelters, taking a simple public health approach. Start with the most vulnerable. Everyone said 'What about me? What about me? What about
me?' And we said 'No. Who is sleeping on the street tonight and who is
going to die?' … so we said shelters" (personal interview 2014).

The first action Robertson took as Vancouver mayor was to open a series of emergency shelters for the winter months. Immediately following his election, he formed the Homelessness Emergency Action Team
(HEAT). Third-sector groups were heavily involved in this process, as
well as city employees, CEO of BC Housing Shayne Ramsey, Pivot Legal Society's David Eby, and three locally elected officials, all of whom
were from Vision Vancouver (Gregor Robertson, Raymond Louie, and
Kerry Jang). The night before his first day as mayor, Robertson called
Ric Matthews at First United Church to ask whether the church, which
at the time was being used as a low-barrier drop-in centre during the
day, could keep its doors open 24/7 and become one of the HEAT

shelters (Burrows 2010). Matthews agreed, and the first announcement made by Robertson on his first day as mayor was the creation of an additional 150 shelter spaces at First United (Paulsen 2008a).[18]

There was excitement that things were happening so quickly. An important bridge between the city and the streets was Judy Graves, a city employee but very much an advocate for homeless people in her own right who would guide the city's actions. Graves formally created the position "advocate for the homeless" for herself within the city bureaucracy in 2010, but her advocacy, effectiveness building relationships with people experiencing homelessness, and ability to find suitable housing for them had given her great credibility within the city administration well before her position became formalized. The role remains unique in Canada because of her independence and reputation across political parties at all levels of government (some cities, like Montreal, have tried to replicate it). Graves's advocacy began slowly, and her bosses did not initially support her work connecting with homeless people and working directly with them to help them find housing, so she had to do this work on her own time. This was in some ways helpful, as someone familiar with this work explained that it can be difficult to identify and connect with people experiencing homelessness during the day: "Homeless people are very busy. You know, survival is actually time-consuming and exhausting. And every social interaction has to be geared towards food, lodging, and anything they can get" (personal interview 2014).

Graves began walking Vancouver's streets at night to build relationships and trust with people, connecting them one by one with housing. Those night-time walks became famous, and she walked politicians from all levels of government and all political stripes through Vancouver between the hours of two and six a.m. While some in the community disagreed with her proposed solutions, her role as advocate for homeless people within a city bureaucracy has yet to be effectively replicated: she was one of a kind. Having worked with the city for decades fighting for the rights of people who are unhoused and experience homelessness and to develop responses that meet their needs, she noted the seismic shift that resulted when Robertson was elected. She told *Vancouver Magazine* that for the first time in nearly twenty years at the city, "I felt like I had the wind at my back" (dev 2011).

Working with allies at city hall and across the third sector, Robertson quickly opened several low-barrier shelters across the city. This process, which heavily involved third-sector groups, is discussed at length in the next section. Bringing people into shelters from the streets required creativity, as the traditional shelter system had multiple barriers to entry – for example, couples were not allowed, nor were pets, nor were belongings (such as carts or bags). Also, people were not allowed to come and go in the evening (a barrier for many, including sex workers), and some shelters required sobriety. The new shelters lowered or eliminated barriers, which allowed some people who had long resisted the shelter system to come inside. Problems arose in certain neighbourhoods, with complaints about increased crime and disorder, and two shelters were eventually closed (Sheffield 2009). The idea, however, of low-barrier shelters that would allow people to come in with their pets and belongings, and without requiring sobriety, is widely credited with immediately reducing street homelessness (CBC News 2011). By one definition – one that distinguishes between street and shelter – this was an immediate success. By other definitions, however, which do not make that distinction, nothing had changed. Indeed, initial street counts in 2010 and 2011 show a drastic drop in street homelessness, a drop accompanied almost precisely by an increase in sheltered homelessness (City of Vancouver 2011).

Robertson's work was criticized for making an artificial distinction: many insist (and continue to insist) that shelter is not housing and even when in a shelter, individuals remain unhoused or homeless. This criticism is fair: shelter is not housing. But it is also true that for some, being in a shelter can be better than being outside and that shelters can alleviate isolation, loneliness, and exclusion. Former NPA insiders, as well as a senior civil servant working on housing and homelessness at the provincial level, described coming around to the idea of low-barrier shelters, an idea to which they were at first openly hostile. Indeed, as a former NPA operative explained: "Everything we had learned before Gregor came into office would have argued against the HEAT strategy. We need something better than shelters" (personal interview 2014). But they continued:

> When it's below zero outside, having some place inside is just better than outside. And I don't want to underestimate that. And in a sense I would say that it was a failing of Project Civil City that we didn't open our eyes to that ... We don't need a system that turns people away because they aren't presenting within the right parameters. "I'm here to apply for welfare but I've got an addictions problem." "Well, I'm not going to give you your welfare until you solve your addictions problem." Well no. If you are alienated in any of the following ways, come in come in come in. And then we'll figure out what to do with you. And if it's a shelter, as long as it has that in mind, as long as there is someone there capable of doing that and seeing that, it's better than no shelter. So I give credit to Vision both

politically, because it was pretty clever, and also from a policy perspective. It is much better to bring people in than to say there is no room for you at any inn. (personal interview 2014)

Robertson and allies who ran the HEAT shelters viewed being indoors as safer than being outdoors; the first step in helping people find permanent housing was to bring them inside and connect them to supports from which they had previously been excluded. The city was able to take on a leadership role in this promise because opening new shelters is within the city's abilities and powers (though the costs would rise quickly, as I outline below). Yet yearly homeless counts made clear that the overall number of people experiencing homelessness, unsheltered and sheltered included, was steadily increasing. Recognizing that shelters are not a lasting solution to homelessness, the city also introduced a ten-year Housing and Homelessness Strategy in 2012. That strategy takes a broad view of housing need, and though the commitment to end *street* homelessness is central, it further aims to provide "a range of housing options… This includes housing that is accessible, affordable and suitable for all income levels, seniors, families, and residents challenged by disability" (City of Vancouver 2012, 5). The strategy places homelessness on a long and diverse spectrum of housing, linking it directly with housing instead of treating it separately, and notes that the city aims to improve housing all along the spectrum. This means not only ensuring adequate shelter space for those experiencing street homelessness but also helping families access rental housing and even reach homeownership.

Driven by an understanding of homelessness that led to a prioritization of street homelessness, the city increased its involvement. Like plans developed by the city in the past, the 2012 housing and homelessness plan developed by Vision Vancouver stressed the importance of senior governments and community partners in homelessness interventions: "Success depends on the support of all our partners. Success cannot be achieved alone. It requires; commitment from all levels of government; support and cooperation of stakeholders and partners; widespread support from the community" (City of Vancouver 2011, 10). While collaboration is important, a section of the 2012 plan outlining lessons learned from the public and partners includes the conclusion that "the City needs to pursue opportunities with new partners to increase the affordable housing supply *with or without* senior government funding" (10; emphasis added). A senior city official noted that the city's willingness to go it alone was sincere: "We didn't specifically engage [the province]. This was about what we could do with our resources and money. There comes a point where you are working in the field and you get so worn down. People were like, 'Okay, what can we do?' Because we wanted to make it a good news story, we wanted to start churning out units and be a part of the solution, not just the only thing we could do was try to advocate" (personal interview 2014).

This marked a significant departure from previous plans, which placed most of the responsibility on senior governments; recall that the 2005 plans on housing and homelessness stressed not only senior government responsibility but also local government limitations. The 2012 plan reflected a clear evolution in ideas regarding the responsibility to produce social protection as city officials came to see a more central role for the city. This evolution was not explained by a left/right divide; rather, it took place within the city's main vehicle for the political left, as previous COPE plans were not prepared to go it alone like the Vision Vancouver plan but rather advocated for provincial leadership. This ideational change coincided with another one regarding the nature of homelessness: the distinction between street and shelter was seen as a matter of life or death, and the city was in a position to make important changes to prevent the worst consequences of homelessness on its own. In a sense, this understanding of homelessness enabled the city to act on its own, because opening more emergency shelters is something that can be done by the city in partnership with local community groups. It is interesting, however, that the city also increased its involvement in housing supply through partnerships with the private sector, an important change from approaches in the past that were more dependent on senior governments.

To encourage other non-governmental actors, particularly private sector ones, to partner in housing developments, the housing plan committed to using the city's housing powers aggressively. Like the 2005 plans, the 2012 strategy focuses on DBAs as a means to create affordable housing without senior government support. The plan goes further than past plans in also using inclusionary zoning powers,[19] which allows the city to *require* that developers include affordable housing in new private developments, or give something else to the city such as land or a cash contribution.[20] This power, though it had been in Vancouver's toolbox since the 1980s, had not been used explicitly in previous plans for housing or homelessness. This new willingness to use it reveals that city officials were serious when they said they would not wait on provincial or federal partnerships.

A city councillor in Vancouver explained the city's approach to ending homelessness and developing more affordable housing on its own, or at least without the province: "We're plugging the holes. The quickest way for us to plug the holes without us having to pay for it was to use our by-laws to incentivize. I think we pushed the envelope in terms of what we can do without government funding" (personal interview 2014). A senior member of the City of Vancouver's housing staff reiterated the importance of institutional powers: "We use every tool in our box [to build affordable housing] ... We'll provide a bunch of relaxations, fast-track the process, we are using rezoning to get developers, in exchange for additional height and density, to provide us with additional turnkey social housing units that they can give to the city. So we are using our regulatory land use tools to create housing" (personal interview 2014). A city councillor was more explicit: "I'll say, use [developers'] greed. They want to make money, so use that. You get accused of being in the developer's pocket ... but the [private developers] did the math and said, 'Yup, works for us'" (personal interview 2014).

As the city sought to end street homelessness and implement its housing plan, tensions between local and provincial officials were palpable, the result of (minor) ideational disagreements regarding the nature of homelessness and somewhat more significant disagreements regarding the responsibility to produce social protection. Local institutions turned these minor disagreements into broader political ones. Recall that before Robertson's plan to end street homelessness was launched, the province had aggressively re-entered the field as well, having just completed a provincial task force on mental health, addictions, and homelessness. The province was now signing MOUs with municipalities across BC to invest in the construction of new supportive housing for people who are homeless.

As the City of Vancouver increased its involvement in an increasingly crowded field, senior municipal bureaucrats noted in interviews that they did not believe the province fully agreed with its specific efforts to end street homelessness, suggesting ideational differences: "I don't think the province is necessarily on board with our goal to end street homelessness. I think they have said that reducing or ending homelessness is a good thing, but I've never heard anyone say, 'Yes, we agree with Vancouver's goal to end street homelessness'... It would seem they have had ample opportunities to get on board the bandwagon that has been rolling for quite some time about ending street homelessness, and I haven't really heard them get on that" (personal interview 2014). Another bureaucrat echoed these sentiments: "Do we share the same goal of ending street homelessness? I don't know if the premier or the mayor or the housing minister all sat down, if they could agree on that specific goal" (personal interview 2014). The differences in goals were small, yet they became politicized. This was further politicized in the context of the development of the StreetoHome Foundation, a non-profit foundation with strong ties to the private sector and the right-of-centre Non-Partisan Association, during this period as well (see below).

Though Robertson's relationship with Premier Campbell was at times tense, he ultimately had a strong ally in the premier (and Minister of Housing Rich Coleman) in efforts to fight homelessness and build more affordable housing. For example, the province stepped in to help fund HEAT shelters, which were more expensive than first expected, but did so grudgingly. The province would also end up taking control of some of the shelters, as I explain below, following irreconcilable conflicts over the nature of homelessness. The municipal–provincial relationship changed in 2011 with the election of Christy Clark as BC premier; as noted, she made clear that the province's role in housing and in fighting homelessness would be limited. Looking back on his record, Robertson regrets that he did not fight harder to get the province on board, citing a lack of senior government involvement as a key reason why his plan to end street homelessness did not ultimately succeed. Reflecting on the current homelessness crisis and his efforts to combat it in 2008, Robertson had this to say in an interview with the *Globe and Mail* in 2020: "We were able to get some housing built, for sure, but it didn't even begin to put a dent in the homeless numbers ... After Gordon Campbell left office, and Christy Clark took over as premier, she had no interest in this issue at all. So it really just stalled for a lack of funding and it's really sad" (Mason 2020).

The lack of provincial partnership posed a challenge to Robertson's efforts to fight homelessness, and he would later reflect that the city alone could not end any form of homelessness without the support of senior governments (Mason 2020). But the municipal–provincial relationship was not the only one that suffered over the course of his efforts to combat homelessness. The powerful, expertise-driven coalition that Robertson had built to implement the HEAT shelters at the local level began to fall apart as well; the reason for this, as I explain more thoroughly below, was a lack of agreement on what it means to end homelessness and competing, irreconcilable understandings of the nature of homelessness. Another high-profile break with Robertson's coalition was Vancouver's advocate for the homeless, Judy Graves, who had been a key supporter of Robertson's early efforts to end homelessness. She retired from her position in 2013, but left retirement to run for City Council in 2017, not for Gregor Robertson's Vision Vancouver, but rather for OneCity, a newly created progressive party. In an op-ed for *The Georgia Straight*, Graves conflated Vision Vancouver with the right-of-centre NPA: "Vision Vancouver and the NPA have depended for decades on luxury condo developers to build homes ... [City Council] pinned its hopes on the idea that affordable housing would trickle down from luxury condo construction" (Graves 2017). Though she was not elected, Graves proposed a new, more involved solution to homelessness: "We need to build thousands of new rental apartments in Vancouver, on land the city already owns. To pay for it, we need a civic revenue stream. I plan to put a fair and progressive surtax on the top five percent of Vancouver's most expensive homes to pay for it" (Graves 2017). Some third-sector groups would also distance themselves from the initial HEAT coalition (see below).

Robertson announced his retirement from municipal politics in 2017. Vision Vancouver, plagued by scandals and weakened by a loss of support from progressive voters, did not run a candidate for mayor in 2018, which left former NDP federal Member of Parliament Kennedy Stewart to battle other independent progressive candidates and a divided right for mayoralty. Elected in 2018, Stewart is the first independent mayor of Vancouver since the 1980s. He has vowed to inject new life into the city's affordable housing market, working closely with the province to build modular housing (and to fight local opposition to it [Dimoff 2018]) throughout the city. The fight against homelessness remains a steady uphill battle: the 2019 homeless count reported the highest number *ever* of homeless people in Vancouver, and Stewart has stated that the DTES is in the worst shape he has ever seen it in (CBC News 2019b). With NDP allies at the provincial level and strong partnerships with community groups across the city, Stewart has turned his attention to the federal government; speaking to CTV, Mayor Stewart insisted that "the missing piece here is from the federal government" (Smart 2019). While housing remains a key concern, his demands to the federal government also include a safe supply of drugs, improving public transit, and contributing to affordable housing solutions.

Interacting with institutions and evolving ideas regarding the nature of homelessness and responsibility to produce social protection is a more stable ideational force: how local officials conceive their role. Throughout Vancouver's history, and with both left-of-centre and right-of-centre parties in power, it has been recognized that while there are important limits on the municipality's capacity, the municipality can and should be more than a mere service provider. A seasoned city bureaucrat pointed to what makes Vancouver different in this respect: "The City of Vancouver has always been more, has had more empathy for marginalized people and is taking on a social agenda in a much more serious way than other municipalities. [Other municipalities] say 'Well, we only collect the garbage and are responsible for roads and the sewage, we don't do social stuff.' But we have always been into making sure that our population is being treated well and looked after" (personal interview 2014).

Given their conceptualization of the city's role, city officials have taken the lead in social policy efforts, which are often related to public health.

Civil Society

Civil society actors in Vancouver, including private-sector and third-sector actors, are influential in the governance of homelessness as well as in broader urban governance dynamics. The third sector is organized in Vancouver, has powerful advocates (including in the BC Civil Liberties Association and the Pivot Legal Society), and participates directly in policy-making. Though groups are influential when it comes to homelessness, they do not have a formal plan on homelessness. Groups that have been well-positioned to lead in local organizing on homelessness, such as the Downtown Eastside Residents Association (DERA) and the Portland Housing Society (PHS), have undergone changes in their leadership or disbanded, and the PHS has long been preoccupied with drug reform. In 2008, private-sector groups increased their involvement in homelessness governance, channelling their efforts through the StreetoHome Foundation, a non-profit foundation created through Sam Sullivan's *Project Civil City* initiative.

The local party system tends to structure civil society in Vancouver: private-sector actors are typically more aligned with the right-of-centre Non-Partisan Association (NPA); community groups and the third sector are more likely to be closer allies of left-of-centre parties, including the Coalition of Progressive Electors (COPE), Vision Vancouver, and OneCity.[21] There are exceptions to this,[22] but the divisions are clear. Though their role is not institutionalized, third-sector groups work closely with elected allies and sympathetic insiders in their efforts to fight homelessness. Private-sector actors are more likely to have close relationships with senior government officials (especially in the NPA and the BC Liberal Party). Furthermore, in 2008, private-sector actors working with the NPA created their own institution through which to channel their involvement in homelessness governance. Private- and third-sector groups tend to channel their involvement in the fight against homelessness through different vehicles because of small differences in understanding of the nature of homelessness, differences that were amplified by the party system. Though these differences have become somewhat politicized, the definition of homelessness adopted by both groups is close enough that they are able to work together when politics is taken out of the equation, prioritizing different forms of homelessness through slightly different approaches. Deeper fragmentation within the third sector, driven by less reconcilable disagreements about the fundamental nature of homelessness, has at times weakened third-sector involvement and influence.

Private Sector

The private sector in Vancouver is less involved in homelessness governance than in Calgary but more involved than in Toronto or Montreal. It emerged as an actor in homelessness governance through the StreetoHome Foundation (STHF), a lasting result of former NPA mayor Sam Sullivan's *Project Civil City*, an initiative that was introduced after the business community pushed the city to do something about homelessness (see above). In 2006, Sullivan's NPA-controlled City Council commissioned, to the tune of $300,000, two consultants to write a report on how to engage the private sector in efforts to fight homelessness. The report originally proposed that a foundation be created that would fundraise for homelessness, but that model was dependent on a federal government change to the tax code to incentivize big financial donations from the private sector. Sullivan personally lobbied for the change to the tax code (personal interview 2014); when the federal government declined to make it, private-sector actors decided to turn the foundation into a more formal actor in the fight against homelessness.

The STHF today works with parties on both the left and the right of the local and provincial political spectrum, but when it was first created, Vision Vancouver was opposed to it. Meeting minutes from City Hall in 2007 show that all Vision Vancouver members voted against a motion to support in principle the creation of the STHF (City of Vancouver 2007). David Eby, then a housing advocate with the progressive and influential Pivot Legal Society and a member of Gregor Robertson's HEAT team (and current BC NDP Minister of Housing), said of the STHF: "I agree that it is important that there be some private-sector funding of social housing. But the idea of forcing charity to pay for it is both unworkable and un-Canadian" (qtd in Paulsen 2007). The STHF was political from the start, but the motion passed, and the NPA-controlled City Council contributed $500,000 in start-up funds.

In 2008, the STHF launched a ten-year plan to end homelessness in Vancouver, which sought to do exactly that: end homelessness in ten years. This plan was informed by a visit from Philip Mangano, then US President George W. Bush's point person on homelessness. Mangano was invited to a BC Leadership Prayer Breakfast in 2008 to speak specifically about homelessness. As he did in many other Canadian cities, Mangano made what is often called the business case for ending homelessness, which is that ending homelessness costs less than managing it, and with the right plan, homelessness can be ended in ten years (Bula 2010). Inspired in part by Mangano's talk, the STHF proposed to end homelessness by prioritizing supportive housing for people experiencing chronic homelessness using a Housing First approach. Though the plan was inspired by Mangano, local research and consultations also were part of the process, and the STFH plan adopted the three-pronged approach (housing, income, support) developed by Vancouver's Regional Steering Committee on Homelessness in 2003.[23] Unlike the Calgary plan to end homelessness, which was implemented in a policy vacuum and was thus able to adopt the US model of a plan to end homelessness more completely, Vancouver efforts to fight homelessness were inspired by the US approach but also aligned with already existing plans, notably the regional plan on homelessness, revealing how institutional differences can shape ideational forces in different contexts. To this end, the plan identified the need to create 2,000 new units of supportive housing for homeless people, in partnership with the city, the province, and the private sector.

The board of the STHF was, in the words of a prominent volunteer, "self-appointed" (personal interview 2014). Clearly, the balance of power was heavily in favour of private-sector actors. Influential mining executive and wealthy philanthropist Frank Guistra donated $5 million to start up the STHF and helped bring together the STHF board (personal interview 2014). There are government and third-sector representatives on the board as well, some of whom worked with the city on its HEAT strategy, including Shayne Ramsey, the CEO of BC Housing, and John MacKay, president of Strand Properties Corporation, but the purpose from the beginning was for the organization to be a vehicle for private-sector involvement. That meant contributing private-sector expertise and money: "[Executive Director Jae Kim] was clear about what the foundation wasn't going to do. It wasn't going to copy the Calgary foundation model, where business provided leadership but not a lot of dollars. 'I'm asking for a lot of cash'" (Bula 2010).

STHF actors proposed to contribute private funding to each unit of government-built affordable housing. STHF actors note that this approach – contributing and leveraging money – was effective and allowed the StreetoHome Foundation to enjoy considerable influence for a time, including by influencing provincial investments: "We brought money ... So when we went to talk to the premier, he said 'Everyone comes and asks me for money. No one brings *me* money'" (personal interview 2014). An actor involved in conversations with the province further explained the pitch: "The Streetohome Foundation was the broker and said 'We'll raise $25 million from philanthropists, the deal is you, the province, have to put in the money, the city has to commit to giving us these properties, and the three of us will make beautiful music together and we'll build social housing.' And the province played ball" (personal interview 2014).

Though they wrote big cheques, private-sector actors insisted they had more than just financial resources. They also insisted that they brought experience, energy, and a new perspective:

> Streetohome will be a positive partner with the non-profit community and with all levels of government. *It will bring private-sector and community leadership understanding and perspectives to the problem* and will provide a clear window on homelessness and the related issues of mental illness and addiction for the community. It will bring more than the resources of the private and community sectors to solving homelessness; *it will bring an action-oriented and implementation focus that generates concrete results*, in terms of projects, research, community awareness and collaboration. (Managing Director of Social Development 2008; emphasis added)

The STHF was meant thus to serve as a vehicle for private-sector involvement, bringing private-sector resources and expertise to the fight against homelessness. Some prominent advocates viewed this as a strength: "They had all the big dogs of business in Vancouver, the guys who are used to 'What's the problem? How much will it cost me? Here's the fucking cheque, do it fast.' That's just the way they operate" (personal interview 2014). Interestingly, this actor also noted that businesspeople are more like people experiencing homelessness than might be first expected: "[Businesspeople] also have an understanding of human nature that is much more applicable to the street than social workers or bureaucrats do. People in the streets are not like bureaucrats or social workers, they are like businesspeople. They think the same" (personal interview 2014). Yet the board was also perceived by some as overlooking important perspectives, notably the expertise of third-sector groups: "The people who are on the board ... know nothing or next to nothing or worse than nothing about what they are talking about. So they are in a high position but have never actually worked in the street, they have never experienced what it's like. They should have had actual outreach workers and supportive housing staff on the board of StreetoHome. I think that would have cut out a lot of mistakes" (personal interview 2014).

Despite these criticisms, various private-sector resources – money, business experience, political connections, and an action-oriented work ethic – allowed the private sector to be seen as a serious and valuable partner. But these resources do not, on their own, explain why the private sector oriented them to the fight against homelessness. Resources were oriented to the fight against homelessness because of ideas. The STHF could easily never have seen the light of day. Sullivan's loss in the 2008 election and the federal government's refusal to implement requested changes to the tax code were seemingly two nails in the idea's coffin. Yet the private sector–led group drove forward with its involvement. Their drive was fuelled in part by ideas regarding the production of social protection: private-sector actors not only saw an important role for themselves in fighting homelessness but also believed that the role of government should be limited. As a senior member of the STHF board explained: "We are a frank, free-enterprise people. I don't think the government should do everything. And the government seems to agree on some level ... When you leave it to the government, it's a cop-out" (personal interview 2014). Another senior official put it slightly differently: "I think the government is looking for direction" – implying that the STHF and its private-sector leadership was providing that direction.

As these actors correctly note, the idea that the private sector has a role in the fight against homelessness was, during this period of NPA governance at the local level and Liberal governance provincially, shared by senior government officials. A City of Vancouver report notes that in the lead-up to the introduction of the STHF, federal, provincial, and local government officials as well as service providers and philanthropists were consulted on the idea. The report notes that following these broad consultations:

> there was broad support for bringing new investment and investors to solving homelessness, not just because of the need for more resources but also to bring new perspectives and new energy to the issue. There was support in particular for the creation of a foundation with a focus and mandate to address homelessness, and *which would provide a vehicle for the corporate sector and the philanthropic community that have not traditionally been involved in homelessness issues to participate in developing and implementing solutions to homelessness.* (Managing Director of Social Development 2008; emphasis added)

An important driver leading to the development of the STHF was the idea that the private sector *could* and *should* be involved in homelessness governance, an idea held not just by private-sector actors but also by the Liberal BC government and NPA council at the time. The financial contribution, energy, and expertise the private sector was offering was warmly welcomed.

The understanding of homelessness was also a key ideational driver of private-sector involvement. The STHF plan adopted the housing, income, support framework developed by the regional network in 2003, along with many of the regional network's proposals in terms of the development of new units of housing. The plan does not include a definition of homelessness, not even in its glossary of definitions, but it does define *chronic* homelessness as "a person who has been homeless for a year or more sleeping on the streets and/or in emergency shelters" (Streetohome Foundation 2010, 54), indicating that its focus is very narrow. Note that there is no difference between people who are homeless on the streets or in shelters. It is also clear that the STHF definition of homelessness is the lack of housing, given its emphasis on housing as a solution. This is important: one thing that stands out in the plan is its clear position on homeless shelters. The first priority of the plan is to prioritize homes, not shelters, and the executive summary of the plan makes this even more clear: *"housing is a basic human need, and shelter is not housing"* (Streetohome Foundation 2010, 2; emphasis in original). In fact, shelters are identified as a contributing factor to homelessness, a view that is not unique to the STHF but that is controversial among service providers (see Streetohome Foundation 2010, 8).

To understand the significance of this idea, it is important to step back and consider what else was happening in the city at the time. Though the original idea for the STHF came from Sullivan's *Project Civil City*, its ten-year plan was being developed at an important moment in Vancouver's fight against homelessness: Gregor Robertson and his Vision Vancouver colleagues were also developing their own response to homelessness, which, in the early days, was focused almost entirely on street homelessness. This is a small difference, but in this moment in history and in this institutional environment, it is a consequential one. The STHF plan to end homelessness positions itself against shelters, stating that they are not housing, whereas Robertson's plan involved, at least as a short-term measure, opening more shelters. Given that the local party system has injected partisan politics into civil society, it was meaningful, and it drove fragmentation and led to two separate plans to end homelessness being developed and implemented at the same time.

Interviews with senior officials with the STHF confirm that their opposition to shelters was deeply held, not just a political point on which they differed with Robertson (though it was that too). A senior official noted that "StreetoHome is not in the business of shelters. No. We are the next step" (personal interview 2014). Another actor involved with the STHF and the NPA local party operations said that as a solution, "shelters are not the answer. They are expedient. Although the STHF has occasionally supported shelters, I think you do that to stay in touch with people. But really my focus and the focus of the handful of people who

were working on *Project Civil City* on the homelessness side was on saying that shelters are not the right response" (personal interview 2014).

Some NPA-aligned actors would eventually appreciate the
HEAT-shelter approach, but as noted earlier, actors insisted that at the
time the STHF and Robertson's plans were being developed, everything
the STHF knew about homelessness led them to believe shelters were
not the answer. This was an important debate, but it had become politicized. Both the NPA and Vision Vancouver, along with their respective
homelessness fighting allies in the private and third sectors, saw the
other side as using the issue of homelessness to score political points.
In an interview with an actor aligned with the STHF and the NPA, the
actor asked *me* a question following our interview: "I was wondering
if, in some of your other interviews, if the undercurrent of the politics
of this came out at all?" The actor noted that there was a "liberal sprin-
kling of politics" in Robertson's HEAT response, notably in "the need
to be seen acting quickly."

The STHF took off just as Robertson was implementing his own approach to homelessness: the two groups started separately and have not
merged. Their different approaches became entrenched because of the partisan origins of their ideas, which resulted in the politicization of the issue
of homelessness. This illustrates not only the magnetic potential of ideas
to attract and build coalitions but also their ability to push groups apart.
It also illustrates how institutions interact with ideas: the disagreement
between the approaches taken by the city and the STHF were meaningful,
but also small, in that both groups were motivated by a housing-oriented
definition of homelessness. The local party system turned this small ideational disagreement into a bigger one, fragmenting local governance.

The STHF set out to not replicate existing efforts; rather, private-sector
actors charged with developing and implementing a ten-year plan believed that they had identified an important oversight in the system. But
when I asked a prominent STHF board member how the different plans
on homelessness fit together, they laughed and said, "They don't" (personal interview 2014). Another actor noted that this fragmentation had
complicated efforts to fight homelessness in Vancouver:

> We've got too many people deciding what to do – the Metro Vancouver
> homelessness whatever, the task force, the interfaith blah blah blah, the
> StreetoHome Foundation, the Aboriginal one, Aboriginal health one, Van-
> couver Coastal Health. So all of a sudden something that is really very
> simple has become an overwhelming, confusing process. It's stagnant. It's
> not moving forward the way it should. It's costing way too much and it
> sucks energy out of everything that is going on. (personal interview 2014)

Third Sector

The third sector in Vancouver also plays an important role in home-lessness governance. Downtown Eastside (DTES) community groups especially have long organized around the questions of housing and homelessness, drug policy reform, harm reduction, and public health. Community leaders have forged unlikely yet strong bonds with politicians at all three levels of government to advocate for their rights and to participate directly in policy-making (see Lupick 2017a). They have been at the forefront of fights for safe injection sites and overdose prevention and had a long and documented history of successful Housing First programs well before these were established and popular government practice. Through advocacy and effective pressure campaigns, third-sector groups have developed practices that have become an important part of government policy, and they work closely with governments to implement those policies.

Third-sector actors often participate directly in policy-making, be it as candidates and elected officials, through relationships with sympathetic insiders, through direct action, or through grassroots approaches such as protests and civil disobedience. While influential, their involvement in homelessness governance has been weakened at times by two factors. First, public health emergencies related to HIV/AIDS, injection drug use, and unsafe drug supplies have absorbed a great deal of time and effort, diverting attention away from homelessness. Groups that would logically lead the fight against homelessness, such as the Portland Housing Society, have long been preoccupied with drug policy reform. Second, there are some divisions between third-sector groups, at times for seemingly personal reasons (Lupick 2017a) and at times for philosophical ones, which can be seen as different understandings of the nature of homelessness. Because of their power and their close relationships with government (especially when their allies are in power), disagreements can destabilize the sector.

Because of the significance of municipal involvement in homelessness in 2008, most of the following discussion will relate to third-sector involvement at that point in time. That said, these groups' advocacy work long predates 2008. For example, the Downtown Eastside Residents Association (DERA) was formed in the 1970s to advocate for housing solutions, and groups organizing in support of tenant rights and social housing have a long history of intense direct action, including in 2002 during the redevelopment of the important Woodward's Building in the Downtown Eastside (Barnes and Hutton 2009). Community groups participated in the city's 2005 plans on housing and homelessness, contributing directly to the draft plans. Much of this advocacy and direct action related to housing and homelessness, and while these issues never fell off the radar of organizers and grassroots movements, considerable attention was directed to efforts to open InSite in the early 2000s.

An important moment for third-sector involvement in homelessness governance was thus in 2008, when specific community actors were invited to be part of Robertson's Homelessness Emergency Action Team (HEAT) in 2008 and co-create and implement the city's response to street homelessness. The plan was to open new, low-barrier shelters before winter so that no one would need to sleep outside. This required locating spaces for the shelters, as well as the capacity to run them – resources available to third-sector groups. Those groups were keen to use their expertise and knowledge to help Robertson craft and implement his plan to end street homelessness. An actor involved with the HEAT team described the mood of the community groups around the table when the HEAT team first got to work: "We were excited. We were really excited. We were getting invited to participate in [the political process] and make a difference" (personal interview 2014).

Another actor on the HEAT team recounted that the mayor brought all the relevant actors together regularly, meeting four hours every Sunday until the shelters were set up: "Things happened really fast. We were in the room with everybody and we had city staff, real estate, housing. [The mayor] would turn to the head of real estate and say, 'What properties do we have?' And [the head of real estate] would pull out a list and we went through them" (personal interview 2014). Explaining the very direct involvement of third sector actors in the opening of a new shelter location, they noted:

> The Mayor turned to me and said, "Okay, we are going to have a tour [of a proposed shelter site] tomorrow morning, can you be there?" … We toured it, and they asked me my opinion and I said sure. We drew up a plan, it was just a diagram, but it was enough to hand to them and say, "This is what we need." And they went ahead and built it. They started right away. Demolition started that week, and we were up and operating within a month I think. Very fast. (personal interview 2014)

With guidance from the HEAT team, four new emergency, low-barrier, twenty-four-hour shelters were opened around Vancouver. Empowered with a mandate to do everything they could to bring people inside, service providers in charge of the HEAT shelters worked tirelessly and with great creativity to eliminate barriers that were keeping people outside. An actor from one of the shelters explained that in practice, this meant eliminating, changing, or breaking rules to get people off the streets and inside the shelters:

> There was a couple outside and I said, "Well, do you want to come in?" And they explained that they couldn't sleep in the same bed [in a different shelter]. And I said, "Well, why not?" They were told by the shelter manager, "No you can't do that." And I said "welllll we can!" ... They've got lots of crap, carts. They asked, "Can we take that stuff in? Dogs?" Well, unless the dog is going to rip someone's throat out, why would we say they can't come in?" ... When there was a shortage of shelter beds it was easy for groups to develop their policies and say, "You can't use drugs, we won't allow you to." [In our shelter we] had a crack smoking room. (personal interview 2014).

This approach "shook up the shelter business" and succeeded in getting more people inside, a key objective in the overall plan to end street homelessness.

Another actor involved with a HEAT shelter also underscored the importance of removing barriers: "In those days, you couldn't take your stuff inside, there was no storage facility, you couldn't take your rat or your dog. So, you just stayed outside" (personal interview 2014). At their low-barrier HEAT shelter, they welcomed everyone as well as their pets and their belongings. They added that their shelter was not like other shelters in the city at the time:

> Our sense was that there were certain people who couldn't sleep in the shelter system because their behaviours were really complicated, their threat of violence really put shelter providers off ... We just knew that there was a group of people, we saw them in the day, who wouldn't function in the shelter system and if all possible just wouldn't go in. And those, we figured, were our people. (personal interview 2014)

There was no intake process, which was the norm at other shelters at the time, so people could come and go freely. When the objective became to get people inside no matter what, barriers were removed and many people did indeed go indoors – that was the point of the HEAT shelters. Implementing this City Hall priority was possible because of the relationships Vision Vancouver had with community groups and leaders, who brought their expertise, compassion, skill, and commitment to fulfilling this promise.

Third-sector groups were intensely involved in this process because of their expertise, but also because they agreed with the objective of ending street homelessness. Service providers in the DTES had been developing innovative and life-saving approaches to homelessness for decades, many of which were low- or no-barrier and permanent. Well before the federal government discovered the idea of Housing First – the commitment to permanent, supportive housing – actors at the Portland Housing Society had committed to a model of housing from which people could not be evicted. This approach was enshrined in the Housing Society's constitution: "The Portland Hotel Society endeavours to find an alternative to eviction in each and every situation. This clause is unalterable" (qtd in Lupick 2017a, 136). In opening low-barrier shelters, Robertson was not teaching community groups anything new, but rather empowering them to scale up their services and provide them with the funding to expand their operations. Because of the close relationships and the extent to which he relied on them to develop, open, and operate the shelters, these groups played an important role in fulfilling his political promise.

Because of the central place they occupied in implementing the vision of ending street homelessness, disagreements between third-sector groups and City Hall, and sometimes even the province, became problematic. In the ultimate breakdown of one relationship – between City Hall and the operators of one of the first HEAT shelters, First United Church in the Downtown Eastside – we see the true force of ideas and the threat that ambiguous ideas can pose to governing coalitions. Senior leaders at the church, which had previously served as a day centre for the community, were involved in designing Robertson's plan and were central to its implementation (Burrows 2010). Originally designed for 150 people, at its peak the shelter welcomed over 300 individuals indoors. Explaining the perspective of the people managing the shelter, a senior actor explained that it was understood by senior leadership to be "pre-shelter":

> In those early months, we were in control of how we were operating ... We weren't in the shelter system. Not to say that shelters aren't important, but we saw ourselves as pre-shelter for that group of people that couldn't deal with the shelter system. We thought there needed to be an alternative for those people. Our belief was that we were meeting the needs of a very complicated, very chaotic group of individuals. (personal interview 2014)

The shelter operated successfully through the first winter season of Robertson's mandate as those in charge of the shelter did exactly what they had been asked to do: remove barriers and create spaces for people to stay inside. Tensions over the shelter's operations began to grow the following year, however. The city warned the shelter it was not following fire safety regulations, though some in the community believed that overcrowding was an excuse to allow the city and province to take control because it disagreed with how the shelter was being run (personal interview 2014).

First United came under increasing scrutiny. In early 2011, there were reports of several sexual assaults in the shelter. In response, the shelter's leadership made comments that were interpreted by many in the community as blaming the victims (CBC 2011a). Community members condemned the comments made by Reverend Matthews, but he insisted that his comments were misconstrued and that he never intended to cast blame. He also insisted that shelter staff were working to create a safer environment. In December, however, a futher damaging article in the *Globe and Mail* referred to the shelter as a "Ghetto Mansion" and painted a picture of disorder and chaos (Stueck 2011). Perhaps more damaging was that the article claimed that up to 40 per cent of the people living in the shelter already had access to government-subsidized housing, implicitly accusing them of double-dipping into public resources. In response to claims made in the *Globe and Mail* and to BC Housing's increasing concerns about whom the shelter was serving and how, the shelter's management wrote an impassioned response in which they made abundantly clear there was a fundamental and irreconcilable disagreement regarding the very nature of homelessness and what it means to end it:

> The increasingly common claim is that First United should exclude those who simply want to be there, but don't really need to be there. *This is a bogus distinction, based on a superficial understanding of the deep need people have for belonging (and the terror many have of being alone). If housing does not provide a genuine home, people need to find other places where they feel at home.* This need is not an easily dismissed "nice to have." It is a very deep, authentic human need. (Severs and Matthews 2011; emphasis added)

Severs and Matthews then stress that ending homelessness requires more than just housing, indeed, more than just *supportive* housing.

> We can build as many new housing units as we like, *but the people we put in them need to feel at home* with sufficient and appropriate support 24 hours a day. Without that, they will continue to cycle through the system ... The fact that First United is "too welcoming and accepting" is not the problem. The problem is that too often these basic needs are not being met in the housing that has been provided.

A few days after writing this, Matthews resigned, and the shelter's operations were transferred to the province. The province had planned on this for 2013 but took control one year earlier. A former leader at the shelter noted in an interview: "It does not get more traditional than what it is now. It is running a 60 bed – 40 men and 20 woman – traditional BC Housing controlled shelter. With case management and an intake process, locked doors. We served anybody and everybody that wanted food three times a day and a snack. That doesn't exist anymore" (personal interview 2014).

Behind this disagreement were fundamentally different understandings of what it meant to end street homelessness. For the people operating First United, homelessness was not just about a lack of housing; it also was about a lack of community and belonging, which they tried to address. For the city, and even for the province, ending homelessness meant finding housing. Allowing people who already had access to government housing, no matter how low the quality, to stay in the shelter was counter to that goal. It is easy to gloss over these differences, especially when exciting albeit ambiguous ideas regarding ending homelessness are being turned into reality. But the unravelling of this relationship reveals how ambiguous ideas can do much to forge coalitions, but that those coalitions may be unstable because of fundamental differences in understanding and motivation.

In other words, the destructive power of ambiguous ideas is in evidence here, and it is a shame. From the perspective of BC Housing and the city, which were funding the shelter and were liable (legally and politically), concerns about overcrowding and the safety of residents were important, but there was also concern that people who were not homeless because they had access to housing were using emergency shelters. Yet those running the shelter had a different perspective. They were motivated by an understanding of homelessness that understood it to be not just an absence of physical housing, but an absence of belonging. They had identified an important oversight in the homeless system – that some people are excluded from the regular system and are not allowed in traditional shelters – and were tirelessly working to address it. Where were they to go? For a time, the answer was to HEAT shelters. And while this disagreement did not result in a complete fracture of the system, local politicians' big promises and bold ambitions did not align, ideationally, with those of all of the groups they had empowered in the rush to implement. The result was struggles over implementation, which led to destabilization.

Robertson's coalition relied on the expertise and capacity of third-sector groups and advocates. Conflict disrupted and destabilized that local coalition. The common story about why Robertson's efforts to end street homelessness failed is that the province was not on board. That is certainly part of it, and the housing crisis worsened under Premier Clark as the province limited its commitment to build and protect housing. But in addition, the local coalition that was so important to

Robertson's plan had begun to fall apart, as seen with Judy Graves's decision to not support Vision Vancouver in the 2018 municipal election and the breakdown of the mayor's important relationship with First United. Homelessness at the local level in Vancouver is political, and there are deep disagreements not just between parties but also within sectors regarding the nature of homelessness.

The third sector remains involved in homelessness governance and in partnerships with the city to develop and operate supportive housing for people exiting homelessness. The above example is not to suggest that all third-sector groups have become alienated from the city or disagree with its approach, nor is it to suggest that the difficulties ending street homelessness were related exclusively to local-level ideational disagreements. In the governance of an area of policy as complex as homelessness, however, where the expertise and involvement of a wide range of actors is needed, it serves as an example of how ambiguous ideas and different fundamental understandings of homelessness can become barriers to cooperative efforts.

NHI/HPS Governance – Metro Vancouver

Of the cities included here, Vancouver delivers National Homelessness Initiative/Homelessness Partnering Strategy (NHI/HPS) funded programs somewhat differently, so these networks are considered separately. The municipality of Vancouver is very small and urban; the suburbs (Surrey, Richmond, etc.) are their own municipalities. The broader Metro Vancouver region is large but fragmented, containing twenty-one municipal governments, one Treaty First Nation, and one "electoral area." The first important feature of Vancouver's NHI/HPS administration is related to this institutional environment. In such a fragmented system of local governance, City of Vancouver actors have joined up with other Metro Vancouver actors to develop a regional rather than municipal plan on homelessness for NHI/HPS purposes. Local actors across the Vancouver region have formed the Regional Steering Committee on Homelessness (RSCH). Second, the RSCH is distinct from other networks considered here in that it coordinates closely with the regional Indigenous network in Vancouver, with representatives from each group sitting on the advisory board of the other group (the Indigenous steering committee chair sits on the RSCH, and vice versa). The explicit purpose of this arrangement is for the groups to communicate and coordinate.

The membership of Vancouver's RSCH is diverse not only in terms of the various municipal governments that are represented but also with respect to representatives from other orders of government and third- and private-sector actors. This network is "a diverse mix of individuals who together bring to the table distinct perspectives and a breadth of knowledge of what is occurring on the ground (in the community and on the streets) and what is coming down the policy pike (from government)" (Doberstein 2016, 69). Furthermore, the fact that there are no elected officials on the RSCH means that actors can be less risk-averse regarding what programs they adopt (Doberstein 2016). The RSCH's 2003 plan, *3 Ways Home*, was influential at the time, and its three-pronged approach to ending homelessness – housing, income, support – was adopted by City of Vancouver plans as well as the StreetoHome Plan in 2008. This shows an impressive degree of coordination across scales and sectors. An updated draft plan, released in 2015, changed priorities following community consultations and a close look at the outcomes of the previous plan, and focuses now on housing, prevention, and capacity-building.

The Indigenous NHI/HPS network meets regularly, and coordinates with other homelessness governance bodies, notably the RSCH. Things got off to a slow start in 1999 because of institutional roadblocks imposed by the federal government (Doberstein 2016) – as was the case for most Indigenous networks at the time. Since the removal of those burdens to implementation, the Indigenous network has gone beyond the requirements necessary to access funding. For example, the Indigenous regional network is one of the only Indigenous networks in the country to develop a plan on homelessness (Indigenous communities are not required to develop plans the way larger designated communities are). Interviews with senior actors involved in the Indigenous network point to the importance of collaboration across and within sectors but also to the importance of having neutral voices on the committee. The chairs of the Indigenous advisory board are not directly affiliated with a homeless service provider. In interviews, actors have noted that this has helped create trust among members, as the chair does not represent an agency that stands to receive federal funding.

The Indigenous network gets considerably less funding from the federal government than the broader Regional Steering Committee. An actor noted in an interview that the funding breakdown is about 90 per cent to the RSCH and 10 per cent to the Indigenous committee, even though Indigenous people make up about one-third of the homeless population. Some see this as problematic given the tremendous, and growing, overrepresentation of Indigenous people among Vancouver's homeless population. Another actor with the Indigenous committee had a different perspective, however; when asked if the funding received by the Indigenous group is sufficient, this person responded: "Mathematically, it isn't. But I don't want to say that the money should be reallocated from the regional table. I think in general, just looking at the overall size and scope of homelessness, that would just be throwing the problem onto another area" (personal interview 2018). This person also noted that the regional table funds programs for Indigenous people and stressed that the overall problem was a broader funding shortfall – all networks are underfunded.

The two regional networks coordinate to an impressive degree, but time is limited. One actor noted that most people involved with the Indigenous network are already stretched very thin and that sitting on the advisory committee is a volunteer job. They noted that they spend twenty-five to thirty hours per week in meetings: "I sit on four or five different tables. It's a classic example of the tremendous amount of need but only a small number of people that are drawn into the same number of tables" (personal interview 2018). Where there are interactions among these HPS networks and the other actors (the city and, to a lesser extent, the StreetoHome Foundation), they tend to be informal. The main interactions among the networks tend to be when individuals sit on multiple committees across the city (not all related to homelessness for that matter), but this places a great burden on the Indigenous people who serve.

One actor I interviewed with the Indigenous governance network in Vancouver was unfamiliar with Thistle's definition of Indigenous homelessness but nevertheless brought up different ways of understanding Indigenous homelessness, underscoring the importance of these ideas for the overall governance of homelessness. Talking specifically about Housing First, this actor noted that there are problems implementing it effectively with respect to Indigenous homelessness:

It is a very good model, but it is a housing-based model. And what I mean by housing is asking them to equate housing with commodities as opposed to homes, which I see as more community-based and maybe more in the relational nature of things. There might be potentially some disconnects in terms of how Indigenous communities see homes, see communities, see all those pieces that have some potential incompatibilities with the underlying constructs of Housing First. (personal interview 2018)

Though there is widespread recognition that Housing First is a promising model for ending homelessness, including among Indigenous people,[24] Indigenous actors overseeing funding specifically for Indigenous people experiencing homelessness indicated that they were motivated by broader understandings of the causes of homelessness and that they tend to fund a wider range of programs: "So whether that's child care, food, life skills, education, it's a pretty broad parameter that we can play in. It's kind of the nature of building a community" (personal interview 2018). While there are differences in understanding, the regional level is again an example of how different groups, with different understandings of homelessness communicate and coordinate closely. Ultimately, however, both regional networks in Vancouver (and across the country) are limited in what they can do. One reason why networks are limited is funding. Many services are underfunded, but in Vancouver, the Indigenous population makes up a significant portion of the number of people experiencing homelessness and the breakdown of funding received by the Indigenous table simply does not reflect that. There was also evidence of a strained relationship with the federal government: "We don't find that the government operates fairly or in good faith ... They are not transparent. They do a lot in secret and then they spring things on you" (personal interview 2014). In that sense, the fact that the Indigenous network (and all networks set up to administer federal funding for that matter) is institutionalized and run by volunteers is not lost on those making decisions: "I'm a volunteer, [Service Canada] can't fire me from anything. What are they going to do?" (personal interview 2014).

This actor gave an example of how the Indigenous table tried to distribute three years' worth of funding in a way that met community needs: "When we did our last contract round in 2011, we opened it up to the community. We tried to be as flexible as possible. We tried to meet as many needs as we could. So we did that, and were quite efficient. We do things quite quickly. Then the federal government came out with its terms and conditions and said, 'You can't do what you did.'" The actor explained that they had spent the federal funding in accordance with local needs, as opposed to spending the same amount of money ($1.8 million) per year for three years: "Some groups said, 'We need money for the first two years but not the third,' or they said, 'We have funding now but need it for later.' And the federal government said, 'No, you can't do that.' Are you serious? They don't like us to have too much initiative" (personal interview 2014). Limitations imposed by inadequate resources mean that Indigenous tables are not fully able to implement solutions to problems they have identified in their communities; but they are further limited by oversight from the federal government. This example also gives pause to those claiming that local communities are given extensive discretion over how to spend the funding; the metagoverning federal government remains a powerful force in the local distribution of funds.

Conclusions

The story of homelessness governance in Vancouver is a long and complicated one. From it, insights can be drawn about the multilevel governance of a complex policy area. A number of groups and actors are involved in homelessness governance, and leadership has at times been contested. Many groups coordinate with one another, though some deep fractures have destabilized the system at times and can weaken the involvement of certain groups. Overall, however, the fragmentation of power is relatively well-coordinated through a mix of institutional and informal arrangements. Institutional features and the distribution of resources are important in understanding the involvement and interactions of actors, but ideas about the responsibility to produce social protection and the nature of homelessness complete our understanding of this vibrant, at times volatile, governance dynamic.

Compared to other provinces, and even compared to its own social policy track record, which has tended to be stingy and punitive, BC has been involved and generous in housing and homelessness for much of its recent history. There have been periods of provincial restraint and decreasing involvement in housing policy, and periods of much stronger involvement as well. In some cases, changes have followed a change of party in power or following changes in party leadership. This includes a change in government in the early 2000s (from NDP to Liberal) that led to decreasing provincial involvement in homelessness governance. It also includes the election of Christy Clark as leader of the governing Liberals and Premier of BC, which resulted in decreased provincial involvement. Yet except for a few years in the early 2000s, the province has been engaged in housing since the federal cuts in the 1990s, during periods of both right-of-centre and left-of-centre governance. Furthermore, a significant change in the province's involvement occurred in the mid-aughts, a change that was not preceeded by a change in party or even leadership. The involvement of the province in homelessness governance is shaped centrally by ideas, held by senior people at key moments in BC history, about there being a role for government in protecting British Columbians from homelessness. It is also informed by an understanding of homelessness that is quite narrow, that prioritizes a relatively small subset of the homeless population, and that is directly related to housing and health, both provincial areas of responsibility.

While some of these changes were ideological, not all were; the same leaders who cut *Homes BC* re-engaged and reinvested in housing development only a few years later. While the reinvestment in housing coincided with an improvement in BC's economy, it was not inevitable that the province re-engaged; ideas regarding the collective, but province-led, responsibility for producing social protection for those in housing need have been important drivers of provincial involvement. Provincial officials' understanding of homelessness, and of their leadership role in producing protection against it, have also led them to seek out collaboration with other actors, including local governments, the third sector, the private sector, and the federal government. While there have been conflicts between governments, intergovernmental action on homelessness has been largely collaborative.

The City of Vancouver has a long history of involvement in housing and homelessness governance as well. This includes local housing and homelessness plans in 2005, though these largely advocated for increased senior government involvement. A more ambitious plan to end street homelessness was introduced in 2008. The promise was not fulfilled, and the number of people experiencing homelessness in Vancouver has continued to rise, yet for years, the fight against homelessness was the city's top priority. Local institutions, including housing-related institutional powers and the local party system, are important for understanding why the city has been so involved in homelessness governance. Though the city does not have jurisdiction over housing, Vancouver has significant powers related to housing, including density bonusing and inclusionary zoning, powers that are made more important by the limited availability of land and space within the city. Ideas regarding the responsibility to produce social protection and a particular definition of homelessness that distinguishes between street and shelter pushed city officials to use these tools and increase their involvement in homelessness governance to the point of assuming leadership of the issue in 2008.

Through the StreetoHome Foundation, private-sector actors increased their involvement in homelessness governance beginning in 2008. Rallying around the idea of ending homelessness, and saving money doing so, key private-sector actors in Vancouver built a powerful coalition of business leaders in 2008 to turn these ideas into reality, though their plan to end homelessness was also unsuccessful. Absent an institutionalized role, private-sector elites drew on personal relationships with senior provincial officials to bolster their role and allow them to collaborate. The STHF exists, despite the strength of community groups and significant municipal government involvement, because it has abundant resources and because of a belief, among private-sector actors as well as governments, that the private sector has a role to play in the production of social protection. Its involvement was also the result of a seemingly small ideational difference regarding the nature of homelessness that solidified in the local party system and resulted in fragmentation. Robertson sought to end *street* homelessness by first opening more low-barrier shelters to bring people inside. This was not his only idea, nor was it his long-term solution. But the STHF and its allies in the right-of-centre NPA positioned themselves against opening new shelters and drew no distinction between street and sheltered homelessness. In the local party system, this disagreement became political. Ideas regarding the nature of homelessness became magnetic, and groups were forced apart; the party system pushed groups even farther apart for a time by turning a small disagreement into a political one. Yet the STHF and Robertson believed in the Housing First approach and shared a definition of homelessness that was linked with housing. The small ideational disagreement, even in a local party system, was eventually overcome. In this sense, fragmentation of small differences, especially when they are motivated by the same housing-focused definition of homelessness, can be coordinated quite easily.

Where they are not coordinated, disagreements regarding the nature of homelessness can lead to fractures in the system, as was the case with a disagreement between city (and provincial) officials and the operator of one of the new HEAT shelters. They were attracted to work together by the magnetic idea of ending homelessness; however, that idea, though appealing, was also ambiguous, and the partners interpreted it very differently. Because they had fundamentally different understandings of homelessness, with city and provincial actors motivated by a housing-based definition and some third-sector groups motivated by one that also emphasized community and belonging, this idea of ending homelessness became volatile, and groups were ultimately pushed apart. Yet we also see evidence that disagreements regarding the nature of homelessness – as is seen with the Indigenous network at the regional level, which tends to adopt a more holistic definition of homelessness than the designated community network – can be coordinated.

6 Calgary

The governance of homelessness in Calgary is centralized in the Calgary Homeless Foundation (CHF). This has not always been the case, and there has been an evolution in the role of all actors – governments and non-governmental groups – in homelessness governance since the 1990s. In the mid-2000s, private-sector actors rallied around the idea of ending homelessness in ten years, funnelling their efforts and lobbying for the orientation of subsequent government investments to the CHF and its implementation plan. Though the CHF has centralized significant power at the local level, key local actors have also been successful at "uploading" responsibility to the province. The Province of Alberta introduced a ten-year plan to end homelessness in 2008, after Calgary's plan was developed. Calgary-based actors have become influential on the national level in advocating for a National Housing Strategy as well as a Housing First orientation to investments in homelessness. The CHF has also become more inclusive of third-sector and Indigenous groups over time. The municipality plays a comparatively small role in homelessness governance.

The private-sector actors who have been behind many of these important governance and policy changes have significant financial resources at their disposal, and though they do not play an institutionalized role in politics, close, personal connections with senior decision-makers allow them informal but influential access to the political process. But it was ideas regarding the nature of homelessness and the responsibility to produce social protection that led these actors to commit their time and resources to the fight against homelessness. In particular, we see local actors (policy entrepreneurs) redefining homelessness as an expensive problem to manage and something that can be ended; this idea, animated by a narrow, housing-focused understanding of homelessness, became magnetic and attracted a wide range of groups to collaborate.

Ideas regarding the nature of homelessness have evolved considerably, as the CHF has gone from seeing a limited role for government in ending homelessness to seeing a much more central one. This change has coincided with the CHF's evolving role in homelessness governance, from one of leadership and ownership to one of partnership and collaboration.

Homelessness History in Alberta

The Province of Alberta has gone from a laggard to a leader when it comes to homelessness governance. From the Second World War until 2008, its involvement in housing and homelessness was minimal. The years 2008 to 2019 were a time of increased involvement, including the development and implementation of a plan to end homelessness as well as a plan to end youth homelessness, and then (following a change in government) a Provincial Housing Strategy and Poverty Reduction Strategy. Many of the commitments made under Rachel Notley's NDP government have been rolled back under Jason Kenney's United Conservative Party's governance, and the provincial role has again decreased. In some instances, these changes have been in line with different party ideologies. But we also see significant changes within the same party.

In Alberta, we can clearly see the power of ideas, which drove government decision-making during periods of economic decline and in times of abundance and institutional power. Guided by local advocates and personal relationships with leaders in the oil and gas sector in the mid-aughts, provincial officials were introduced to new ideas about the nature of homelessness and became convinced that it was possible to end it. They were further convinced that ending homelessness would require a significant upfront investment but in the end save money. This framing was driven by a narrow understanding of homelessness, as calculations regarding cost savings tend to focus the most on people who experience chronic homelessness (as opposed to those whose homelessness is more hidden). Ideas regarding the nature of homelessness did not originate at the provincial level; rather, local level entrepreneurs, many of whom were Calgary-based, succeeded in redefining homelessness and used that new definition to build a political coalition of supporters, including powerful actors at the provincial level.

After the Second World War, the Province of Alberta, like other provinces, built social housing in partnership with the federal government. Slowly but steadily, the province added to its housing supply through the 1970s and 1980s, largely targeting this housing at seniors. Indeed, for much of its history, housing in Alberta was the responsibility of the Minister for Seniors, a clear indication that government-built housing was (and to a large extent still is) for that population. The 1981–2 annual report explains: "More than half of the corporation's unit commitments, 2,070, were to the Senior Citizens Self-contained Program; a further indication of the priority which the government places on affordable housing for Alberta's many *pioneers*" (Alberta Housing Corporation 1982; 3 emphasis added). An additional 366 units of "hotel-like" accommodation for seniors were also included. Less than one-third of the units committed for construction in 1981 (1,138) were through the Community Housing Program and intended for low-income families.

By 1992, there were just under 40,000 units of social housing in Alberta, including municipal non-profit housing that was provincially subsidized (Alberta Ministry of Municipal Affairs 1992), 21,906 units of which were for seniors. By prioritizing seniors who were (and continue to be) framed as "pioneers," Alberta's early housing policy made clear its very narrow understanding of its role in producing social protection for those in housing need and those, also narrowly defined, as most deserving. The government's responsibility to produce social protection was limited to those who were perceived to have done their share, following a model more of social insurance rather than protection. While some government-funded housing was made available for low-income Albertans (approximately 25 per cent), the idea that tended to prevail and guide provincial involvement was that the private sector provided most of the social protection needed by vulnerable people.

Following federal cuts to social housing in the 1990s, the province stopped funding new social housing developments, going so far as to halt developments and commitments already under way. As a result, the province's social housing stock did not grow during the 2000s. Indeed, Maroine Bendaoud (2016) notes that while a small number of units of social or affordable housing were constructed during the 1990s and early 2000s (drawing on funding that had been dedicated to housing in 1992–3), the province also sold off stock: "The ministry disposed of a total of 35 housing units that were surplus or no longer suitable for the ministry's housing portfolio" (Alberta Seniors 2002, 26). Some units were built, but some were "disposed of," meaning the total stock remained virtually unchanged.

In 1992, Ralph Klein was elected premier. He inherited an annual deficit of $3.3 billion and a provincial debt of $23 billion from his predecessor, Progressive Conservative Premier Don Getty (Gregg 2006). Bringing the party back to the "Conservative" side of Progressive Conservative, Klein made the economy his top priority and turned a deficit into a surplus within a very short time, all without raising taxes. This change in the provincial economy was achieved through cuts, sometimes very deep. This was an ideological project. Social assistance incomes were cut by 20 per cent and eligibility requirements were heightened. In the early 1990s, Alberta already had the second-lowest social assistance rates in the country; by 2003, the province was second to none. Provincial cuts to housing were combined with these drastic cuts to social spending, earning Progressive Conservative Premier Ralph Klein the nickname "King Ralph the Deficit Slayer" (CBC News 2013b; Dabbs 2006). As a result of a growing population in Alberta, a federal freeze on new social housing developments, a booming economy (when not busting), lack of provincial interest in the housing sector, and further social spending cuts, the homeless population began to increase rapidly throughout Alberta in the 1990s and 2000s (Gaetz, Gulliver, and Richter 2014). The government's actions and inactions during this period made clear that it did not view homelessness as a political or structural problem; rather, it was seen as an individual problem. People experiencing homelessness were met with indifference or worse by provincial public officials (CBC News 2013a).

In 2002, incentivized by the federal government's new cost-sharing Affordable Housing Agreement, the Government of Alberta committed some funding to housing, matching the $67.12 million (over five years) federal investment. It would continue to match funding as the agreement was renewed. Between 2001 and 2011, Alberta produced 4,308 units of housing (CMHC 2011), much of which was for seniors but some of which was targeted at low-income Albertans and those with special needs (CMHC 2002). These provincial interventions were, however, modest when compared with those of other provinces (see Suttor 2016, 167). This is particularly interesting in light of the fact that by 2006, Alberta had amassed a significant budgetary surplus. But rather than investing that surplus in social policies, the government sent $600 to each Albertan. Nicknamed "Ralph bucks," this use of a surplus underscores how resources on their own are not enough to drive policy involvement. This may be seen as ideological, and indeed it was consistent with Klein's conservative agenda to reduce the size of government. But consider the case of BC during this same period: that province, also led by a right-of-centre party, having embarked on a similar cost-reduction exercise a few years earlier, made the different decision to reinvest in housing a few years after making cuts. This comparison with BC makes clear that ideas regarding the nature of homelessness and the responsibility to produce social protection structure governments' decisions about what to do with their resources.

By 2007, under the leadership of Ed Stelmach, housing needs were growing across Alberta, particularly in big cities like Calgary and Edmonton (Falvo 2017). Drawing on personal connections to key government officials, including the premier himself, Calgary-based actors communicated their concerns about the growing number of people experiencing homelessness in the province. These actors, primarily from the private sector, succeeded in placing homelessness on the province's agenda and effectively manipulated ideas regarding the nature of homelessness to convince the province to join its efforts to combat it. Some of these ideas were partial or mistaken, and subsequent work in Calgary and at the provincial level made adjustments in light of an evolving understanding of homelessness, as will be noted below. At this key moment in history, however, homelessness was understood to be expensive and solvable; motivating this understanding of homelessness was a narrow definition of it, one that focused primarily on chronic homelessness and that viewed causes and solutions on the individual level.

In 2007, private-sector actors who had worked with the CHF on its ten-year plan met with influential officials at the provincial level, including ministers and deputy ministers responsible for housing, to explain the logic of an upfront investment to end homelessness and to make the case that this would result in significant long-run savings. As I will explain below, Calgary-based actors, including oil and gas mogul Steve Snyder, had been recently exposed to the idea of ending homelessness by Philip Mangano, former US President George W. Bush's "point-person" on homelessness. Indeed, Mangano visited all cities under study here and is a key source spreading the idea of ending homelessness across the country. Journalist Susan Scott describes an important meeting in September 2007 between Premier Ed Stelmach and Steve Snyder, who was chair of Calgary's committee to end homelessness (discussed below):

> As soon as [Premier] Stelmach sat down, Snyder drew out a piece of paper and started to scribble diagrams explaining the effectiveness of ten-year plans both in human and economic terms. The catch? They required funding upfront before things could happen ... Snyder, of course, had done his homework and had all the facts to back up the request for $1 billion over ten years. It took him twenty minutes to outline his case. "Will this work?," Stelmach asked. "Yes, it will," they assured him ... Basically, Stelmach committed there and then to make something happen. (S. Scott 2012, 164–5)

As revealed by this focus on the cost-saving promise of ending homelessness, Snyder's idea regarding the nature of homelessness was narrow, and the involvement he was asking for from the province was accordingly also narrow (though it was significant compared to what other provinces were doing at the time, and certainly compared to what had previously been done in Alberta, in that it included requests for provincial investments in housing).

One month after meeting with Snyder, Premier Stelmach announced an Alberta Secretariat for Action on Homelessness. Yvonne Fritz, a Progressive Conservative MLA representing Calgary as well as Minister of Housing and Urban Affairs, would lead the secretariat; Snyder would chair it, all but ensuring that it would align with and indeed follow the work that had been done in Calgary: "Once again, it was a cut-and-paste job taking the best from other jurisdictions. Snyder brought with him all the knowledge and expertise acquired in putting together Calgary's recently released plan.[1] They also went to the US" (S. Scott 2012, 167). Plans to end homelessness were showing signs of success in places like Portland and New York, giving committee members confidence in their Housing First approach to ending homelessness, as Snyder explained in an interview: "That gives us confidence, if we can head in that direction, we should get the same results and hopefully we will get there first" (qtd in CBC News 2009).

In March 2009, following the implementation of seven local plans to end homelessness across Alberta, the province introduced a ten-year plan to end homelessness, the first such provincial plan in the country. Informed by a Housing First philosophy, the plan listed five priority areas for action: "Better information; aggressive assistance; coordinated systems; more housing options; effective policies" (Alberta Secretariat for Action on Homelessness 2008, 18). It promised to house 11,000 homeless Albertans within ten years and estimated that to do so it would need to construct some 8,000 new units of affordable housing *specifically for people experiencing homelessness*. In addition to this commitment to housing, the plan insisted on a new approach to ending homelessness:

> Addressing homelessness requires integrated, cross-ministerial work, and efforts from a number of sectors and social organizations. It will also require a fundamental change in thinking. This is the crux of the Plan for Alberta. The Plan changes the way homelessness is addressed. Rather than spending money on more shelter spaces to accommodate more homeless Albertans, the Plan shifts the system to focus on housing and moving the homeless to more self-reliance. (Alberta Secretariat for Action On Homelessness 2008, 7)

An important part of Alberta's efforts, then, was extensive coordination between levels of government and within the local service system.

Alberta was an early adopter of this coordinated approach to homelessness, particularly between the provincial government and local groups, but also at the local level and within the provincial administration as well. There are important strengths to this approach, and Alberta should be given credit for identifying the need to work across departments at the provincial level as well as across scales of governance in its efforts to fight homelessness (Quebec has also made efforts to coordinate different departments at the provincial level). In the end, the plan did not succeed; even so, Alberta's intergovernmental, multilevel, internal coordination is (along with Quebec's effort) an important case study in the importance of coordinated and collaborative governance.

In Alberta's plan, the causes of homelessness were seen to be multiple, though no formal definition was given: "The reasons behind the increase in homelessness are many and complex, rooted in fiscal, social and policy decisions over many years" (Alberta Secretariat for Action On Homelessness 2008, 2). The plan also identified four "types" of homelessness: chronic, transient, working, and family. Alberta's plan is the only one considered in this book to include the category of "working" homelessness. Like the broader definition, this understanding of "working homelessness" hints at structural causes and reveals an important assumption made by those writing the plan – that people experience homelessness because of a simple inability to access housing. This assumption was bolstered by some evidence from the local level, notably a study titled *Homeless Not Jobless* by a large homeless shelter in Calgary that found that many homeless people were working part- or even full-time. Indeed, interviews with key local and provincial actors suggested that many private-sector actors in Calgary felt that the increase in the number of people experiencing homelessness was in part due to their own efforts to create a booming economy in an environment that did not have enough housing for everyone attracted to the city for work (Calgary Drop-In 2007; personal interviews). On the one hand, this is naive, as homelessness is much more complicated than that. Yet on the other, it is also insightful and opens the door to a way of understanding homelessness much more broadly and as simply related to poverty and the unaffordability of housing. This "type" of homelessness has not appeared in any other Alberta plan since 2009.

The problem of homelessness was further conceptualized, repeatedly and in great detail in the plan, as costly. The provincial approach consistently noted that ending homelessness was "socially the right thing to do" but also insisted that "ending homelessness also makes economic sense for Alberta taxpayers" (Alberta Secretariat for Action On Homelessness 2008, 8). To elaborate on the cost savings, the plan

noted that the Government of Alberta was incurring direct and in-
direct costs related to homelessness, claiming that a person experiencing chronic homelessness cost taxpayers over $114,000 a year and
that 3,000 people in the province were experiencing chronic homelessness.[2] By contrast, the cost of providing housing and services to
a person experiencing chronic homelessness was around $34,000 per
year. Other forms of homelessness were less costly to "manage" as
well as less costly to resolve, resulting in less significant cost savings,
but savings nonetheless; an "employable" person was estimated to
cost the system $21,600 per year while homeless, but the cost of pro-
viding housing and services would be $6,000 per year. In insisting
that homelessness is an expensive problem and by going into such
great detail about the costs associated with managing versus ending
homelessness, government officials revealed that their understanding
was narrow and that efforts would be focused on people experiencing
chronic homelessness and thus assumed, by the province's own calculations, to be most costly.

The Alberta plan also included a definition of what it means to *end*
homelessness: "Even though there may still be emergency shelter available for those who become homeless, those who become homeless will
be re-housed into permanent homes within 21 days" (Alberta Secretariat for Action On Homelessness 2008, 14). If achieved, this would
mean the eventual closing of a significant number of homeless shelters in the province. This was an incredibly audacious goal given what
studies have shown about the average length of chronic homelessness
(710 days in Ontario [Aubry et al. 2013], 471 in BC [Rabinovitch, Pauly,
and Zhao 2016]). The budget for Alberta's plan was $3.316 billion over
ten years (Alberta Secretariat for Action On Homelessness 2008, 11) but
promised that ending homelessness would *save* $7.1 billion by 2019.

Seeking to update and adapt its plan, and responding to a recommendation of the Homelessness Secretariat (which had created the
plan), in 2012 the province established an Interagency Council on
Homelessness. Inspired by similar American institutions, the council
was designed to bring different perspectives and stakeholders together
to develop holistic solutions to homelessness and to advise the province on how to implement its ten-year plan. One of the actors involved
described the council as "a very large cross-section of people. It has
shelter providers, housing first providers, community-based organizations, private-sector people, police commissions, housing management
bodies ... There is a lot of diversity, and it is both rich and challenging"
(personal interview 2014). This actor went on to note that the council included very senior members of the Alberta government, including five

deputy ministers (senior government officials are not usually included on similar American bodies, making the Alberta model comparatively more inclusive and collaborative [Doberstein and Reimer 2016]).

An immediate concern raised by the Interagency Council in March 2013 was youth homelessness. An actor involved on that council noted that certain groups had been overlooked in the original provincial plan: "We are constantly looking at how to make the plan successful. There were gaps, specialized populations that were not being served" (personal interview 2014). Following the council's recommendation, in 2015 the province developed and implemented a plan to prevent and reduce youth homelessness. This youth plan was directly coordinated with the broader plan to end homelessness and was seen as important to its success:

> The 10-year plan states that Albertans from specialized groups, including homeless youth, are dealing with particularly challenging issues, and require targeted responses to be rehoused. *Supporting Health and Successful Transitions to Adulthood: A Plan to Prevent and Reduce Youth Homelessness* aligns and is integral to work being led through the 10-year plan. The Youth Plan represents the next step in the 10-year plan and is a targeted response to a specialized population. (Government of Alberta 2015, 4)

A five-year review of the ten-year plan again identified "risks to the Plan's success," this time stressing the need to recommit to government-funded housing: "Development of new affordable housing for those experiencing homelessness has not kept pace with needs" (Alberta Interagency Council on Homelessness 2014). The following year's progress report identified "an approximate $1 billion shortfall in capital housing investments required to achieve the goals of Alberta's Homelessness Plan" (Alberta Interagency Council on Homelessness 2015, 17). The Interagency Council recommended that the Government of Alberta develop and implement a provincial housing strategy and prioritize housing supports.

Indeed, it was clear that the government *was* contributing to the 11,000 promised units of affordable housing, but they were not being targeted as promised. Interviews reveal that early on, the province succeeded in housing more than 9,000 previously unhoused people (personal interview 2014). Yet the number of homeless people remained high across the province. This is in part because the province fell far short of creating 8,000 new units *specifically for people experiencing homelessness*, as it originally committed to doing, meaning the affordable and supportive housing stock did not grow enough to permanently include all those experiencing homelessness. In 2009–10, for example,

2,899 units of housing were developed, but only 933 were for homeless people (Housing and Urban Affairs 2010); in 2010–11, 1,936 units of housing were developed, 581 for homeless people. In other words, about one-third of the new units developed in Alberta were for homeless people, as opposed to the promised two-thirds, meaning provincial contributions to supportive and deeply affordable housing stock were nowhere near what they needed to be in order to fulfil the promise to end homelessness.

While these risks to the plan's success were being identified, the political winds in Alberta were changing, leading to the historic election of the NDP in 2015, led by Rachel Notley, after more than four decades of governance by the Progressive Conservatives. Under the NDP, the plan to end homelessness fell off the provincial government's radar; it was mentioned specifically in the PCs' 2009–12 fiscal plan (see Alberta Finance 2009, 35), yet it was not mentioned at all in the 2013–16 fiscal plan, nor was it in the NDP's 2017–20 plan. Perhaps this was partly because the plan, by every indication, was not headed toward success. Indeed, the ten-year plan did not achieve its promised result of ending homelessness: the 2018 coordinated homeless count identified 5,735 people experiencing homelessness in the province (Turner Strategies 2018).[3] The NDP government did not engage directly with the ten-year plan to end homelessness; however, it did recognize the increased need for housing and responded to an important recommendation from the Interagency Council by introducing a Provincial Affordable Housing Strategy in 2017. In that strategy, the province promised to invest $1.2 billion over five years in housing with the goal of creating 4,100 new and regenerated housing units by 2021 (2,100 new units and repairs to 2,000 existing affordable housing units) (Alberta Seniors and Housing 2017). Though the plan noted that it sought to help people "graduate" from Housing First programs into more independent forms of housing, it did not specifically identify ways of reducing or ending homelessness, or even the need for supportive housing for people experiencing homelessness. Rather, it focused on increasing the availability of affordable and government-supported housing and making that housing more inclusive and mixed.

After four years of NDP governance, the political pendulum swung back to the right. After winning the provincial election in 2019, Jason Kenney's right-wing United Conservative Party cut funding to emergency homeless shelters in the province and announced a review of affordable housing (CBC News 2019a). Tellingly, the review sought to identify ways to minimize the government's involvement and specifically to make it more efficient and more reliant on the private sector:

"[The review panel's] work was guided by 3 questions: 1) How can we get more value for government spending on housing? 2) How can government address housing needs through the private sector? 3) What are the reasons people need subsidized housing and what role should government play?" (Government of Alberta 2020). The second question was a direct nod to ideas aligned with conservative ideology regarding the responsibility to produce social protection. Notably, according to provincial officials, the lead actor in social protection as it related to housing ought to be the private sector, with the province limiting itself to a support role.

Calgary Homelessness History

The local government in Calgary is not very involved in homelessness governance; indeed, of all municipal governments studied here, Calgary is the least involved by far. Calgary was the first city in the country to conduct a regular homeless count, beginning in the 1990s, but even that minimal role was transferred to the CHF in the mid-2000s. The city was an early supporter of the CHF's ten-year plan to end homelessness and helped build an influential coalition of local actors to implement it and get the province on board. But this role was a supporting one, and even a former mayor of the city has said repeatedly that efforts to fight homelessness must be led by the business community. Under former Mayor Naheed Nenshi, the City of Calgary increased its involvement in poverty reduction, and though the city remains minimally involved in homelessness, Nenshi later became a powerful advocate for efforts to end homelessness as a part of broader COVID recovery efforts.

The city's limited involvement in homelessness has been in part for institutional reasons, but actors in Calgary tend to overstate those reasons. It is true that the city has no formal jurisdiction for housing and that its housing-related powers are weak, but the same can be said for Montreal, which has recently increased its involvement in homelessness despite these institutional constraints. As I will explain, ideas regarding the responsibility to produce social protection have led the municipal government in Calgary to stand back in the fight against homelessness and instead support and advocate for other actors, first the province and then the CHF.

The city's involvement in homelessness governance has been minimal. Even so, it is interesting that Calgary was the first big city in the country, by well over a decade, to regularly conduct homeless counts. Beginning in 1992, it began doing so every two years; this continued until 2008, when the responsibility was transferred to the CHF. The counts run by the city were designed to measure visible homelessness only, though the methodology for who that included would expand slowly and then suddenly in 2004. To help guide the counts, the city adopted a housing-based definition of homelessness: "Homeless persons are considered to be those who do not have a permanent residence to which they can return whenever they so choose" (Community and Neighbourhood Services, Policy and Planning Division 2006, 1). This strict emphasis on permanent residence, with no mention of adequate or affordable housing, meant that people living in overcrowded or unsafe environments were not necessarily considered homeless. This was a narrow understanding of homelessness, though the inclusion of choice ("whenever they so choose") opens up the definition to a broader interpretation; people living in unsafe environments to which they cannot always return, for example, may be considered homeless.

In 1992, the homeless count included a survey of about twenty services providing emergency shelter to people experiencing homelessness. The survey included questions regarding shelter occupancy rates, as well as an observational count of people sleeping outside; it identified 447 people experiencing homelessness, five of whom were identified as sleeping outside (Policy and Planning Social Research Unit 2004). Through the 1990s, the counts gradually collected more information about people experiencing homelessness, including "observational" information regarding age, sex, and "racial features." The subjective nature of the data collection (surveyors were asked for their observations, as opposed to asking people how they identified) renders these results highly questionable. The counts between 1992 and 2002 revealed a steady increase in the number of people experiencing homelessness, reaching 1,737 in 2002, including 117 people on the streets.

Significant changes were made to the city's methodology in 2004, including the inclusion of an additional thirty-one services (which already existed in the city but had not been included in past counts) and an expanded street survey. This was in response to a community plan on homelessness, *The Calgary Community Plan* (reviewed below), which "resulted in the inclusion of many facilities and services that were not surveyed in previous counts" (Policy and Planning Social Research Unit 2004, iii). This had significant implications for the 2004 results and how they would be compared with past and future results. A perceived dramatic rise in the number of homeless people in Calgary would eventually be deployed to create a frightening, but exaggerated, scenario of a rapidly growing homeless population. Homelessness was growing rapidly during this period, to be sure, but putting the numbers in their proper context reveals that the growth, particularly after 2004, was overstated. Indeed, there were reasons to believe that the trend was reversing:

> In total, 2,597 homeless persons were enumerated [in 2004] ... This represents an overall growth rate of 49% from 2002. *However, had the number of facilities and service agencies surveyed in 2004 not been increased (by 138%)* ... *the growth in homelessness over 2002 would have been only 23% –* a substantial drop from the 2002 increase of 43% and a reversal of the "over 30% growth rate" trend seen in the preceding four counts" (Policy and Planning Social Research Unit 2004, iii; emphasis added)

The report went on to note that this was a cause for *optimism*, given the reversal of past trends, but that the good news risked being overshadowed by the stark increase in the final number.

In 2001, the province consolidated the provincial and municipal housing societies and transferred the responsibility for administering housing to municipalities (though the province kept the responsibility for funding housing, making this transfer not as disastrous as the Ontario government's decision to transfer administration *and* funding responsibility; see chapter 6). To bring coherence to its housing interventions, the City of Calgary adopted a Corporate Affordable Housing Strategy in 2002, which identified a continuum of housing ranging from emergency shelters to homeownership and specified the city's role in producing social protection across that continuum. Informed by the results of city-run homeless counts, which showed growing numbers of people experiencing homelessness, the Corporate Affordable Housing Strategy proposed that Calgary develop a homelessness strategy with the objective of clarifying the respective roles of the city, the Calgary Homeless Foundation, and the province (City of Calgary 2002). This was in part a response to a challenge faced by the city: the province was refusing to cover the costs associated with emergency shelters. The municipal government was left to provide emergency assistance to growing numbers of people needing emergency housing, an increasingly complex and expensive endeavour. To the extent that the city was involved in homelessness governance at this point, it was minimally and begrudgingly; the Homelessness Strategy was designed specifically to further limit the city's involvement by pressuring the province to step up and fund. Ideas regarding the responsibility to produce social protection led city officials to seek to limit their role in homelessness; city officials now made clear that they viewed the province, not municipal government, as primarily responsible for producing social protection for those experiencing homelessness (including the provision of emergency shelters).

To develop the Homelessness Strategy, municipal officials first held a "deliberative dialogue" with people living in Calgary to determine how they understood homelessness and to ask for their perspectives on what the municipal role in homelessness should be. Tellingly, the title of the dialogue was "Who should pay to shelter the homeless?," an indication of how core ideas regarding the responsibility to produce social protection were in guiding city actions. The conclusion of these deliberations was that the city had a responsibility to meet the emergency needs of those experiencing homelessness *when the province would not do its share*. Participants expressed scepticism that the province would do what was needed, however, and insisted that the city must be prepared to fill the gap:

> Not only does the province have the constitutional mandate to see that the most basic needs of Albertans are met, but it also has responsibility for many areas that affect homelessness ... However, citizens are not confident that the Province will fulfil its role ... There must be a City budget allocation for homeless shelter costs *when the Province's allocations are insufficient*. If this means increased taxes, the increase should be specified as necessary to fund care of the homeless *because of the Province's insufficient allocations*. (Hargroup Research and Consulting 2004; emphasis added)

Though this was from the perspective of people living in Calgary, it is interesting to note their insistence that homelessness was not the city's responsibility and that the city should step in only when absolutely necessary. What's more, this suggested that when the city was forced to act (and spend), it should be prepared to assign blame to the province.

In addition to the deliberative dialogue, the city also consulted with key stakeholders, again asking who was responsible for paying the costs associated with emergency shelters. Immediately apparent was how few stakeholders were engaged during this consultation: when municipal homelessness plans and strategies were being formulated in Vancouver and Montreal, even during the early 2000s when homelessness was only just emerging as an important issue, hundreds of people and stakeholders were consulted. In Calgary, only three stakeholders participated – so few that they can be listed here by name: the CHF, the Salvation Army (an emergency shelter), and the Mustard Seed (an emergency shelter). The purpose of the engagement was to resolve the question of who should pay. In response, CHF CEO Terry Roberts clearly pointed to the province: "We are glad to see that it is the intention of the City to remain a key participant, even though the primary responsibilities lie with other orders of government" (Roberts 2004).

John Rook, writing on behalf of the Salvation Army, pushed for a centralized but collaborative approach: "Imagine what would happen if all funds received federally, provincially, and locally were the autonomous responsibility of one body. Then prevention, care and cure could all be part of a single, integrated plan which would also result in considerable cost savings throughout the entire system" (Rook 2004). Rook was describing the model that would eventually take hold in Calgary, with the CHF centrally controlling funding. Rook would become the CHF president a few years after writing this letter.

Floyd Perras, operating officer with the Mustard Seed, wrote a strongly worded letter in which he expressed some disagreement regarding the responsibility to produce social protection, accusing the city of not doing nearly enough: "There is much talk that homelessness is a provincial responsibility. Well homelessness is all our responsibility" (Perras 2004). He continued to push the city to increase its involvement, or at least to be more proactive and then request reimbursement from senior governments – an indication that he agreed that senior governments should ultimately be responsible:

> The buck is just continuing to get passed off or blamed on another department or level of government. Who has the courage to say the buck stops here and we will take [sic] of our people. I believe the City of Calgary should take action and incur costs and if they feel it is provincial or federal responsibility send them a bill and if they do not pay take them to court. How important is it this winter to ensure everyone has a warm place to sleep. (Perras 2004)

In 2004, the city tabled its Homelessness Strategy, which was shaped by these ideas about the responsibility to produce social protection. Clearly, the city was seeking to limit its involvement in homelessness: "This Homelessness Strategy is an important clarification because *care of the homeless falls clearly within the mandate of the Province of Alberta* (Canadian Constitution 92:7) but is a very local issue, and one which the municipality often feels pressure to address" (Community Services 2004; emphasis added). It stressed that the city should continue to advocate for the province to invest, but if the province would not, "contributions of City resources should be publicized as the City covering Province's cost" (Calgary Neighbourhoods 2004). Incredibly, the city's involvement in homelessness governance during this time was limited to strategizing ways to limit its involvement and push the province to act. And though the city's involvement in the homeless counts was significant, even reports of the counts noted that providing homelessness services was not a responsibility of the municipal government, illustrating how deeply held this idea regarding the responsibility to produce social protection was at the time, and how that responsibility was believed to lie with the province: "Municipalities are not mandated to provide for the basic needs of residents such as food, shelter, health care, or education, which are provincial responsibilities" (City of Calgary 2008).

City officials accepted, albeit reluctantly and only when absolutely necessary, a role in funding some services for those experiencing homelessness. However, by 2008 the CHF was gaining strength and in the process of creating a ten-year plan to end homelessness. In 2008, the city transferred the responsibility to conduct the homeless counts to the CHF. The CHF has been organizing the counts ever since, and the city's involvement has remained minimal. A Calgary city official said that this transfer from the city to the CHF was in keeping with the city's role in social issues: "The purpose of [the community and neighbourhood services that conducted the early homeless counts] unit was really to identify emerging issues, do the research, bring it to light. And then, in an ideal world you can transfer it to the community to own and to move forward. You might say that this is an example of how this has worked really well" (personal interview 2014). We again see the idea here that the city should not lead the fight against homelessness. But there was a more significant shift in its understanding of the responsibility to produce social protection. Until the mid-aughts, the city viewed the province as primarily responsible; that changed in 2008, when city officials came to see the CHF as the lead actor. This change happened, as I will note below, as the CHF was growing in influence and began to develop and implement a ten-year plan to end homelessness.

City officials were strong supporters of the ten-year plan and contributed to its development. David Bronconnier, who was mayor of Calgary while the ten-year plan was being developed, has stated repeatedly that fighting homelessness is not and should not be the responsibility of the city of Calgary: "It couldn't be a City of Calgary solution; it had to be a community-based solution" (qtd in S. Scott 2012, 55). A senior city official confirmed this in an interview: "I said 'Look, I was born and raised in this city. This will not be successful if it is the mayor standing up and saying 'I am going to run it.' It needs to be seen as a community-driven initiative. It needs to be owned by the community" (personal interview 2014). To specify what they meant by "community," they added: "It needs a private sector business leader to lead."

Mayor Bronconnier's support of the plan was important to its evolution, for it signalled that it was a serious plan with support of people across society. But even city councillors who were interested in homelessness contended that other actors were better positioned to respond to the needs of the homeless population. Responding to a question about why the municipality was not involved in homelessness governance, a Calgary city councillor first insisted, in keeping with a long line of city officials before them, that homelessness was not a matter of local jurisdiction: "Officially, the city doesn't really do anything with homelessness. It is not the city's role, not the municipal government's role to deal with homelessness. It is fully provincial or federal sphere. The city doesn't officially play in the homeless world" (personal interview 2014).

When pushed to consider that homelessness could be seen as the responsibility of a number of actors and does not fall neatly into any single jurisdiction, this councillor acquiesced:

> There are a lot of things that the city does that are not in its jurisdiction, but it steps in and does it out of necessity. Hell, we were just talking about that this morning in Council. We haven't done it [with respect to homelessness] because we actually have some active and strong organizations – the CHF, the Drop-In Centre, the Mustard Seed – that are working reasonably well. So we support them as opposed to stepping in and doing the job ourselves. (personal interview 2014)

Many highly placed actors, even those deeply interested in and sympathetic to the issue of homelessness, limit their involvement because they understand that the CHF has assumed leadership of the issue and is better positioned to produce social protection.

To be clear, the City of Calgary's institutional powers *are* limited. The city obtained density bonusing powers in 2013, but that has not led to much affordable housing, in part because rental and condominium developments in Calgary have been slower to roll out than in Vancouver and Toronto. Former Mayor Nenshi tried to use the power of persuasion to convince developers to contribute to affordable housing in the city, but with little success (Mason 2014). Cities in Alberta were given power over inclusionary zoning in 2017 through amendments to the Municipal Government Act, which will allow Calgary to apply leverage to current and future developments so as to generate affordable housing. While these powers could be used in a meaningful way in the future, especially if private-sector development expands, they were not available to the city when the CHF was gaining power. And in any event, these powers are weaker in Calgary than they are in Vancouver and Toronto. With respect to density bonusing, the city's ability to forge agreements is limited to certain neighbourhoods, and developers are given the choice of which public amenity they will give. As affordable housing is expensive, public amenities tend to be public art (Barrett 2014). Furthermore, Calgary developers may not even be interested in entering into DBAs or building new developments that require, through inclusionary zoning by-laws, something in return. These agreements eat into their profits, especially because developers can always build less dense developments at the edge of the city (where land is plentiful, unlike in Vancouver).

In other words, land in Calgary is not as limited as it is in Vancouver and Toronto, so developments can and do sprawl. A senior official at the Calgary Housing Corporation put this very plainly in an interview. Walking over to their corner-office window, they said to me:

> Look anywhere you want, look at the skyline. The only place that has high-rises is the core of the city. When you look everywhere else you won't see more than 2 or 3 stories... When you get ten feet out of Vancouver heading east, you run into Burnaby, then Coquitlam, and on and on. Ten feet outside of Calgary in any direction, you are in fields. So the land has a different pressure. [In Toronto and Vancouver] you can't go out, so you have to go up. In Calgary, we can keep going out, there is no one for hundreds of miles. (personal interview 2014)

The value of the density bonusing power in Calgary's context is thus limited by the ready availability of land on which to build new developments. In this context of increasing population, low vacancy rates, and rising housing prices, rental housing is becoming somewhat more common as developers have begun to see value in rental developments (Mason 2014), though not nearly enough are being built to meet the acute need for rental and affordable housing in Calgary.

When it comes to conceptions of local government, officials in Calgary have historically seen a limited role for the municipality beyond day-to-day, bread-and-butter issues. A former senior official with the city acknowledged that municipalities are sometimes left to deal with issues that no one else wants to, such as homelessness, and said that in a sense this is appropriate, as municipalities are well positioned to intervene: "In fairness to other orders of government, local governments generally speaking can respond much quicker than a provincial or federal government. Cities are the closest to the people" (personal interview 2014). They went on, however, to stress that in their opinion, the city's role tends to be day-to-day – "this building, the bus that just went by, that police officer, the water that made this cup of coffee" are responsibilities of City Hall, whereas what they called "larger issues" like employment are provincial ones.

None of this is meant to imply, however, that city officials are not bothered by homelessness or do not feel compelled to act. The resistance to funding emergency shelters is well-documented and goes back nearly two decades, but that does not mean the city is disengaged from all areas of social policy. Under Mayor Nenshi, the city adopted a Poverty Reduction Strategy in 2011. Working in partnership with Vibrant Communities Calgary and the United Way, Calgary has extended its involvement in poverty reduction to 2023. The plan *Enough for All 2.0* seeks to reduce poverty rates in Calgary by 30 per cent by 2023 and, in so doing, ensure that "all Calgarians live in a strong, supportive, and inclusive community; all Calgarians have sufficient income and assets to thrive; all Indigenous People are equal participants in Calgary's future" (Refresh Steering Committee 2019). With this project, the city is seeking to work inclusively and collaboratively to reduce poverty. In this instance, the city has remained involved in poverty reduction instead of fully passing it off to a foundation, as one city official noted tends to happen.

The city's Corporate Affordable Housing Strategy (2016–25) is another example of increasing involvement in the production of social protection. That strategy notes that other cities, such as Vancouver and Regina, are making significant contributions to affordable housing, and concludes that Calgary, too, must take more meaningful action (City of Calgary 2016). This interest in increasing its involvement in housing and poverty reduction is meaningful and speaks to a willingness on the part of city officials to engage in areas extending beyond their delineated powers. As made clear by Nenshi's efforts for a City Charter, which were successful in 2018, city officials are seeking more powers so as to play a larger and more meaningful role. In light of what we just learned about the city's reluctance to involve itself in homelessness, this may seem puzzling. Ideas regarding the responsibility to produce social protection explain why this is so. The city has been particularly reluctant to become involved in homelessness because other actors, first the province and then, more enduringly, the CHF, have been seen as primarily responsible for producing social protection for those experiencing homelessness. The CHF has a particularly important role in this history and in structuring the actions of municipal, provincial, and even federal governments, and it is to this final piece of the puzzle that we now turn.

Civil Society

The private sector is more involved in homelessness governance in Calgary than in the other cities in this study. The third sector was organized outside of the Calgary Homeless Foundation (CHF) in the 1990s, but the CHF slowly, then suddenly, took up more space in homelessness governance in the mid-aughts. There were two important changes in the involvement of local groups in homelessness governance: first, in the mid-2000s the CHF significantly increased its involvement in homelessness governance; then, in the mid-2010s, local actors, led by the CHF, began lobbying more aggressively for increased senior government, particularly federal involvement. Much of the following section, therefore, considers how the private sector channelled its involvement in homelessness governance through the CHF.

The private sector's strong involvement is in part a function of its substantial resources, notably its financial resources and business knowledge, as well as the informal, personal connections many business leaders have with senior government officials. Leveraging personal connections, private-sector actors have been able to convince local and provincial governments to support and invest in their efforts. They also brought money and expertise to the table. But the availability of resources does not on its own explain the significant involvement of the private sector; to fully understand this, we also have to consider ideas. Ideas regarding the nature of homelessness and the responsibility to produce social protection exerted a powerful influence on these changing governance dynamics. In the mid-2000s, there was broad (but not universal) agreement across scales of government and sectors that the responsibility for ending homelessness is not a sole or even primary responsibility of government and that there is and should be a leadership role for the private sector. Over time, actors have come to see a more substantial role for governments in the production of social protection for people experiencing homelessness, and the CHF has become more proactive in building relationships and interacting with local groups and senior governments. This change in the CHF's involvement and interactions with other actors was driven by key officials at the CHF as they broadened their understanding of homelessness. Though homelessness has always been understood as directly related to housing, and though there has consistently been a prioritization of people who are chronically homeless, there has also been an important shift in focus, from individual causes in the early aughts to more structural and systemic causes in the mid-2010s.

In the 1990s and early 2000s, before the CHF gained significant influence in homelessness governance, third-sector groups in Calgary were organized in the area of homelessness. Drawing on the expertise and local knowledge of service providers, in 1996, city councillor Bob Hawkesworth and PC MLA Bonnie Laing led an Ad Hoc Committee on Homelessness; as the name suggests, this was designed to be a temporary body created to address homelessness in the city. This committee was concerned about the increasing number of people experiencing homelessness and set out to understand the problem by conducting a number of influential studies, including *Homelessness in Calgary* and the Street Speaks survey (Doberstein 2016). The committee eventually changed its name to the Community Action Committee on Housing and Homelessness (CACHH) and would remain influential for more than ten years. It brought together not just service providers but also an impressive number and variety of sectors across the city, creating a space for organizations to learn from one another and to collaborate. With eight subsections representing different sectors and interests, it was, according to Doberstein, "the most elaborate community deliberative process of decision making on homelessness programs among the networks compared in Canada" (2016, 141).

Working with the CHF, the committee created a plan on homelessness, the *Calgary Community Plan 2004–2008*. The community plan used the UN's definition of homelessness, which distinguished between "absolute" and "relative" homelessness and noted that all homeless people have two things in common: "the absence of safe, affordable housing and the experience of poverty" (CHF 2004, 6). In linking the experience of homelessness with poverty, and in insisting that homelessness results not just from a lack of housing but from a lack of "safe" housing and poverty, this early community plan adopted a definition of homelessness that was comparatively broad in both the Canadian context and the Calgary context. While the plan noted the importance of prevention and of prioritizing services for people who experience homelessness despite no perceived "barriers" to housing (such as untreated mental illness or drug use), it proposed to focus the majority of its resources (62.5 per cent) on people with so-called multiple barriers who experience chronic homelessness.

The 2004–8 plan developed by the CACHH highlighted the need for more housing in Calgary, specifically the need for 1,000 transitional units and 2,000 non-market units. The insistence on the need for transitional housing is important, as it indicates that this plan followed the "treatment first" model. The plan itself defined transitional housing as "short or long-term accommodation while assistance is obtained to address problems such as unemployment, addictions, mental health issues, educational deficits, physical and cognitive disabilities, and domestic violence" (CHF 2004, 9). Before accessing permanent housing, people experiencing homelessness were in many cases required to pass through this transitional phase, which, in the treatment-first model, was implemented to ensure they were "housing ready." As I will explain below, only a few years later, the CHF would position itself in total opposition to this approach. Yet when the 2004 plan was first introduced, the CHF was tasked with implementing it.

Though the CHF began to increase its role in homelessness governance in 2006, it was originally set up by prominent Calgary businessman Art Smith in the 1990s when he was distraught to learn about increasing homelessness in the city (Scott 2012). Ideas regarding the nature of homelessness and the responsibility to produce social protection, strongly linked at this time, drove this involvement of private-sector leaders. According to the CHF documents recounting this history, Art Smith was a giant in the city, referred to as an "elder statesman" (CHF 2008) and earning the nickname "Mr Calgary." He cared for his city and the people who lived there. These accounts also suggest that he was driven by an understanding of homelessness that was partial and viewed it as largely resulting from a housing shortage. He also felt that the business community, having created so many jobs, was responsible in that it had attracted people to the city at a time when there was not enough housing. It followed, for Smith, that the private sector held some responsibility for finding solutions. John Currie, a former oil and gas executive, told Calgary-based journalist Susan Scott, "'[Smith] thought corporate Calgary could solve [homelessness]'" (quoted in Scott 2012, 16).

Smith's wife, Betty Ann, reinforced the perspective that Smith felt business had a responsibility for the sudden increase in homelessness in Calgary. Scott writes: "[Smith's wife] Betty Ann adds that Smith felt that corporate Calgary was largely responsible for the crisis by 'painting a golden picture of the West enticing people to come. And, they did. They piled their families into cars and came'" (16). Behind this were important assumptions about the nature of homelessness – that it was about a lack of housing supply. Furthermore, and this is a common theme in a number of interviews and documents regarding private-sector involvement more generally, there was a sense that Calgary was becoming a great city, and that homelessness, for economic and public perception reasons, stood to get in the way of that. There was a group of businesspeople who believed they were helping transform Calgary into a major city: "[Smith] was part of that group and if he saw anything that would detract from becoming that city, he would jump on it" (16).

Ideas regarding the nature of homelessness and the private sector's responsibility for addressing it led Smith to work with a small group of friends and allies to build the CHF. Things started off somewhat modestly, with a limited private-sector role. Smith took to lobbying friends in the oil and gas industry and the provincial government for contributions ranging from $1 million investments to office space to get the foundation up and running. In the 1990s and early 2000s, the CHF was involved in raising awareness about homelessness and starting a few small pilot projects, but homelessness did not become a significant issue on the public agenda until the mid-2000s, when the number of people experiencing homelessness began to grow quickly. Noticing this, a few key entrepreneurs, including oil and gas mogul Jim Gray and then-president of the CHF Terry Roberts, felt compelled to do more with the CHF to respond to the needs of those experiencing homelessness. Doing more, however, required a coalition, and they set about building one. Specifically, Roberts knew that the CHF needed a powerful coalition, including private sector buy-in, to respond more effectively to the needs of those experiencing homelessness; to that end, he invited Philip Mangano to hold a breakfast event in Calgary in 2006.[4] Mangano had been US President George W. Bush's point-person on homelessness in the United States, and this lent him authority in policy discussions and credibility with the business community in particular. The goal was to attract private-sector support for the mission to build the CHF into a more powerful agency capable of ending homelessness.

Mangano's visit to Calgary had the intended effect of galvanizing powerful groups to rally around the goal of ending homelessness. Key to his pitch was a different way of understanding homelessness. Central to this story are ideas; homelessness would be redefined in Calgary in 2006 and then promoted across the city (and the country) to facilitate the construction of powerful coalitions. At the breakfast event, Mangano made what is often called the "business case" for ending homelessness. This new way of understanding homelessness had two important dimensions: the fact that it is possible to end, not manage, homelessness, and that doing so would save money: "Mangano spoke passionately about the economic case for addressing chronic homelessness and about a new ten-year planning model that was showing some remarkable results south of the border" (Calgary Homeless Foundation 2008, 44). This involved orienting services to people experiencing chronic homelessness and adopting the Housing First approach, which would provide immediate access to permanent housing with supports. This approach was effective, Mangano insisted, and would result in cost savings.

Ending homelessness through a ten-year plan based on a Housing First approach stood in contrast to the way things were being done in Calgary at the time: recall that the 2004–8 plan developed by the CACHH identified the need for new transitional housing, identifying that form of housing as the first step out of homelessness before permanent housing. Following this redefinition of homelessness, and a belief in the promise of Housing First, actors involved with the CHF created a new committee comprised mainly of private-sector groups, which would draft a new plan motivated by these ideas. The CACHH was thus sidelined as a growing coalition, led by private-sector actors, committed to ending homelessness.

At the breakfast in Calgary, Mangano was well-received by the crowd, particularly by the business-sector attendees: "Excitement rippled through the business crowd; they looked like they 'had discovered the moon,' recalls a social worker. Roberts remembers thinking that the visit was at just the right moment to give the cause a boost and that Mangano had the credentials in the US to prove ten-year plans could work" (Scott 2012, 74–5). CHF reports identify this event as the spark for future action, not mentioning the previous community-based work that had been done since the 1990s to respond to homelessness (CHF 2008). Won over by Mangano's redefinition of homelessness and the idea of ending it (and saving money while doing so), Gray and Wayne Stewart, who had replaced Terry Roberts as CEO of the CHF, set about using the idea to build a coalition committed to that goal, specifically a plan to end homelessness in ten years.

This marked the beginning of a prolonged period of private-sector involvement, even leadership, in homelessness governance in Calgary. This involvement of the private sector in homelessness governance was in part due to the financial resources at its disposal. Drawing on the example of a pilot project the CHF wanted to run, but that was being held back by a lack of funding, an actor explained the significance of these resources for enabling action and involvement: "[A pilot project we wanted to run] was going to cost $400,000 and we didn't have the money. We had a sense that the money was coming, we had put in a grant application. Then one of the guys on the committee said, '$400,000 eh? If you don't get the money, I'll write you the cheque. Just start'" (personal interview 2014). Using the example of Mayor Nenshi's poverty reduction strategy, which is a partnership between the city and the United Way, as a contrast to the CHF, an actor explained: "[Mayor Nenshi] constructed the poverty reduction strategy and it had to represent all facets of community ... He has two co-chairs, they are pretty good but they are not CEOs ... Neither one of them could write a cheque for $400,000. So we are fumbling around, playing on the edges, running pilots, and I don't think we have helped a poor person yet" (personal interview, 2014). Saying that private-sector leadership was needed to make the CHF successful, this person concluded, "We know that in Calgary. We know that is how you get things done."

There was a further sense that business-sector expertise was needed in the fight against homelessness. This is not, to be clear, information about the homeless population or the most innovative solutions to homelessness; rather, it is about project management. Reflected in many interviews and directly in the early plans was the sense that the resources required to solve homelessness – health care, rental housing, social services – were already mostly available in Calgary but were not being properly used or accessed. The private sector just needed to put things together. Given their experience managing complex problems and the guidance they had received from Mangano, private-sector leaders were considered to have valuable expertise in this respect. And while the private sector does not have an institutionalized role in policy-making at the provincial or local level, their informal, personal connections with senior policy-makers, including premiers and mayors, have allowed them to in many ways drive the public agenda, as noted earlier in this chapter (Feng, Li, and Langford 2014; Miller and Smart 2012).

Yet these resources still needed to be oriented to the fight against homelessness. Powerfully directing these resources toward homelessness in the mid-aughts were ideas. Private-sector actors were motivated by the idea that social protection production should not be left to governments alone. A former president of the CHF was clear that the private sector's role in this process was key: "In my view, major changes to policy in something as revolutionary as ending homelessness, the impetus for those changes rarely comes from within government. It is the political influence of players in different communities. But typically, if you look at major changes in policy, there is an external stimulus" (personal interview 2014). Interestingly, this "external stimulus" and the private sector's role in policy development ultimately led to a re-engagement with governments, albeit in a limited way at first that did not involve major institutional or structural changes.

Another actor was more pointed: "The problem with government, and you can quote me on this, is it's bureaucratic. Process becomes more important than results" (personal interview, Stewart 2014). Curious about these views regarding the responsibility to produce social protection, I asked him: "Is government better suited to ending homelessness than a foundation?" He responded: "Really?! Who is going to say that?" I replied: "Government people." "They are full of shit!," he replied, adding that "we do more with less." A former president of the CHF had a slightly different view, explaining that the foundation was not giving the provincial government a reason not to act, but in fact was doing the opposite: "In Calgary, the CHF taking on a plan to end homelessness and the other seven cities were able to get the Province of Alberta to commit to ending homelessness specifically. So it's the opposite of letting the government off the hook, it is making them accountable for the things they should have been doing anyway" (personal interview 2014).

Indeed, the province and the municipal government were persuaded to support the ten-year plan and then the province was persuaded to adopt its own and to increase investments in supportive and affordable housing. So while the government has a role to play in producing social protection, it is interesting to note here that the private sector saw itself playing a leadership role in guiding government toward the right solutions. Yet even this is consistent with ideas regarding a limited role for government in the production of social protection: the province became involved but followed the advice of private-sector actors in what to do.

Though important, ideas regarding the limited role of government in the production of social protection do not explain the drastic increase in private-sector involvement in homelessness governance, which would turn the CHF into a much more powerful organization than it had originally been designed to be. A second idea, a particularly magnetic one – that ending homelessness is possible and will save money – led to the creation of a powerful local governance network committed specifically to ending homelessness. After the breakfast with Mangano where the business case for homelessness was made, Steve Snyder, the influential CEO of TransAlta, was asked to oversee the effort to develop a ten-year plan to end homelessness in Calgary. Snyder was recruited to lead the plan's development in part because of his position in the community and his extensive network; recall that it was Snyder who had sat down with Premier Stelmach and persuaded him to invest provincial money in housing and homelessness. At first, Snyder resisted, recalling to journalist Susan Scott that his initial response to being asked was "No, I don't know anything about [homelessness]. I'm an observer. I don't know the facts. I'm not qualified. I'm just a business guy." But when presented with the business case, and with the idea that homelessness can be ended, "I knew then they had me" (qtd in Scott 2012, 92).

Having been won over, Snyder set to work building the Calgary Committee to End Homelessness (CCEH), which was tasked with overseeing the development of a plan to end homelessness. Tim Richter, a former oil and gas lobbyist with TransAlta, was approached to lead the development of the ten-year plan. Richter accepted and has been one of the most powerful leaders in the field of homelessness ever since. These leaders were key to the development of a powerful coalition in Calgary, a city where private-sector leadership is needed to "get things done," as was explained in many interviews. This is consistent with past studies of urban governance in Calgary, which have found that influence is not evenly spread among private-sector actors; instead, there are a small number of people – around 300, according to the title of one book chapter on urban governance in Calgary – who exercise considerable influence (Feng, Li, and Langford 2014). While I did not hear mention of a specific number of influential people, several people I interviewed told me there is a small number of influential actors in Calgary and that if you want to get something done, you need one of them on board. A former CEO of the CHF told me: "Calgary has some very big, very wealthy, heavy hitters who try to run things. They only get one vote, but they have tons of influence. More than anywhere I have ever worked. And they want it their way. So you have got to get those guys on your side" (personal interview 2014). Steve Snyder, by all accounts, is one of those people who can get things done, so long as he can be won over. Roberts and Gray won him over with the idea of ending homelessness, and he set to work building a coalition, and influencing government, to implement that vision.

The idea of ending homelessness was used to build a larger coalition. Snyder and the oil and gas CEOs he recruited to the CCEH and the CHF undoubtedly felt a human concern for homelessness (personal interviews 2014). But over and over again in interviews, people identified the idea that homelessness could be ended and that money could be saved in the process as key to their decision to join the coalition to develop and implement the plan to end homelessness. One actor who had previously refused to align with the plan explained how they were ultimately won over to the effort:

> I was approached by two people from the CHF... They walked into my office and said: "We would like to invite you to join a committee to end homelessness in ten years." I said: "You are going to end it? I am used to people walking in the door and saying 'we have a problem with homelessness let's cut it back by 25 per cent or something like that'"... So I said "I'll join and do whatever I can." ... It costs you less money, you save money. There are people out there who have no faith, but they understand economics. The current situation costs $110,000 but our solution costs $45,000. They understand there's a big change there. There is a lot of savings here.

This same idea was used to convince others to join the coalition: "We just said 'Hey, this is a cost saving measure'" (personal interview 2014).

The idea of ending homelessness also attracted service providers, reflecting the power of a magnetic idea to attract a wide range of groups. Perhaps some were attracted to the idea of ending homelessness by its money-saving potential, but for others in the homeless-serving sector, the idea was attractive for its human rights and social justice orientation to homelessness. Coming from this second perspective was Alpha House, an important ally in the CHF's efforts and itself something of a black sheep in Calgary because of its commitment to harm reduction. It was the lowest-barrier shelter in a city where many churches and other faith-based services required sobriety and ran abstinence-based programs. Working with a population that was excluded elsewhere, often because of intoxication, service providers with Alpha House were quickly on board with the idea of ending homelessness through permanent, Housing First solutions. Kathy Christiansen, the Executive Director of Alpha House, told Scott: "I always thought it was weird that you shouldn't be housed, especially with addictions, that you had to earn the right through sobriety" (qtd in Scott 2012, 78). Permanent housing, rather than transitional housing or more shelter spaces, as a solution to homelessness was intuitive for the people at Alpha House, who were early supporters of the CHF as a result of their ideational agreement on the idea of ending homelessness through Housing First. Their support lent community credibility to the effort.

Yet these powerful, magnetic ideas also pushed some actors away from the CHF in the early days of the ten-year plan's development. Actors that did not join in the CHF efforts also referred to this magnetic idea – and their opposition to it. One actor who opposed the CHF's plan early on laughed when I asked whether it is possible to end homelessness: "Oh god no" (personal interview 2014). This actor went on to explain the role shelters play: "I don't think closing shelters is the issue, nor should it be. I think shelters play an important role in providing wraparound services to individuals. And I can only speak for our shelter, but I know that when there is a need, we will create a program to address the need" (personal interview 2014). Though this disagreement was profound, actors who disagreed with the CHF's approach were unable to effectively challenge the CHF because they failed to craft a counter-narrative powerful enough to win over and draw the support of influential private-sector actors in the city. In other words, they were unable to identify ideas that were powerful enough to build a coalition of their own and counter those advanced by the CCEH and the CHF. As a result, previously powerful actors, including community groups with significant influence and experience in the area of homelessness, such as the Drop-In Centre, were marginalized early on by the CHF and its governance network.[5]

Though the coalition that was built included third-sector groups, senior leadership of the CHF would become dominated by the private sector. This was following a recommendation from the CCEH (led by Snyder) (CHF 2008). A former CEO of the CHF said in an interview: "We said okay, we'll get input from [service providers and community groups], but not on the leadership team. So those people were on the subcommittees" (personal interview 2014). This is in contrast to the CACHH, which existed in the 1990s and directly involved service providers and put their expertise to use for developing solutions to homelessness. The decision to prioritize private-sector leadership on the board was criticized by some community groups, including the Executive Director of a large shelter, who felt that the CCEH and the CHF were ignoring their expertise during the development of the new plan:

> We have been in the business for almost fifty-three years ... Look at the homeless foundation, they have had a number of people leading the organization, CEOs, who wanted to bring in a business model. The board was more heavily weighted with people from the business community. They felt that we didn't know what we were doing. That it needed a business model to turn homelessness around. What they didn't realize is just how complex human behaviour is. (personal interview 2014)[6]

The development of the CHF plan was led by private-sector representatives. It involved community groups, to be sure, but it was heavily influenced by American plans to end homelessness, as confirmed in interviews and CHF documents: "We were importing a model from the US, hook, line, and sinker. Everything was off the shelf. We relied a lot on the [American] National Alliance to End Homelessness and Housing First stuff. We constructed our plan to end homelessness following the essentials of the American model and adapting it to Canada and to Calgary" (personal interview 2014; see also CHF 2008). With a powerful leadership committee, guidance from American cities, and support from enough service providers to run pilot projects and participate in the plan's implementation, the first version of the CHF's plan was introduced in 2008. It was bold in its language, promises, and targets: "Efforts to end the homelessness crisis have focused in recent years on increasing the number of beds, shelters, and services available to the homeless. These efforts have increased our capacity to manage homelessness. We believe a new approach is needed to end it" (CHF 2008, 6). Those approaches included a strong focus on Housing First, which showed (and continues to show) promise in helping people experiencing chronic homelessness to access and maintain housing.

Targets were audacious. They included "the elimination of family homelessness in two years, the retirement of 50 percent of Calgary's emergency shelter beds within five years, an 85 percent reduction in the chronic homeless population within five years with the complete elimination of chronic homelessness in seven years, and a reduction in the maximum average stay in emergency shelters to less than 7 days by the end of 2018" (CHF 2008, 3). This is similar to what had been promised in the provincial plan, evidence of cross-level and sector collaboration during this period, albeit to achieve an all but impossible target. The first principle of the plan was cast as follows: "Ending homelessness is a collective responsibility. This includes those experiencing homelessness who must take personal ownership and accountability in ending their homelessness" (CHF 2008, 9). There would also be heavy reliance on the private sector: "This is not a plan that expects government to shoulder the full burden" (CHF 2008, 2). As a principle, "the use of markets will be maximized by involving the private sector in the implementation of our 10 Year Plan" (CHF 2008, 9). The role of individuals and the private sector in the production of social protection was built right into the plan.

The plan called for major policy changes, but a close read reveals that those changes were not the systemic changes that advocates have long called for, such as increased social assistance incomes and, crucially, government investment in housing; rather, they involved tweaks around the edges of policies and systems. For example, in the ten-year plan there was no demand for government-built, or at least government-supported, housing. Rather, to limit the government's investment in housing and to maximize "the use of markets," the plan insisted that the members of its powerful leadership committee lobby governments for legislative changes to provide the city with density-bonusing and inclusionary-zoning powers. These changes would place the primary responsibility for building housing on private-sector developers. Furthermore, rather than reform systems often viewed as "creating" homelessness, such as the child welfare system and the justice system, the plan proposed to manage people's transitions out of these systems so they would have access to housing.

The plan used facts and figures to rally support around the goal of ending homelessness and the need to do so. The plan estimated that if nothing was done about the growing number of people experiencing homelessness in the city, 15,000 people would be experiencing homelessness in Calgary by 2016. This was based on past homeless counts, which reported a 30 per cent increase in the number of people experiencing homelessness every two years since the early 2000s. Homelessness was rising rapidly in Calgary, and it is clear that something needed to be done, but the suggestion that it would reach 15,000 people by 2016 was unfounded. Recall that changes to the city's methodology between 2002 and 2006 resulted in a broader definition of homelessness and the inclusion of services that had been excluded in previous counts, and this created the appearance of a large jump in the number of people experiencing homelessness. A 2004 homeless count reported that when the difference in methodology was factored in, the 30 per cent rise in homelessness appeared to be reversing in 2006. Furthermore, the 2008 count, conducted just as the plan to end homelessness was being implemented, identified 3,601 people experiencing homelessness, compared to 3,436 in 2006. So there were indications that even before the plan was implemented, growth in the number of people experiencing homelessness in Calgary had slowed. This is not to say that homelessness was not a problem, or even a crisis. It is, however, important to note that the calculations regarding cost savings that were so influential in driving private-sector involvement were likely exaggerated and that the tremendous growth seen in the early 2000s appeared to be slowing.

Ideas regarding the nature of homelessness were powerful during this period and drove the creation of a strong coalition of actors that worked to end it. Understandings of homelessness and of whose responsibility it is to produce social protection have evolved considerably in recent years, going far to explain important changes in multilevel governance dynamics in Calgary since 2008. The CHF's ten-year plan was rewritten in 2011 and again in 2015. This was not unanticipated; the 2008 plan had divided implementation into three stages and noted that changes would be made based on what had been learned. The first update was released in 2011, and noted that changes to the plan had been made based on the need for "added attention to the unique needs to vulnerable subpopulations, including youth, women, families and Aboriginal peoples" (CHF 2011, 2). Interviews confirmed that much had been learned about the homeless population between 2008 and 2011: "We had to make the changes because we learned so much more about the population ... We didn't have the right assumptions, but we were close" (personal interview 2014). The updated plan also tightened its focus on prevention while shifting more resources toward those in greatest need. The update was based on wide consultations, in the course of which the community was provided with broad opportunities to contribute, though Indigenous groups were only minimally involved (see below). The updated plan maintained the commitment to Housing First as well as to the audacious goal of retiring the majority (85 per cent) of the shelter beds in the city and reducing the maximum shelter stay to seven days by 2018.

The number of people experiencing homelessness had declined in Calgary, an important achievement. By 2015, however, it was clear that many of the CHF's original goals would be difficult to achieve, including the ultimate goal of ending homelessness (no matter how it was defined). Results of the 2014 homeless count concluded that there were 3,555 homeless people in Calgary on the night of 16 October (two years later, the number would remain virtually unchanged, at 3,430) (Turner

2015; Turner Strategies 2018). After an additional four years of experience working with service providers and the homeless population, in 2015 the plan was again rewritten and, this time, largely reframed. The new plan made clear that important assumptions had changed significantly regarding the nature of homelessness and the responsibility to produce social protection. Importantly, the plan adopted the Canadian Homelessness Research Network (CHRN) definition of homelessness, which identifies causes as individual-level but also systemic and structural. The 2015 plan insisted that approaches to homelessness must "meet those at risk or experiencing homelessness where they are at and offer them real choices when it comes to services and housing. There is no 'one size fits all' housing or support program: our approach has to be nimble and adaptive to the needs of unique individuals" (CHF 2015, 1).

Rather than identifying goals or milestones, as had been done in the two previous versions of the plan, the 2015 update instead noted several "conditions for success" (2015, 4) as well as "critical risks" (2015, 6). These were some of the biggest changes to the plan and made clear how drastically the understanding of homelessness and ideas about the responsibility to produce social protection against it had changed. Conditions for success now included substantially increased government funding for housing and homelessness services (rather than simply plans to lobby for inclusionary zoning powers announced in the 2008 plan), intra-governmental alignment, coordination across ministries and departments, and more significant systems reform. The significance of these ideational changes was evident with income supports, for example. Whereas the first version of the plan suggested changing regulations regarding income support eligibility, notably regarding additional income-earning exemptions and liquid asset retention, the 2015 plan now suggested increasing these incomes through more generous income supports, access to living-wage employment, and poverty reduction measures more broadly. Critical risks to the plan's success now included a growing and aging population, and again, the 2015 plan insisted that additional funding would be required to mitigate these risks.

Marking a significant evolution in understanding of the responsibility to produce social protection, the 2015 plan called upon several government partners to do more: "Unlike previous updates of the Plan, this is first and foremost a call to action to our system partners to take ownership of their accountabilities and to own this community effort. An effective and coordinated strategy for responding to homelessness will necessarily have to grapple with the myriad of social issues that accompany housing instability, including mental health, addictions, poverty, family violence, child intervention and justice system involvement." The plan continued:

"To 'turn off the tap' into homelessness, a coordinated effort among the service delivery agencies and government departments involved in these areas is critical to advance progress" (2015, 10). In previous versions of the plan, the CHF had positioned itself as leader and champion; where it called on government support, it was to fund the implementation of its plan and to make minor policy changes such as to allow inclusionary zoning. By 2015, the days when the CHF sought to limit government involvement and claimed that all the tools were already available were long gone. The CHF was now asking the government to shoulder a much more significant burden and greatly increase its involvement.

A 2018 Collective Impact Report reviewing the results of the 2008 plan makes these ideational evolutions even clearer and came out even more strongly for system reform than even the 2015 update: "The higher incidence of homelessness among those who exit the Children's Services system requires us to examine how that system prepares young people for transitions to adulthood ... The higher incidence of people experiencing mental illness in shelters compared to the general population would suggest a gap in the health care system related to this vulnerable population" (Turner, Balance, and Sinclair 2018, 34). Homelessness was no longer viewed as an individual level problem, but rather as a deeply structural and systemic one. This was a significant ideational change. Another important evolution in the nature of the problem of homelessness related to shelters. Across the country, homeless shelters are controversial and people disagree on what their role is and should be. The CHF had come out strongly in 2008 with its promise to close 85 per cent of emergency shelter beds. Looking back, CHF actors note that this was a mistake: "One of the most noteworthy key lessons over the past decade was the failure to recognize the essential role of emergency shelters in our homeless-serving system. We have learned increasingly how critical emergency shelters are in our system of care" (Turner, Ballance, and Sinclair 2018, 53). This acceptance that shelters are necessary and always will be marked an evolution in the understanding of homelessness and what it means to end homelessness, and an appreciation of the need for a strong and permanent safety net.

As these documents make clear, following the experience implementing the ten-year plan to end homelessness, which made significant contributions to the homeless-serving system but did not achieve its ultimate goal, the ideas of key CHF officials evolved. It is of course to be expected that people learn from experience. Yet this was more than tinkering with implementation or adding or expanding programs: there had been changes in the fundamental assumptions regarding the nature of homelessness and whose responsibility it is to produce social protection. Homelessness was now understood not as an individual issue or something related to economic growth in Calgary, but rather as a consequence of policy decisions and structural failures. It followed that solutions could not simply involve putting services together, for those services themselves were the problem; required instead were substantial reforms, government investments, and commitments.

NHI/HPS

The story of NHI/HPS implementation in Calgary has in many ways mirrored the evolution we saw regarding the role of the CHF in the production of social protection, especially in terms of the CHF's expanding definition of homelessness and its relationship with other actors. The CHF has been the Community Entity (CE) for federal NHI/HPS funds for both the designated community and the Indigenous community from the very beginning of the program. When the federal government announced NHI funding in 1999, including the requirements for a community advisory board (CAB), a community plan, and a community entity (CE) to administer the funds, existing actors in Calgary quickly snapped into place: the Calgary Action Committee on Housing and Homelessness (CACHH) would become the NHI/HPS CAB, and the CHF would be the CE, responsible for overseeing the funding. An Aboriginal Standing Committee on Housing and Homelessness (ASCHH), established in 1996 as a part of the Ad Hoc Committee on Homelessness's work, would become the CAB for the Indigenous community and the CHF would eventually become the CE for the Indigenous community. While the CACHH had a formal role developing a community plan, the CHF developed its own community plan in 2008, effectively diminishing the influence of the CACHH within the NHI/HPS process.

The fact that the CHF – with its own board – was also the CE for the designated and Indigenous communities and needed to follow the advice of separate CABs (per federal funding requirements) made for a difficult institutional arrangement:

> The intention of the CABs makes a lot of sense when you may have a municipality governing the CE's function. Having an independent community advisory group to advise into that space makes a lot of sense. When you're a non-profit, we already have a board of directors which should and do fulfil the need of the community advisory group. There is some tension around that – our board of directors are all independent community members, and I've got this other advisory body. Who am I supposed to listen to? (personal interview 2018)

Interesting here is that the CHF's board is primarily private-sector representatives, whereas the CAB is comprised of service providers and community groups. These groups (the CHF board and the CAB membership) are actually comprised of different people representing very different sectors; yet in Calgary, "community" and "private sector" are often conflated, hence this actor's insistence that the CHF board can perform the role assigned to CABs.

The CACHH disbanded in 2014 and is no longer the designated community's CAB. An actor with the CHF explained that "[the CACHH] wasn't really advancing the agenda anymore, it was too fragmented and disorganized. There were too many competing agendas" (personal interview 2018). This actor stressed that the CHF had also changed considerably in terms of its relationship with community groups throughout Calgary since the early aughts, and the CACHH as the voice of the community was less needed in light of this. As noted earlier, ideas regarding the nature of homelessness have changed considerably since the early aughts, with key officials at the CHF shifting from an individualized understanding to a more structural one. This had led to collaborative relationships with other groups in the city: "There's been a huge move to acknowledge that the CHF is one player of many who are influencing and/or partnered in this whole movement to end homelessness. We control some of the funding, but we control nowhere near all of it" (personal interview 2018). This actor, who is involved with HPS operations at the CHF, continued: "We aren't *the* funder. We are one funder, and an influential one. But there have been a number of conversations around really positioning the CHF in a new light. That has changed [since 2008] and I think you'd find a very different relationship here within the community." When asked who else is responsible, they pointed to various government ministries at the provincial and federal levels, stressing that ending homelessness in Calgary is not something that a single agency or foundation can do. They later said this change came about from what they called a "big learning" from ten years' experience implementing the CHF plan to end homelessness: "That holy shit, this requires everybody on the wheel!" (personal interview 2018). In light of this, the CHF now sees itself as more responsive to community needs, as evident in its evolving relationship with the city's two CABs.

This evolving relationship and understanding of the need for "everybody on the wheel" is visible in the CHF's new relationship with the network representing Indigenous-led services in the city, ASCHH. In the early to mid-aughts, the relationship between the CHF and the Indigenous CAB was fraught. A member who had served for a long time on the Indigenous council repeatedly referred to the early relationship between the Indigenous CAB and the CHF as "a dictatorship" (personal interview 2018). When I asked whether input from the Indigenous community had been sought in the development of the CHF's original ten-year plan on homelessness in 2008, this person laughed, and then explained that the lack of consultation was the reason why the ASCHH had written its own plan. Though some Indigenous CABs have written plans for federal funding (including in Vancouver), Calgary was the only city in Canada with a separate ten-year plan to end Indigenous homelessness during this time.

Calgary's Indigenous plan to end homelessness was, and remains, influential across the country. It includes a definition of Indigenous homelessness that centres Indigenous culture: "The Definition of Aboriginal Homelessness: Self-identifying Aboriginal persons (including First Nations, Métis, and Inuit) of any age, situated as a single person or within a family who is lacking permanent nighttime residence with appropriate cultural recognition supports. This includes individuals 'precariously housed' within institutions settings such as jails, prisons, and unstable, unsafe, and/or inappropriate child intervention settings" (ASCHH 2012, 5). This definition is much broader than the definition being used by the CHF at the time, not only in its insistence on cultural supports, but also in its inclusion of people who are precariously housed. It remains influential, though more recently it has been adapted to include elements of Thistle's definition (Atlohsa Family Healing Services 2020).

An actor involved with the Aboriginal Standing Committee noted that they wrote their own plan because the CHF was not responsive to feedback they had offered while the original CHF plan and the 2011 update were being written:

> That's why we did our own plan, to be honest … We gave a bunch of feedback and then we went to take the feedback to [the CHF] and they go "Oh, no. We've got it written. It's already done. It's being published." They didn't take any of our feedback. There was a page and a half that was developed, but again it was from a colonial view, it wasn't from the committee's perspective or an Indigenous perspective. (personal interview 2018)

After this, the ASCHH decided to do their own plan. An actor recalled that once it was complete, the CHF would not recognize it for years:

> [The CHF] didn't want us to publish it. They didn't want us to put it out. They said "publish it as a report, it's not a plan." …At the time, they said

"Well, we can't fulfil any of these recommendations," and we said, "We never asked you to fulfil the recommendations, we didn't ask you to be a part of this plan" (personal interview 2018).

Not until 2015, after a change in leadership at the CHF, was the ASCHH plan recognized by the powerful CHF, at which point the relationship between the CHF and the ASCHH began to improve. A member of the Indigenous CAB explained: "We've started to build an extremely positive relationship [with the CHF], because that was where the other problem was. It was a dictatorship for a number of years" (personal interview 2018).

ASCHH members have learned from the past and are now more assertive when it comes to their role in homelessness governance in Calgary and with the CHF. This includes not letting the CHF take anything for granted. For example, an actor with the Aboriginal Standing Committee explained that they had no choice in the CHF becoming their CE and thus responsible for distributing federal funding for the NHI/HPS: "[The CHF] was always the Community Entity. It wasn't defined by us, for example. It was just dictated to us that this is your CE now, by the government" (personal interview 2018). When an opportunity arose for the Indigenous Standing Committee to vote on the continuation of this arrangement (CABs can vote on the continuation of their relationship with their CE one year prior to funding renewal), they were not provided with enough notice to make a change: "Service Canada didn't alert us [to the vote]. We didn't know about it, nobody informed us about it. So when it came down to it, we were late in making our vote" (personal interview 2018).

Explaining that they weren't going to let that happen again, this person continued:

So this time, I've already informed the [CHF] and Service Canada, I said "it's likely we are not gonna change, because the relationship is there and the processes are there. But, at the same time, we wouldn't be doing due diligence if we didn't explore all our options." And so we are gonna have conversations with the city, the United way, we've had a conversation with the CHF. What we're doing is just gathering information so an informed decision can be made. Versus it being one choice, one option.

This was acknowledged by non-Indigenous officials at the CHF as well: "We will be seeing our Indigenous CAB and leadership in the Indigenous community saying, 'Hey, we should be self-governing this. Why would we have a non-Indigenous agency like the CHF continue to be the CE?' Which would ... yeah ... There's a very good argument to be made there, but also a complex political and operational and deliverable space to be navigated and negotiated" (personal interview 2018).

The importance of Indigenous voices being included throughout the policy-making process and provided with the necessary resources to implement solutions on their own was made clear by an actor involved with the Indigenous Steering Committee. This person said there is what they believe to be a sincere commitment to implementing Truth and Reconciliation Calls to Action among community groups, including those that are not Indigenous-led. While this was viewed positively, they expressed some concern as well, worrying that this rush to incorporate Indigenous culture into non–Indigenous-run services might be damaging: 'It's almost out of desperation, it's like people want this checkbox toolkit around reconciliation" (personal interview 2018). They gave an example of why autonomous and adequately resourced Indigenous-led service providers is so important. Using the example of a sweat lodge, they noted that for people who are using drugs or have not been sober for long, it can be dangerous from a spiritual and physical perspective for sweat lodges to be led by a non-Indigenous person, insisting that

> there are healers that are specific to dealing with people that are under the influence of alcohol and drugs, for example. So, we'd have somebody who really had that experience, who's really capable of taking someone who's still using, who can't just stop, and bringing them into the sweat lodge to heal them. But it's a different perspective than having a general sweat lodge and allowing people who have not had the sufficient clean time. Because there's a safety issue in that, physically. And there's a spiritual safety issue there as well. (personal interview 2018)

This actor also discussed the relationship between the Indigenous Standing Committee and the federal government: though the CHF is the CE, there is a Calgary-based Service Canada representative to liaise between the federal government and Indigenous CAB members. They noted that on a high level, the relationship with the federal government is strained, but emphasized that on the ground, relationships were better:

> Our representative of Service Canada, she's been on the ground with me [for years], and we work together. She comes to us all the time to say, "What do you guys think? Really? What's your feedback to us on how this is working?" And she's a voice, she's taking it back and saying this is how we see it, this is how our community is seeing it ... Overall, I think that in Calgary we feel very heard. (personal interview 2018)

Conclusion

Compared to the other cities studied here, Calgary has grown rapidly in terms of both physical size and population, exploding from 768,082 in 1996 to 1,239,220 in 2016 (Statistics Canada 2001, 2016).[7] Throughout those years, the province was largely disengaged from the area of affordable housing. Between 2001 and 2009, the city actually *lost* 7,500 units of rental housing, mostly through conversions to condominiums (CMHC 2010). As the city's population began to rise, so did rents and housing prices, resulting in a housing crunch. This housing and market dynamics are important context, but government actions and inactions also mattered, profoundly so, in that the failure to keep up with the need for affordable housing resulted from federal and provincial decisions to stop investing in it.

The governance of homelessness in Calgary is centralized in the Calgary Homeless Foundation. That foundation, which was founded in the 1990s and expanded its influence in the mid-aughts, was created primarily by private-sector elites. It has been the lead agency in homelessness governance in Calgary, though its role has changed considerably since 2008. The CHF has since retreated from its leadership role; it has prioritized collaborations and relationships since the mid-2010s and, crucially, has become an important advocate for increased government funding and system reform. Ideas regarding the nature of homelessness and the responsibility to produce social protection have driven these changes.

For much of the postwar period, the province was minimally involved in producing social protection for those in housing need, making only modest contributions to affordable housing and targeting that housing at seniors. After the federal government stopped investing in housing in the 1990s, the province followed suit, even halting projects that had already been promised. As a result, the stock of affordable housing decreased across the province, particularly in Calgary. After a change in leadership of the governing Progressive Conservative party and in response to local activism, led powerfully by the CHF in the mid-2000s, in 2008 the province introduced a ten-year plan to end homelessness, the first province to do so (by about a decade). Its involvement included investments in housing; however, an Affordable Housing Strategy would not be introduced until 2017, under an NDP government.

Institutions and resources alone do not explain the evolution in provincial involvement. Even with federal dollars on the table in the early 2000s, a substantial surplus (following Klein's "slaying" of the deficit), and jurisdictional authority, the province remained uninvolved in housing and homelessness governance. It took efforts by local actors, who redefined homelessness as a costly problem that could be ended, to push the province to become involved. This shift in involvement was due not to a change in resources, but rather to changing ideas; as this chapter has made clear, this change in ideas was facilitated by Calgary-based policy entrepreneurs (inspired by Mangano) who redefined homelessness and used that new definition to attract provincial officials to their coalition. We also see the importance of personal connections in Alberta, perhaps more so than anywhere else. Private-sector actors did not have an institutionalized role in policy-making in the early to mid-2000s when actors were organizing around homelessness; rather, private-sector individuals drew on personal connections with key government officials to push government involvement and investment, a dynamic also observed in BC. In this sense, the story of the governance of homelessness confirms that in Alberta, private-sector actors are at times more influential than public ones (Feng, Li, and Langford 2014).

The City of Calgary is minimally involved in the governance of homelessness; the city conducted homeless counts in the 1990s but transferred this responsibility to the CHF in 2008. This minimal involvement was for a number of reasons. Historically, Calgary has had few institutional powers (such as density bonusing and inclusionary zoning) to contribute to the fight against homelessness, which means there are few tools to use in the governance of homelessness. In recent years, that has changed somewhat: the municipality has been granted inclusionary zoning powers, which may increase its ability to contribute to the affordable housing stock (if it is willing to use that power). But like density bonusing, inclusionary zoning powers in Calgary are weak given the city's geographic landscape, in that there is always more land to develop on the edge of the city. The municipal government is thus under institutional and resource constraints, but ideas regarding the responsibility to produce social protection have also structured its involvement. Since the early 2000s, city officials have sought to limit their involvement in homelessness governance, seeking greater provincial leadership and expressing a grudging willingness to become involved only when the province would not. In 2007–8, as the CHF became increasingly powerful, the city continued to limit its involvement and instead supported and advocated for the leadership of the CHF.

The CHF has had considerable power and influence since 2008, both in Calgary and nationally. It was built into the powerful foundation it is today by private-sector actors who drew on their resources, including financial and political connections, to develop a powerful governance network. Yet ideas have been powerful forces as well, including ideas regarding the responsibility to produce social protection. Especially early on, the private sector believed that to win their battle against homelessness, "You take it out of government," reflecting the idea that governments do not necessarily have a leadership role to play in the production of social protection. This idea was especially powerful because governments in Alberta, both local and provincial, agreed to some extent.

The CHF's influence has long been buttressed by powerful and magnetic ideas regarding the nature of homelessness as a problem that can be ended, and regarding the responsibility to produce social protection. Those ideas served as a powerful coalition magnet after Mangano proposed this redefinition of homelessness during his visit to the city. Entrepreneurs used those ideas to build a powerful coalition, one that included actors who had not previously been allied. Actors who disagreed with the CHF's efforts failed to win the support of influential actors in Calgary's governance and were marginalized. More recently, though, ideas about homelessness have evolved considerably and, along with them, the CHF's interactions with other actors. As the first version of their plan was being developed, CHF officials sought to maximize the role of markets and did not expect extensive government involvement. As the plan was being implemented, key officials came to understand and appreciate the importance of collaborative governance. Driven by the CHRN's more complex definition of homelessness, one that focused less on individuals and more on structures, the CHF sought to collaborate with more actors. The CHF has been willing to adapt and has updated its plan regularly. Senior officials reflect on past mistakes and even failures and have committed to implementing lessons learned into future efforts to reduce homelessness. Its definition of homelessness has become more inclusive and complex over time, though it remains focused on housing (as opposed to community or poverty).

Local governance networks that implement the federal NHI/HPS have consolidated the CHF's position of power in Calgary, but we also see an evolving relationship with these groups, including the one between the CHF and the ASCHH. The CHF became the Community Entity for the federal funding, including Indigenous funding. Isolated from the development of the first two versions of the CHF plan, the ASCHH developed its own plan, a Plan to End Aboriginal Homelessness in Calgary. The CHF's relationship with Indigenous groups has improved since 2015, as Indigenous people continue to seek increased involvement and collaboration and as the CHF learns to recognize and value their expertise.

7 Toronto

Homelessness governance in Toronto is centralized, with the city taking the lead role. While there were periods of innovation and expansion in the city's response to homelessness, that response was also stagnant for several years. Until recently, the city has jealously guarded its power related to homelessness. The Province of Ontario downloaded responsibility for housing policy to municipalities in the 1990s, the only Canadian province to do so. After downloading responsibility, the province re-emerged as an actor in homelessness governance in 2005 and even more so in 2014, with a commitment to ending homelessness by 2025, though municipalities maintain significant responsibility in this effort.

Private- and third-sector actors have been involved in homelessness governance for decades. While both have at times exercised great influence in the city, these actors have long struggled to establish institutionalized or long-term roles in the governance of homelessness (though institutionalization is not always the goal of advocacy groups and activists). The involvement of civil society groups in homelessness governance changed in 2014 with the emergence of the Toronto Alliance to End Homelessness (TAEH), comprised of service providers and other stakeholders. The TAEH made significant progress in building and institutionalizing a relationship with the city; the result was a significant shift in local power dynamics so that by 2017, the city and the TAEH were collaborating closely. This evolving role of civil society in Toronto policy is also evident in relation to the federal Homelessness Partnering Strategy.

Institutions loom large in explaining the centralized but increasingly inclusive governance dynamics in Toronto. Most obviously, the city has formal jurisdiction over this power. The lack of institutionalized third-sector involvement in homelessness governance can similarly be understood in part as a result of the political/institutional realities of Toronto; the city covers an enormous territory and has a huge population, so its sheer size makes it difficult for social actors to coordinate and join forces. Yet a focus on institutions alone leaves unanswered important questions. For example, the city was long closed to civil society involvement in homelessness governance, but this changed in 2017 when it shifted gears and created an institutionalized venue of co-governance. Why? Also, why did third-sector groups persist in political organizing to overcome institutional barriers and form a powerful network, the TAEH? Why was the TAEH willing and able to collaborate institutionally with the municipal government while other third-sector advocacy organizations, including the Toronto Disaster Relief Committee and the province-wide but locally active Ontario Coalition Against Poverty (OCAP), were not? Institutions loom large in the governance of homelessness in Toronto, but ideas complete the explanation for these significant changes, particularly with respect to the interactions of different groups over time. These changes came about as a result of evolving ideas regarding the nature of homelessness and the responsibility to produce social protection, interacting with Toronto's unique, centralizing institutions.

Homelessness History in Ontario

In the 1960s and 1970s, the Province of Ontario was a Canadian leader in terms of housing policy, developing expertise and capacity in the field before other provinces. Indeed, Ontario was influential on the national stage in advancing progressive housing policy (Suttor 2016). This changed dramatically in the 1990s, when the province washed its hands of housing as well as the responsibility for homelessness, passing the buck (but not the *bucks*) to local governments. Since then, the province has gradually re-emerged in housing and homelessness policy, culminating in 2014 in a commitment to end homelessness by 2025. With the political pendulum swinging back to the right with the election of Doug Ford's Progressive Conservatives in 2018, this commitment to ending homelessness is in jeopardy. What is clear from this history is that ideas regarding the responsibility to produce social protection, not strictly ideological ones, have driven some of Ontario's most important changes.

Between 1964 and 1975, the "peak" of public housing production in Canada (Suttor 2016), an astonishing 84,145 units of social housing were built in Ontario alone (Ontario Non-Profit Housing Association 2011). Housing investments were maintained by both Progressive Conservative and Liberal governments throughout the 1970s and 1980s, decades during which Ontario maintained a diverse housing policy that included social housing developments as well as subsidies for private developments (Suttor 2016, 155). Though housing developments were expanding in Canada during this period, Ontario was particularly aggressive: "In 1971, over 60% of Canadian social housing (47,000 out of 77,000 homes) was in Ontario, with half of this (23,000) in Toronto" (Suttor 2016, 91). This leadership role changed in the mid-1990s, following an economic downturn and increasing provincial debt. 1995 marked the beginning of an austerity-focused period led by Mike Harris's Progressive Conservative government. Besides inflicting direct cuts, the Harris administration placed unprecedented burdens on municipal governments.

Ideas regarding the responsibility to produce social protection are clearly visible at this point in Ontario's history. Having campaigned on a promise to get out of the housing business, Harris cancelled provincial housing programs just days after being elected premier of Ontario in 1995 (Shapcott 2001). Not only did Harris make no new commitments to build housing in the future, but he also went further than other premiers (even those who had eliminated new investments in housing programs, like BC Premier Gordon Campbell) and cancelled 17,000 units that were under construction at the time (Shapcott 2007). Harris also announced that he would sell 84,000 units of social housing, though he ultimately abandoned that plan. As the Common Sense Revolution platform and subsequent actions taken by the Harris government made clear, the dominant idea was that the private sector should play a large role in the production of social protection; as the platform stated (in **bold**, no less), **"the best social assistance program ever created is a real job"** (Ontario PC 1995, 9).

This was part of an ideological project to reduce the size of the provincial government. To that end, the Harris government announced a realignment of provincial and municipal government responsibilities (the Local Services Realignment, or LSR). The LSR was intended to be revenue neutral, but municipalities ended up with a much bigger bill than they could afford to pay (personal interviews 2014). This is in large part because the cities were not provided with new revenue tools to fund their new responsibilities, which included housing. By consigning the housing power to municipal governments without also transferring the funding required to fully implement that power, or even providing inclusionary zoning powers, the province had *de facto* (and perhaps by design) obliterated government-supported housing.

This decision to download responsibility to local governments has had long-lasting and devastating effects on the housing market across Ontario, notably in Toronto. This local burden was, ironically, partly a result of Ontario's historic leadership in progressive housing policy, which led to a large stock of social housing being built in Toronto. In the 1990s, there was a growing need for *new* affordable housing in Toronto and across Ontario; in addition, the high concentration of old and deteriorating social housing in Toronto made maintenance and repairs a pressing and expensive municipal issue for Toronto. Built between the 1960s and the 1990s, this housing was and continues to be in need of expensive repairs, estimated at around $1.6 billion (Pagliaro 2017).

The federal government began signing cost-sharing Affordable Housing Framework Agreements with provinces in 2001, but this opportunity was received with little enthusiasm in Ontario. The federal government offered up to $25,000 of funding per unit for new affordable housing, with the requirement that the funding be matched. Given that housing had been downloaded to municipalities, Harris had little interest in the federal dollars. Instead, he passed the opportunity along to municipalities, agreeing only to provide provincial grants of $2,000 per unit and leaving it up to municipalities to contribute the remaining $23,000 per unit (City Clerk 2002). Given the municipalities' limited resources, it is no surprise that little housing was built during the early years of the Affordable Housing Agreement in Ontario, despite the federal dollars on offer. A comparative perspective on the success of the Affordable Housing Agreements in Canadian provinces shows that Ontario was among the worst performers in those early years (Suttor 2016).

The Harris years were characterized by unprecedented provincial retrenchment and downloading onto municipalities; the city still struggles with these changes today. In the late 1990s and early 2000s, when almost no social housing was produced in Ontario, homelessness in Toronto began to rise (Crowe 2019; Layton 2008). Following the influential Golden Report on homelessness in Toronto (reviewed below), which detailed the scope and scale of homelessness in Toronto, the province implemented a program in Toronto called Off the Streets, Into Shelters (OSIS). While reports and interviews suggest that individuals were moved from the streets into housing as well as shelters during this period, the very title of the program makes clear that the province had adopted a narrow understanding of homelessness as street homelessness. Provincial policy was designed to move people off the streets and, cynics might insist, out of sight and into emergency shelters (though it does not take a cynic to point out that shelter is not housing and that people in shelters are still unhoused). It is significant that the OSIS program coincided with the Safe Streets Act, which was designed to target aggressive panhandling. The Safe Streets Act was seen as counterproductive to efforts to fight homelessness, particularly youth homelessness, for it characterized homelessness as a nuisance, even criminal, rather than a result of policy failures (O'Grady, Gaetz, and Buccieri 2013).

The Liberal Party came to power after defeating the Progressive Conservatives in the 2003 provincial election. Upon assuming power, they introduced new homelessness programs, though these were small at first and included a rent bank and a homelessness prevention fund. In 2005, the province began to show a little more interest in the federal affordable housing dollars and signed a new Affordable Housing Agreement with the federal government. As advocate Michael Shapcott has written, "almost four years after the original framework was signed by the Ontario government, the investments started to flow in significant numbers" (Shapcott 2011, 22). Between 1996 and 2017, around 20,000 units of housing were built in Ontario (Shapcott 2011; Auditor General of Ontario 2017). This was more than had been built in the past; even so, it came nowhere near the pace of housing development during the postwar era. Indeed, Shapcott notes that the provinces that were best able to benefit from the federal housing agreement in 2001 were BC and Quebec, "which already had relatively strong affordable housing infrastructure" (2011). Having dismantled the province's role in housing in the late 1990s, Ontario got off to a slow restart in housing developments; even so, 2005 marked a renewal of provincial investment in housing policy following Harris's total shutdown of the system.

There was also the important question of how affordable this housing really *was*, in that Affordable Housing Agreements allowed provinces to define affordability. Rather than defining affordable housing as costing no more than 30 per cent of one's income – the definition of affordable housing used by the Canadian Mortgage and Housing Corporation (CMHC) – Ontario's definition required that affordable housing be 80 per cent of the average market rate. The result was that housing was still out of reach for many low-income people (see Shapcott 2011). In 2009, an Auditor General's report concluded that "more than half of the units in this program would still be unaffordable for households on [social housing] waiting lists, or eligible to be on wait-lists" (Auditor General of Ontario 2009, 290; see also Shapcott 2011).[1]

In 2008, the province introduced a timid Poverty Reduction Strategy (PRS). Its primary commitment was to reduce child poverty by 25 per cent, but the plan noted the importance of fighting homelessness as well. The provision of supportive housing to those who needed it most was stated as a priority, but the PRS offered no indication of how this would be done, nor did it include targets. The PRS also introduced an Ontario-wide Long-Term Affordable Housing Strategy (LTAHS), which included binding requirements on municipalities to develop ten-year affordable housing and homelessness plans, along with some guidelines for how to do so. The LTAHS also merged the funding for five extant homelessness programs[2] into the Community Homelessness Partnership Initiative (CHPI), whose intent was to "consolidate the current patchwork of provincial housing programs and allow municipalities to use funding in a more flexible manner, reflective of local need" (Ministry of Municipal Affairs and Housing 2010, 9). The consolidated funding model was a block payment to municipalities that gave them control over housing, though the province transferred less money to the municipalities for homelessness services than it had under the previous arrangement. This highlights a recurring theme in intergovernmental welfare state funding: flexibility comes at the cost of decreased transfers.

The first PRS emphasized the idea that that federal government, the province, and the private sector shared the responsibility for fighting poverty and homelessness: "Ontario can't do this alone – meeting this target depends on having a willing partner in the federal government and a growing economy" (Government of Ontario 2008, 2). Provincial officials saw an important role for themselves in the production of social protection but also insisted that the federal government had to involve itself as well (at the time, Stephen Harper's Conservative Party was in power in Ottawa). So when the provincial objective of reducing childhood poverty by 25 per cent was not achieved in 2015, the minister responsible for the PRS, Deb Matthews, blamed the federal government: "We did everything we said we would do when we released that strategy in 2008 … Had the federal government done its part we would have come very close, if not had achieved, our goal of a 25-per-cent reduction in child poverty" (Jones 2014).

In light of the province's failure to achieve even the modest goals contained in the 2008 PRS, it is interesting that a second PRS was introduced in 2014. It was much bolder than the first and included a promise to end chronic homelessness by 2025. An Advisory Council on Homelessness, created to inform and guide the province's implementation of this promise, wrote a detailed report with a number of recommendations for how to achieve this goal, including: adopting a common definition of homelessness, prioritizing Housing First interventions, and gathering consistent data so as to track progress and learn more about the homeless population. Speaking to an audience at the Conference to End Homelessness in Montreal in 2015 in the early days of the implementation of the PRS, the minister responsible for the PRS continued to stress the shared responsibility for producing social protection, and expressed optimism that the second PRS would achieve its goals given that the province had Liberal partners at the federal level (the Liberals had been elected federally earlier that year).

In 2020, a third PRS was introduced in Ontario under Doug Ford's Progressive Conservative government. Homelessness does not feature as prominently in this PRS as it did in previous plans, and the Ford government has indicated a desire to limit government involvement. Ideas regarding the province's role in producing social protection have changed, in line with ideological differences between the Liberals and Progressive Conservatives. The first objective of the 2020 PRS is to encourage job creation and to connect people to employment, evidence that ideas, in line with ideology and past PC governments, regarding the private sector's role in producing social protection are again limiting provincial involvement. Whereas the second PRS in 2014 planned to end homelessness, the third PRS under Ford's government identifies homelessness as a barrier to employment. The PRS's primary objective is job creation, a not so subtle return to the old Harris approach to social protection (i.e., the best social policy is a job).

Ideas regarding responsibility to produce social protection have been particularly powerful in driving provincial involvement over this history (including increases and decreases in involvement). These ideas have also, however, created gaps in the governance system, in which there is no clear leader. Intergovernmental dynamics in Ontario, and Toronto in particular, are therefore quite peculiar: the level of government that has the responsibility for housing and homelessness (municipal) does not have the adequate resources to implement effective solutions. The levels that do have resources (provincial and federal) look to each other for leadership. A 2017 Auditor General's Report noted how difficult this institutional reality made developing affordable housing and combating homelessness: "Although the federal, provincial and municipal governments all play a role in the provision of social and affordable housing in Ontario, none take ownership of ensuring that everyone in Ontario has an affordable and suitable home" (Auditor General of Ontario 2017; 715).

City of Toronto

Toronto is unique among the cities studied here because of its official role in housing and homelessness policy. The city has been actively involved in housing since the early 2000s, including in one of the first formal Housing First plans on homelessness in Canada. Though its responses were innovative and expanded in the mid-aughts, city actions became stagnant toward 2010. Under Mayor John Tory, the city has made more bold commitments to housing and homelessness, but these municipal contributions to the production of social protection risk

being overshadowed by intense protests against the violent displacement of a small number of people living in encampments in Toronto's
parks in mid-2021 (Bingley 2021).

The city has formal jurisdiction over housing, and this institutional
reality goes a long way in explaining its leading role in housing and
homelessness. But the way in which it has wielded this power and its
interactions with other locally based groups have changed over time.
If anything, the city's institutional strength has increased in recent
years when the province granted municipalities inclusionary zoning
powers, yet Toronto has gone from a so-called command-and-control
approach (personal interview 2015) in the early 2000s to one of co-
governance and inclusion of third-sector groups through its relationship with the Toronto Alliance to End Homelessness. This co-governing
relationship is an important change in local governance dynamics, but
it has been criticized by groups such as the Ontario Coalition Against
Poverty (OCAP), as I will explain below. While the city's involvement
in homelessness governance is largely explained by institutions, ideas
regarding the responsibility to produce social protection have shaped
its interactions with civil society. In the early 2000s, those ideas led city
officials to guard their powers jealously. But in recent years, they have
evolved and city officials have taken a more collaborative (if selective)
approach to governance. This change in governance dynamics was also
facilitated by ideas regarding the nature of the problem, a dynamic that
will be explored more fully in the next section regarding civil society.

It is worth noting that City of Toronto officials strongly objected to
the transfer of housing policy powers to the local level in the late 1990s
because of funding concerns. An actor involved with the municipality
during that period recalled the vehement opposition among senior officials, including then Mayor Mel Lastman:

> There was a lot of resistance, because [housing responsibility] also came
> with the responsibility to fund it. So not just the management, but the
> cost of funding it. The mayor was pretty angry about it and contem-
> plated a constitutional challenge. I think we should have constitutionally
> challenged it just to highlight opposition. It has turned out to be not too
> terrific, because cities do not have the tax base to deal with it. (personal
> interview 2014)

Unsurprisingly, housing accounts for a significant portion of the City
of Toronto's annual expenditures. The budget for Toronto's Shelter,
Support and Housing Administration (SSHA) has ebbed and flowed
over the past decade, reaching $862.605 million in gross expenditures

in 2018 (Shelter, Support & Housing Administration 2018). That funding is mostly operating funding for affordable and supportive housing, but it also includes what the budget calls Homeless and Housing First solutions, notably the Streets to Homes program. Around 70 per cent of SSHA's budget goes to social housing, a figure that has not changed much since 2013 (Shelter, Support & Housing Administration 2014, 2018). Funding comes from all levels of government, including the federal Homelessness Partnering Strategy[3] and provincial Community Homelessness Prevention Initiative funding. The most important source of funding, however, is the municipality itself (53 per cent). Housing is a serious policy responsibility, one that exerts great pressure on the city's budget.

In what would later be seen as a key moment in the history of homelessness in Toronto, mayoral candidates in the 1997 municipal election for the newly amalgamated City of Toronto were asked about homelessness. Former North York mayor Mel Lastman (who would go on to win the mayoral election) responded simply that there was no homelessness in North York, implying that homelessness was not and would not be a priority for him. Tragically, a homeless woman named Linda Houston died at a gas station in North York the following day (Queen 2010). Showing humility and regret for his comment, Lastman pledged to study homelessness in Toronto if elected mayor.

Upon his election, Mayor Lastman made good on his promise and launched an influential study of homelessness in Toronto. To lead the study, he recruited Anne Golden,[4] a well-known historian and then president of the United Way of Greater Toronto. The resulting Golden Report (formally titled "Taking Responsibility for Homelessness: An Action Plan for Toronto") identified several barriers to effective homelessness responses, including increasing poverty, a decreasing supply of affordable housing, a dearth of coordinated efforts to fight homelessness, as well as institutional features such as jurisdictional gridlock. Targeted solutions were proposed for each problem, such as improved service planning and investment in affordable and supportive housing.

Ideas regarding the responsibility to produce social protection are evident throughout the Golden Report. Its authors emphasized that all three levels of government are needed in the effort to respond effectively to the needs of homeless people: "Everyone, including all three levels of government, must take ownership of the problem and responsibility for solving it" (Golden et al. 1999, iii). The appropriate role of each level of government was identified for each action, indicating that Golden and her collaborators, as well as the mayor himself, who endorsed the report, saw homelessness as primarily a *government* responsibility. This idea is apparent in the very title of the report ("Taking Responsibility for Homelessness"), perhaps a diplomatic clap-back to Lastman and his comment that there was no homelessness in North York and the implicit suggestion that there is thus no role for government in solving it.

Published in 1999 after the local government was given housing powers, the Golden report identifies a leading role for the municipality in homelessness: "the City of Toronto should take the lead in planning and managing the overall system ... The City should spearhead a rental housing development strategy to produce new affordable housing and to preserve existing housing" (Golden et al. 1999, x). Accepting that the province was not involved in housing and homelessness directly, the Golden Report recommended that the province increase social assistance rates and improve access to health care. The federal government was called upon to reverse cuts to social housing and "provide capital assistance for the construction of new affordable housing and the rehabilitation of existing affordable housing" (Golden et al. 1999, ix–x). Buried deep in the report is a reference to civil society, including community agencies, private-sector actors, and faith communities, an indication that the city has a long history of *not* prioritizing the collaboration and involvement of civil society in the production of social protection. The report proposed that the city involve third-sector groups in homelessness governance by liaising with a homeless "Facilitator," a position the report proposed creating to help coordinate actions on homelessness. (This position was not created.)

The Golden Report also included an early attempt to define homelessness in Toronto: "We have included in our definition of homeless people those who are 'visible' on the streets or staying in hostels, the 'hidden' homeless who live in illegal or temporary accommodation, and those at imminent risk of becoming homeless" (iii). While this definition relates homelessness entirely to housing, it also encompasses a wide range of experiences, including individuals in unstable environments or at risk of becoming homeless, meaning the definition was innovative by the standards of the time.

As noted, not all of the Golden Report recommendations were implemented, though the report did provoke some increased municipal involvement including for an improved information system and harm reduction strategies. It was in this context that the federal government introduced its National Homelessness Initiative in 1999. The City of Toronto, having recently been given responsibility for homelessness by the province and having assumed a role in its governance following the Golden Report, became the Community Entity (CE) and was thus responsible for administering federal homelessness funding. In the early days, most of this funding was absorbed into the city's planning process. Though community groups were federally mandated to form a Community Advisory Board (CAB) to create a local plan and advise the CE on how to spend the federal funds, the city's strong institutional position meant that the CAB's influence was minimal. Carey Doberstein explains that Toronto's CAB, which should have written the local plan and set priorities for the city to act on, was weak compared to similar boards in other cities in part because it was "inserted into a pre-existing and active policy space in Toronto" (Doberstein 2016, 116). The strong centralization in the city during this period was thus the result of multiple ideational and institutional forces. The NHI maintained and reinforced that status quo.

In the early 2000s, in the wake of the Golden Report and the introduction of the NHI, homelessness continued to emerge as a visible and politically sensitive issue in Toronto, and City Council engaged in several debates about the rising costs associated with the issue (Falvo 2010). A senior official explained how troubling it was for municipal officials to be confronted with the realities of homelessness at the very doors of City Hall: "So the fact that Nathan Phillips Square ... was completely occupied by street homeless people was symbolic that the City was not able to deal with this problem" (personal interview 2014). Other senior bureaucrats recall that on their way to work they often had to step over homeless people who were sleeping in the square (personal interview 2014).

This period also saw a tense and bitter end to the Tent City encampment, when more than 100 people were forcefully evicted from what had become their homes along Toronto's waterfront. In one of the longest acts of civil disobedience by a group of people experiencing homelessness in Canadian history (Crowe 2019), more than 100 people occupied the land that was owned by Home Depot and created homes on it. With the support of the influential Toronto Disaster Relief Committee (see below), including then city councillor Jack Layton, Tent City residents created homes and installed composting toilets, showers, places to cook, and more. A political problem emerged when Home Depot planned to evict those people, many of whom had purposefully avoided the emergency shelter system; in *Shelter from the Storm* (Connolly 2001), a film about the conflict, a man living in Tent City explained that he had just left prison and wanted to live in Tent City because he had no interest in living in a shelter where every aspect of his life would again be controlled.

As the threat of eviction increased, advocates drew considerable media attention to the city's response. Advocates proposed moving Tent City residents to a new location on city-owned land. The city disagreed and proposed a much different solution. A senior administrator with the city at the time of the Tent City evictions recalled the pressure this placed on the city to find a solution, and how the city moved quickly to do so: "Then one night, the landowner evicted everyone. So, one day this was front page news in *The Star* – we had 104 people who didn't want to use the regular system, and so we said 'well what do we do?' So we said, 'well, we will house them'" (personal interview 2014). Partly in response to pressure from advocates, and partly to find housing for people who had avoided the shelter system under the spotlight of increasing media attention, the City of Toronto used rent supplements to fast-track people from Tent City into private housing and brought intensive supports to them depending on their needs and requests.[5]

Bypassing shelters and other temporary housing and ensuring quick access to permanent housing was at odds with the way things were done in Toronto at the time. Recall that the provincial program then being implemented in Toronto was Off the Streets into Shelters. An actor reinforced that this shift to Housing First was contrary to the way things had long been done: "Instead of the traditional approach, where the service providers said 'What do you need?' – the answer was usually 'Well, food and a sleeping bag' – we changed the question to 'What do you need *to find housing*?' And then the conversation became quite different. So that is how it all started, how we moved from managing to ending homelessness" (personal interview 2014).

Interesting here is that while the balance of power is normally tilted heavily toward the city as opposed to third-sector groups, the TDRC exerted considerable pressure on the city to find a solution. That pressure largely succeeded in forcing the city to respond by using rent supplements to ensure immediate access to permanent, supportive housing for the people of Tent City. Though the TDRC did not have an institutionalized role, it had good relationships with key officials (including Mayor Lastman's senior aide, Sean Gadon) as well as a crucial relationship with insider Jack Layton. Thus, it was able to exert pressure at key moments. Even so, city officials maintained control over solutions. The city outright rejected the idea of relocating Tent City, and when TDRC advocates pushed for social housing commitments, the city instead resorted to rent supplements for private-market housing.

A.J. Withers explains the opposition among some community groups to the use of rent supplements as opposed to social housing: "OCAP is deeply critical of housing allowances as a social policy solution because they are individual interventions that do nothing to alleviate the causes of homelessness ... OCAP wanted funds to be invested in creating more social housing, not to go towards subsidizing private landlords – including slumlords" (Withers 2021, 99). Tent City evictions presented a challenge, in a context where social housing waitlists are extremely long and social housing takes a very long time to build. Rent supplements ensured that people living in Tent City did not end up homeless following the eviction (a key demand of the TDRC). There is a tension between the immediate solution enabled by rent supplements and the longer-term solution and preventative measure of increased social housing investments. This reveals that the city's response to the Tent City evictions was seen by the TDRC and OCAP as at best a partial victory.

The use of rent supplements and intensive wrap-around services that followed the Tent City evictions led to an unplanned pilot study of Housing First. This would guide the city's future responses to homelessness, notably the Streets to Homes Program. That program is often viewed as Canada's first official Housing First program (Falvo 2010), though as noted throughout this text, service providers had long been espousing Housing First approaches; many insist that the first "Housing First" program was actually HouseLink in Toronto in 1977 (Withers 2021; personal interviews 2014). The goal of the Streets to Homes program was to end homelessness (though no timeline was given) by immediately connecting people experiencing homelessness with permanent, affordable housing and the social supports they required and requested. It sought to "serve homeless people who live outdoors, which includes individuals living in parks, ravines, under bridges, on sidewalks, laneways, alleys, stairwells, building alcoves, squats and living in vehicles" (City of Toronto 2007, 61). This marked a much narrower understanding of homelessness than the one proposed in the Golden Report, and certainly narrower than how community-based advocates with the TDRC and OCAP understood homelessness (see below).

Interviews with senior city officials about the development of the Streets to Homes program in the early 2000s reveal that they had a clear idea of what they wanted to do in terms of responding to homelessness and that they did not collaborate extensively with civil society, though there were efforts to communicate with service providers and seek their input. One senior official recognized the important role played by advocates but maintained that the city's job was to *lead*:

What [the TDRC] did and what I think they were very capable at, was hold the city to account ... Activism always has a central role in terms of identifying issues, identifying solutions, being part of that process. But it also takes leadership at senior levels of government to establish and support policy change. And that did happen. There was a seismic shift ... It really is the obligation of senior public servants to identify needs, to make recommendations to council, and to advance responsive approaches to serving marginalized communities. (personal interview 2014)

Disagreements over the nature of homelessness and the solution the city was proposing led to continued friction between the groups. The TDRC decried city policy, including the expansion of Housing First approaches and to the city's first homeless count (the Street Needs Assessment). Influential TDRC member and street nurse Cathy Crowe disseminated a newsletter for years in which she criticized government policy and raised awareness about homelessness. After the city implemented the Streets to Homes program, her newsletter featured a column by fellow TDRC member Beric German. German criticized the prioritization of Housing First programs through Streets to Homes, insisting that other services, such as shelters, would lose their funding. And he went further: "Now the city is expanding their policy, cleaning the streets, which is the real intent of 'streets to homes.' Canadian neoliberal policy does not include a national housing program. Window-dressing will do just fine ... We must consistently oppose this neoliberal policy ... This regressive approach to homelessness cannot take the place of a fully funded national housing program and a fully funded emergency shelter" (German 2008).

Opposition to Housing First continues even after the dissolution of the TDRC. Withers gives a thoughtful analysis of Housing First and the Streets to Homes program from the perspective of OCAP. They concede that Housing First has been a successful approach to ending homelessness for some vulnerable individuals (Withers 2021, 89) but insist that it does nothing to address the causes of homelessness:

> Housing First policies have been enacted by city staff to displace homeless people from the downtown core and reconstruct them as self-sufficient neoliberal actors. By rendering homelessness a technical problem, [Housing First] proponents create a mirage in which homelessness is not caused by unjust social relations but rather by individual problems requiring individuals solutions that can be resolved within the neoliberal policy frameworks of ruling relations. This is one of the falsehoods of Housing First. (Withers 2021, 101)

Though there were and still are protests and opposition, the continuation of Housing First as the main tool used by the City of Toronto to combat homelessness, and the fact that its use has only been expanded, underscores the power dynamics in Toronto that privilege the city. It also underscores important ideational differences regarding the definition of homelessness between city officials and social justice advocates, which remain very much in evidence. Introduced under Mayor David Miller in 2005, the Streets to Homes program expanded in 2008 (also under Miller's leadership). Following new provincial requirements for local housing plans announced in 2008, the city introduced a ten-year housing plan in 2010. This first plan, Housing Opportunities Toronto 2010–2020 (HOT), highlighted the city's efforts to fight homelessness. It prioritized ending homelessness, but provided no timeline for that goal and relied on Housing First approaches to do so. The lack of a timeline or other specific targets was intentional, explained a former senior official with the city: "One thing we never did, but that others did, was to set targets. Like reducing homelessness by 10 per cent. We had no idea how well the program was going to go, given that it was the first one in Canada. People are not widgets, they are people … Looking back, it is good that we never did that" (personal interview 2014). HOT set a target of 1,000 new affordable rental units per year for ten years and introduced a Housing Charter, a symbolic but important document outlining the rights of Toronto residents when it comes to housing. The city's homelessness response would remain largely untouched during Rob Ford's mayoralty, a period remembered as one of policy stagnation and lack of innovation or political will to invest in homelessness (Doberstein 2016).

A more recent housing plan, HousingTO 2020–2030, is bolder than the first. It remains committed to the goal of ending homelessness through Housing First approaches and still provides no firm timeline for doing so. Its commitment to housing, however, is greatly increased; HousingTO commits to supporting the creation of 40,000 units of supportive housing over ten years, 18,000 of them for vulnerable residents, including those who are homeless or those who are at risk of homelessness. The increased commitments from the city may be related to the 2018 provincial decision to give the city inclusionary zoning powers.[6] Inclusionary zoning is an important institutional tool in efforts to create affordable housing and potentially to combat homelessness, albeit one dependent on the continuation of private housing developments. The battle for inclusionary zoning powers to be given to Toronto had been ongoing since at least 1999, when Anne Golden recommended that the province grant Toronto that power (Golden et al. 1999, 165). The province was reluctant to do so to the enormous frustration of local actors: the province had dumped the responsibility for housing on Toronto without transferring funding or even allowing for inclusionary zoning as a means of exercising this power. In 2018, Kathleen Wynne's Liberal government finally reversed course and announced plans to grant municipalities inclusionary zoning powers. (The Ford government currently in power remains committed to inclusionary zoning.[7]) By the fall of 2020, the City of Toronto was engaging in consultations regarding inclusionary zoning and a definition of "affordable housing" to accompany it.

The city has become institutionally more powerful, and it was already in a strong position; its bolder commitments to housing coincide with the addition of inclusionary zoning powers, which may explain some of this increased involvement. Yet the city has also become more inclusive in its style of governance and how it interacts with community groups. To understand why, it is important to look at the evolution of ideas since the 1990s, specifically ideas regarding the responsibility to produce social protection. In the early aughts, the institutions that centralized power in the local government were bolstered by ideas regarding the city's primary role in the production of social protection. Indeed, the belief from the very top during this period was that the municipality was *the* important producer of social protection. A senior official with the city during the aughts explained:

> In the bottom half of the income scale, it is very hard to find housing. And that has to be subsidized somehow by government. The only way the market will build it is if we create slums. So, if we don't want people to live in slums where they are going to catch on fire and die – and you might think I'm exaggerating, but that has happened … Rooming houses caught fire and people died … there is a very important place for government. (personal interview 2014)

This actor also stressed that it was the municipality that should fill this role. And when I asked local actors about the origins of the Streets to Homes program, for example, they pointed to the municipal bureaucracy. Indeed, one bureaucrat, in response to the question "Whose idea was Streets to Homes?," raised their own hand. A senior elected official confirmed this: when asked where the Streets to Homes idea came from, they responded, "Mostly from the civil service doing really good work" (personal interview 2014). Even when the community sector was organized and the TDRC active, the City of Toronto understood its relationships in a hierarchy: advocates could advise and lobby, but the responsibility to produce social protection belonged primarily to the city.

In the years leading up to the second housing plan, the city's approach to homelessness governance changed and it began to guard its powers a little less jealously. The relationship between the City and the TAEH started slowly but evolved into a close, constructive working relationship fairly quickly. The City, for its part, indicated a willingness to engage and involve third sector groups in their efforts to combat homelessness, including by adopting a new engagement and planning process around homeless shelters in 2017. This process proposed to use "respectful dialogue and non-threatening language." It further noted that the homeless need "a champion or champions" and specifically mentioned the Toronto Alliance to End Homelessness as a group to be engaged in this process (along with other groups from the third and private sectors). Importantly, the item adopted by the city notes that this is not just about obtaining approval, but also about planning and improving services together (City of Toronto 2017).

As I explain in the following section, environmental and cognitive mechanisms were at play and led to this change in governance. The city has worked closely with the TAEH to create a venue of co-governance in 2017, the Toronto Housing and Homelessness Service Planning Forum (THHSPF), a development that is explored from the perspective of the TAEH (and their critics) more fully below. Once city officials came to understand that third-sector groups had an important role to play in producing social protection for people who are homeless, policy-making opened up and allowed for direct participation by these actors. Withers considers this collaboration between the city and TAEH in a different light, noting that the city benefits from the relationship with the TAEH in a number of ways beyond the benefits of collaborating to end homelessness. They write, "this is a forged alignment; in this governing practice of assemblage, the two groups align their objectives and both groups benefit through this alignment/alliance. SSHA benefits from its alignment with TAEH because it legitimizes SSHA's appearance of community engagement" (Withers 2021, 112). They go on to note that this community engagement is strategic in that it excludes and can even discredit other voices, notably OCAP. While some criticisms of this arrangement are valid, TAEH members include some of the oldest and most established service providers in the city. This arrangement allows for their expertise to be regularly and directly brought into policy-making processes.

Finally, local officials with the city tend to have a broad and comprehensive conception of the municipal government's role in governing homelessness in Toronto. This is understandable, given the size of the city and the scope of its policy responsibilities. In interviews, several actors stressed that Toronto is the fifth-largest government in Canada, sometimes directly comparing Toronto to provincial governments. A senior official explained how Toronto stacks up against provinces: "Quebec and Ontario are larger by population and budget. Alberta is larger by budget, but about the same population as Toronto. Toronto is Canada's fifth largest government after Alberta and BC, but is close to both" (personal interview 2014). This view that Toronto is a major government in Canada, comparable even with large provinces, is the broadest conceptualization seen among city officials regarding their own role. This understanding of the city's role extends to housing policy. The frustration that the city is not treated as an equal or as a legitimate government by the provinces is palpable. A senior official recalled efforts in the early 2000s to get Toronto invited to a federal–provincial conference on housing: "One of the things I said is, 'Toronto is Canada's biggest landlord. How can you have a conference on housing without having the biggest landlord there?' We lost, though."

The city's institutional strength was often acknowledged and highlighted in interviews. Looking back on the history of Toronto's involvement in housing and homelessness, however, senior officials with the city consistently emphasized the very real limitations under which they were operating, many of which related to financial resources. Housing is an expensive infrastructure to build and maintain, and without additional funding or revenue sources (and without even inclusionary zoning powers being granted from the province until 2018) the municipality was limited in what it could accomplish. One actor said in an interview, "Could we have done more? Absolutely. But we needed more money" (personal interview 2014). Another stressed: "Have you noticed the elevated expressway at the bottom of the city? The Gardiner Expressway is falling down and it needs hundreds and hundreds and hundreds of millions of dollars to keep it standing up. Our subway system needs billions and billions and billions of dollars of investment. That is what we are up against. And City Council makes those choices. Money is an issue" (personal interview 2014).

Civil Society

Private-sector and third-sector community groups in Toronto have at times exercised important influence over homelessness policy, though they have not been formally involved in the policy-making process until recently. As noted, the city is powerful and has historically been closed to civil society involvement not just in homelessness but in broader urban governance dynamics as well (Bramwell and Wolfe 2014). This institutional environment, combined with the difficulties associated with organizing groups across such a large space, is a major barrier to the involvement of civil society actors in homelessness governance. Though some groups have sought formal involvement, others see collaborating with governments as ineffective and prefer to engage in direct action and protest; for them, a lack of institutionalization is not a problem. Though not institutionally involved until recently, third-sector groups have a long history of involvement in homelessness governance and have exercised considerable influence during key periods. That involvement has been driven by ideas about the responsibility to produce social protection: third-sector groups see an important role for themselves, alongside government leaders, in homelessness governance. Ideas about the nature of homelessness have also structured involvement but have been more influential in structuring the relations and interactions of local actors, notably with the city. To the extent that some third-sector groups collaborate more closely with city officials now than they did in the past, this is in large part because of evolving ideas among key third-sector leaders, about the nature of homelessness (and changing ideas among municipal officials regarding the responsibility to produce social protection, as explained in the previous section).

The private sector in Toronto has at certain moments demonstrated an interest in and even leadership around the question of homelessness, though this has been fleeting. In 2000, the Toronto Board of Trade wrote an influential report on homelessness that characterized it as a crisis that was negatively impacting businesses in Toronto: "For Toronto's business community, homelessness affects the size of our productive and motivated workforce. It has an impact on tourism and business, particularly the retail sector" (The Toronto Board of Trade 2000, 2). The report continued: "Unless it is addressed, homelessness will reduce Toronto's global competitiveness." This reflected the idea, also held among private-sector actors in Calgary and to some extent in Vancouver, that homelessness is an obstacle to urban economic growth. The report insisted that governments have a leading role to play in solutions, notably that they should work together to create a National Housing Strategy, but it also concluded: "Traditional programs designed, funded and implemented exclusively by government will not suffice. The Board believes that innovative approaches, particularly the use of Public Private Partnerships are a far more efficient and cost-effective way" (10). Interestingly, the suggestion here was that private-sector involvement in the production of social protection was in some ways motivated by a desire to limit government's involvement.

While the report was briefly influential in terms of framing and defining homelessness as it related to Toronto's global competitiveness (Hanna and Walton-Roberts 2004), there has been no sustained private-sector involvement in the governance of homelessness as there has been in Calgary. In Toronto, there is some degree of consensus that homelessness policy and service delivery is not the responsibility of private-sector actors. Private-sector actors have at times indicated a willingness to participate in implementation through public/private partnerships (PPPs), but they have not demonstrated an interest in a more significant role in policy development. One senior municipal official recalled that while developing Toronto's response to homelessness, city officials approached private-sector leaders for ideas about how the private sector could contribute long-term to the city's efforts to fight homelessness: "Their response was very clear – 'We pay our taxes already, you are asking us to pay more?' And we said, 'Hmm, good point'" (personal interview 2014).

The third sector's involvement in homelessness has been more sustained and at times highly influential, not just in Toronto but on the national scale as well. Lacking institutionalized venues through which to participate regularly during the 1990s and 2000s, third-sector actors pushed their ideas into policy-making circles through various forms of advocacy and direct action. The TDRC was the most visible locally based organization. It was formed in the 1990s by a group of activists and academics and a small number of private-sector actors (notably David Walsh, the President of Realco Property Ltd). Until it disbanded in 2012, the TDRC defended the rights of people who were unhoused and experiencing homelessness. While it never advanced a plan to end or reduce homelessness, it was a strong, highly critical voice advocating for better standards in emergency shelters and more government investments in social and affordable housing. Formed in 1990, the Ontario Coalition Against Poverty (OCAP)[8] is another important network that remains active. Though the network is active province-wide, it has a strong history of involvement in Toronto.

The TDRC sought to influence homelessness policy through protests, direct action and highly (and *surprisingly*, by their own admission) successful efforts to push homelessness onto the agenda of policy-makers. A major achievement of the TDRC, aided by TDRC member and city councillor Jack Layton – one of the few politicians at any level of government prioritizing homelessness at the time – was getting big city mayors across the country to declare in 1998 that homelessness was an unnatural, national disaster (see Connolly 2001; Crowe 2019; Layton 2008 for a full account). An actor involved with the TDRC explained how it happened:

> So we thought, just as a publicity stunt, let's get a bunch of mayors to declare a disaster. We didn't think anyone would take us seriously, we thought mayors would laugh us out of the room. But it was Jack [Layton]. We were sitting around with Jack and he said "I will go talk to the Mayor ..." Mel [Lastman] was this weird guy, but if you got him on the right day ... Lastman said "Hey, that's a great idea ..."
>
> Big city mayors used to all get together in the city the Grey Cup was in. So Mel said, "We are getting together in Winnipeg, there are going to be thirteen other mayors." So he said when the mayors get there, "I'll say, 'Okay, boys (because they're all men), what do you think about this idea?"

It was November 22, 1998. Much to our complete delight and surprise, all the mayors immediately signed on. On November 22 every year, we celebrate National Housing Day ... People don't realize that it came out of a crazy idea that a bunch of activists had, that then went to Jack Layton that went to Mel that went to all the other mayors ... But it became really powerful, and was the founding document for the TDRC[9] because as the name suggests, our basic message was that homelessness was a disaster, governments have an obligation for short-term relief and long-term redevelopment ...

Nothing came of it, from the provincial government or the federal prime minister. They did not unfortunately do anything about it. But symbolically, all of a sudden we had a bunch of energized mayors who were saying, "Wait a second. We have got a problem and you, provincial and federal governments, are abandoning us" (except for Quebec, which still had a fairly robust social policy program). (personal interview 2014)

The TDRC defined homelessness in disaster and emergency terms, which may have inadvertently contributed to the narrow prioritization of people experiencing chronic homelessness in future responses. Despite this original framing, the TDRC understood homelessness, and solutions to it, in broad terms. According to TDRC documents, "having no place to live means being excluded from all that is associated with having a home, a surrounding neighbourhood and a set of established community networks. It means being exiled from the mainstream patterns of day-to-day life" (TDRC 1998, 2). Homelessness was understood to be much more than a physical or even legal and social space associated with four walls and a roof. In this respect, the TDRC definition aligned with the broader definitions of homelessness adopted by the RAPSIM in Montreal as well as by some actors in Vancouver's Downtown Eastside. (The TDRC and Quebec-based groups collaborated, including during protests in Quebec City to advocate for increased federal investment in housing and responses to homelessness [Connolly 2001; Crowe 2019]).

The TDRC was guided by this understanding of homelessness and motivated by emergency conditions in Toronto. Former TDRC member Michael Shapcott described their approach to advocacy and to engaging with policy-makers. Referencing the report on homelessness in Toronto produced by Anne Golden in 1999, Shapcott explained how the TDRC engaged:

We kind of stood on the outside and we pushed and pushed and pushed. We said, "Not good enough, you have to do more." Because Dr Golden ...

would have her finger in the wind and would say, "I think I can push this far but I can't push any farther. It won't work." And we would say, "No, you have got to push farther." So we created a political space for her to be a lot more bold. (Shapcott 2014)

Implicit in this interpretation of the TDRC's role was the responsibility to produce social protection. The TDRC clearly saw that responsibility as lying with government. It also saw the TDRC's role as pushing the government to do more in terms of that production. In creating a "political space" for bolder government action, the TDRC did not simply advocate: that group made it possible for government responses to be more expansive. Linked to their understanding of the government's role was their understanding of the problem: in pushing the government to go farther and in creating space for it to be bolder, the TDRC was expanding the city's understanding of homelessness.

Though their influence at City Hall was never institutionalized, it was strengthened by a crucial insider, Jack Layton, a city councillor and TDRC member. According to many, Layton was the key bridge between the city and the advocates. The TDRC targeted key political leaders, including Mayor Lastman's high-ranking aide Sean Gadon (Lastman refused to meet with the TDRC for years, but the activists had a good relationship with Gadon). TDRC advocates also went to great lengths to spread their message beyond the halls of power. They advocated in direct ways, at times involving civil disobedience (Crowe 2011), with a focus on educating the broader public, changing minds, all while pressuring those in power. Amplified with a megaphone, which it sometimes raised even in City Hall, the TDRC pushed successfully for reforms to shelter standards, including maximum capacities (personal interviews 2014).

The TDRC dissolved in 2012, partly due to funding challenges. A senior bureaucrat noted: "It is hard to sustain any type of political organization ... They were not able to get donations" (personal interview 2014). This was confirmed, in somewhat more bitter terms, by a TDRC founding member: "Advocacy is extremely, extremely weak right now ... Agencies are very much silenced by the funding streams they have got" (personal interview 2014). This actor went on to explain how funding had become tied to Housing First. Groups that did not agree with that approach faced consequences, according to this actor: "An agency will be ostracized or have their funding cut because of advocacy." OCAP remained active and continued to organize and engage in direct action with respect to poverty reduction and homelessness interventions, though some city officials interviewed noted that even OCAP advocacy was quiet and went through a period of weakness shortly after 2010 (personal interview 2014).

In addition to funding challenges, important ideational divisions had arisen within the group. Divisions between third-sector groups are not uncommon at the local level in Toronto, where community groups sometimes split between centre-left and far-left (see Hudson and Graefe 2012; Isin 1998). In interviews, former TDRC members shared different interpretations of the group's history and what it had accomplished, revealing disagreements regarding ideas about the nature of homelessness and what constitutes progress in efforts to fight it. One former member was sarcastic about the state of homelessness in the city: "A positive step is that shelters are now closer to refugee camps than they were. It is not a big win." A different version of the story, told by another founding member of the TDRC, Michael Shapcott, is more optimistic:

> Most of the people I have worked [in the TDRC] with have gone by the wayside. I feel sad about that. Many of them are bitter, and when they look at the history I just told you, they see it as a history of failure. That despite all our incredible efforts, the conditions are still worse, more people in poverty, more people are precariously housed, more are homeless than ever since the end of World War Two. So objectively, we have failed.
>
> I think slightly differently. This is a very personal thing for me, and I don't want to discount that there are lots of people who are suffering and dying. We know that. Many of them are people I have known. I go to the homeless memorial every month. I feel strongly a continuing sense of anger and loss ... But one of the dangers of housing advocates is that we start to really believe our own rhetoric, like the world is ending and so on. It is terrible. Objectively, the conditions are awful. But in the midst of these terrible conditions, we have actually had some important successes. (personal interview Shapcott 2014)

When the TDRC disbanded in 2012, it left an important advocacy gap. Though its role had been contentious, city officials who were interviewed shortly after the group's dissolution remembered it fondly and even hoped it might return: "I think the advocates are terrific. They help make better public policy. So it is a bad thing that the Toronto Disaster Relief Committee does not operate anymore" (personal interview 2014). Another senior official said, "I'd like to see the TDRC reinvent itself and come back" (personal interview 2014). OCAP was able to fill some of the advocacy gap, though that organization also went through a period of relative calm in the early 2010s. Still, the role of OCAP was also acknowledged by city officials: "they come and storm city hall every once in a while … God they are frustrating as hell sometimes. But there needs to be someone out there raising banners on empty housing" (personal interview 2014).

After a few years of comparatively weak advocacy at the local level, the Toronto Alliance to End Homelessness (TAEH) was founded in 2014, incorporating dozens of service providers and supporters from across the city, including some (though certainly not all) former members of the TDRC. The TAEH was founded in the wake of the CAEH's first annual conference to end homelessness, held in Ottawa. A founding member recalled returning to Toronto after the conference: "I know I came back [to Toronto] with a very strong feeling that there were a whole bunch of other municipalities and cities that were well ahead of Toronto in terms of having a coordinated and more effective approach" (personal interview 2018). Inspired by efforts elsewhere (primarily in Alberta, for Alberta-based presentations dominated that first conference in 2013), the TAEH set out to improve the coordination of homelessness efforts between the city and third-sector groups and to streamline those efforts toward permanent solutions. It has sought to do this through collabora-tion, and it supports Housing First approaches to ending homelessness. Like other Alliances to End Homelessness and their allies, the TAEH is critical of shelters and respite centres as solutions to homelessness, but it has supported them on certain occasions (including during winter months or when faced with evidence that Toronto's emergency shelter system is overrun). Where the TDRC was positioned more as a critic of, and outsider to, governmental efforts, the TAEH seeks to work more closely with city officials.

Remembering what homelessness governance in Toronto was like in the early 2000s, an actor involved with the TAEH underscored the local conflict that characterized that period: "The advocates at the time had very little time for the government and politicians and some bu-reaucrats and agencies. And the agencies have had little time for the City. And the City hasn't trusted the agencies because they feel every time they put something forward, they get slammed" (personal inter-view 2018). Suspicion, disagreement, and distrust abounded. A senior official explained that while they tried to involve community groups, some were much more difficult to engage: "With OCAP, you just can't tell what they want. You answer their problem and they still protest. Just nothing to work with there" (personal interview 2014).[10] From the perspective of third-sector groups and service providers who wanted to collaborate, the city wasn't any easier to work with. Carey Dober-stein has argued that the local governance dynamics in Toronto have historically lacked inclusion and consultation of third sector groups, noting that "policy-making in Toronto has generally been municipal-ized" (Doberstein 2016, 88). This perspective was confirmed in an inter-view, when an actor said there was "a good deal of frustration among many people in the [TAEH]. Not just about the sort of interventions and their effectiveness, but the fact that communications from the city ... and engagement in community consultation was lacking ... Frankly, we weren't being used in an optimal way" (personal interview 2018). The TAEH wanted to be used optimally, and its members indicated that they saw a larger role for themselves in homelessness governance be-yond advocating and implementing.

There was also frustration that concerted and heartfelt efforts by all in-volved were not leading to reductions in homelessness, a reality that led to "an unbelievable sort of exhaustion with banging our heads against the wall and getting very frustrating results" (personal interview 2018). In an effort to do things differently, and recognizing the value of col-laboration, the TAEH sought a new, closer relationship with the city. The external situation had not changed, but frustration with a lack of progress led to changing ideas regarding the responsibility to produce social protection. The mechanism by which these ideas shaped the gov-ernance dynamics was therefore environmental, which allowed to the exploration of new solutions to the same problem in the same context.

In the words of another senior actor, "What we are trying to do is really do something ... We are not trying to be another traditional ad-vocacy organization. We are trying to create a table where people can come and work together, people that have never been able to work together before" (personal interview 2018). This seeming nod to tacti-cal differences between the TAEH on the one hand and the TDRC and OCAP on the other indicates that they take starkly different approaches to seeking this change. For example, a film about the Tent City evic-tions shows several antagonistic interactions between TDRC members and senior bureaucrats, including Sean Gadon (Connolly 2001). At one point in the film, TDRC member Beric German storms City Hall with a megaphone, demanding to know the location of Mayor Lastman. With-ers notes that this kind of direct action is almost inevitable from the per-spective of OCAP. To the extent that OCAP engages the city in formal institutional contexts, it is strategic:

> The strategy behind making deputations isn't simply to be heard through the formal democratic process. Indeed, OCAP's experiences demonstrate that there is good reason not to believe these processes will lead to change. However, OCAP takes institutional avenues, at various points in its

campaigns, so it can say that it did – as a means of legitimizing the nearly always necessary disruption that will follow. While OCAP is a direct-action organization, it cannot simply rush into direct action without attempting to resolve an issue through another avenue first. (Withers 2021, 131)

They contrast this approach with that of the TAEH, which has become aligned with the city and therefore has close relationships with senior decision-makers: "TAEH has direct access to decision makers in the ruling regime and the organization has forged an alliance with them. Consequently, disruptive tactics are unnecessary" (Withers 2021, 166).

TAEH leadership did not dispute this, and implicitly agreed in interviews that there are substantial differences in terms of tactics and definitions of homelessness motivating their actions when compared with OCAP or historically the TDRC. This type of divide between third-sector groups, operating in different ways and with different assumptions regarding homelessness, is also clearly seen in Montreal (see the next chapter). From its early days, the TAEH planned to do its work in a more targeted, behind-the-scenes way: "We fairly quickly migrated towards and then refined a position of 'Look, we have to work effectively with stakeholders here. Municipal government probably being number one on that list'…Consultation has been very high level, and then people go away and make decisions" (personal interview 2018). The TAEH has achieved considerable success, and quickly. It became the Community Advisory Board for the HPS in 2015 – an important step toward a better relationship with the city.

Efforts to work with the city were further eased by a strengthening ideational convergence between city officials and community advocates regarding the nature of homelessness. Having aligned itself with the national movement that had inspired its creation and with local experts who had pioneered the Housing First approach in Canada, the TAEH now fully espouses a data-driven, Housing First approach to ending homelessness. This marks a break with what advocates and coalitions demanded in the past. But as a lead actor with the TAEH noted, "it didn't take a rocket scientist to figure out that what was being done wasn't working, right?" (personal interview 2018). This ideational convergence around the definition of homelessness underscored the value of working cooperatively with the city. When discussing the factors that allowed the TAEH to work more cooperatively with the city, one actor explained that "[our approach] was in line with the Housing First direction that the city has held for a long time" (personal interview 2018). Another actor confirmed that this ideational shift at the service provider level allowed the TAEH to work more effectively with the city: "The city said back to us, "if our vision is the same as the TAEH's to reach zero chronic and episodic homelessness, and to do so through this sort of data-driven approach, then why would we not want you to co-chair as our community leaders?'" (personal interview 2018). In an sense, then, this change in governing arrangement is a fairly safe one for the city; as Withers notes, the city is able to hold up its relationship with the TAEH as evidence of consultation with community groups (which, in fact, it is), but the city has managed to foster a relationship with a group that agrees with its approach in the first place.

In 2018, the city and the TAEH together founded the Toronto Housing And Homelessness Service Planning Forum (THHSPF). The original plan was to work together for one year and reassess in 2019; by all accounts, the forum is going well, and as of 2022 it still meets each month. These meetings allow city officials and service providers to learn from one another and exchange information, both formally and informally (though this is harder than it used to be now that meetings have been forced online by COVID restrictions). These meetings are open to the public and service providers who are not formal members of the TAEH are free to attend and participate. In its draft terms of reference, presented to and approved by the THHSPF on 28 March 2018, the forum's mandate is clearly identified: "The forum collaborates together to create a shared vision for Toronto's housing stability service system, and to improve housing stability outcomes for residents of Toronto. It supports a mutually reinforcing and inclusive environment in which the city, its relevant agencies, boards and commissions, and the community work together to develop collective approaches that draw on the strengths, expertise and powers of each." The forum's authority is broad: "The forum considers issues relating to the whole Housing Stability Service System administered by the City of Toronto. This includes, but is not limited to, emergency shelters, housing help, street outreach, drop-ins, housing supports, housing access, and affordable housing" (City of Toronto and TAEH 2018).

THHSPF meetings are co-chaired by the city and the TAEH. The two work hard to build a strong and trusting relationship; attendees from both sides suppress their well-honed combative instincts. Since 2014, however, the TAEH has sought a more cooperative relationship with the city. A letter from TAEH founding president Mark Aston, sent to the city in 2015, noted that for twelve months, the TAEH had been working constructively with the city to "effectively address the crisis of homelessness." He then noted that efforts were well-received: "We have spoken to the General Manager of SSHA, Phillip Abrahams, and he has committed to working constructively and meaningfully with the Alliance" (Aston 2015).

While the two groups are working hard to collaborate, and are succeeding in many respects, some tensions remain. One recent contentious issue has been the development of "respite sites," that is, city-run facilities that provide additional shelter space during the winter. Respite centres are low-barrier, accessible emergency services for populations that might avoid or might not be able to access the traditional shelter system. TAEH members claim that such shelters risk undermining efforts to end homelessness. A letter written by Kira Heineck on behalf of the TAEH illustrates the TAEH's perspective regarding the nature of homelessness, but also the diplomatic approach taken by senior leadership when engaging the city on matters of disagreement. Heineck walks a very careful line, not fully opposing new shelters, but also pushing the city to make them a truly temporary response: "For right now, of course immediate emergency action was and is needed this winter. The current challenges people face in finding good shelter, appropriate health care and other supports demand it. As we have stated before, however, we cannot address homelessness through an expansion of shelter services alone" (Heineck 2018).

The letter goes on to compare the cost of emergency shelter ($27,500 per year) to supportive housing ($17,000 per year), and concludes: "There is no doubt that this committee and City Council are grappling with an unhappy, dire situation in regards to homelessness in Toronto. The TAEH supports you in doing the right thing and make [sic] decisions that will end homelessness rather than just manage it" (Heineck 2018). While the instinct to criticize one another remains strong, the institutionalized forum has positively structured interactions and allows groups to communicate and coordinate in a way that is respectful and collaborative. A different perspective on this disagreement, articulated by Withers, is that the TAEH has become compromised by its close relationship with the city. This has led the TAEH, which is generally opposed to new shelters, to support the city in its opening of new respite centres, or at least to self-censor. The same might be said for the TAEH's publicly diplomatic response to Toronto's violent clearing of homeless encampments in the summer of 2021; though the TAEH was opposed to encampment clearances, when the city went ahead, its opposition was muted. Of course, behind the scenes lobbying and advocacy may have taken place, making it difficult to know if the TAEH did self-censor, or only did so publicly.

The TAEH is seeking to build a relationship with Toronto's Aboriginal Community Advisory Board, which administers federal HPS funding, so that at the very least information can be shared more easily. A senior official with the TAEH explained that "we are *slowly* finding our way to the Aboriginal CAB. It's a key goal for this year" (personal interview 2018). In a recent THHSPF meeting in 2021, senior leaders of the TAEH reflected on their role in the context of Black Lives Matter and struggles for reconciliation with and inclusion of Indigenous people, acknowledging that their own leadership lacked diversity and that they were seeking to change this. Historically, there has been little interaction between the Indigenous CAB and the Designated Community CAB. Toronto's Aboriginal CAB is small compared to Vancouver's, containing representatives from just seven service providers, including the Native Women's Resource Centre, Native Child and Family Services of Toronto, and Nishnawbe Homes. This lack of interaction is jarring: Toronto's Designated Community CAB has historically dedicated 20 per cent of its HPS funding to Indigenous programs, yet it has done so without formal coordination with the Indigenous CAB (Doberstein 2016). Coordination with the Indigenous CAB would likely make efforts to combat Indigenous homelessness more effective, for it would align services toward the same, or at least coordinated, goals.

Indigenous groups have not historically been included in broader homelessness governance dynamics in Toronto. A leader at an Indigenous-led service in Toronto said: "At the city level, often Aboriginal people are not consulted on how to solve homelessness ... You put yourself out there. They don't come to you" (personal interview 2014). This is consistent with what has been found in other work on Indigenous involvement in urban multilevel governance in Ontario: "In Ontario cities, urban Aboriginal populations are often not visible to municipal government officials" (Peters 2012, 4). Sometimes, Indigenous people are even prevented from implementing programs that are specifically for the Indigenous community. One actor explained how the Indigenous-led organization they manage was able to purchase housing and run it as a supportive development, a good example of both the importance of Indigenous-led services and the barriers faced by Indigenous service providers in providing them. When I asked where the funding for the housing project came from, they said, "We found out some time ago that the province was holding on to Urban Aboriginal Housing dollars. It was not being administered." When I asked why, they responded:

It's really stupid. There are a lot of systemic barriers from the province, and ignorance, I'm sure. They said they didn't feel that there was any Aboriginal organization that had the capacity to administer those dollars. Or the experience. But lots of Aboriginal agencies had administered funding dollars through the assets agreement, so they were able to demonstrate that they had a track record of administering funding. They had all the risk management in place, they had been fiscally responsible. It took a long time to convince the province to administer those dollars. Once they started administering it, we applied to them for that funding. (personal interview 2014)

Third-sector groups often face scrutiny over their budgets, to be sure, and some have been forced to change their leadership (this is perhaps most famously the case with the Portland Housing Society in Vancouver). But in this case, Indigenous-led organizations not even being given the opportunity to apply for funding is systemic racism in action. When Indigenous people do "put themselves out there" to be part of the solution, they frequently must first address problems and barriers that are unique to the Indigenous community. This is labour-intensive work that requires Indigenous people to identify problems, explain them, and educate others before working toward solutions, all while responding to the crisis of homelessness. A senior official at one of the oldest services for Indigenous men in the country gave an example of this:

> At one point some of our guys were profiled by the police. Sometimes some of the boys will go to the park to play Frisbee or soccer. Sometimes the police go to the park. They don't stop the other guys, but they stop the Native guys, ID them, run their names through the system. They ask them why they aren't drinking. Our programs are abstinence-based, we don't allow drinking. I tell the guys to get [the officers'] names and badge numbers. Eventually I started complaining to the unit commander. He wasn't responding. So I got smart and emailed some of the high-ranking officers I know, and City Council. The city counsellor facilitated a meeting with the key players and we worked through it. And it resulted in me training every front-line officer in Unit [redacted] on how to work more collaboratively with us…
>
> We talk about the treaties, some of the unjust laws that Canada has had that have put Native people in conflict with police. Sometimes when Native people see the uniform, it puts them on the defensive. After all, it was police officers in uniform who would force Aboriginal children to go to residential schools. Or back in the sixties, when they took children from homes, it was usually an officer who accompanied them when they did that. A lot of baggage comes for certain people when they see that uniform.

Indigenous-led services not only face increased barriers but also are made responsible for identifying them and for education (in this case, educating the police on the history of policing and relationships with Indigenous communities). Furthermore, during the aughts and

2010s, Indigenous knowledge was not sought systematically in local responses to homelessness. This exclusion of Indigenous knowledge and approaches to homelessness places the success of those programs at risk, given the unique ability of Indigenous-led services to connect and produce social protection from an Indigenous perspective. In an interview with the leader of a shelter for Indigenous men, drumming can be heard in the background of the interview, a reminder of how Indigenous traditions are constantly centred in that service. This leader explained the resurgent approach taken by their organization and how centring Indigenous ceremonies and traditions has been healing:

> We have a unique approach to outreach because we work with elders. They go in our vans. A lot of our staff know the different parks and ravines, they know where the homeless guys sleep out in encampments, the drop-ins. So they go with elders. Two of them are Ojibwe and speak their language. They are well-known and respected. Some of the folks who have been homeless for many years are difficult to engage, even for our staff. With our elders, they seem to break down those barriers. They will do some counselling and a ceremony. They bring the cultural connection, they speak to the guy in their language. They have a way of engaging the people who maybe our staff can't engage so easily. It creates a trusting bond a little more quickly. They are a great help. (personal interview 2014)

Conclusion

Toronto is unique among the cities included here because of its formal jurisdiction over housing and homelessness, a power transferred to municipalities in 1999 by Premier Mike Harris. The ways in which the city has exercised this power have changed considerably: the city has gone from jealously guarding its power to governing collaboratively with some third-sector groups. If anything, the city gained institutional strength while this was happening. These changes occurred because of changing ideas regarding the responsibility to produce social protection among city officials, and regarding the nature of homelessness among the advocacy group representing third-sector groups city-wide.

The Province of Ontario has gone from a leader to a laggard with respect to its involvement in housing. In the 1960s, Ontario was a Canadian leader in housing policy, developing expertise and capacity early on and influencing policy in other provinces as well as at the federal level. This changed dramatically in the 1990s when the province downloaded responsibility for housing and homelessness to municipalities, making clear that the province saw no role for itself in this part of welfare state governance. Even more than resources, ideas regarding the limited role of government in the provision of social protection explain the province's decision to step back from housing policy during the 1990s.

The province has since become more involved in efforts to combat homelessness, which became a core component of efforts to fight poverty under Premier Kathleen Wynne's Liberal government. Yet even with renewed provincial involvement under Liberal governments, provincial involvement is minimal. Ideas regarding the responsibility to produce social protection, interacting with the institutional reality that assigns authority to municipalities have created a situation in which authority and resources are mismatched. Provincial actors have re-embraced an understanding that they have a role to play, but in partnership and collaboration with other multilevel actors, especially the federal government. The province has further limited its involvement under Doug Ford's Progressive Conservative government; to the extent that the province seeks partnerships, it is now with the private sector, as the province's poverty reduction strategy prioritizes jobs as a primary means of social protection, consistent with ideological differences between provincial parties.

The governance of homelessness in Toronto is centralized in the city, but the way in which the city governs has evolved considerably since the 1990s, when it was first given the responsibility. Over time, the city has gone from a so-called command-and-control approach to one of co-governance with community groups. This important change in governance has led to power-sharing despite an increase in institutional power (after being granted inclusionary zoning powers). This dynamism in the governance of homelessness is explained by two ideational changes operating through environmental and cognitive mechanisms. First, the city's understanding of the responsibility to produce social protection changed as city officials became frustrated by a lack of progress and increasingly aware of the need to work with community groups in efforts to fight homelessness.

The second ideational change is seen in the third sector, where the most powerful group representing service providers and people experiencing homelessness, the TAEH, espouses the city's understanding of homelessness and preferred approach to ending it. This is a significant shift in community dynamics, as up until 2012, the main body representing service providers and people experiencing homelessness, the TDRC, positioned itself in opposition to much of what the city was doing. OCAP remains active in Toronto and continues to criticize the city and oppose Housing First approaches. The TAEH for its part was frustrated with not being included in policy-making and advanced a different approach to engaging with the city than the TDRC and OCAP, working collabora- tively with the city even if that may mean muting its criticisms (publicly at least). Convergence around both of these ideas, which involved each of the parties moving toward the other's position, has allowed for a part- nership to emerge at the local level. Indigenous actors in Toronto have long been excluded from policy-making. Where they are involved, it has tended to be at their own initiative, which means it is frequently up to them to identify and explain problems and to advocate for solutions. Even with these additional burdens, Indigenous-led groups are effective in their approaches, which centre Indigenous culture and ceremonies.

8 Montreal

A number of actors are involved in the governance of homelessness in Montreal. Though there are some deep divides, there is also extensive coordination and collaboration. The Province of Quebec has a long history of involvement in homelessness, including with an interministerial plan on homelessness since 2010 and a policy on homelessness since 2014.[1] Provincial officials are also involved in the administration of non-Indigenous federal NHI/HPS funds in Quebec, though community plans are developed at the regional level by civil society actors. Following funding changes imposed by the federal government in 2014, which required 65 per cent of HPS funding to be allocated to Housing First programs, an *additional* regional plan, based on the province's plan, was created for Montreal. This regional plan prioritizes non-Housing First programs. The City of Montreal has become increasingly involved in homelessness governance in recent years as well. Montreal's first formal homelessness plan was introduced in 2010. A new plan, introduced in 2013, broke away from provincial priorities and advanced a distinct municipal vision. A 2018 municipal plan has continued to assert the city's viewpoint and increased its involvement, while also moving toward alignment with future provincial plans in terms of timing and approach.

Third-sector groups have an institutionalized role in policy-making in Quebec, affording them greater legitimacy and influence than what is seen in other cities and provinces. One of the most important local third-sector actors is the Réseau d'aide au personnes seules et itinérantes de Montréal (RAPSIM), a group that advocates on behalf of people who experience homelessness as well as for service providers. It has existed since the 1970s. The RAPSIM does not have a formal plan on homelessness, but it is influential in policy-making across all three levels of government and in advocating for its preferred solution to homelessness: social housing with community support. A second locally based network, the Mouvement pour mettre fin à l'itinérance à Montréal (MMFIM), was formed in 2015. The MMFIM takes a different approach to homelessness than the RAPSIM, advancing Housing First programs and prioritizing chronic homelessness.

Some of these groups work together, aligning and coordinating their actions. Others, however, are at odds with one another and advance different approaches to homelessness. Ideas and institutions interact in Montreal to create a vibrant but divided – especially at the local level – governance structure. Ideas regarding the responsibility to produce social protection interacting with ideas regarding federalism have led the province to enthusiastically exercise its powers over housing and homelessness. The city's involvement in homelessness is relatively limited due in part to its institutionally weak position, but changing ideas regarding the responsibility to produce social protection and an increasingly comprehensive conceptualization of the city's role have led the city to push its way onto the crowded policy field in recent years. With an institutionalized role in policy-making, third-sector groups have considerable power at the municipal and provincial levels. Powerful ideas regarding the nature of homelessness, however, have broken this influential sector in two, resulting in two distinct approaches to homelessness. The institutional structure of the National Homelessness Initiative/Homelessness Partnering Strategy, which involves the province, has reinforced these ideational divisions but also illustrates the productive potential of coordinated fragmentation (the NHI/HPS is reviewed under the provincial history, because of the province's involvement in its administration).

Homelessness History in Quebec

The provincial welfare state developed later in Quebec than it did in other provinces. It also developed differently: compared to other provinces, Quebec's welfare state tends to be more interventionist, with more universal programs, and civil society participates more in policy development. These differences should not be overstated: Quebec is not the most generous province in the federation when it comes to social assistance, for example (Tweddle and Aldridge 2019). Quebec differs substantively, nevertheless, from other provinces, not just in the content of some of its social policies but also in terms of their governance and development, which is very inclusive of third-sector groups.[2] The province is heavily involved in housing and homelessness policy, having developed two provincial action plans on homelessness and a policy on homelessness as well. Civil society was involved in developing these, particularly during periods of Parti Québécois (PQ) governance. Ideas regarding the responsibility to produce social protection, interacting with ideas regarding federalism, explain initial provincial involvement, and provincially developed ideas regarding the nature of homelessness explain the endurance of its leadership.

Quebec is the only province to have continually funded social housing ever since the federal cuts, though its commitment in the 1990s was lukewarm. Social housing production was comparatively slow in the 1960s and 1970s when other social policies were expanding in the province: "Quebec's Quiet Revolution, which started in the early 1960s, sparked tremendous reforms in the fields of education, health and welfare. But other fields – housing among them – had to wait longer" (Vaillancourt and Ducharme 2001, 12). This began to change, albeit slowly, with the creation of the province's housing agency, the Société d'habitation du Québec (SHQ), during the Quiet Revolution. While housing was not a government priority *per se* during the 1970s, evolving ideas about federalism and sovereignty led to a more assertive provincial stance in the provision of social protection to Quebec citizens. In other words, standing up to the federal government against what were seen to be intrusions into areas of provincial jurisdiction *was* a priority, and housing fit with this agenda.

In a commemoration of the fiftieth anniversary of the SHQ, a 2017 publication explains that before the Quiet Revolution, "the Quebec government was reluctant to intervene in the housing sector" and instead "considered housing a responsibility of the private sector" (Société d'habitation du Québec 2017, 3; author's translation). A document commemorating the twenty-fifth anniversary of the SHQ further explains: "The government of Quebec was not very happy with the conclusion of direct agreements between municipalities and the federal government. It thus decided to create its own organization" (Société d'habitation du Québec 1992, 17; author's translation). Ideas regarding federalism led the province to assert its responsibility for housing policy in the 1960s. Evident in these documents is the fact that this original engagement in housing was less about a belief in government responsibility for the production of housing; indeed, as indicated above, it was seen to be a private-sector responsibility. Rather, a more powerful idea about *federalism* led the province to increase its involvement so as to block federal involvement in areas of provincial jurisdiction.

Quebec expanded its role in housing production in the late 1970s and 1980s, and the development of social housing across Quebec began to pick up considerably toward the late 1970s. Logipop was Quebec's main housing program at that time, existing from 1977 to 1986.

This was a broadly targeted housing program geared toward low- and moderate-income people wanting to form housing cooperatives. By 1980, there were just over 35,000 units of broadly targeted social or public housing in Quebec (Vaillancourt and Ducharme 2001). A 1986 Canada–Quebec housing agreement, based on private-sector–built and non-profit managed projects, brought a more targeted, low-income focus to social housing. Maroine Bendaoud writes that "the generalist goal of the Logipop program was gone" (Bendaoud 2016, 187; author's translation). Alongside the more targeted orientation of housing policy were decreased future commitments to new housing developments in Quebec; these changes (which preceded the federal government's withdrawal) would guide provincial policies developed in the absence of the federal partner in the 1990s.

When the federal government cut and downloaded social housing in the mid-1990s, the province was facing several political and economic challenges (Vaillancourt et al. 2016). The province had been through a divisive referendum on sovereignty, and its finances were suffering as a result of an economic downturn that affected the entire country. Vaillancourt and colleagues (2016) write that this timing both increased and decreased the likelihood that the province would step up and continue to fund social housing on its own. On the one hand, the province was experiencing financial precarity, and housing is expensive to build; but on the other, the province was in the process of nation-building, and social policies can be powerful tools in that process (Banting 2005).

In this context, the PQ government introduced a provincial housing policy, though Gabriel Arsenault specifies that this "commitment to expand the provision of social housing was highly fragile" (Arsenault 2016, 16). The province initially committed to building 1,500 units of social housing per year for three years only; however, it fell far short of this objective, producing only 1,142 units in all (see Arsenault 2016; Vaillancourt et al. 2016). Despite a weak commitment to housing policy in the 1990s, community groups succeeded in pushing the PQ government to increase its investment in housing. The PQ has historically had stronger ties to civil society groups than the provincial Liberals, ties that were strengthened during a series of economic summits in the 1990s, during which "a coherent and credible coalition in favour of new policies had coalesced and gained recognition by government officials" (Noël 2010, 2). Maroine Bendaoud notes that during these summits, influential third-sector members of this coalition were strongly in favour of an expanded provincial role in housing policy: "Third sector groups mobilised to encourage the government to continue to support their efforts to develop new affordable housing. The pilot project that would become *AccèsLogis* was conceived of by these groups" (Bendaoud 2016, 182; author's translation).

During the 1980s and 1990s, the province slowly increased its involvement in the area of homelessness as well. In 1987, the UN's International Year of Shelter for the Homeless, Quebec undertook an initial study of homelessness. This effort was exploratory; even so, it revealed that the understanding of the nature of homelessness in Quebec has long related to more than just a lack of housing: "Housing instability results from economic, social, and psychological instability" (Ministère de la Main-d'ouevre et de la Sécurité du Revenue 1988, 13; author's translation). Though homelessness was loosely defined and no clear methodology or time period was explained, the study concluded that between 10,000 and 15,000 people in Montreal became homeless in the 1970s (Ministère de la Main-d'ouevre et de la Sécurité du Revenue 1988).

Informed by the results of the study, the province's Policy on Health and Well-Being (1992–2002) identified homelessness as an issue of concern. That policy sought to prevent homelessness, identifying Montreal and Quebec City as cities to prioritize. Actions to prevent and end homelessness included supporting families and prioritizing social re-insertion, the development of community housing for women, help for youth to complete schooling, and investments in detox, housing, and mental health services. The policy also identified three forms of homelessness – chronic, episodic, and transitional – and adopted the definition of homelessness developed in a 1987 Montreal plan (reviewed below): "A homeless person presents one or many of the following characteristics: does not have a fixed address or access to stable, safe, adequate housing for the following 60 days; has a very low income; does not have access to services available to citizens because of discrimination; has problems related to mental health, alcohol, drug use, or social disorganization; and is not a member of any stable group" (MSSS 1998, 52–3; author's translation). Though there was a strong focus on individual-level causes, the province's early conceptualization of homelessness indicated that homelessness was understood to be more than just the absence of housing, but related to inclusion and relationships as well. Homelessness was not a priority of government action during this time, but these documents nevertheless reveal early ideas regarding the nature of homelessness.

The province expanded its involvement in housing in 1997 with the introduction of the AccèsLogis program, which enabled the provincial government to work with community partners to build new social housing and to renovate older housing stock. It initially proposed the creation of 1,820 provincially funded units of housing per year (Société d'habitation du Québec 1997, 22).[3] This was a far cry from the 8,000 units per year demanded by advocacy groups (FRAPRU 2015), but it was nevertheless an important political commitment at a time when eight of the other nine Canadian provinces were completely ignoring housing development. AccèsLogis was initially set to expire after five years (Société d'habitation du Québec 1997); however, it has remained in place in Quebec ever since its inception in 1997, surviving changes in government,[4] economic downturns, and even periods of austerity.[5] Quebec is thus the only province in the country to have continually committed to funding new housing developments since the federal cuts in the 1990s.

The province was thus involved in housing, was slowing engaging in the governance of homelessness, and had adopted a definition of homelessness when the federal government introduced the National Homelessness Initiative (NHI) in 1999. Often considered an early example of "place-based policy" (Bradford 2005; Leo 2006), the NHI was seen by many in Quebec as a federal intrusion into provincial jurisdiction because it was designed to jump over the provinces and resulted in what effectively amounted to a transfer of money from the federal government to local groups to fight homelessness. Quebec objected to the arrangement. Indeed, when minister Claudette Bradshaw was developing the NHI, her federal Liberal cabinet colleague from Quebec, Stéphane Dion, then Minister of Intergovernmental Relations, opposed the program because he viewed it as intruding on provincial jurisdiction (Klodawsky and Evans 2014). Quebec had been studying and defining homelessness for ten years and was prepared to defend its jurisdictional responsibility from federal intrusion. The federal government would not simply transfer the funding to Quebec and allow it unilateral control as the province initially requested; however, a complicated but ultimately effective process was put in place, at Quebec's insistence, to allow for extensive provincial involvement in NHI/HPS operations in Quebec. At this time, we clearly see ideas about the responsibility to produce social protection, shaped by ideas about federalism, driving provincial involvement.

The process for implementing the NHI in Quebec began with a Canada–Quebec agreement, which stipulated that NHI/HPS funding for communities in Quebec must be transferred from the federal government to the province and that federal and provincial governments would be *jointly* responsible for overseeing the program. Canada–Quebec agreements make note of the priorities of each government, which include respecting Quebec jurisdiction and the organizational structure of services in Quebec while also acknowledging the orientations and priorities of Canada. While only one federal minister signs off on the agreements (Claudette Bradshaw herself, in the early days), two Quebec ministers sign off: the Minister Responsible for Social Services and the Minister of Intergovernmental Affairs, again underscoring the importance of ideas about federalism in shaping welfare state governance dynamics in Quebec.

The first agreement took two years to negotiate, resulting in a delay in NHI implementation in Quebec. The governance relations that are spelled out in these agreements point to a process that is bureaucratic and complicated, but one that allows for extensive community input into the plan development and project selection (though final decisions are made by provincial and federal bureaucrats). Flowing from provincial health structures, the NHI/HPS is administered by Regional Agencies of Health and Social Services,[6] which coordinate the development of community plans and oversee their implementation. To develop its early plans, the Regional Agency in Montreal relied on the expertise of two committees: a newly created NHI/HPS partners committee (Comité des partenaires[7]) as well as an older and more established homelessness liaison committee in Montreal (Comité liaison en itinérance[8]). Once drafted, the plan is approved by provincial and federal bureaucrats. Following approval, the agency issues a call for proposals to community groups seeking NHI/HPS funding. The agency then passes proposals on to a regional committee,[9] which recommends projects for funding, but this is not the end. The recommended projects are then sent for final approval to a bilateral committee comprised of two federal bureaucrats and two provincial bureaucrats.

Provincial officials note that Canada–Quebec agreements spell out provincial and federal priorities in advance, so that there are no surprises when it comes time to select projects, and few disagreements. Federal officials agree that the process works well but also note that from their perspective, projects are not truly jointly selected:

> The regional committee selects the top ten projects that go to the joint management committee. So they say, "It's jointly done." Well, no, because I never saw all the projects. [Quebec] is doing the priority setting, because they're only giving me the projects that they want to jointly fund. They say, "Oh, it's a wonderful model, it's all joint," but it's not actually. It would only be joint if I also had Service Canada people sifting through all the projects as well. (personal interview 2018).

In interviews, actors who were involved in NHI implementation in those early days noted that over time, the NHI/HPS has come to operate smoothly in Quebec. From the beginning, regional plans in Montreal have been critical of the federal program and outspoken about unrealistic timelines and inadequate funding, a reflection of the fiercely independent nature of third-sector groups in Quebec who criticize the governments that fund them routinely (Laforest 2011a; 2011b). The timeline of the NHI/HPS was frequently raised as particularly problematic. Recall that the NHI/HPS was, until 2014, only ever implemented for periods of one to three years at a time. This placed community groups in a very difficult position in terms of their programming and the services they could offer to the homeless population. The 2003 regional plan for Montreal, for example, stated that "the [renewed] program has been highly anticipated by the Montreal community notwithstanding the difficulties associated with the non-reoccurrence of the funding" (Régie régionale de la santé et des services sociaux de Montréal 2003, 13).

Through this model, Quebec has managed to wrestle considerable control from the federal government in terms of program implementation. Though the process works smoothly and a new Canada–Quebec agreement is signed every time the program is renewed, there is still evidence of power struggles between the governments. This was notably the case when the federal government imposed new requirements on HPS funding in 2014, requiring that 65 per cent of funding received by big cities by oriented to Housing First programs. There was strong resistance to this among some community groups in Montreal, as I will explain below. The importance of ideas about federalism are also in evidence as driving forces (even beyond ideas regarding the production of social protection) when it comes to the administration of federal funding for Indigenous homelessness. In other cities and provinces, in addition to the "Designated Community," there is also an "Aboriginal Community." In Montreal, there is no "Aboriginal Community," so there is no transfer of federal funding to an Indigenous-led entity to administer as they see fit. In Quebec, the province is only involved in the administration of non-Indigenous funding, and it does not have a similar agreement with the federal government regarding the implementation of funding for Indigenous communities (though Indigenous-led organizations can apply to the general regional network for funding). Indigenous groups seeking federal NHI/HPS funding apply directly to the federal government.

When it comes to the relationship between the federal government and Indigenous people in Montreal, therefore the province does not interfere, and the Indigenous stream of this funding is not included in Canada–Quebec agreements that govern the NHI/HPS. Ideas regarding federalism may be at play here, indicating that the province may view the responsibility for producing social protection for Indigenous people specifically as a federal responsibility, a reflection of the colonial division of powers that continues to give the federal government responsibility for Indigenous people and their lands (see Jago 2021). In the interviews, I was unable to determine the effectiveness of this dynamic; provincial officials did not know whether Indigenous groups in Montreal access all the funding for Indigenous communities to which they are entitled from the federal government (details on how general NHI/HPS funding has been spent have been nearly impossible to find as well, including through access to information requests). They did, however, stress that Indigenous groups can apply for funding through the main Designated Community plan, as is the case in other cities as well.

Advocacy groups advancing the rights of people experiencing homelessness, poverty, and social exclusion have been active in the province for decades; provincial policy began to more meaningfully catch up to these groups in the mid- to late 2000s. In 2008, in the wake of increases in the number of people experiencing homelessness, a provincial health and social services commission began to conduct extensive community consultations on homelessness. Provincial officials were concerned that their lack of understanding about homelessness risked weakening efforts to fight it. The consultation's work was guided by the 1987 definition of homelessness developed in Montreal (see below). Armed with a dense and detailed consultation document, the province asked community groups a number of questions related to the effectiveness of service delivery, to differences in the composition of the homeless population across the province, and to what could be done better to prevent homelessness.

The commission held twelve public meetings across the province, received 145 submissions, and heard from more than 100 individuals and organizations. The final report, released in 2009, made more than thirty recommendations. Illustrating the importance of community feedback in the design of government policy, that report[10] presents transparently what was heard during the consultations, including contradictory opinions in many cases, and then presents a final recommendation. For example, some groups said that the province and community actors needed more and better information about homelessness, whereas others said they already understood the problem (and the solutions as well). Acknowledging the disagreement, the commission recommended that a thorough, and regularly updated, portrait of homelessness in the province be developed. Importantly, the report also noted that all community groups and most institutional partners insisted that a provincial *policy* on homelessness was necessary: "Only a government policy, based on a global and inclusive vision … can respond to the multiple challenges that this phenomenon presents" (Commission de la santé et des services sociaux 2009, 53; author's translation). The report endorsed this call for a policy on homelessness, recommending that the government introduce one to guide government actions and to coordinate the different partners involved. It also called for an action plan on homelessness.

While the consultation was under way, the province was already developing a plan on homelessness, which was released in 2010 under a Liberal government. That plan was informed by the same process that had informed the commission's 2009 report. The plan on homelessness notes that the "democratic exercise" of the 2008–9 consultations had called for the development of a plan on homelessness, though no mention was made of a homelessness policy – an important omission considering that many community groups and the commission had advocated powerfully for one. The 2010 plan on homelessness involved nine ministries,[11] demonstrating significant internal collaboration, and invested $14 million in efforts to combat homelessness over three years (2010–13). It applied a narrow, housing-based definition of homelessness developed by the Library of Parliament (a federal institution): "By definition, a homeless person does not have a fixed address, stable, secure, and adequate housing" (MSSS 2009, 23; author's translation).

This departure from past understandings of homelessness in Quebec is curious. It confirms what others have found – that the Liberal Party has long had weaker links with community groups (Laforest 2011b; Arsenault 2018), which had advanced and developed a broader and more inclusive definition of homelessness since the 1990s. Buried in the province's first homelessness plan, Recommendation #63 called for a portrait of homelessness; the portrait had been Recommendation #1 of the 2009 final report on homelessness. It would take five years for the first portrait of homelessness in Quebec to be released due to a lack of political will and difficulty finding a group to lead the development of the portrait.

Montreal-based homelessness advocacy group the RAPSIM, and the RSIQ, a province-wide advocacy body,[12] criticized the provincial plan for not investing enough resources in housing and poverty reduction. Further, these groups and others across the province had long advocated for a homelessness *policy* before a plan, and criticized the government for skipping what they saw as a necessary first step that would allow for a "coherence in the actions undertaken by the government. Simply put, so the right hand knows what the left is doing, which is not currently the case. The best example of this concerns public space; with the left hand, the state finances aid organizations … but with the right, it criminalizes homeless people" (RAPSIM 2009; author's translation). The Quebec Liberal Party, however, went straight to an action plan in 2010, creating an opening for the PQ. The 2012 provincial election campaign saw PQ leader Pauline Marois lean on her party's relations with community groups and service providers and promise a provincial homelessness policy and a province-wide portrait of homelessness. Shortly after the PQ was elected to lead a minority government, the new PQ Minister Responsible for Homelessness, Véronique Hivon, held a two-day forum on homelessness and conducted extensive community consultations on the subject across the province.

A senior official with Quebec's housing society recounted that the process for developing the policy extended considerable power to community groups. During the consultation, for example, provincial officials were not allowed to so much as speak: "Community groups from across the province where there, and only they had the right to speak. [Provincial officials] were backbenchers" (personal interview 2014; author's translation). The PQ brought advocacy groups right into their policy-making, thus reinforcing a partisan difference in terms of the role of third-sector groups in the production of social protection. Indications at this time were that while the province was the leader, the responsibility to produce social protection was to be exercised in partnership with community groups. This led to the unveiling of a long-demanded homelessness policy in 2014 (the 2010–13 homelessness plan, introduced by the PLQ, had been extended for one year to maintain continuity of services).

The involvement of third-sector groups in the development of the provincial policy allowed them to contribute directly to a made-in- and made-for-Quebec definition of homelessness. The new definition replaced the previous definitions, including the 2010 plan's narrow one (federally developed) and the inclusive but highly individualized 1987 one. In the homelessness policy introduced in 2014, homelessness was defined as follows: "Homelessness refers to a process of social disaffiliation and a situation of social rupture that manifests in a person's difficulty maintaining a stable, safe, adequate, and clean home as a result of the unavailability of housing or of his or her inability to maintain it and, at the same time, by a person's difficulty maintaining functional, stable and safe relations in the community" (Gouvernement du Québec 2014, 30; author's translation).

As was made clear in chapter 2, this definition is much broader than past ones in terms of structural (versus individual) causes, but it continues to stress the importance of community relations and inclusion. It follows that the solutions to homelessness that flow out of this definition entail more than just housing, or even supportive housing; they are also community-based. The definition does not specifically mention Indigenous homelessness, though the policy identifies homelessness among Indigenous people as a concern and recognizes that Indigenous people face additional barriers to accessing housing. These barriers include trauma arising from recent experiences in the residential "school" system, as well as other forms of discrimination. Colonialism – either historic or contemporary – is not identified independently as a cause of homelessness, and this indicates that for Indigenous people in Quebec, homelessness is still quite individualized.

Applying the province's definition of homelessness, the portrait of homelessness released in 2014[13] found that there were 1,263 shelter beds in the province, including 130 for women, 967 for men, and 166 in mixed shelters. It noted that over the course of one year, the shelters were at an average capacity of 78.8 per cent, albeit with considerable variation depending on location and type of shelter (the occupancy rate in youth shelters, for example, tended to be much higher) (MSSS 2014; see also Withers 2021). The portrait noted that its methodology had been designed to reflect different forms of homelessness, not just chronic or visible homelessness but also invisible forms of homelessness such as couch-surfing. Furthermore, the province positioned itself in opposition to homeless counts as a means of understanding homelessness, noting that they overrepresent chronic homelessness and underrepresent episodic and other, more hidden forms of homelessness.

In addition to all these developments, in 2014 the federal government announced new requirements for HPS funding: large cities would have to dedicate 65 per cent of their funding to Housing First programs. Advocacy bodies across Quebec immediately pressured the province to refuse this new funding orientation and called on the federal government to reinstate the "generalist" HPS, which allowed Quebec actors to fund whatever homelessness programs they wanted (RAPSIM 2013a, 2013b). For groups that oppose (and continue to oppose) Housing First, their opposition was in part because the new rules would require the use of a narrower definition of homelessness than what was developed in Quebec. Some groups in Quebec also objected to the forced prioritization of chronic homelessness. The province ultimately agreed to the federal terms, stressing that Housing First aligned with Quebec's policy goals and objectives (Saint-Arnaud 2015a, 2015b). Of course, the province's choices were to accept the money and the terms or reject both. Federal funding being oriented to Housing First meant that non-Housing First service providers in Montreal that had previously relied on federal HPS funding would likely lose it. Recognizing this, and motivated by a broader definition of homelessness than the federal HPS, provincial and regional officials developed a second regional plan for Montreal, one that would promote the implementation of the province's plan on homelessness and be guided by a broader definition of homelessness.

One of the main differences between the two regional plans for Montreal related to the place of Housing First. In the community plan made for HPS purposes, 65 per cent of the funding was allocated to Housing First projects in accordance with federal requirements. In contrast, the province's regional plan adopts a "global" approach to reducing homelessness, in which interventions are to be varied and would not prioritize Housing First (indeed Housing First is barely mentioned at all in the document). The regional plan has a budget of $4 million per year (Barnabé 2015); the HPS funding for the region amounts to nearly $8 million per year, divided between Housing First programs ($5,114,008 per year) and non–Housing First programs ($2,753,696). The provincial funding will thus allow many non–Housing First service providers (that had in the past been dependent on federal funding) to continue their operations. Ideational disagreements regarding the definition of homelessness drove the development of this second regional plan (the first regional plan being the one developed for federal HPS purposes).

At the regional level, therefore, there is a mix of services: some are targeted at people who are chronically homeless (funded by the federal HPS) and based on Housing First principles, while others are more general and are accessible to a much broader population (funded by the province). Significant here is that these ideational disagreements are managed through an institutionalized process; notably, there was considerable overlap in terms of people and organizations involved in developing the 2014–19 HPS community plan and the 2015–20 regional plan, including, importantly, the person in charge of overseeing them both, Manon Barnabé. The two regional plans are thus highly coordinated despite their conceptual loggerheads, and include not just informal but also institutionalized ways of liaising with each other and with the province. This allows them to attack the challenge of homelessness on multiple fronts, without fighting each other for funding (though some proponents of Housing First continue to believe that their work may be undermined by the more generalist approach taken by the province).

The PQ government increased provincial involvement in homelessness governance significantly, but that government did not last long, and the PLQ assumed power again in 2014. A second action plan on homelessness, this time involving eleven ministries, was introduced for 2015–20. Recall that there were differences in how the PQ and PLQ defined homelessness, with the PQ adopting a much broader definition of homelessness in 2014 than the PLQ did in 2010. So it is significant that the second homelessness plan, introduced under the Liberal government in 2015, used the policy's broader definition word for word, including its emphasis on community relations. Instead of updating the policy with a narrower definition or returning to the definition used in the first plan, which related solely to housing, the PLQ maintained the broader definition. This suggests an evolution in how PLQ officials understood homelessness and an enduring role for third-sector groups – which developed the definition with the province – in homelessness governance.

The second plan was applauded by the RAPSIM for its coherence and continuity with the provincial homelessness policy, notably its continued use of the policy's expanded definition of homelessness. Despite this important ideational shift, the 2015 plan was again criticized by community groups for not investing sufficient funding in social assistance and social housing. In 2016, RAPSIM leaders wrote that the two-year anniversary of the second homelessness plan would be a sad one. Contrary to the title of the policy, *Ensemble pour eviter la rue et en sortir* (which translates to Together to Avoid and Leave the Street), the authors said that austerity measures and cuts to housing indicated that the priority of then Premier Couillard and his government was rather *"Ensemble pour faire que davantage de personnes se retrouvent à la rue"* (which translates to Together so that more people end up on the street) (Bonnefont and Gaudreau 2016).

Though the province is increasingly involved and multiple approaches are taken, Indigenous-led organizations to not always have similar access to and influence in the policy process. One recent study of Indigenous homelessness in Montreal has identified a language barrier faced by many Indigenous people, who may speak their own language, or English, or their own language and English, but less often French (Latimer, Bordeleau, and Méthot 2018). This can make it difficult to access services in Montreal, which may contribute to the isolation of some Indigenous people who experience homelessness. Perhaps related to this last point, when asked about solutions and what forms of housing they would prefer, many Indigenous respondents said their preference would be to live in a building specifically for Indigenous people. This is not the case for everyone, however; others (particularly women, according to the study's findings) indicated that they would prefer their own apartment with a subsidy. Though this research does not get specifically at ways of understanding homelessness among Indigenous people, these different solutions point to the coexistence of different understandings of homelessness, and the importance of language and culture in solutions (familiar concepts in Quebec). Future work should continue to interrogate the role of Indigenous-led networks in homelessness policy-making in Quebec, an environment in which multiple approaches can coexist but where language and institutional barriers can contribute to the exclusion of Indigenous involvement and leadership.

François Legault, elected premier in 2018 as leader of the majority right-of-centre Coalition Avenir Québec has maintained the province's commitment to combat homelessness, including continuing to fund the development of social housing through AccèsLogis. Influential advocacy groups have been highly critical of Legault and of past governments as well, saying that investments have not been adequate and contend that as of 2018, between 12,500 and 15,000 units of social housing promised over the previous ten years had not been built (FRAPRU 2018, 2019). Yet even one of the most right-of-centre governments in recent history has remained committed to building social housing. This ongoing commitment to housing policy has meant that the city and third-sector providers have never been abandoned by the province and left totally on their own in the fight against homelessness, as others have been at various times in every other major city in the country.

The province's most recent plan for homelessness covered the years 2015 to 2020. In the middle of this period, the federal government introduced the National Housing Strategy. Early discussions between federal, provincial and territorial governments led to the development of a multilateral agreement to endorse a framework for implementing the National Housing Strategy. All provinces except Quebec have agreed to the Housing Partnership Framework. Footnote 1 on the news release notes Quebec's objections:

> While it shares many of the objectives sought by other governments, Québec intends to fully exercise its own responsibilities and control over the planning, organization and management of housing on its territory to benefit Québec's population. Accordingly, Québec does not subscribe to the NHS and hopes to undertake as soon as possible discussion to reach an asymmetrical bilateral agreement, distinct from the NHS, which fully respects Quebec's exclusive responsibility in the area of housing and allows Québec to obtain its share of all federal funding dedicated to housing. (Canadian Intergovernmental Conference Secretariat 2018)

Federalism continues to operate with a literal footnote to this day, as Alain Noël famously wrote (Noël 2001), and intergovernmental agreements involving the federal and provincial governments are not universally collaborative. Thus, federalism remains contested, with Quebec's actions and involvement in policy fields structured by ideas regarding the responsibility to produce social protection and ideas regarding federalism.

A bilateral agreement to implement the NHS has since been signed by Canada and Quebec (bilateral agreements have been signed with other provinces as well). Additional agreements have been signed for the federal housing allowance, and more recently to allow federal funding from the Rapid Housing Initiative, a COVID-19–specific policy response that involves a transfer of funding to the local level, to flow to Montreal. All of these agreements take time to negotiate; though the RHI was introduced in October 2020, for example, a Canada–Quebec agreement was not signed until January 2021, resulting in a delay in implementation. Ideas regarding the responsibility to produce social protection and regarding the nature of homelessness have led provincial actors to take a consistent leadership role in homelessness governance, working with the federal government when necessary but with as much autonomy as possible.

Homelessness History: City of Montreal

The City of Montreal has been involved in homelessness since at least 1987, the International Year of Shelter for the Homeless, but it was not until the 2000s that the city began formally developing local plans. When the municipality began its formal efforts to fight homelessness, it respected and acted within its limited jurisdiction; recent plans, though, have been more ambitious and had sought to extend and expand the city's authority. Increasingly, the city has sought to bring its own contributions to the policy-making table while also working collaboratively with the province. While the municipal government in Montreal is institutionally weak, ideas about the responsibility to produce social protection and increasingly comprehensive conceptualizations of the city's role have led city actors and officials to push their way onto this already crowded policy field. City officials have balanced their relationship with a divided civil society, as well as pressures from the province and opportunities from the federal government. These efforts are structured by nuanced ideas about the nature of homelessness and the responsibility to produce social protection.

The year before the UN's International Year of Shelter for the Homeless – an important event that drew the attention of many governments in Canada to homelessness – Montreal councillor John Gardiner, a member of the city's powerful executive committee, invited the city to consider adopting a policy on homelessness. This resulted in a 1987 report written by Montreal's Committee on the Homeless titled *Towards a Municipal Policy for the Homeless*. The report's authors consulted widely with community groups, reviewed the literature on housing (including several reports from the 1970s and 1980s on rooming houses). The report's authors travelled to Toronto to learn from their experiences with housing and homelessness; reporting back on the experience, they stressed that "regular contact with actors in Toronto would be of benefit for any Montreal group involved in homelessness" (Comité des sans-abri 1987, 3; author's translation). The report recommended that the city work to develop 5,000 units of housing over five years, as well as create at least three new emergency shelters with at least twenty-five beds each. It also called on the federal and provincial governments to dedicate funding specifically for housing for people experiencing homelessness.

It also offered a new definition of homelessness that would remain influential in Montreal and at the provincial level for almost thirty years: "A homeless person presents one or many of the following characteristics: does not have a fixed address or access to stable, safe, adequate housing for the following 60 days; has a very low income; does not have access to services available to citizens because of discrimination; has problems related to mental health, alcohol, drug use, or social disorganization; and is not a member of any stable group" (Comité des sans-abri 1987, 2). Like the 1988 Quebec study referenced earlier, the Montreal report estimated there were 10,000 homeless people in Montreal; also like the Quebec study, it did not indicate how this number was reached. What is clear from these early reports is that a very broad definition of homelessness was being used and that causes of homelessness were viewed as both structural – no access to housing, discrimination – and individual – alcohol or drug use, though the strong emphasis was on the latter. It also noted the importance of inclusion. This very broad definition is important to keep in mind when considering enduring disagreements between actors regarding the solution to homelessness. Disagreements, which continue to this day, did not appear out of nowhere; rather, they reflect a long history of actors in Montreal grappling with the definition of homelessness.

The 1987 report contained forty recommendations. As with many reports with a similar number of recommendations (including the Golden Report in Toronto and the Homelessness Action Plan in Vancouver), few were adopted. Some recommendations identified what the city could do to combat homelessness and to protect the housing rights of vulnerable people; for example, it was proposed that the city could prohibit the conversion of buildings into condominiums and create additional rooming houses out of abandoned buildings in the city. It further recommended that existing services be considered for consolidation before new ones were introduced, and recommended the formation of a permanent committee on homelessness to advise the city on matters related to housing and homelessness. This committee was created in the early 1990s – Comité de liaison en itinérance – and it has become influential and continues to advise the municipal government, as well as provincial government and regional agencies, in the development of plans and policies on homelessness.

In 2007, the Comité de liaison en itinérance tabled a proposed plan on homelessness for the City of Montreal (Comité de liaison en itinérance de Montréal 2007). The plan began its overview of homelessness with a list of lead organizations in the fight against homelessness, including the City of Montreal, the Agency of Health and Social Services (an arm of the provincial government), and a Montreal-based advocacy body, the RAPSIM (reviewed below). The 2007 report also identifies the federal government as an actor insofar as it contributes funding through the NHI/HPS. The proposed plan uses the 1987 definition word for word. A City of Montreal commission drew on the 2007 draft plan, including the same five priority areas it identified, to again consult broadly on the issues of homelessness through a series of public meetings. The 2008 report that resulted from these consultations notes that

> for over twenty years, the City of Montreal has been involved in the issue of homelessness through interventions, measures and programs that have been put in place with the objective of fighting it. Indeed, on April 13 1987, the committee on homelessness submitted a report to the municipal council entitled: Towards a municipal policy for the homeless. In 2008, homelessness is still present in Montreal, but its faces have changed and its causes have become more complex. (Commission permanente du conseil municipal sur le développement culturel et la qualité du milieu de vie 2008, 6)

Like the 2007 draft plan, the city report notes the primary partners in the fight against homelessness – the Agency for Health and Social Services, the city, and the RAPSIM – but it does not mention the federal government, an indication that city officials have come to view the primary producers of social protection as Quebec-based (local and provincial).

The 2008 report made twenty-six recommendations. The first was for the city to lobby the province for a policy on homelessness. It also recommended that the city lobby for both a homeless count and a portrait of homelessness and that the city study the approaches taken by other large cities in North America as a means of learning how best to prevent and combat homelessness. City Council adopted recommendations to implement the plan (Ville de Montréal 2008a); however, a formal plan on homelessness was not introduced until 2010 under the mayoralty of Gerald Tremblay. The city's 2010 plan differed in important ways from the proposed plan for 2007–10: there was no emphasis on a homeless count or a portrait, for example, and it curiously did not include a definition of homelessness. Protecting rooming houses and building new social housing in partnership with community partners were, however, priorities, as was consolidating day-time services.

While Montreal's 2010 plan involved community voices and consultation, a primary focus was alignment with the 2010–13 provincial plan on homelessness, and it was designed to act specifically within Montreal's jurisdiction. This may explain the absence of key elements noted above (e.g., a definition of homelessness); city officials viewed the province as the primary producer of social protection and intended to follow its lead. The municipal plan thus lacked ambition in terms of increasing its involvement. The introduction to the plan noted that the city could not replace the province when it came to homelessness and went on to note that the actions outlined in the plan "respect [the city's] jurisdiction" (Ville de Montréal 2009, 5). Under the 2010 plan, the city would spend around $1 million per year on homeless services, mostly by supporting organizations or small projects throughout Montreal.

Elected in 2013, mayor Denis Coderre took an interest in homelessness and attempted to change the nature of the city's involvement in it (CBC News 2014). Under his administration, a new plan on homelessness was introduced, and municipal homelessness investments were more than doubled to $2.2 million per year for three years. Whereas Tremblay's plan was timid, looked to the province for leadership, and sought to work with very limited city powers, Coderre's plan announced that it was time to rethink the role the city can and should play: "The time has come for Montreal to take on a new role in this fight" (Ville de Montreal 2014, 3; author's translation).[14] Taking a more expansive view of municipal powers and obligations and seeking to expand those powers even further, Coderre wrote in the plan's introduction that homelessness should be Montreal's responsibility.

Specifically, Coderre argued that the highly localized nature of homelessness meant that actors at the City of Montreal knew the problem best and were accordingly best able to produce social protection for people experiencing homelessness, yet they lacked the necessary powers (legal, financial, and political) to do so. Coderre told Le Devoir: "We have the numbers, we know what the needs are. The concrete solution is to have the capacity" (Paré 2015; author's translation). That the city was best placed to respond to homelessness based on its local knowledge and experience was a powerful argument for why powers should be decentralized from the province. That, indeed, was Coderre's broader and more ambitious goal: to achieve metropolitan status for the city. Metropolitan status would, in his view, give the city sorely needed policy authority and full control over its budget, allowing it to better meet the needs of Montrealers and act with enhanced autonomy.

This was a clear ideational shift from the approach taken under Tremblay, which saw a more limited role for the city in the production of social protection for people who are homeless. Coderre's stance, in contrast, was motivated by a broad conceptualization not simply of what the city could do, but of what it could do *with more powers*. Coderre's plan on homelessness, introduced in 2014, resulted in the creation of a local watchdog over issues relating to homelessness – based on the role of City of Vancouver advocate Judy Graves – and the implementation of regular point-in-time counts of the homeless population. These actions *did not* line up with the provincial plan, notably with respect to the point-in-time count, which the province did not initially support (personal interviews 2014; MSSS 2014). Importantly, Coderre's 2014 plan did not include a definition of homelessness. His plan was expansive in its understanding of the city's role, and federalist in its understanding of the partners involved in the fight, which included the federal, provincial, and municipal governments as well as the health sector and community groups. It did not specifically mention the RAPSIM as a key partner (though the RAPSIM was involved in the plan's development, along with the newly created MMFIM).

In the homeless plan's introduction, Coderre linked the fight against homelessness with the fight for metropolitan status: "We are confident that being given Metropolitan status by the government of Quebec will lead to a redefinition of power in terms of social development" (Ville de Montréal 2014, 3). This expansive conceptualization was aspirational, but that does not matter for our purposes. That the city should play a primary role in the production of social protection for those experiencing homelessness – indeed, play a more comprehensive role more broadly – was a powerful idea that changed the nature of the city's involvement in 2014, and its interactions as well.

The province agreed but only in very small part, to Coderre's request and granted the city metropolitan status in 2017. Quebec Premier Philippe Couillard characterized the Metropolitan Status Agreement as "the biggest decentralization of power to municipalities in Quebec's history" (Plante 2016; author's translation), though this says more about the province's historic reluctance to relinquish powers to municipalities than it does about the nature of the powers transferred. The agreement fell far short of Coderre's stated ambition of acquiring increased financial powers for Montreal, and crucially, it did not give the city the financial control it sought. Metropolitan status was nevertheless an important development for Montreal's governance structures and for municipal–provincial relations. Notably, it included the devolution of inclusionary zoning powers, which would allow the city to leverage private developments so that they must include affordable housing.

The extent to which the city will use its new inclusionary zoning power remains to be seen, but current Montreal mayor Valérie Plante leaned heavily on inclusionary zoning powers during her first campaign for mayor, indicating that she would require that all new housing developments in Montreal in 2021 include 20 per cent social housing, 20 per cent affordable housing, and 10 to 20 per cent housing for families (M. Scott 2019), the most aggressive inclusionary zoning policy considered here (if only in the form of a campaign proposal). These requirements would apply even to developments with as few as five units, though for these smaller developments (five to fifty units), there would also be the option for the developer to make a financial contribution to the city, which would go to a housing fund. This so called 20-20-20 policy has since been adapted to the point that it is much less aggressive, and new by-law requirements give housing developers more flexibility and even choice. The requirement for 20 per cent of affordable housing has been limited to a small section of the city, for example, and developers are only encouraged to create 10 to 20 per cent of the units for families (M. Scott 2019, 2020). The requirement for 20 per cent of units to be social housing remains; even without the other requirements for affordable and family housing, this use of inclusionary zoning in Montreal is aggressive in the Canadian context.

Inclusionary zoning has increased Montreal's institutional strength, though only fairly recently. Montreal is also able to enter into density bonusing agreements, though they are dependent on private-sector interest and further weakened by the city's two-tiered governance structure, that assigns certain zoning powers and responsibilities to boroughs. For the city to enter into density bonusing negotiations with developers, boroughs must also agree to the necessary zoning changes that would be required. Some boroughs are cooperative and willing to work with the city, but support is far from universal (Ville de Montréal 2008b). Density bonusing powers, in light of their weakness, have not factored into municipal plans on homelessness, in contrast to Vancouver, where they feature quite prominently in more recent local efforts to fight homelessness and contribute to affordable housing.

Since defeating Coderre in the municipal election in 2017, Mayor Valérie Plante has been committed to a collaborative approach to homelessness, locally and intergovernmentally. She introduced a new homelessness plan in 2018. Though the two-year plan clearly stakes out the city's place in the fight against homelessness, actors involved in its development noted that the city set aside its preference for a longer-term plan (five years) so as to directly align the subsequent local plan with the province's new plan in 2020 (personal interview 2018). Importantly, the 2018 plan uses the provincial definition of homelessness, signalling the city's alignment with provincial (as opposed to federal) understandings of homelessness and, flowing from that, solutions to it as well.

Though she was critical of her campaign rival Coderre, it is significant that Mayor Plante has maintained two of his centrepiece interventions in homelessness: the local watchdog (though the name was changed from "protector" to "commissioner"), and the homeless count (it helps that the province no longer opposes homeless counts and in fact participated in the federal government's coordinated count in 2018). In a list of partners with whom the city works on the production of social protection for people experiencing homelessness, Plante reverses the order in which she presents the key actors, beginning with community organizations, including both the RAPSIM and the MMFIM. She also notes the importance of citizen engagement and philanthropy, marking the first time a Montreal-based plan has mentioned anything relating to the private sector: "Contributions from private foundation[s] bring an essential support to the fight against homelessness" (Ville de Montréal 2018, 15). The plan goes on to note the importance of the federal and provincial governments, as well as regional efforts (including the Integrated University Health and Social Service Centres,[15] which replaced regional health and social service agencies). It also insists on the importance of collaboration: "Our responses will only be realized in collaboration with different partners, including the network of health and social services and community groups" (6). The list of partners is longer, and more diverse, than similar lists from the past.

Interviews reveal that behind the scenes in the bureaucracy, municipal-provincial relations have changed, and are continuing to do so, as a result of the city's increased involvement in homelessness. City of Montreal respondents expressed great respect for the province and its role in fighting homelessness, but also an increasing willingness to push for a greater role in policy development and governance. One senior official emphasized the legal realities of the Montreal–Quebec relationship: "Legally speaking, we are within the jurisdiction of the province. I can't make an agreement directly with the federal government, I first need to get a derogation from the province" (personal interview 2018).

Senior officials argued that the City of Montreal will never be able to solve homelessness on its own, nor should it try. Yet while they recognized the importance of respecting the province, they also insisted that the city's voice needed to be heard as well, emphasizing that Montreal could and should play a greater role in the production of social protection: "We have to tell [the province] that we are the ones who manage the impacts of homelessness. So, we certainly have something to say, and we can't be shy. We have to say it" (personal interview 2018; author's translation). Asked how the province was responding to this assertiveness, the official noted that "there are some bureaucrats who are starting to understand, 'Yes, okay, we should work together.' But still, they still have their foot on the break – 'It's our responsibility.'" This actor added that these conversations with provincial officials needed to be cautiously respectful.

This same sentiment was expressed by a political aide with Projet Montréal, the party that won the 2017 and 2021 local elections. They declared that Montreal has a role to play in producing social protection: "We have a responsibility at the City of Montreal to respond to the needs of homeless people" (personal interview 2018). Explaining that the city has no interest in replacing the province, which does most of the policy-making and funding related to homelessness policy, they added: "But we want to specify a little what Montreal can do, how we can do more, in the logic of shared-responsibility" (personal interview 2018). From a governance perspective, these ideas about an increased role for the city under continuing provincial leadership, as well as a clear alignment on the definition of homelessness, have shaped the city's interactions with the province and have resulted in a strong willingness to partner and collaborate rather than fight and compete, as we see in some other cities. Coderre was less collaborative, of course, and he did have some successes in increasing city powers and involvement. But as we also saw in Vancouver, local officials in Montreal seem to also understand that homelessness requires collaboration after all.

The development of a new municipal (indeed, a new provincial) plan on homelessness has been put on hold, partly because of changing arrangements with the federal National Housing Strategy and the Reaching Home homelessness program and due to the evolving COVID-19 situation. A new City of Montreal plan on homelessness has yet to be developed, but the city is moving forward with efforts to rapidly house people who experience homelessness and to develop longer-term solutions in partnership with the provincial and federal governments. The City of

Montreal received $56.8 million in federal funding through the Rapid Housing Initiative and is using it to build around 250 units of non-profit housing in partnership with local service providers (Montréal 2021).

This policy field is ideationally divided at the local level, as I will explain in the next section, but this has not necessarily been a problem for city officials. Regarding the advantages of a more centralized governance model, such as Calgary's, one official said that Montreal was used to working in an environment of fragmented authority and competing visions: "In the city we have 19 boroughs, which have all kinds of responsibilities. So we are used to governing with people who have a different vision and who will sometimes develop a better practice. I have heard people say, 'This is so complicated, we should consolidate everything.' I don't think like that" (personal interview 2018). This actor added that a centralized governance model like Calgary's was unlikely to take hold in Montreal, even suggesting that a centralized model would be inappropriate in Montreal.

The city has been cautious about aligning itself fully with either of the third-sector groups at the local level, the RAPSIM or the MMFIM, all while maintaining productive and positive relationships with both. On the one hand, the author of the MMFIM's plan on homelessness, Serge Lareault, was appointed to the position of protector (now commissioner) of the homeless. Lareault had been appointed by Coderre, then Plante kept him in the position. On the other hand, the MMFIM-allied Robert Beaudry was elected to City Council with Projet Montreal but was not immediately given a direct role in homelessness policy, which seems to indicate that Plante has been reluctant to fully align with the MMFIM. And while the MMFIM adopted the Canadian definition of homelessness and used it during Montreal's first homeless count in 2015, the 2018 city plan uses the Quebec definition of homelessness, which the RAPSIM prefers. Under Plante's leadership, the city has taken an inclusive and collaborative approach to homelessness governance, finding ways to work with anyone (private sector, federal government, MMFIM and the RAPSIM) willing to partner. Broad ideas regarding the nature of homelessness and the responsibility to produce social protection have enabled this current dynamic.

Civil Society

The private sector[16] plays a relatively small role in homelessness governance in Montreal. The third sector, by contrast, is afforded a significant institutional role in policy development in both Quebec and Montreal. Third-sector actors expect to co-govern, not simply advocate or be

consulted. The idea that the third sector has a role to play in the production of social protection is influential for all involved in homelessness
governance, including governmental leaders (as the above has demonstrated), though there is widespread (but not universal) agreement that
the government should lead. Ideas about federalism interact with this
idea, resulting in divisions among third-sector groups, while ideas about
the nature of homelessness contribute to that divide. The result has been
the creation of two powerful, locally based groups: The RAPSIM, which
advocates a Quebec-based approach to homelessness and understands
homelessness broadly, as related to housing and community; and the
MMFIM, which understands homelessness more narrowly, as related to
housing, and argues that chronic homelessness should be prioritized.

The RAPSIM was founded in 1974 by service providers concerned
about growing homelessness in Montreal. It was one of the first such
groups in Canada. Its website notes the group's early emphasis on
speaking with a unified voice: "People involved in the sector saw the
importance of raising, with a single voice, the needs of homeless people
to all levels of government" (RAPSIM 2019; author's translation). From
the start, the RAPSIM has positioned itself as a defender of the rights
of homeless people as well as the interests of service providers, including their autonomy and financial support. Today it boasts more than 100
members, all of whom are service providers. There is, nevertheless, considerable diversity among them, as an actor involved with the RAPSIM
in the 1990s explained: "There are a lot of diversified practices in terms
of ideology, many different orientations, religious traditions, secu-
lar traditions, traditions of autonomous communities, groups that are
more combative in terms of defending rights. So it's a very interesting
group" (personal interview 2014). The RAPSIM's administrative council
is elected by its members, and all of them are members of the RAPSIM;
thus, its leadership council is comprised exclusively of service providers.

The MMFIM formed in 2013 after some service providers in the city
grew frustrated that the homeless-serving system was not operating as
effectively or efficiently as it could, and they felt that leadership was
lacking. This was after the first annual Canadian Alliance to End Homelessness conference, when the CAEH began disseminating the idea of
ending homelessness across the country. In part, it was ideas about the
responsibility to produce social protection that caused this new group
to form. A senior actor with the MMFIM explained: "The community
has been calling for the province to take leadership. The province has
been putting up its hand politically to say that it will take leadership,
but it hasn't ... So a few of us kind of said, 'Okay, we'll do it'" (personal
interview 2014). As I will explain, a second ideational disagreement

with the RAPSIM regarding the nature of homelessness led this small group of Montreal-based actors to form a new group instead of channelling their efforts through the RAPSIM.

There is overlap between the groups; some RAPSIM members were founding members of the MMFIM; but other MMFIM members – including the largest homeless shelter in the city, the Old Brewery Mission – have never been members of the RAPSIM. The MMFIM's membership is smaller but more broadly constituted than that of the RAPSIM: it includes not just service providers but also governmental and agency representatives, institutional representatives (from hospitals and universities), and private-sector members, such as the local Chamber of Commerce.[17] The MMFIM's board is similarly diverse, and while the balance is tilted toward third-sector community groups, there are institutional and private-sector representatives as well. The RAPSIM was invited to join the MMFIM, but declined, saying that it would continue to support provincial efforts to implement policy and to participate in the province-wide portrait of homelessness that was under way at the time (RAPSIM 2014).

The RAPSIM does not have a plan for homelessness, though it produces yearly plans that lay out its advocacy efforts and strategies. An important intervention in the fight against homelessness involves advocating for social housing and community support. That solution flows directly out of the RAPSIM's understanding of homelessness, which aligns with the provincial definition and which it helped develop. RAPSIM members understand homelessness broadly, as related not just to housing but to poverty and inclusion as well. Community support is thus seen as a non-negotiable part of the solution. They discourage prioritizing any form of homelessness, particularly chronic or long-term homelessness, over other forms of homelessness. The multi-dimensional understanding of homelessness makes them critical of efforts to prioritize interventions based on chronicity, because they understand homelessness to be about more than the lack of housing.

Many MMFIM members criticize this approach to homelessness, arguing that chronic homelessness should be prioritized and that solutions to that form of homelessness require not just community supports but also highly specialized social supports (including mental health supports). While the MMFIM notes the importance of prevention, its members insist that chronic homelessness must be ended *first*; that will enable the homeless-serving system to deal more effectively with other, less severe forms of homelessness. A leader with the MMFIM insisted: "5% of the homeless population are consuming 50% of the resources. Why on earth have we not adapted our services to first of all get those people out of shelter life and into something that is better for them? And then we have 50% more resources to help the rest" (personal interview 2014).

In contrast with the RAPSIM, the MMFIM has written a plan on homelessness, one rooted in the realities of Montreal but informed by best practices in Canada, the United States, and Europe. The plan is based on numbers recorded in Montreal's first point-in-time homeless count, which MMFIM members advocated for and led (see below).[18] The first count was conducted in 2015 and found 3,016 people experiencing homelessness. The plan relies on a Housing First approach and comes with a significant price tag: $37 million, but with a promised savings of $28 million.[19] The plan is unfunded and has not been fully implemented. The RAPSIM denounced the MMFIM's plan to end homelessness for focusing too narrowly on chronic homelessness on the one hand but also for duplicating efforts to fight homelessness that are already being made in the province on the other.

Members of both groups expect to be involved in homelessness policy-making, though both acknowledge the province's important role. MMFIM members focus less on protest and grassroots advocacy than members of the RAPSIM and are more elite-driven in their efforts to influence policy, though the RAPSIM has strong relationships with political insiders and leaders as well. The Executive Director of a large Montreal homeless shelter, who is aligned with the MMFIM, discussed their constant contact with government officials, reflecting ideas regarding the responsibility to produce social protection: "We have something to say. So yes, I have been in contact with the minister's office this week ... I saw the Minister of Health on Tuesday, the mayor a week and a half ago ... We are influencing policy, we see it as a responsibility of our organization" (personal interview 2014).

The RAPSIM also does advocacy work and has engaged in grassroots protests and pressure campaigns, besides being persistently and directly involved with policy-makers over the course of policy development, from advocacy through to implementation. One actor told me in 2014 that RAPSIM members had spoken with the Minister of Social Services and Youth Protection the night before our interview, and had been told that the province would be releasing its homelessness policy imminently – an indication that the RAPSIM was deeply involved in provincial policy-making. Much of the RAPSIM's work focuses on the province, a direct reflection of their understanding of the responsibility to produce social protection, which in their view lies with the provincial government: "The government of Quebec is primarily responsible in the fight against homelessness, as all actions in this fight are under its responsibility" (RAPSIM 2019b; author's translation). That said, the RAPSIM lobbies all three levels of government (RAPSIM 2019a) and has worked and partnered with other groups, notably the Toronto Disaster Relief Committee (TDRC; see chapter 8), to protest and to make coordinated demands on the federal government.

These two very different groups exist because of profound ideational disagreements. There are subtle but consequential differences regarding the responsibility to produce social protection. The RAPSIM supports the province's plan and provincial leadership, though it participates heavily in provincial policy-making processes. The MMFIM is more critical of the province, and has developed its own approach and plan as a result. The MMFIM and RAPSIM also use different definitions, showing clear differences in understanding the nature of homelessness. RAPSIM actors rely on Quebec's broad definition. This definition notes that there are different kinds of homelessness – temporary, cyclical, and chronic – a typology that has existed for a long time in Quebec. The RAPSIM nevertheless laments, looking squarely at Housing First, that some present-day approaches to homelessness concentrate solely on chronic homelessness. RAPSIM-aligned actors insist that "it is imperative to not simply consider and address chronic homelessness. Contrary to the Housing First approach, which only targets people living on the streets in urban centres, the diversity of approaches implemented by Quebec allow us to act with respect to all forms of homelessness, including people who are not on the streets but who are in unstable housing situations" (RAPSIM 2013a, 2013b; author's translation).

Throughout the RAPSIM's published media, reports, and outreach we find this contrast between what the RAPSIM says is a partial approach to homelessness advanced by the MMFIM (Housing First, a focus on chronic homelessness, and the federal government's 2014 orientation to Housing First in HPS funding) and the approach that it supports, which is "global" (social housing with community support, broad applicability and orientation, and no prioritization of any type of homelessness). In practice, this means an approach to homelessness that is much broader than getting people into housing and ensuring that they can remain there: "Our concern is not just to find a homeless person housing, but also to find them a place *socially, relationally,* as best as possible" (personal interview 2014).

Conversely, the mandate of the MMFIM is to end chronic homelessness in Montreal, and it aims to do so through Housing First programs. While recognizing the breadth of the problem, the MMFIM explicitly prioritizes those who are chronically homeless.[20] Underscoring what this difference means, the MMFIM plan specifies that "even when housed, many of these individuals will remain vulnerable and will experience recurring problems, which is why a permanent system providing variable supports according to their needs is necessary. **But they will no longer be homeless**, and will be better equipped to claim their place in the community" (MMFIM 2015, 3; original emphasis). To make it perfectly clear, and to contrast directly with RAPSIM, the MMFIM asserts that once housed, people no longer experience homelessness.

These profound disagreements over the definition of homelessness, and what it means for the policies and programs the two groups support, have implications for services on the ground and for the agencies and organizations that provide them. One senior and influential third-sector leader with the MMFIM implicitly referenced the RAPSIM in explaining these different approaches: "We want to close our doors … A lot of organizations are looking to keep themselves going. We are trying to not keep ourselves going. Other organizations say, 'We need more money for all these hundreds of organizations.' We are saying we don't need a hundred organizations'" (personal interview 2014). They continued: "I am not trying to build an empire here, I am trying to close down." For the RAPSIM, on the other hand, a multitude of agencies taking diverse approaches is a strength, indeed a necessary feature, of a community-based welfare state: "We believe that the diversity of interventions is a strength.[21] Yes, there are small organizations, but they will respond to needs that another organization can't meet. Yes, there is a multiplication of administrations, of councils, of structures, of buildings, and maybe a consolidation might be interesting. But this diversity of approaches, of the way of working, seems to me to be something positive" (personal interview 2014, author's translation).

If the definition implies that homelessness is not just about housing, then non-housing related support services are required and should be funded by homelessness plans. If the definition emphasizes housing as the end to homelessness, then these services are superfluous, at least from the perspective of a homelessness plan. This is not to say that support services are not required and that integration is not important; rather, it is saying that finding housing for those without it is the top priority. As Dion Oxford, a Toronto-based proponent of this view explains, "First, we must recognize that housing is not the same as home but also that home is not possible without housing … Once the housing piece is resolved, we can explore what else is needed to make a home" (Oxford 2018, 115–17).

Interacting with these ideas about the nature of homelessness are ideas about federalism. Montreal is the only city among those being studied here where we see these latter ideas exerting influence. The

MMFIM is closely aligned with pan-Canadian organizations, and its members have strong ties to Canadian projects such as the At Home/Chez Soi project and the CAEH. Matthew Pearce (former CEO of the Old Brewery Mission) was on the board of both the MMFIM and the CAEH. Influential MMFIM member Eric Latimer was At Home/Chez Soi's principle investigator in Montreal. These national connections have allowed actors to learn rapidly from others in the CAEH network across the country; as a result, the MMFIM was able to punch above its weight as soon as it was formed.

For some, Montreal is not all that different from other cities, so relationships with national leadership and leaders in other communities is a strength. An actor involved with the MMFIM noted that the profile of the homeless population in Montreal is very similar to that of the homeless populations in other cities, such as Ottawa, Toronto, Seattle, and New York: "So then when Montreal keeps saying 'Quebec is a distinct society, it is very special, things work there but won't necessarily work in the Montreal context' – in fact, they are dealing with the same profiles as we are here. So let's take a look at what they are doing – Housing First, StreetoHome, whatever … We are not that distinct, at least when it comes to homelessness" (personal interview 2014). It follows, for these actors, that solutions to homelessness developed outside of Quebec – including Housing First, informed by a point-in-time homeless count, for example – should work just as well in Montreal as they do in other cities. An actor involved with the MMFIM remarked: "I'm pretty sure that if they found a cure for cancer, it would work here, even if it was discovered in New York" (personal interview 2014). Endorsing this perspective, MMFIM founding member Matthew Pearce has written that

> the next critical step is to lift our heads and look around at what is actually in place and happening elsewhere – regionally, nationally, continentally, internationally. This reflex is not as well developed in Quebec community organizations as it could be, partly due to the language obstacle, partly to an excessive and limiting pride in how we work within our distinct society. We reflexively deny the value of what comes from outside. (Pearce 2018, 94)

This insistence that Quebec is no different from other parts of the country is controversial with some community members. In interviews with RAPSIM-aligned actors, there was no explicit negation of the value of ideas that "come from outside," though RAPSIM documents do refer dismissively and critically to Housing First and homeless counts as "in vogue in Canada [and] the US" (RAPSIM 2014). There is, however, a distinct pride in policies that are seen as having been developed in Montreal rather than discovered by the federal government. An actor involved with the RAPSIM explained that innovation does not happen on the federal level: "The federal government did not invent social housing. The development of social housing with community support was done in a very specific way in the 1980s, right here in Montreal" (personal interview 2014, author's translation). This actor added that service providers in Montreal do not want models or approaches imposed on them "top down." Speaking of the MMFIM's approach to the governance of homelessness, this RAPSIM-aligned actor explained that "[the MMFIM] works in contrast with the way we work. Them, they want to work differently, they want a more Canadian model with the three levels of government around the table. Unfortunately, it isn't possible to work that way in Quebec. It's kind of the two solitudes" (personal interview 2014; author's translation).

It is, however, possible for all three levels of government to sit down together, at least in theory. In interviews with some Montreal-based community leaders, there was some evidence of a misunderstanding of the role of cities in other parts of the country and that this has led them to justify a distinct Quebec approach to homelessness. For example, an actor involved with the original negotiations to implement the federal NHI in Montreal in 1999 explained why it took two years to negotiate the original agreement: "The model that the federal government wanted to impose across Canada didn't work in Montreal. Minister Bradshaw negotiated with cities – Toronto, Calgary, et cetera. Because the responsibility for social services is a city responsibility in other cities in Canada. Whereas in Quebec, the responsibility for health and social services is provincial. It's an important distinction that is not political, but structural and organizational" (personal interview 2014, author's translation). Another RAPSIM-aligned actor insisted that certain policies or approaches might work in Toronto because Toronto holds responsibility for health policy, whereas in Quebec it is a provincial responsibility. Neither assertion regarding the responsibility for health or social services broadly defined[22] is entirely correct, as other provinces have health and social policy regimes similar to Quebec's. This view that other provinces play a smaller role in social protection than Quebec does has, for some local actors, led them to dismiss approaches taken elsewhere as fundamentally irreconcilable with Quebec's institutional structure. But this is not always warranted.

To be clear, plenty of actors in cities across Canada were, often by their own admission, quite simply ignorant of the approaches to homelessness taken by Quebec and Montreal. A Vancouver-based actor admitted that even when they were involved with the provincial government in a senior capacity, their understanding of Quebec politics was limited: "It's always harder to get a sense of what is happening there" (personal interview 2014). Another Vancouver-based actor who referenced responses to homelessness in Toronto, Ottawa, Winnipeg, and Whitehorse admitted: "I don't know Montreal so well" (personal interview 2014). Whether it is because of disinterest or oversight, this is regrettable, for there is much to learn from Montreal and Quebec. To the extent that the actor above references two solitudes, it would perhaps exist not simply because of differences between provinces but because of a lack of understanding between them. In Montreal, we see among certain actors a misunderstanding of how policies are developed and implemented elsewhere, and this is at times used to justify why those national policies do not work in Montreal. Previous Montreal reports, including the first from 1987, insisted on the benefits of keeping in touch with actors in Toronto, and a 2008 report recommended studying other North American cities, indicating a willingness to learn from other North American contexts. What some criticize as Quebec pride and a sense of "things are different here" may not, in fact, be pride, but rather misunderstanding. Montreal *is* different, and Quebec *is* different, but not in the ways these actors insist it is, and misunderstanding may create divides where there actually are none.

These ideational disagreements have led to divides at the local level. Those divisions are unfortunate, as both actors have important insights to bring to the table regarding homelessness and how to fight and prevent it. Though ideational disagreements about the nature of homelessness run deep, we find at the regional level that it is possible to coordinate between two different approaches so as to ultimately create a system that offers a wide range of services without actors competing against one another. But at the local level, groups do not formally coordinate, and that is to the detriment of homeless people and those working in the sector. An example of this was the effort in 2015 to understand the homeless population. The MMFIM ran the city's homeless count (a key promise in Denis Coderre's homelessness plan), an exercise that provides a snapshot of homelessness on a given night. It is useful particularly for understanding how many people experience chronic homelessness, as it involves conducting interviews to get a sense of a person's housing history and to identify needs that the current system does not address well. Such counts are limited in their scope, to be clear, for they are restricted to one night and do not capture hidden homelessness, nor do they give a sense of how many people over the course of a given year experience homelessness. They can nevertheless capture a useful image of homelessness when it is understood in this context.

The RAPSIM did not formally try to prevent its members from participating in the homeless count in 2015, but it never endorsed the effort, repeatedly pointed out the limitations of the exercise, and insisted that it supported the province's portrait of homelessness that had been released the previous year. Most Montreal groups eventually participated in the count, though convincing them to do so took time, in part because of RAPSIM's persistent scepticism. After the homeless count's findings were released, RAPSIM reiterated its concerns; later, it released its own report, which presented the different forms (many of them hidden) that homelessness takes in Montreal. Titled *Homelessness in Montreal: Beyond the Numbers* (author's translation), that document questioned the value of quantification, strongly and directly challenging the homeless count. Yet that report could also have been framed as, and understood as, a valuable complement to the count. Both reports provided important insights into the different ways people experience homelessness, and collaborating could have produced one of the most detailed and comprehensive studies of homelessness in any Canadian city.

It is important to note that while these groups criticize each other, neither has sought to formally block the work of the other. This is in keeping with the Quebec model of governance (Arsenault 2016; Bourque 2000), which historically has seen collaboration between different groups, even those advancing slightly different visions. It is also in keeping with what Withers identifies as a common practice among organizers that criticizing other social movements or organizations is to be avoided (Withers 2021). While various groups have advanced different approaches or solutions to, for example, poverty reduction or proposed tuition increases, they actually tend to support one another's inclusion in discussions and policy-making, appreciating that policy challenges require that everyone be at the same table. This was seen, for example, during the 2011 student strike in Quebec. The three groups representing students – the FEUQ, the FECQ, and the CLASSE – had different visions and approaches, with the CLASSE being more radical in its demands. When the province sought to negotiate with just representatives of the more moderate FEUQ and the FECQ, these two groups insisted that CLASSE also be invited and refused to participate until they were all at the table. In this sense, the fact that the RAPSIM expressed so much concern with the first homeless count, yet did not use its power to block the initiative (which it could have done), speaks to the endurance of the Quebec model even in a strongly divided sector.

Recent changes to the RAPSIM's membership underscore the growing divide between the two groups, however. Three influential homelessness service providers[23] announced their decision to leave the

RAPSIM in 2018, saying that the organization no longer reflected their priorities or points of view. This was significant, for they were all founding members of the RAPSIM in the 1970s (Robichaud 2018). Having left the RAPSIM, they are now working closely with the Old Brewery Mission (recall that that organization has never been a RAPSIM member) to coordinate their work, focusing on what they call "proven approaches" to ending homelessness, including Housing First. While few in number, the four non-RAPSIM members are the largest service providers in the city. This points to a growing ideological and philosophical divide in terms of how to approach homelessness and the deepening divisions among third-sector actors.

Montreal Conclusions

The governance of homelessness in Montreal is complex and involves several actors, some of whom collaborate and some of whom do not. The province has long been the leader in the governance of homelessness. The municipality has become increasingly involved, sometimes in conflict but more recently in collaboration with the province. Indigenous groups in Montreal do not have an institutional structure to allow for the local administration of NHI/HPS funding, another dynamic that is unique to Quebec. Rather, Indigenous groups apply directly to the federal government for funding allocated to Indigenous communities through the NHI/HPS. It is not clear whether Indigenous groups fully access this funding or whether it remains unspent as a result of this institutional set-up. Third-sector groups in Montreal, and in Quebec more generally, are powerful policy-making actors in their own right. They play an institutionalized role in the governance of homelessness; however, third-sector groups are divided regarding the nature of homelessness and organize through two different groups. Resources and institutions matter in understanding the involvement and interactions of these actors, but ideas about the responsibility to produce social protection (shaped at all levels by ideas about federalism) and the nature of homelessness are powerful forces shaping this unique governance dynamic.

Despite changes in political parties, the Quebec provincial government has guarded and fully exercised its responsibility for housing and homelessness since the federal government withdrew from the policy sector in the early 1990s. This includes involvement in implementing the federal government's NHI/HPS from its beginning, in a co-governance arrangement that no other province has sought. The province introduced a plan on homelessness in 2010 and again in 2015.

Furthermore, Quebec is the only province to have a policy on home-lessness (introduced in 2014), one that has assembled nearly a dozen government departments to work together, in the same direction, in the fight against homelessness.[24]

There are disagreements between political parties, of course, including with respect to ideas regarding the role of other actors in the production of social protection. Consistent with past research on the Quebec model (Arsenault 2018; Laforest 2011a, 2011b), this chapter has found that the Parti Québécois maintains stronger relationships with civil society than the Liberal Party and allows non-governmental actors to participate more fully in homelessness policy development. There is, however, evi-dence of significant ideational agreement among political parties as well. Consistent involvement of the provincial government, in a leadership position, in homelessness governance is the result of ideational agree-ments across political parties that areas of provincial jurisdiction should be protected from federal intrusion and that the province has a lead role in the production of social protection for people who are unhoused or experience homelessness. Furthermore, we see the *disappearance* of dis-agreements between parties regarding the nature of homelessness. The Liberal Party's definition of homelessness changed between 2010 and 2015, from one based just on housing to one (introduced in the 2014 policy) related to social inclusion as well as housing. During periods of changes in power, ideas have broken down ideological barriers and driven consistent government involvement. Quebec governments strive to produce social protection for people living in Quebec, including those who experience homelessness, which, along with housing, has become a *projet de société* in Quebec (Vaillancourt and Ducharme 2001).

The City of Montreal was an early and influential actor in homeless-ness governance, particularly with respect to the definition of home-lessness that was developed at the local level in 1987 and was used across the province for almost thirty years. The city also created a com-mittee of third-sector representatives, which allowed for the continu-ous input of homeless service providers in decision-making at various levels of governance. Since the 1980s, plans and studies have shown a willingness on the part of Montreal actors to work with different gov-ernments and actors at the local level, though the federal government is at times not seen as a meaningful partner in efforts to combat home-lessness (except for being a funder). The first formal municipal plan on homelessness identified the province as the lead actor and stressed municipal constraints. 2014 was a turning point, when Mayor Denis Coderre announced that the city would be playing a larger role in the fight against homelessness; to that end, he sought additional powers from the province. The current mayor, Valérie Plante, has maintained, with some adjustments, the city's heightened involvement in homelessness. Unlike the Coderre administration, however, which introduced priorities with which the province did not fully agree at the time (notably the point-in-time homeless count), Plante's administration has been more willing to work with the province. This includes compromising on its preference for a five-year municipal plan; instead it adopted a two-year plan in 2018 so as to allow the municipality and the province to coordinate on the development of new plans in 2020.

The change in the city's involvement in homelessness has been the result of two closely linked ideational changes related to the conceptualization of the city's role and the responsibility to produce social protection. Before 2014, city officials addressed homelessness within the confines of their limited powers. Coderre conceived of a more expansive role for the city, one that would require a transfer of powers from the province. He envisioned the city playing an important, even leading role in the fight against homelessness, noting that the only reason the city was unable to take on that role was a lack of legal and financial resources. The city's ability to respond more effectively to homelessness, if only it was empowered to do so, was a leading argument in his case for increased municipal powers and metropolitan status. Taking a more collaborative tone, Plante recognizes that everyone, including the federal government and local actors (including disagreeing ones), needs to be involved in homelessness governance and social protection. While her government has maintained the city's increased involvement (and relies heavily on some of the tools Coderre was able to get for the city, notably inclusionary zoning), ideas about the collective responsibility to produce social protection alongside the province have shaped her involvement.

Institutions have long empowered third-sector actors, including the RAPSIM and the more recent MMFIM, in social policy development at the municipal and provincial levels. The "Quebec model" refers not only to the content of policies (which tend to be more generous as well as more universal) but also to their governance. But ideas regarding the nature of homelessness also play a powerful role in structuring the involvement and interactions of local actors in homelessness governance. Local groups are divided, and there are competing local approaches to homelessness. There is clear disagreement between the MMFIM and RAPSIM on the nature of homelessness. The MMFIM embraces a narrower interpretation of homelessness that focuses on housing. Its approach is to start by targeting, and aspiring to end, chronic homelessness, after which it will turn to less severe forms of homelessness and to preventing it outright. The RAPSIM defines homelessness in more general terms, seeing it as related not just to physical housing but also to social inclusion and stable and functional relationships. They advocate a "generalist" response to homelessness as opposed to a "partial" one, and that means offering a wide range of services for people experiencing all types of homelessness, with a strong focus on prevention.

The NHI/HPS governance model in Montreal has reinforced some of these governance dynamics, including an active province and a heavily involved third sector. It has also underscored divisions within Montreal society. At the regional level, ideational disagreement has led to fragmentation of plans and a system in which approaches are both specific (Housing First) and expansive (prevention, as well as addressing more hidden forms of homelessness). Because these plans are coordinated, they are able to expand the terrain and fill any gaps. At the regional level, then, competing ideas about the nature of homelessness are coordinated. In other words, institutions bridge competing ideas and have fostered a rich and diverse array of services. Members of the distinct local groups may still oppose the approach taken by the other, but this disagreement is managed. This should provide inspiration for the local level, where competing groups interact informally but do not formally coordinate.

Furthermore, there is evidence of differing ideas regarding federalism. Montreal is the only city in this study in which we see these ideas exerting a powerful influence at the local level. The RAPSIM is a nationalist, Quebec-based group, whereas the MMFIM strongly identifies with Quebec *and* Canada. This leads to different ideas regarding the responsibility to produce social protection, with the RAPSIM looking to the province for leadership (and the federal government for funding), whereas the MMFIM accepts provincial and federal leadership and involvement in collaborative governance efforts. These different ideas have led to the creation of two different third-sector groups involved in the governance of homelessness in Montreal.

Conclusion

"What causes homelessness?"

"Ah shit. What doesn't cause homelessness?" (personal interview 2014)

Across the country, people have poured their hearts, minds, and resources into the task of ensuring that everyone has a safe and adequate home. Indigenous-led organizations and local service providers have been at the forefront of these efforts. Despite their work, the number of people who are unhoused or underhoused continues to grow. Faced with a seemingly never-ending task, groups have come together to develop plans, responses, and strategies to produce social protection for people who are unhoused and are experiencing homelessness. In big cities across the country, the governance networks that have developed to do so (and continue to evolve) vary greatly. The municipality has been a powerful and leading actor in Toronto and, at some points in recent history, in Vancouver as well. Third-sector groups work closely with governments in Montreal, and the private sector has driven the agenda in Calgary. In addition to different lead actors, we see varying degrees of involvement of other actors as well as different levels of coordination and collaboration among them, with some groups collaborating extensively and others working at odds with one another.

This book has been motivated by a desire to understand why these different governance networks emerge. I began with the assumption, grounded in the literature, that governance matters for social policy. It matters for policy innovation, the quality of outputs, the responsiveness of interventions, and the ability of a complex system to make sure individuals do not get lost and cycle through homelessness for years on end. This book takes a necessary step back to ask what shaped these governance networks in the first place. To better understand these dynamics, I conducted nearly 100 semi-structured interviews with actors from all levels of government, as well as third- and private-sector and Indigenous actors about their involvement in advocacy, policy development, and the financing and implementation of responses to homelessness. I closely reviewed hundreds of primary documents, including a multitude of plans, reports on plans, policies, and reviews; and I participated in meetings, conferences, and homeless counts. What I found sheds light on what we know about multilevel governance, the welfare state, and homelessness in Canada.

What Have We Learned

This research has documented what some may find to be a surprising number of plans, policies, and actors dedicated to fighting homelessness. Some actors joked that there are more plans than there are people experiencing homelessness; this is an exaggeration, but it makes clear the fact that there is some frustration with the governance of this complex policy. Recall the actor in Vancouver who said: "We've got too many people deciding what to do ... So all of a sudden something that is really very simple has become an overwhelming, confusing process. It's stagnant. It's not moving forward the way it should. It's costing way too much and it sucks energy out of everything that is going on" (personal interview 2014). This underscores an important descriptive element of this research: it is the first attempt to systematically document multilevel responses to homelessness. It brings to light the sheer number of actors involved in combating homelessness and recounts their efforts across twenty years, four urban centres, all levels of government, and various sectors of society. This has involved some degree of storytelling (or story-retelling), with history-making actors generously and thoughtfully sharing their memories, giving us an insider's look at twenty years of efforts to respond to homelessness. These stories also shed light on what we know about multilevel governance, ideas, and the welfare state.

Multilevel Governance

The four in-depth case studies offer insight into the forces that structure the involvement and interactions of actors in multilevel governance. This close look at a single policy area allows for extensive within-case analysis of the forces that drive involvement and interactions, as well as across-case comparison of how those forces play out in different institutional environments. Many of this study's findings confirm the conclusions of Robert Young in his groundbreaking work in the Fields of Governance research series, including those related to the structuring role of resources. Indeed, extensive cuts across the social safety net have in many instances been made during times of economic recession and decline, including during the 1990s at the federal level and a few years later at the provincial level in BC, Ontario, and Alberta. Private-sector actors were also able to leverage money (many of them called it "new money") into fast action, and at times drove government agendas through partnership.

Other sorts of resources, including locally based expertise, Indigenous knowledge, and private-sector management expertise, have allowed groups to become involved. These resources are not always equally valued, however; this study has shown that to date, private-sector management and locally based expertise have been the most valued forms of expertise. Institutions also matter, notably jurisdiction (or the lack thereof), and so do locally based housing powers such as density bonusing and inclusionary zoning. Toronto is the most extensively involved municipality in the governance of homelessness because it has formal jurisdiction. Absent jurisdiction, other institutional powers can enable municipal involvement as well; this has been the case in Vancouver, where powerful density bonusing and inclusionary zoning powers have put the city in a position of power. Furthermore, Indigenous leaders are in some cases involved institutionally – through Indigenous HPS networks, for example – and third-sector groups are involved in policy-making at different levels in Quebec. Institutionalization enables these actors to be more outspoken, to criticize, and to exercise greater influence in the process.

Yet we have seen governments and other actors defying the expectation that they act in accordance with their resources and institutions. To shed light on why, this study has looked carefully at the role of ideas, specifically regarding the responsibility to produce social protection, the conceptualization of local governments, and the nature of homelessness. An important conclusion of previous work on multilevel governance has been that resources are sometimes more powerful than institutions (including jurisdiction) in structuring involvement. This present work demonstrates that ideas may be more powerful still.

Ideas and Multilevel Governance

Ideas regarding the responsibility to produce social protection go a long way toward explaining some of the most puzzling cases. Those ideas relate to the actors' understanding of their own role in homelessness governance as well as that of others. For example, they help us understand the *lack* of municipal involvement in homelessness governance in Calgary. The municipal government there has sought to limit its involvement because its officials view the responsibility for producing social protection for people experiencing homelessness as lying elsewhere. From the 1990s until the mid-aughts, city officials viewed that responsibility as lying primarily with the provincial government; later, as the Calgary Homeless Foundation gained more power, those same officials insisted that they had not become more involved because the Calgary Homeless Foundation was responsible. In other cases – notably Vancouver and Calgary – the private sector increased its involvement in homelessness governance in the mid-aughts. This was in part because of a belief in the role of the private sector in contributing to this effort, but also because of a belief that the role of governments should be limited.

Ideas about the responsibility to produce social protection can interact with ideas about federalism. In this book, this is most clear in Quebec, where the province increased its involvement in housing in the 1960s and 1970s in order to limit the federal government's involvement in areas of provincial jurisdiction. Ideas about federalism have led provincial officials in Quebec (from all political parties) to jealously guard their jurisdiction. In fully and energetically occupying this policy field, the province is simultaneously engaged in acts of jurisdictional offence and defence: in offence, the province is exercising its powers by fighting homelessness; in defence, it is protecting the policy field from federal encroachment. This is also seen in the provincial–federal bilateral governance model for implementing the NHI/HPS in Quebec; elsewhere in the country, this relationship is strictly federal–local. As I explain below, Quebec is one of the most deeply involved provinces in the country because ideas about federalism and the responsibility to produce social protection have combined with some of the broadest ideas in evidence about the nature of homelessness. Federal involvement has also been shaped by these ideas, with Stephen Harper's conservative government viewing housing and homelessness as provincial jurisdiction, whereas Justin Trudeau's Liberal government views them as shared.

At the local level, this book confirms Martin Horak's findings regarding the importance of how local officials conceive the role of the local government. In Vancouver, city officials insist that they do more than just pick up the garbage – they are engaged in taking care of the people who live there. InSite is often cited as an example of this. It is in Toronto that the conceptualization of the local government's role is the most expansive, and senior officials went to great lengths to stress the ways in which the municipality is more like a province than other municipal governments. The idea that Toronto is a large, democratic government has for years led officials there to exercise and defend housing policy the way a jealous province would, almost as though the responsibility for housing policy is proof that Toronto is more than a municipality. In Montreal, we see nuanced ideas regarding the city's role: city officials are careful to point out the primary responsibility of the province, including over municipalities, noting that Montreal is a "creature of the province"; also, ideas regarding federalism have permeated the local level in Montreal, as this book has shown. Yet officials in Montreal are becoming more assertive in their relationship with the province, insisting that they can and should do more than fix potholes (a never-ending job in Montreal). Coderre's quest for Metropolitan status, and the central role that the fight against homelessness played in his justification for increased city powers, is another clear example of how this idea drives municipal involvement.

Conceptualizations of local government and ideas about the responsibility to produce social protection tend to drive cities' involvement, whereas ideas about the nature of homelessness tend to structure the interactions of groups. There has been considerable evolution in how homelessness is understood. In the 1990s and 2000s, dominant understandings of homelessness emphasized individual-level causes, including drug use, and mental illness. These were understood at the time to be the individual-level barriers to housing. Over time, definitions have come to identify structural and systemic causes of homelessness, including, fundamentally, a lack of affordable housing but also a host of other structural and institutional failures and weaknesses. These barriers can interact with individual-level factors to contribute to homelessness, but there is now an understanding that barriers to housing exist not just within individuals but also within systems.

Yet there have also been persistent disagreements over the nature of homelessness. One definition relates homelessness to the absence of housing; homelessness is always, in this understanding, a lack of housing. Housing is sometimes defined narrowly as a permanent residence; other times, it is defined more broadly as safe, adequate, and affordable. Federal officials and many provinces outside of Quebec, as well as private-sector groups (where they are involved), understand homelessness to be the absence of housing. Another definition understands homelessness as resulting not just from a lack of housing but from a lack of community integration as well. Accordingly, homelessness is the lack of a *home*, which is understood as more than four walls, a door, and a roof; it is also something that facilitates social inclusion and participation. Solutions must therefore involve social and community supports. This definition has been broadly, though not universally, adopted in Quebec.

This might be understood as a divide between English and French Canada, but I found evidence that both definitions of homelessness are used by different actors across the country; for example, the TDRC and some third-sector groups in Vancouver espouse this expansive understanding, and Montreal-based groups (such as the MMFIM) use the housing-based definition. Meanwhile, an Indigenous definition of homelessness has been articulated by Jesse Thistle. This definition identifies homelessness as not just the lack of a physical structure or even a lack of integration. Rather, it is the result of forced displacement from land and culture, and ongoing colonization that leads to a separation from "All My Relations." Indigenous actors across the country, even those who were unfamiliar with this specific definition, explained in interviews that homelessness is more than a lack of housing, because a home, from an Indigenous perspective, is understood in a different, more holistic sense.

Where actors agree on the nature of homelessness, they are likely to coordinate and even collaborate. In Calgary, widespread agreement on the nature and definition of homelessness has allowed for a great deal of power to be centralized in the Calgary Homeless Foundation. In Toronto, changing ideas have led to ideational convergence among powerful actors regarding the nature of homelessness and the responsibility to produce social protection, leading to collaborative co-governance between the city and third-sector actors. In Montreal, by contrast, we see strongly conflicting ideas regarding the nature of homelessness, with one group (RAPSIM) advancing a broad definition of homelessness that relates to housing and inclusion, and another group (the MMFIM) proposing a narrower definition linked to accessing and maintaining housing. Neither of these groups blocks the other's actions, but they are critical of each other and do not formally collaborate.

Where homelessness governance is fragmented, disagreements over the nature of homelessness can raise barriers to stable, responsive governance. Yet ideational differences, when coordinated institutionally, can lead to a rich and diverse service system. This is seen at the regional level in Montreal, where two plans with two different sources of funding advance different approaches to homelessness. These plans are highly coordinated. Because these two plans are overseen by the same person, liaise regularly, and involve many of the same groups in their development, they are able to fill each other's gaps. They are not fighting over funding because they have different sources; thus, each can do its own work implementing its own plans without stepping on the toes of the other, or worse, undoing the other's work. Similarly, at the regional level in Vancouver, groups implementing the federal NHI/HPS coordinate closely. This includes an Indigenous group that is motivated by a definition of homelessness that is not just housing-based, but more in line with Thistle's definition of Indigenous homelessness. Fragmentation, and even irreconcilable ideational disagreements, are not fatal blows to efforts to combat homelessness. Indeed, a diverse but coordinated system can be highly effective because it allows genuine space for different approaches to meet the needs of a highly diverse population.

Ideas regarding the nature of homelessness tend to structure the interactions of groups, but they can also influence actor involvement. The Government of Quebec has adopted a broad definition of homelessness, which has driven the involvement of not just a lead Ministry (health, in Quebec), but a number of ministries and departments. By contrast, homelessness has been understood in BC as more strictly related to housing. As a consequence, BC Housing leads in efforts to combat homelessness and does not collaborate as extensively with other provincial departments, though this has changed under the NDP government and more Ministries are increasingly involved. Also, in Vancouver we find that different understandings of the nature of homelessness drive actor involvement. This was particularly the case in 2008, when Gregor Robertson was beginning to implement his plan to end street homelessness. Disagreeing with this focus on street homelessness, the StreetoHome Foundation moved forward with the implementation of its own, separate ten-year plan.

To be sure, is not always clear that ideas on their own exert an independent force in every instance of changing involvement or interactions; in some instances, something else may well be at play. For example, changes in governance dynamics are sometimes driven by ideological differences. Conservative governments tend to see a more limited role for themselves in the production of social protection than Liberal or NDP governments. Provincial and local government involvement has at times changed in line with what we would expect from ideology; for example, the Progressive Conservative Ford government in Ontario limited its involvement in governance, whereas the NDP government led by Horgan in BC expanded its role.

A change in leadership can also lead to a change in ideas. There can be subtle ideological differences between leaders of the same party, with some leaning more to the left (or right) than their predecessors.

For example, after Christy Clark, a Liberal, was elected BC's premier, the provincial role in the production of social protection for people experiencing homelessness became much more limited than it had been under Gordon Campbell, also a BC Liberal. Also, a change in leadership at the Calgary Homeless Foundation in 2015 led to more positive interactions between the CHF and the Aboriginal Standing Committee on Housing and Homelessness. So changes in leadership or ideology sometimes explain changes in involvement and interaction; other times, though, they do not. This is seen at the federal level, where the NHI/HPS remained virtually unchanged for nearly twenty years of Liberal and Conservative governments. Similarly in Quebec, we see consistency in definitions of homelessness between Liberal and PQ governments. And there was no leadership change in BC in 2005/2006, when the province reengaged.

Ideational Theory

In instances where changes do not align with what we would expect, ideas have been important. Below I consider two ideational mechanisms have been at play. First, in a number of instances across the country, groups were starting to feel that their work was not succeeding. Some actors went so far as to frame their work as having failed. This recognition that the status quo was not working and that something needed to change can be understood as an environmental mechanism, one that "works to expand the space for discussion of alternatives" (Jenson 2010). It can lead to a changing degree of involvement of different actors but also, importantly, to a change in the nature of their interactions. Importantly, there is no external change, but rather ideas lead groups to understand their environment differently. With respect to homelessness, this meant that actors come to understand that they are limited in what they can do to end or reduce homelessness and that responsibility for the production of social protection is shared. This was seen with the Calgary Homeless Foundation as well as the City of Toronto. An actor in Calgary explained that by the mid-2010s, the CHF was taking a step back from its leadership role in the community after what they called a "big learning" that everyone needs to be "at the wheel." The CHF has come to collaborate, and call on senior government involvement, more than it originally did. And in Toronto, an actor recalled that people were frustrated with banging their heads against the wall and not getting the results they wanted and needed; this led groups to create new partnerships.

The second mechanism of ideational change we have seen is a cognitive mechanism (Jenson 2010). Because of their ambiguity and positive valence, actors can use ideas to redefine a problem and create coalitions of people working toward new solutions. In this way, particularly powerful ideas can transform into coalition magnets. Recall that according to Béland and Cox (2016), an idea becomes a coalition magnet when it results in the redefinition of a problem, is promoted by key actors, and brings together a group of people, some of whom may disagree on politics. As the empirical chapters in this book have demonstrated, these ideas tend to be specific and are informed by a particular definition of homelessness. The most notable coalition magnet has been the idea of ending homelessness.

In a number of cities across the country in the mid-aughts, homelessness was redefined by key entrepreneurs. Motivated by a new and narrow understanding of homelessness, some key community leaders (entrepreneurs) argued that homelessness could be ended and that doing so (as opposed to managing homelessness) would save money in the long run. This idea was introduced by a powerful policy entrepreneur – Philip Mangano – who visited Vancouver, Calgary, Toronto, and Montreal to redefine homelessness. The idea of ending homelessness, and saving money in the process, was appealing to a wide-range of people, including private-sector business leaders, faith-based organizations, and social justice activists. With homelessness not clearly defined in early efforts, ending homelessness was also somewhat ambiguous, allowing groups to bring their own values, assumptions and ideas regarding the nature of homelessness to their collaborative efforts. These groups were drawn to work together by the idea of ending homelessness: for some, that idea was a human rights solution to a violation of human rights and a failure of public policy, whereas for others, it was a cost-cutting solution to an expensive problem.

Magnetic ideas attract groups and draw people to work together, but they can also push groups apart. That happened at the local level in Montreal, where the MMFIM sought to end homelessness through Housing First. The MMFIM invited the RAPSIM to participate in its efforts and join the coalition, an invitation that was strongly rebuffed. The RAPSIM expressed scepticism about Housing First and the idea of ending homelessness. Specifically referencing the provincial definition and approach to understanding homelessness, which it supported, the RAPSIM refused to collaborate (RAPSIM 2014). So disagreements over powerful and magnetic ideas can push groups apart, a novel contribution of this study.

The ambiguity of ideas can also make them volatile. This was seen in Vancouver, where a strong local coalition came together around the idea of ending street homelessness. But as conflicts among actors arose, it became clear that while coalition members agreed on the idea of ending homelessness, their actions were driven by different understandings about its nature and what ending it actually meant. City officials and other powerful actors involved in implementing the coalition's plan, including other local groups and provincial officials, were motivated by a housing-based definition. They therefore viewed low-barrier shelters as a short-term solution to the longer-term objective of using Housing First programs to find supportive housing for people experiencing homelessness. Others involved in the coalition, including those at First United Church, did not necessarily disagree with this objective, but they also sought to create a community in the low-barrier shelter, one that would welcome anyone who wanted to use the space. For them, homelessness could not be ended if people, even when housed, remained isolated and excluded. Their shelter space welcomed everyone, including people who, by the definition used by the city and the province, were not experiencing homelessness because they had access to subsidized housing. So the powerfully magnetic idea of ending street homelessness brought together an ambitious and committed coalition, but disagreements about what ending homelessness meant were fomented by the idea's ambiguity, which made it volatile and led to the breakdown of part of that coalition. This underscores an important contribution of this work to ideational theory: ambiguous ideas are powerful coalition builders, but they are also volatile.

This book has also examined how ideas and institutions interact. The ideational disagreement between city and Vancouver actors and the StreetoHome Foundation was very small, for example, but was amplified by local institutions – notably the local party system – that turned minor differences into political ones. As a result, the two approaches solidified and a chasm between them developed. Once the initial shock of the partisan origins of the StreetoHome Foundation wore off, the foundation was able to work with city officials along the continuum of homelessness, with the city focusing on shelters (as well as permanent and transitional housing) and the STHF on Housing First approaches. Institutions can also enable groups to overcome significant barriers posed by different understandings of homelessness; as noted, formal coordination between two different plans at the regional level in Montreal – one motivated by a housing-based definition of homelessness and the other by a community-based definition – has managed this profound disagreement, allowing these different groups to coexist.

Welfare State

This book also makes a number of contributions to the study of the welfare state. The federal nature of Canada's welfare state has received considerable attention in the academic literature. This is unlikely to change, and scholars should continue to examine how federalism and competing interpretations of federalism have shaped the welfare state. But the federal welfare state is also urban. This presents an additional challenge, both theoretical and practical, to social policy governance and the production of social protection. Complex policy challenges tend to concentrate in urban centres, spaces that in Canada are increasingly unaffordable and unequal, thus posing even greater challenges to equitable social protection. And complex social problems like homelessness tend to be hyper-localized: things are different in Vancouver than they are in West Kelowna , but they are also different in East Vancouver than they are in Kitsilano. Local groups are the ones that know this best, but their expertise has often been overlooked, and they usually do not have the resources, mandate, or both to respond on their own.

Much of what has been learned in the preceding pages comes from locally based actors. Federal and provincial governments took scissors and in some cases a chainsaw to the social safety net, carving out large gaps through which people could, did, and continue to fall. Local actors, mainly third-sector and Indigenous-led groups, have reinforced the safety net when no one else would, stretching it to cover more people and mending the holes with duct tape. Understanding social protection in Canada, including how inequality is reproduced, how social risks change over time, where ideas come from, how policies are developed and why, who is prioritized and who is not and why, all of these questions require a close examination of local and even hyper-local levels, actions, and actors. Studies of complex social policy are incomplete without a careful consideration of local groups, Indigenous actors, and municipal governments. And the success of complex policy-making depends on the inclusion of the knowers – Indigenous leaders, lived experts, and service providers – so understanding barriers to their participation is urgent.

This work also buttresses a path-breaking conclusion drawn by urban scholars like Kristin Good: municipal governments are democratic governments in their own right (Good 2009). This is evident in the different degrees and types of involvement we see among municipal governments, which are partly a consequence of variations in institutional realities and choices informed by specific ideas identified here. Most obviously, Toronto is responsible for housing and homelessness. Other, less obvious institutional features also matter to this involvement, such as density bonusing and inclusionary zoning powers, which some cities have and use aggressively. Municipal officials have made it clear that they belong at the policy-making table; if not invited, many have simply invited themselves and pulled up a chair. If anyone still believes that municipalities are uninvolved in social policy or are all the same and should be treated as such, this simple reality is powerful evidence otherwise.

This research also reveals an important conclusion regarding housing and the welfare state. Housing policy has not typically been considered central to the welfare state in Canada, or even internationally; Ulf Torgerson famously called housing the "wobbly pillar" of the welfare state (Torgersen 1987). While ending homelessness may be about more than housing, depending on the definition, homelessness is *always* the absence of housing. The centrality of housing to so many aspects of health and well-being should once and for all put this debate to rest: while housing has at times been considered an economic good or infrastructure, it is and always will be social protection from a host of social risks as well. Given that it centrally determines so many other measures of health and well-being, housing is not the welfare state's wobbly pillar but rather its load-bearing wall. Especially given the housing crisis in many large Canadian cities, future studies (and governments) should treat it as such.

To the extent that housing has been studied, it has tended to be prior to the federal cuts in the 1990s. This present research reinforces some of the conclusions drawn in previous studies of the welfare state, including how housing policy and federalism interact, but gaps in our understanding of housing in the federal welfare state remain. Consistent with studies from the past, this research has found that not all provinces are concerned about protecting their jurisdiction from what can be interpreted as federal encroachment. This is notably the case with the federal NHI/HPS. Quebec is the only province to co-govern this program with the federal government, a fact that one federal bureaucrat admitted was baffling. Yet for decades, provinces have behaved differently when it comes to protecting their jurisdiction over housing (Banting 1990, 129). This study also finds that federalism continues to operate with a footnote, as Alain Noël so aptly noted in 2000: the multilateral agreement between federal and provincial governments regarding the implementation of the NHS contains that famous footnote to indicate Quebec's protest against federal encroachment into provincial jurisdiction. Continuing to explore federal, urban, and place-based dimensions of housing and the welfare state will provide important insights to these literatures.

Finally, this book contributes to a small but growing body of research on the governance of homelessness. In this careful documentation of the involvement of multilevel and multisector actors in homelessness governance, I have identified the ways in which actors are involved in the production of social protection across the country. Many of these actors are deeply engaged. This multitude of highly involved actors can in some cities lead to fragmentation. This does not necessarily diminish the effectiveness of governance networks, especially when different groups collaborate or coordinate. This finding challenges some of what has been concluded about homelessness governance in other studies, including Nienke Boesveldt's study of homelessness governance in Europe and Charley Willison's study of homelessness governance in the United States. The conclusion that homelessness governance requires a central agency (Boesveldt 2015) or recentralization (Willison 2021) is useful in some contexts. But it is difficult to apply in others, such as Vancouver and Montreal, where a number of actors are involved and centralizing authority in one body would risk alienating some groups. The alienation of some groups can result in an uncoordinated and less complete network or, at worst, a fragmented system where groups work at cross-purposes. Besides which, we would lose their expertise. Centralization is not, therefore, necessarily necessary, and in some instances the productive potential of coordinated fragmentation is clear to see.

The existence of multiple definitions of homelessness in Canada is important to document and keep in mind as policy-makers develop responses to ensure that people living in Canada have adequate, safe homes. This suggests that the understandings of what is motivating the actions of decision-makers may be even more complicated than previously thought. In the United States, Charley Willison (2021) identified two "social constructions" of homelessness: individual and structural. That a community-centred definition of homelessness was identified across Canada but was not identified by Willison suggests there are perhaps important differences in social protection between Canada and the United States, or perhaps community-based definitions are present in cities not covered in Willison's study. Similarly, a comparison of the results of Canadian and American studies raises the important question of the role of Indigenous people in homelessness governance in the United States. What is their role in the production of social protection in the US? Is there no Indigenous perspective on homelessness in the United States? Why or why not? These are some questions to consider in future studies, informed by the Canadian experience.

Erin Dej also considers two of the definitions identified above: the housing-focused one and the Indigenous one proposed by Thistle. Her book, *A Complex Exile*, was based on extensive fieldwork, including participant observation, in two homeless shelters in Ottawa, Ontario. This intensive look at two services allowed her to invest considerable time in each resource and with the people using the services, which made for a rich empirical study of how the services provided in those shelters do and do not respond to the causes of homelessness. Dej concludes that homeless shelters, through mental health supports, pathologize homelessness, reinforcing the exclusion and isolation of homeless people. Given the existence of another, community-focused definition of homelessness, and given the centrality of community and inclusion in Dej's recommendations for policy, my research suggests that it would be fruitful to also consider services offered by agencies that adopt a community-focused definition of homelessness in future research to see how they compare and if they are more success at addressing the root causes of homelessness than interventions motivated by the housing-based definition.

Theorizing the Multilevel Governance of Complex Policy Problems

Individual Canadians, however, might wonder whether all this really matters. Are federal/provincial battles simply a game beloved by bureaucrats and politicians, driven by a territorial imperative, but devoid of real consequences – "full of sound and fury, signifying nothing"? Or do subtle shifts in the models that structure the distribution of power have major impacts that are visible at the grassroots, where real people need better housing? The complexities of federal/provincial relations do, in fact, have important implications for the broad patterns of public policy. (Banting 1990, 144)

Drawing on studies of multilevel governance and the welfare state, this book has sought to explain why different governance configurations have emerged with respect to homelessness across the country. This variation in governance dynamics is not unexpected, but we know that governance shapes policy. As this book has found, it is not just federal–provincial dynamics that matter, as Banting noted thirty years ago, but broader multilevel dynamics do as well. The following sections walk through what we have learned about how resources, institutions, and ideas shape the involvement and interactions of third-sector groups, private-sector actors, Indigenous groups, local governments, provincial governments, and the federal government in the multilevel governance of homelessness in Canada.

Third-Sector Involvement and Interactions

Though many third-sector groups have the expertise and capacity to develop and implement measures to end homelessness, they are not always involved, or not always involved at *all* stages of policy development. A variety of forces structure the involvement of third-sector groups in the governance of homelessness. Institutionalizing their involvement ensures that their expertise is brought right into policy-making and affords them some degree of independence in the process. This is the case in Quebec, at both local and provincial levels, where third-sector groups are government-funded and independent and have access to the policy process through a number of venues and channels (Laforest 2011a). Where they have not been invited or institutionally involved, third-sector groups employ a number of methods to push their knowledge into decision-making processes. Absent formal institutional structures, third-sector groups in other parts of the country are sometimes able to leverage connections with sympathetic "insiders" in government. The Toronto Disaster Relief Committee, active for about fifteen years in Toronto, benefited from an important insider on Toronto City Council: Jack Layton. Layton championed TDRC ideas, including a plan to declare homelessness a disaster. Judy Graves, the City of Vancouver's advocate for the homeless, brought the perspective of service providers and people experiencing homelessness to decision-makers at City Hall. Libby Davies was another important insider: as house leader for the federal New Democratic Party, she championed the concerns of third-sector groups from Vancouver, notably regarding the creation of a National Housing Strategy.

Third-sector groups also engage decision-makers more broadly. Emily Paradis contrasts grassroots activism with advocacy.[1] They write that grassroots advocates "embrace a radical and intersectional analysis ... They often take a direct approach, and their campaigns tend to be reactive to local events." This contrasts with the lobbying approach to engagement, which is more moderate: "While the role of inequities based on race, gender, and disability is often acknowledged, fundamental critiques of capitalism and institutionalization are typically absent, and state-led solutions are promoted" (Paradis 2016, 100). Paradis also notes that groups can adopt an insider or an outsider stance, referring to "the extent to which their discourses, activities and demands align with or are contrary to those of the powerful entities they seek to influence" (2016, 101).

The CHF, the TAEH, the MMFIM and the CAEH tend to adopt the lobbying approach from an insider stance, whereas the TDRC, OCAP, and RAPSIM adopt more grassroots methods. The TDRC and OCAP have approached their work as critical outsiders, an interesting contrast with the RAPSIM, an organization that believes government is part of the solution, not the problem. Because of institutionalization in Quebec, the RAPSIM is both an insider and an outsider. These two methods of engagement, advocacy and grassroots, are effective, but in different ways. The lobbying approach is targeted and behind the scenes. Groups or their leaders carefully select a small number of officials (both elected and bureaucratic) to target with key messages, solutions, and demands. CAEH president Tim Richter is a clear example of this; indeed, he had a background in lobbying prior to his work in the homelessness sector, and his lobbying efforts are rapid and razor sharp. On her second day on the job as Minister of Veterans Affairs, Jody Wilson-Raybould received a letter from the CAEH regarding veteran's homelessness, a priority for the CAEH. The TAEH also takes a more targeted approach with the City of Toronto, distinct from the grassroots method the TRDC employed and that OCAP continues to take. Senior actors with the TAEH explained that they do not want to be simply another advocacy group; they want to participate in decision-making.

A concern raised by Withers (2021) is that proximity to power may leave these groups compromised, unable to criticize governments and needing to self-censor when they do. The grassroots approach is employed by groups that tend to be more critical or radical in their approach, and their actions seek to build broad support. In the film *Shelter from the Storm*, we see TDRC officials storming City Hall with a megaphone, demanding to know the location of Mel Lastman. The use of a megaphone was not required in order to find Lastman, but of course finding Lastman was not their only goal: it was also to make their presence, their discontent, and their demands known widely throughout City Hall. RAPSIM members also use a megaphone at rallies and spread their message broadly. Their objective is to inform not just policy-makers but a wider constituency, who will help apply pressure on decision-makers. The ultimate objective, as Michael Shapcott so eloquently explained, is to create space for political leaders to go further. Grassroots approaches, especially when taken by radical movements, risk alienating decision-makers, though this is not always seen as a problem by organizers. A former senior official recalled with exasperation that they found working with OCAP nearly impossible, and that you give them what they want and they still protest. Another senior city official said they are "annoying as hell" but still appreciated the need for advocacy.

Though some groups tend to use more grassroots approaches than lobbying ones, as defined by Paradis, most groups employ a variety of methods for making themselves heard. The RAPSIM carries out grassroots organizing, but at the same time, its leaders communicate directly – and more quietly – with elected officials. The CAEH also does grassroots organizing, an example being its 2021 Vote Housing campaign, which sought to build a movement to pressure political parties to commit to housing and ending homelessness in the upcoming federal election. It can be difficult to employ different methods of engagement, but many third sector leaders insisted on the importance of relationships with political decision-makers. One highly respected insider advocate explained their strategy for how to maintain a critical stance without alienating allies: "In my own experience, [politicians] are like dogs – if you whack them all the time, it just confuses them. But if you whack them a few times, and then the next time you fluff them behind the ears, they start paying attention" (personal interview 2014).[2] Scholars interested in the different approaches taken by social movements will find a closer look at this history exciting and theoretically enriching.

Ideas lead third-sector groups deploy their resources to connect with insiders and advocate. One of these ideas is the deeply held belief that they have a role to play in the production of social protection. Across the country, third sector leaders generally agree that the main responsibility for homelessness governance lies with governments, though some groups – notably the Calgary Homeless Foundation[3] and the Movement to End Homelessness in Montreal – have sought to assume more of a leadership role. There is nevertheless widespread agreement among the third sector that effective and responsive governance of homelessness requires substantial input from third-sector groups.

Ideas regarding the nature of homelessness are powerful in structuring the interactions between third-sector groups and other actors. In some instances, we see little disagreement. This is the case in Calgary, though the understanding of the nature of homelessness has evolved considerably since 2008. The CHF was able to use the highly magnetic idea of ending homelessness and saving money doing so to build a powerful coalition, in the process crowding out or winning over groups that disagreed. By contrast, there were divergent understandings of the nature of homelessness in Toronto in the late 1990s and early 2000s, with the city adopting a more narrow definition than the then powerful TDRC and allied network OCAP. This contributed to climate of hostility and distrust. In 2015, the Toronto Alliance to End Homelessness emerged, espousing an understanding of homelessness that largely aligned with that of the city. This ideational convergence on the nature of homelessness has done much to ease the friction that characterized past relationships between the city and the third sector, enabling the two to collaborate.

Disagreements about the nature of homelessness can also cause conflicts *within* the third sector. We see this clearly in Montreal, Toronto, and Vancouver. Some groups, such as the RAPSIM in Montreal, the leaders of a former HEAT shelter in Vancouver, and the TDRC and OCAP in Toronto view homelessness as related not just to housing but to poverty, inclusion, and community as well. These groups are critical of plans and strategies that prioritize people who experience chronic homelessness, because their understanding of the problem is related to much more than housing. Other groups, such as the MMFIM, the CHF, the TAEH and the national CAEH have a narrower understanding of homelessness as related to housing and believe that people who experience chronic homelessness should be targeted first. These different understandings of homelessness can coexist; groups can work together by targeting specific forms or types of homelessness, filling gaps left or created by others. But disagreements can also raise barriers to the development of effective governance and ultimately an effective service system. The MMFIM and RAPSIM have at times worked at cross-purposes, competing for funding or to influence government agendas. Given the importance of third-sector involvement, particularly in Montreal, these conflicts can destabilize and weaken the overall governance dynamics.

As this makes clear, the third sector involves a great diversity of actors advancing different approaches and visions, and who often compete with one another for limited funding. This is not a novel finding, as anyone who studies or works in the third-sector will know, and is consistent with the literature on civil-society and community-led efforts to produce social protection (Hudson and Graefe 2012). This is a strength; the homeless population is diverse, meaning many different types of services are required, including harm reduction in some cases, abstinence-based programs in others. Further, while some shelters are safe for people of all genders, some women or trans people feel safer in segregated spaces. Youth, queer people, seniors, and people with disabilities also have unique needs that are not always met in large homeless shelters, and may find better support in smaller environments where services are more sensitive to them. As is often said, one size does not fit all.

What is notable about the third sector when it comes to serving people who are homeless is that some agencies or services believe that the work of others is undermining their own. For example, Matthew Pearce, who ran the Old Brewery Mission in Montreal for years, wrote that "shelters had inadvertently become facilitators of homelessness; they enabled people who had nothing to stabilize their lives within a state of homelessness. Shelters allowed homelessness to become more than a difficult period in someone's life – they allowed it to become normalized as a lifestyle" (Pearce 2018, 88–9). That is a controversial statement, but Pearce is not afraid to speak up about what he thinks it will take to end homelessness in Montreal, and across the country for that matter. And he is by no means the only one to criticize services and how they are producing social protection. The deep commitment of service providers to their work leads some groups to criticize others, a dynamic that leaves third-sector groups involved in homelessness particularly divided. These criticisms and divisions are frequently the result of different understandings of homelessness, and fundamental disagreements can indeed be very difficult to coordinate.

Private Sector Involvement and Interactions

Where they are involved, private-sector actors are influential in the governance of homelessness. Different kinds of resources, primarily money and management expertise, help explain why these actors are involved. The private sector is the least involved in homelessness in Montreal; actors attribute this to a lack of resources and to the fact that private philanthropy in the province has historically been minimal. In Calgary and Vancouver, however, where private-sector groups are influential in homelessness governance, the ability to bring "new money" to the table was important in driving this involvement. Actors in Vancouver recall meeting with a former premier who was pleasantly surprised to learn that they did not simply want to influence decisions about provincial spending but were prepared to co-fund solutions as well. In Calgary, the ability to write a big cheque to fund a pilot project allowed the CHF to hit the ground running and not wait on government funding or a long grant processes. Besides bringing material resources, private-sector actors pride themselves on offering management expertise; what they lack in knowledge of homelessness, they purport to make up for with their proven ability to manage complex problems and systems. In the mid-aughts, the homeless system was understood to be something of a technical challenge; community groups were told that they had what they needed to end homelessness, they just needed to put the parts together. An experienced private sector leader was seen has having the skills to do this, and in Vancouver and Calgary, there is strong evidence that government officials also valued this private-sector experience and expertise.

Private-sector actors can also draw on personal connections with top, and sometimes *very* top, elected officials. In Calgary, for example, some scholars have concluded that there are around 300 people, mostly private-sector individuals from the oil and gas sector, who are powerful and connected enough to influence government agendas (Feng, Li, and Langford 2014). In other words, private-sector actors are not always connected to an insider who is sympathetic to their cause, but they have strong enough relationships with senior officials that they can win them over, effectively creating not just a sympathetic insider for their cause, but a sympathetic mayor, premier, or minister. This is an important insight of this research and allows for a more nuanced understanding of power dynamics between third sector groups and private sector groups. Private sector leaders in some cases have access to the very top elected officials, often in a personal way that allows them to ask for a meeting, even just a few minutes, with political leaders; this is valuable access that other sectors tend not to have.

Ideas allow us to more fully understand why private-sector actors have chosen to leverage their connections and bring their resources to the governance of homelessness in particular. Ideas regarding the responsibility to produce social protection – both whose responsibility it *is* and whose it is *not* – have been important. In Calgary and Vancouver, private-sector actors noted that they believe they have a responsibility to help those in need. In both cities, however, actors also noted that homelessness should not be left to government alone. In fact, the private-sector has often increased its involvement as a means to *limit* government involvement in efforts to make the overall system more efficient.

Ideas regarding the nature of homelessness have also driven involvement. In Vancouver, Calgary, and Toronto, at key moments, private-sector actors organized around homelessness out of concern about what homelessness was doing to local economic activity and productivity. In Vancouver, business leaders wrote a letter to then Mayor Sam Sullivan in 2006, imploring him to do more to address an "urban malignancy" that was interfering with economic activity. In Calgary, business leaders in the early-aughts believed that Calgary was on the cusp of becoming a global economic hub and that homelessness threatened that future. Similar concerns were expressed by business leaders in Toronto in a report by the Toronto Board of Trade. In these cases, private-sector actors sought rapid solutions to a problem they had defined in negative and stereotypical terms (crime, disorder), reflecting a narrow understanding of homelessness. Involvement in solutions were at least in part self-interested.

While continuing to embrace a narrow understanding of homelessness, and sometimes out of self-interest, private-sector leaders in Canada have also been interested in long-term evidence-based solutions to homelessness, and they have been some of the most enthusiastic champions of Housing First programs in Canadian cities. Private-sector support for Housing First was based in part on presentations made at various breakfasts (many of them Prayer) by Philip Mangano, who insisted that plans to end homelessness through Housing First were succeeding in US cities. Interestingly, this private-sector support of evidence-based policy measures contrasts with findings in the United States, where Charley Willison's work on homelessness governance found that business leaders tend to support individualized and criminalized responses to homelessness as opposed to Housing First (which she finds is more often supported by local governments) (Willison 2021).

There is ample evidence that the private sector deeply respects the work being done by third-sector groups and that it is willing to partner. Private-sector actors at times collaborate effectively with third-sector groups. But also evident are disagreements between sectors over the nature of homelessness. As the CHF was developing its ten-year plan, some third-sector groups in Calgary came to feel that they were being pushed off their own turf. The CHF eventually won over many sceptics (a process helped by CHF officials' evolving ideas regarding the nature of homelessness); even so, early disagreements on the nature of homelessness (and whether it can be ended) created a rift between some service agencies in Calgary and the CHF. As private-sector–led organizations have spent more and more time in the field, and have experienced failures or at least slower successes than they had expected, third-sector groups have come to be seen in a much more positive light, as necessary partners rather than obstacles. The same can be said of governments.

Indigenous Leaders

I think the non-Indigenous community needs to step back a little bit and give the lead to the Indigenous community to say, "This is what we need and what we want. Thank you very much for listening to our voice and please don't interpret it from your perspective."

Member of an Indigenous Community Advisory Board

Indigenous groups across the country are involved in the governance of homelessness, producing social protection in accordance with

Indigenous knowledge in a colonial country. Because of its focus on urban spaces, this book has considered a small dimension of Indigenous involvement in homelessness governance, which has generally been in terms of networks that have been created to implement federal NHI/HPS funding and with other local advocacy groups. Indigenous knowledge has not been systematically included, or perhaps more accurately it has been systematically excluded, by all levels of government and sectors of society in the development of responses to homelessness. To the extent that Indigenous people are involved and interact with other groups in homelessness governance, it tends to be informal and at their own initiative (as opposed to by invitation) – as one actor explained in an interview, "You put yourself out there."

Even when they do put themselves out there, Indigenous leaders are frequently met with resistance, illustrating the additional burdens that are placed on Indigenous people to identify and push to resolve problems. This was the case for Indigenous service providers concerned about the over-policing of Indigenous men, for example. One leader interviewed had to fight to have their voice heard; once they were listened to, they ended up educating local police officers on the history of policing and Indigenous-police relations. In addition to this practice of putting themselves out there to have their voices heard, a number of Indigenous people interviewed referenced the fact that they serve on a number of local committees (frequently on a volunteer basis) and that they use those opportunities to advocate. Not all these committees are specifically related to homelessness, but people interviewed said they used every opportunity to speak and advocate. This approach is in contrast to what was seen among third-sector leaders, who tend to rely on a sympathetic insider, and private-sector leaders, who often have personal connections with senior political leaders.

An important lesson emerged regarding the necessity not only of regular and institutionalized involvement, but also of different channels of communication. An Indigenous leader involved in developing a municipal response to homelessness explained that were frequent meetings that brought together all the partners involved in developing and implementing the plan, but that this environment was not the best place for this person to advocate:

> I guess I found it a bit difficult to be heard in that scenario. The city had developed what it thought was its mission, so they were going forward. The only way you could be heard in that is if you were a Type A personality and just wanted to be heard and were not afraid to speak out. Not

that they were excluding voices. But it's a bit intimidating sitting in that room with council and the chief of police and say, "uuuuuuuum I have a question." One of the ways around that I found was to be strategic in how you get your voice out there. So I would send emails or speak to people outside the room. The mayor is very open in terms of being able to be in contact with him. (personal interview 2014)

Through the Community Advisory Boards required to access federal homelessness program funding, Indigenous people have some degree of institutionalized role in NHI/HPS implementation, though the institutional structure is imposed and was originally set up by the federal government in a way that could only have failed. The original NHI model for Indigenous communities sought to use Indigenous labour-based organizations, to implement NHI funding. Because of that institutional set-up, projects funded by the NHI had to have an employment element to them in order to receive funding, a totally inappropriate set-up for funding intended to combat homelessness that was changed within two years. Additional constraints remain, however. Indigenous CABs have tried to be flexible with regard to what programs they fund and how they fund them; this includes allowing groups to use a larger up-front investment instead of spreading the funding out over three years. However, they have been told by federal actors that they cannot release the funding that way. Their choices are constrained, but Indigenous groups are resisting. The NHI/HPS structure, which relies on volunteer members, has emboldened some of those who serve. They note that, as volunteers, they can't be fired. Relying on volunteers who are already overburdened cannot be a best practice. This structure does give some power to community groups (indeed, this structure relies on them), however, and it means some Indigenous leaders can and do push back against federal requirements and constraints.

A lack of adequate funding is also a major obstacle to Indigenous involvement. Indigenous people are significantly overrepresented among the homeless population across the country, a legacy not just of social policy failures but of ongoing colonization. Members serving on Indigenous CABs have noted that the funding breakdown between what they get and what the Designated Community CAB gets does not reflect the breakdown of the homeless population. The fact that the NHI/HPS has been so underfunded means that Indigenous services and the people who use them have been hit particularly hard. While the Designated CAB funds Indigenous services as well, some Indigenous CAB members suggest that they should be the ones making those decisions, or at least have a say.

In addition to institutional and resource constraints, two further barriers exist to the involvement of Indigenous people in particular in the governance of homelessness: systemic racism as it specifically relates to policy-involvement[4] and the exclusion or devaluing of Indigenous knowledge. Recall an actor who ran an Indigenous service in Toronto who had to convince provincial officials to release Aboriginal Housing dollars. The province held on to this funding, certain that no Indigenous service could administer it. Indigenous capacity was drastically underestimated. Similarly, in the original set up of the federal NHI, the federal government chose to administer funding for Indigenous communities through existing labour-market focussed agencies, seeming to suggest a lack of trust in Indigenous service providers to administer the funding themselves.

Furthermore, Indigenous knowledge has not been valued and has been excluded from policy development. In that regard, this book has not presented anything new, but rather has confirmed what has been found in reports and studies and what has long been known among Indigenous groups – that Indigenous people must do the work of making connections, of educating, and of convincing governments that their experience and knowledge is valuable. These barriers risk undermining responses to homelessness by excluding Indigenous knowledge that is so important to efforts to combat homelessness. Though this knowledge has not been centred in policy development or governance, Indigenous leaders have taken up a resurgence approach to produce social protection. This was made clear in an interview with senior officials involved with Indigenous services across the country, including one who works with elders who do ceremonies during outreach: "[The elders] seem to break down those barriers."

Interviews pointed to the importance of Indigenous leadership at organizations serving Indigenous populations. One leader gave the example of sweat lodges: without Indigenous knowledge and experience, sweats can be dangerous for some people, including people who use or are early in their recovery, but they can be healing and safe (physically and spiritually) when led with by Indigenous healers and knowledge-keepers. Indigenous leaders noted with some appreciation a growing awareness of the importance of incorporating Indigenous knowledge in services and of reconciliation efforts, but expressed concern that this was being done in some cases without the guidance or involvement of Indigenous leaders, healers and elders. Faced with failures of social protection and of reconciliation, Indigenous elders have stepped into outreach vans to drive into ravines to perform ceremonies with some of the most isolated people experiencing homelessness.

This connection to culture and ceremony has been profoundly healing for many people experiencing homelessness, illustrating the need to include this knowledge and expertise not just in vans during outreach, but in the design and reform of systems to end and prevent homelessness in the first place.

Indigenous leaders understand that homelessness is about more than a lack of housing or even housing and community integration. Murray Sinclair explained how common conceptions of homelessness overlook the reality that homelessness is experienced in different ways: "Today, when we think about homelessness, we tend to think about somebody on the street in downtown Ottawa asking for money, without putting it more in the Indigenous context of landlessness, moving around, not having that settled home space, whatever form it may take" (personal interview, Murray Sinclair 2018). Ideas translate into different approaches to producing social protection, including funding projects that are not technically eligible for NHI/HPS funding and according to the housing-based definition that motivates that federal program. Guided by a different definition of homelessness, Indigenous networks have nevertheless funded a wider range of programs to meet those needs.

Homelessness is understood in different ways across the country, but those different ways are not necessarily incompatible. Different definitions can coexist and be coordinated, as is seen in Vancouver, where the two HPS networks – one Indigenous, the other non-Indigenous – coordinate formally. Because the two groups coordinate and communicate regularly, these different approaches can coexist without getting in each other's way or undoing each other's work, though both groups are so underfunded that they are limited in their ability to meet existing needs, let alone duplicate services. This is increasingly happening in Toronto as well, but only very recently. That said, disagreements about the definition of homelessness can also result in fragmented governance dynamics and the exclusion of the Indigenous perspective. This was the case in 2008 in Calgary, where the Aboriginal Standing Committee on Housing and Homelessness was isolated from the Calgary Homeless Foundation's plans on homelessness and ended up creating its own plan. Diverging perspectives regarding the responsibility to produce social protection (the exclusion of Indigenous knowledge by the CHF) and regarding the nature of homelessness (Indigenous-leaders did not find the housing-focussed approach taken by the CHF to respond to their experiences) led to fragmentation. The relationship between the two groups has since improved, following a change at the CHF and a recognition that the Indigenous plan is valuable.

Indigenous knowledge has not always been sought, or has been ignored or rejected, but there are indications that this may be changing.

The federal government has acknowledged an Indigenous definition of homelessness, one that identifies colonialism as a cause. There is increasing agreement that there is a need for an Indigenous housing strategy at the national level, and that this strategy must be Indigenous-led, and important work is being done locally to inform groups that Housing First can and should adapt to Indigenous definitions of home and homelessness (Distasio et al. 2019). Though ideas among federal officials have evolved so that they now recognize there are different causes and experiences of homelessness among Indigenous people, the federal government has historically been unwilling to fully share power, even in the NHI/HPS, which is often seen as early example of place-based policy (Leo and August 2006). The effectiveness and justice of future interventions requires this to change and for power to be shared.

The involvement considered here has mostly been through a federally imposed structure. Future work should consider Indigenous involvement in homelessness governance outside of urban spaces and beyond these federally created networks. That includes the North, where Indigenous communities are seeking increased authority over housing in a nation-to-nation relationship with the federal government. For example, Jason Snaggs of the Yellowknifes Dene First Nation said recently that "if the federal government sincerely wants to improve its nation-to-nation relationship with First Nations, prioritizing Indigenous-led housing initiatives would be a good way to do that" (Taylor 2020; see also Yesno and Maher Lopez 2020). Further study of recent developments in urban spaces should be conducted as well – developments such as the landmark agreement between the Squamish First Nation and BC Housing to develop the first provincially funded on-reserve housing for people who are unhoused or underhoused (Chan 2020).

Local Governments

The municipal government in Vancouver, Toronto, and Montreal are all involved in the governance of homelessness. Whatever their involvement, municipal officials in all cities referenced a lack of financial resources as a key constraint on what they were able to do with respect to homelessness. A Toronto official recalled that their top three priorities in municipal efforts to combat homelessness were "funding, funding, funding" (personal interview 2014). Another, reflecting on the city's efforts in the mid-2000s, concluded: "Could we have done more? Absolutely. But we needed more money" (personal interview 2014). A former mayor said that mayors are always going to other orders of government, cap in hand, asking for more money. Yet another said that their role was to be a professional fundraiser (they also noted, almost as an afterthought, that they had always hated fundraising).

Though the resources are scarce, municipal officials in three large cities have found ways to become involved in homelessness to various degrees. This is in part thanks to another type of resource: expertise. Councillors, bureaucrats, and mayors noted that their locally based understanding of homelessness allowed them to develop more responsive plans. In Montreal, Mayor Denis Coderre explicitly linked the city's increased involvement in homelessness governance with knowledge of local needs: "We have the numbers, we know what the needs are" (Paré 2015, author's translation). As a Calgary city councillor explained: "As politicians and decision-makers, we are not in Edmonton or Ottawa, we are [in Calgary] and we see it and live it every day. We don't just show up on Friday. When you are here and you see it, you can sit there and close your eyes and say 'not my jurisdiction' for only so long" (personal interview 2014).

Institutions have also enabled some municipalities to increase their involvement in homelessness governance. Indeed, the differences in involvement among the four cities studied here can be understood to be in part a function of institutions. The most obvious is jurisdiction: Toronto is the only city that is officially responsible for homelessness and housing, which explains why Toronto is so involved. Expanding our understanding of institutions to include other features and tools that municipalities have, however, I find that some cities have other meaningful powers for fighting homelessness. Density bonusing and inclusionary zoning are two important tools. All cities have both powers, though in Calgary, Toronto, and Montreal, inclusionary zoning has only recently been introduced. Furthermore, these tools are not equally powerful across the country. Land is particularly valuable and limited in Toronto and Vancouver, and developers are eager to increase their profits by building taller and denser (others might point out that in this context, the use of these powers should be limited in favour of the development of more deeply affordable housing). With density bonusing or inclusionary zoning, municipal governments can leverage that eagerness into public contributions (Dingman 2021). Where developers are less eager (Calgary and Montreal), these powers are of less consequence. Also, inclusionary zoning in Toronto is currently not allowed city-wide but only near transit hubs. In Calgary, where land is less limited, incentives to build "dense," especially when something must be given in return, is not as strong as it is in Vancouver and Toronto, which makes these powers less meaningful.

Interacting with these institutional forces are ideas. First, consistent with the literature, I found evidence that conceptualizations of the local government matter. Where a municipality was involved in homelessness governance, the local government was understood by key local officials to be more than just a policy-taker or a garbage collector. This was clearest in Toronto, where officials repeatedly compared the city to a province. I also found evidence that municipal involvement is strongly structured by ideas regarding the responsibility to produce social protection. Interestingly, in some cases, the lack of involvement in homelessness was in part justified by the understanding that other actors are responsible. Calgary's former Mayor Naheed Nenshi was one of the fiercest advocates for increased city powers, and the city is involved in poverty reduction and affordable housing; yet in Calgary, homelessness in particular has been understood to be either a provincial or third sector responsibility.

Former Vancouver mayor Gregor Robertson tried to some extent to go it alone in his plan to end street homelessness, or to at least go it without the province, believing that the municipal government could and should fill the gap created by a lack of senior government efforts to produce social protection. Looking back on those efforts, he now sounds somewhat regretful. Gary Mason, after interviewing him for the *Globe and Mail*, summarized Robertson's retrospective analysis: "And [Robertson] said, unless you have Ottawa and the provincial government willing to bankroll housing and the necessary health supports to help people overcome their various problems, it's a lost cause. Cities simply don't have the ability to raise the funds necessary to have a critical impact on the homeless situation" (Mason 2020). It seems that this lesson has been learned, if he needed to learn it, by the current mayor, Kennedy Stewart, who has switched back to advocacy, asking senior governments for more and playing the role of Vancouver's lobbyist-in-chief (McElroy 2019); Mayor Plante in Montreal has also been more collaborative than Mayor Coderre, who tried to assume leadership over homelessness when he was Mayor.

When it comes to cities' interactions with other actors, ideas regarding the nature of homelessness are of great importance. Small but sharp disagreements over the nature of homelessness in the mid-2000s in Vancouver interacted with the local party system, leading to the fragmentation of homelessness governance. The city and the StreetoHome Foundation worked on different plans, implementing their efforts at the same time, but separately, because they understood the problem differently. Toronto further illustrates how ideas regarding the nature of the problem can structure relations at the local level. In the 1990s and early 2000s, discord over the nature of homelessness led to conflict between the city and the Toronto Disaster Relief Committee. A new civil society group has since emerged in Toronto, the Toronto Alliance to End Homelessness, which espouses a view of homelessness that is closer to the city's, including support for Housing First, efforts to collect data, and a belief in ending homelessness. The relationship between the city and the third sector as represented by the TAEH is now much more collaborative.

Ideas regarding the nature of homelessness also shape intergovernmental relations, particularly municipal–provincial. For example, the Province of Ontario re-engaged only timidly in homelessness policy in the early 2000s. Its program, Off the Streets Into Shelters, was implemented as the city began to expand its housing and homelessness responses. A senior Toronto official explained: "In 2005, if I wanted to *shelter* 3,000 homeless individuals, the province would pay a portion ... if I wanted to *house* the same people, which is more cost effective, I couldn't get a dime" (personal interview 2014). City officials had related homelessness squarely to housing and were working to find housing for people experiencing homelessness. Provincial officials, by contrast, did not understand homelessness as related to housing; rather, they viewed it as a short-term emergency, and these ideas risked undermining municipal goals. Frustrations with the province were also seen in Vancouver, where city officials sensed that they were not on the same page as the province in their efforts to end street homelessness. A municipal official involved in housing and homelessness said with exasperation: "I don't know what their goal is" and noted that the city's planning process did not specifically engage the province.

Municipal officials understand that their relations with the provincial government are important, however, and that they need some degree of support from the province to achieve their goals. An actor involved in implementing Gregor Robertson's plan described the city's relationship with the province in family terms, with the city playing the role of annoying little brother and the province the annoyed big brother. Though the relationship was difficult, they were still family. Respect for the provincial role was particularly evident in Montreal, where city actors are working to acquire a greater say in issues related to homelessness but are doing so slowly and cautiously. Montreal officials are well aware that their city is a creature of the province and that they cannot engage directly with the federal government, for example. On this last point, no city official outside of Montreal mentioned that cities are creatures of the province in this way, suggesting that ideas about federalism have uniquely penetrated local government actions in Montreal.

Municipal officials saved their harshest words for the federal government, which may not surprise students of urban politics in Canada. The Vancouver actor who had called the province big brother had this to say about the federal government: "It always feels a little unfair to bash the province around these issues because the real people who should be on the hook are the feds" (personal interview 2014). Many actors declared that for most of the past twenty years, the federal government simply hadn't shown up. This was particularly the case with interviews conducted in 2014, when calls for a National Housing Strategy were falling on deaf ears in Ottawa: "The federal government, I can tell you, they are not a player" (personal interview 2014). This person went on to say that when they were involved in implementing a municipal response to homelessness in the mid-aughts, "the feds were not in any meaningful way at the table." A city councillor put this in less diplomatic terms: "[the federal government] is nowhere. Bunch of assholes. They are bums in seats and they don't understand the individuals. I haven't seen one of those motherfuckers out here. Not one has come out and meet with us" (personal interview 2014).

There was a sense that municipalities were being disregarded and that their role was not being appreciated or respected. When asked how to improve Calgary's relationships with the province and the federal government, one city councillor insisted that the relationship needed to change: "When I look at who we are as a country, 75 per cent of us live in urban areas now. And I say we have a governance structure that no longer reflects the reality of where we live. The governance structure reflects who are were one hundred years ago, but not who we are now." When asked how that change could be made, they implied that they were tired of being treated as a child: "The federal and provincial governments need to recognize that municipalities are grown-ups. It's as simple as that. We are grown-ups" (personal interview 2014).

Provincial Involvement and Interactions

Over time, the provinces have become more involved in the governance of homelessness, though some have a longer history of involvement than others and there is variation in their degree of involvement. In some respects, this involvement is structured by resources. After the federal government decided to cut investments in social housing in the mid-1990s, most provinces, having lost significant revenue through the new social transfer program, also ended their commitments to housing. Yet BC and Quebec continued to develop housing, including supportive housing for people experiencing homelessness, evidence that resources alone do not explain provincial involvement. Furthermore, Alberta was *not* involved in housing or in the rising challenges related to homelessness in 2005 during a period of surplus. Instead of investing in efforts to alleviate and reduce homelessness, Ralph Klein's Progressive Conservative government sent a $600 cheque to every Albertan.

Indeed, in many cases we see changes in a province's involvement without a change in party and even without a change in party leader. Resources can constrain or facilitate provincial involvement, but these alone do not explain different degrees of provincial involvement in homelessness governance or variations over time. This points to the importance of ideas, notably regarding how homelessness is understood and whose responsibility it is to produce social protection against it. While some ideas align with what we would expect from parties given their left or right ideology, in other cases, ideas lead to actions that defy those expectations, illustrating the powerful role they can play independently of political ideology.

In some cases, provincial officials devolved responsibility for the production of social protection to the local level, be it formally or informally, actions that were intended to limit the province's role in the production of social protection. In 1999, PC Premier of Ontario Mike Harris devolved responsibility, but not additional funding, for housing to the local level. This can be understood as consistent with a broader ideological project to limit government involvement. This new context makes future provincial re-engagement very difficult. Liberal premiers of Ontario have focused on collaborative partnerships in producing social protection, primarily with the federal government but also with the local level. Intergovernmental and multilevel collaboration in an area of complex policy such as housing and homelessness is important and necessary for effective responses, but in Ontario there is a particularly challenging mismatch of resources at the provincial level and authority at the local level. This has made identifying a leader in this governance network difficult. Responses to homelessness in Toronto have been most productive when there has been ideational alignment across levels of government and sectors of society responsible for producing social protection. When there is ideational disagreement, however, this mismatch can be nearly impossible to overcome because of the institutional context.

Ideas about the responsibility to produce social protection have structured provincial involvement in BC as well, but in a way that is not so closely related to ideology as what we saw in Ontario. For all but five years in the early 2000s, the government of BC has been involved, mostly as a leader, in housing and homelessness governance because housing and homelessness have generally been understood to be government – specifically *provincial* – responsibilities. In 2001, the province announced plans to stop investing in housing, but only five years later it reversed course and began investing again. In the early 2000s, housing was understood to be a private-sector responsibility, but this changed after key senior officials embraced a redefinition of homelessness as having not just individual-level causes. Though actions under the Liberals have prioritized a relatively narrowly defined group of people, the prioritization of people who use drugs or live with mental illness reinforced provincial involvement because homelessness was now defined in terms of housing and health, both of which are usually understood to be provincial responsibilities.

Ideas about the responsibility for producing social protection are also at times shaped by ideas about federalism. This has notably been the case in Quebec. Federalism has tended to be understood differently there, where provincial jurisdiction is jealously guarded (Rocher 2009), though Western premiers also have strong history of protesting federal encroachments on provincial jurisdiction (Banting 1990). Quebec's initial commitment to housing in the 1990s was driven more by ideas about federalism than by ideas about the responsibility to produce social protection; yet changing ideas have led the province to assume a strong leadership role in homelessness governance from which it is now difficult to step back. There are ideological differences between parties, on both the left/right spectrum and the federalist/sovereigntist spectrum. But all Quebec provincial parties (Liberal, PQ, and CAQ) have been consistently willing to exercise and defend areas of provincial jurisdiction, including housing and other areas of social policy related to homelessness and have continued to fund plans consistently.

Ideas about the nature of homelessness structure interactions, but with the provinces we also see these ideas shaping provincial involvement. The Province of Quebec has developed a broad definition of homelessness and a strong propensity to defend and exercise its powers. These ideational and institutional forces have converged, resulting in strong provincial involvement in homelessness. The province's broad definition of homelessness has contributed to the development of a significant coalition of twelve provincial ministries working together on homelessness plans and policies; these are viewed as having to work together to reduce homelessness. It was also the understanding of the nature of homelessness that drove increased provincial involvement in Alberta in 2008, when the CHF announced that it would develop and implement a plan to end homelessness in ten years. The province re-engaged, but its ensuing actions were motivated by a narrow understanding of homelessness as largely an individual-level issue, albeit one requiring access to more housing. Convinced by these ideas about the nature of homelessness (and more specifically the possibility of ending it), the province limited its involvement to inadequate investments in housing and to tinkering with other related policy areas, such as income security. This involvement was at the direction of local groups and can be almost pinpointed to a meeting between an oil and gas executive and an Alberta premier. This changed again in 2014, though this was by all accounts an ideological change that followed the election of an NDP government for the first time in the province's history. While governance matters, provincial efforts to end homelessness in Alberta are an important reminder that resources are also necessary. The interagency council was a sophisticated governance network that brought various governmental and non-governmental leaders together, but was undermined by the lack of investments in affordable housing.

When asked about cities' involvement and their interactions with municipal officials, provincial officials noted – sometimes with mild condescension – that municipal efforts were appreciated but that political and financial leadership came from the province. A senior provincial actor noted: "The strategy is being built with 90 per cent of the funding from the province. It's great to have city land and philanthropic contributions, but they represent 10 to 12 per cent of the total cost. And no operating funds" (personal interview 2014). City actors do not deny this, but they also point out that given the distribution of revenues and resources, the province is better able to provide most of the funding. In other words, given the unequal resource availability, this partnership is more equal than a strict financial breakdown would lead one to conclude. Quebec provincial actors similarly insist on provincial leadership over housing and homelessness. While the province works in partnership with municipal governments and community groups (which play an institutionalized role in policy development in Quebec), it is with the understanding that the province is the lead actor.

Interestingly, before the National Housing Strategy was announced in 2017, some provincial officials expressed concern when questioned about the fact that the federal government could play a greater role, though again this concern was typically expressed in provinces that were already engaged in housing and homelessness. The concern was that a greater federal role would reduce the provinces' authority and leadership. When asked about the desirability of a National Housing Strategy, a senior BC official explained:

It's interesting, I always love that question. What do you mean by a National Housing Strategy? ... You don't want the federal government setting standards or administering programs. So what do you mean? Do you want CHMC to come back and directly administer programs in an area of provincial jurisdiction? Well, no. No. But do you want them to set standards that apply across Canada? Well, probably not. When you narrow in down, you want a stable form of funding, which I believe needs to be administered by the provinces who partner with local governments to identify local needs and deliver the programs and services. (personal interview 2014)

After the federal government introduced the National Housing Strategy, BC enthusiastically partnered with it, and it has used that funding to implement Homes for BC (in addition to implementing federal priorities, a condition of the funding). So too did the other provinces (including Quebec). Where they are involved in homelessness, provinces like having the upper hand to set priorities and make policies. They want and need funding from the federal government, but they define homelessness as a provincial responsibility.

Federal Government Involvement and Interactions

The federal government cut housing expenditures during a period of economic decline in the 1990s. Yet in 2008, it increased investments in housing at a time of economic decline in addition to investing in extensive studies of homelessness. Investments in homelessness have remained virtually unchanged for twenty years, surviving economic and ideological changes. This involvement has depended not just on resources and institutions but on ideas as well. At the federal level, ideas about the responsibility to produce social protection often interact with ideas about federalism to structure involvement. Justin Trudeau's Liberal federal government insists that housing and homelessness is a shared jurisdiction rather than a provincial one (which is how the previous Conservative administration saw it). But the main idea we see shaping federal involvement and interactions with other actors has to do with the definition of homelessness. In 1999, the federal government introduced the National Homelessness Initiative (NHI) for three years. The NHI was consistently renewed for one- to three-year periods until 2014, when it was renewed for five years. Implicit in this governance structure, which bypassed the provinces and all their social policy might, was the dominant understanding of homelessness as a short-term problem requiring emergency-type interventions. Advocates remember with great frustration how Claudette Bradshaw, the minister responsible for developing and overseeing the NHI, insisted that homelessness was *not* related to housing.

In understanding homelessness in such limited terms, the federal government confined its role to that of a short-term funder, directly transferring money (if wholly inadequate amounts) to the local level, bypassing all provinces except Quebec. In a sense, it is appropriate that the federal government got out of the way of local officials who know the problem best, and local groups appreciated this element of the program's design. Yet the federal government kept to itself a key aspect of the process – the definition of homelessness. The TDRC was instrumental in igniting federal involvement in what its members decried as an emergency; however, those same advocates also insisted, loudly, that homelessness was related to housing, a perspective that the federal government at the time ignored. In defining the problem so narrowly, the federal government prevented local groups from implementing the most effective and lasting solutions related to housing, and from doing so in partnership with provinces that had the authority to reform systems related to homelessness and could have contributed material resources to the effort.

This has changed with the advent of the National Housing Strategy. For the first time ever in Canada, homelessness is now directly linked to housing, marking a sea change in how the problem is understood. It is no longer viewed as just a short-term problem requiring emergency responses; instead, it is seen as related to social policy – notably housing – and as resulting from structural rather than individual forces. This is a striking ideational shift, and it is significant that it occurred *within* the Liberal Party, the same party that created and defended the NHI as a short-term, emergency, non-housing-focused program and the same party that cut investments in housing entirely. Though they insist that the NHS has been developed in close collaboration with community groups and provinces, federal officials see themselves taking a leadership role: "we are setting up a very specific direction and expecting everyone to follow that direction" (personal interview 2018).

An actor involved in developing Reaching Home was aware of the resentment other levels of government felt toward the feds, noting that federal officials "are used to getting yelled at" when they make decisions. But this actor also insisted that the federal and provincial governments were on the same team and share blame strategically:

I talk to provinces and territories quite regularly and they say, "Please be the bad guy. We really want this too, but it's too hard for us at our level to go out and publicly say X. But if you go out and say it, then we can say, "Oh, the feds are making us do it"... A lot of what gets said publicly and what happens behind the scenes are often two different things. (personal interview 2018)

This actor added that some federal–provincial tensions are, from the federal perspective, simply politics: "We have very good working relations with Ontario, but at the same time, if we implement something they are going to grumble publicly but behind the scenes, they're going to absolutely help us to implement it." Moreover, there were advantages to collaborative governance other than just pooling resources and expertise: "That's one ... advantage of a shared governance model, or of a partnership or shared jurisdiction. Risks can be shared and blame can also be shared" (personal interview 2018).

Can We End Homelessness?

The answer to that question depends, of course, on how you define homelessness. If we broadly define homelessness as related to social inclusion, poverty, *and* housing, the answer may be no. Indeed, actors who espouse a broad definition of homelessness tend to be the least likely to also demand an end to it. When it comes to a narrower definition of homelessness, the answer is different. Those who do push for an end to homelessness tend to have a housing-based definition in mind, often refer to chronic homelessness, and have become increasingly specific about what that means (Turner, Albanese, and Pakeman 2017), perhaps having learned from the mistakes of the past when this was left open to interpretation. They also specify that there will always be a need for emergency supports, including shelters, as well as for a sturdy social safety net to ensure that supports are there when people need them. We may not put an end, once and for all, to every kind of homelessness, but by the same token, we should not be trying to convince ourselves that large numbers of unhoused or underhoused people is an inevitable reality of Canadian society. It is not. We can and should drastically reduce the number of people who are without safe, adequate homes.

The lack of investments in permanent solutions, in prevention, and in robust health and social supports, along with a failure to commit to meeting the most basic prerequisites for reconciliation as defined by Indigenous people, has meant that for many years, service providers were left on their own to paddle upstream. Through a storm. Without a paddle. This was tremendously unfair to those providing services as well as to those needing them. That people in Canada so often find themselves without a home is the result of government decisions and lack of investment. Ensuring that everyone in Canada has access to a safe and adequate home will require investments and system reform, and as this book has shown, it will also require inclusive, collaborative governance. This means ensuring that all the actors are at the policy-making table through all stages of policy development and that they are talking to one another, listening to one another, and working together. It may mean senior governments need to get out of the way in some instances. Of utmost importance are voices that have been excluded for far too long: those with lived expertise and Indigenous knowledge. Beyond investments and reforms, this requires a shift in power.

***

The COVID-19 pandemic has been devastating for many people. Given the centrality of home in public health precautions, this has particularly been the case for people who are unhoused or underhoused. The tent cities and homeless encampments that emerged in 2020 and 2021 across the country revealed what had long been known to service providers, advocates, and people experiencing homelessness – the social safety net is not sturdy enough to protect people from becoming and remaining homeless. Leilani Farha, the former UN ambassador on the right to housing and current leader of The Shift, an organization committed to the right to housing, explains that to some, encampments represent the deprivation of the right to housing. Yet she explains that in the context of an inadequate housing and social security system, encampments are also a *claim* to housing by those who live in them (Farha 2021). They are a demand that governments do more, that they stop ignoring fault lines and weaknesses in the welfare state. They are a challenge to do better.

Encampments are a demand for housing but also a reminder of the importance of community. The pandemic has been an intensely isolating experience for many. While we were told to remain home, we were also told to limit contact with others and maintain only a small bubble. Prolonged periods of isolation, also imposed by public health mandates, have made clear the need for community and the consequences of being isolated from it. In this sense, homeless encampments have not just been a claim to housing; for many people living in them, they have been a claim to community as well. The voices of people living in encampments reveal that many feel they found a community and a family in those environments (Dawson 2021; Encampment Support Network n.d.; Jewell 2021; Winter 2021). There were safety concerns as well (CBC News 2020; Winter 2021),[5] though safety concerns (including fire safety) are present in supportive housing developments as well (Miller 2021). Encampments are not generally understood to be a long-term solution to homelessness (Farha and Schwan 2020). But the emergence of so many encampments, the fact that many of them continued through the winter, and the conflicts that resulted from efforts to put an end to them (including violent clashes with police in Toronto) are sending important messages about the nature of homelessness and what it will take to ensure that everyone has access to a home.

Recognizing the pressure under which the emergency shelter system was operating, provinces and cities have rushed to buy or lease hotels, arenas, and other temporary forms of housing to allow for isolation and distanced service use. Some of these spaces have been offered to people living in encampments; some of these offers have been declined (Encampment Support Network n.d.). A former resident of an encampment in Victoria, BC, said in a CityTalks webinar hosted in 2021 that she accepted temporary housing after living an encampment. She experienced homelessness for the first time in her life during COVID, and spent four months in an encampment, which she described as a community, even a family. The housing she was offered was, in her eyes, inadequate, and the experience was isolating. In her own words, "I'm inside. But that's it." *That's it.* For her, no longer being homeless needs to be about more than just being inside.

This makes crystal clear that for many people, home is more than a physical structure. This is not too much to ask. The pandemic has made abundantly clear the importance of home, but also the importance of place and the importance of community. Ending homelessness for some people may mean more than getting people inside and keeping them there. The people best-suited to explaining how to do that are people with lived experience, who should be involved and centred throughout the policy-making process. That includes Indigenous people, who have developed some of the most effective interventions in Indigenous-led services. Involving and valuing the expertise of people with lived experience and Indigenous knowledge will require acknowledging that like it or not, homelessness means different things to different people.

Appendix: List of Interviews

1 Member of Vancouver Mayor's Task Force on Homelessness, Aboriginal Steering Committee on Homelessness
2 Member of Vancouver Mayor's Task Force on Homelessness, Senior City of Vancouver Official working in the area of homelessness
3 Member of Vancouver Mayor's Task Force on Homelessness, City of Vancouver councillor
4 Senior City of Vancouver official working in the area of homelessness
5 Senior City of Vancouver official Working in the areas of housing and planning
6 Greater Vancouver Regional Steering Committee on Homelessness member
7 Vision Vancouver Member, Provincial MLA
8 Former Provincial MLA, former senior City of Vancouver official working in the area of homelessness, former Streetohome Foundation board member
9 Executive Director of a homeless serving organization, Vancouver
10 City Of Vancouver Police
11 Member of the Streetohome Foundation board
12 Executive Director of a homeless serving organization, Vancouver
13 Executive Director Of A homeless serving organization, Vancouver
14 Former Executive Director of a homeless serving organization, Vancouver
15 Greater Vancouver Regional Steering Committee on Homelessness member
16 Senior official with BC Housing
17 Executive Director of a homeless serving organization, Vancouver
18 Director of a faith-based organization, Vancouver
19 Former mid-size city mayor

20 Senior City of Vancouver official working in the area of housing
21 Former City of Vancouver mayor
22 Former vice-president, CHF
23 City of Calgary councillor
24 Former City Of Calgary mayor
25 Executive Director of a homeless serving organization, Calgary
26 Senior City of Calgary official working on the Poverty Reduction Strategy
27 Executive Director of a homeless serving organization, Calgary
28 Former president, CHF
29 Executive Director of a homeless serving organization, Calgary
30 Senior Official with the City of Calgary Housing Corporation
31 Executive Director of a homeless serving organization, Calgary
32 Executive Director of a homeless serving organization, Calgary
33 Former president, CHF
34 Former president, CHF
35 City of Calgary social worker
36 Executive Director of a homeless serving organization, Calgary
37 Former president, CHF
38 Director of a homeless serving organization, Calgary
39 Provincial Interagency Council on Homelessness member
40 City of Calgary Police
41 Senior Member of the City of Lethbridge's Homelessness Taskforce
42 City of Toronto activist
43 Former City of Toronto Mayor
44 City of Toronto, Street to Home staff
45 Executive Director of a homeless serving organization, Toronto
46 Former Senior City of Toronto official working in the area of housing
47 Executive Director of a homeless serving organization, Toronto
48 Senior City of Toronto official working in the area of housing
49 Former senior City of Toronto official working in the area of housing
50 City of Toronto activist
51 City of Toronto councillor
52 Former senior official with City of Toronto Social Services And Housing Administration
53 Senior official with City of Toronto Social Services And Housing Administration
54 Senior Official with City of Toronto Social Services And Housing Administration
55 Toronto researcher and physician

56 Executive Director of a homeless serving organization, Toronto
57 Executive Director of a homeless serving organization, Montreal
58 City of Montreal official working in the area of housing and homelessness
59 City of Montreal police
60 Former Executive Director of a homeless serving organization, Montreal
61 Director of a homeless serving organization, Montreal
62 City of Montreal official working in the area of housing
63 Montreal area researcher
64 Former Executive Director of a homeless serving organization, Montreal
65 Executive Director of a homeless serving organization, Montreal
66 Official with the Provincial Housing Association (*la Société d'habitation du Québec*)
67 Former Executive Director of a homeless serving organization, Montreal
68 Former Canadian prime minister
69 Senior official with the Federal Homelessness Partnering Strategy
70 Federal Member of Parliament responsible for housing and homelessness
71 City of Montreal Councillor
72 City of Lethbridge department of housing and homelessness
73 City of Calgary faith-based organization
74 Former City of Vancouver mayor
75 City of Vancouver official working in the area of housing
76 Journalist, *Megaphone* magazine
77 Former City of Calgary Councillor
78 Calgary-based researcher
79 Calgary-based social worker
80 Director of External Relations of a homeless serving organization, Calgary
81 Calgary-based journalist
82 Executive Director of a poverty fighting organization, Calgary
83 Executive Director of a homeless serving organization, Kelowna
84 Executive Director of a homeless serving organization, Trois-Rivières
85 City of Montreal bureaucrat
86 City of Montreal bureaucrat
87 Political attaché, Projet Montreal
88 Toronto Alliance to End Homelessness, senior management
89 Toronto Alliance to End Homelessness, senior management

90 Vancouver Aboriginal Homelessness Steering Committee member
91 Senator Murray Sinclair
92 Federal Bureaucrat, HPS
93 Federal Bureaucrat, HPS
94 Former senior official, Ministry of Housing, British Columbia
95 Calgary Aboriginal Standing Committee on Homelessness member
96 Quebec bureaucrat, intergovernmental relations
97 Quebec bureaucrat, HPS
98 Vice-President Community relations, CHF

Notes

1 Introduction

1 Willison considers Housing First to be the evidence-based response to homelessness.
2 The federal government was an important partner for provinces in the postwar era, and when the federal government left the field of housing, eight out of ten provinces followed suit.
3 There is overlap between these groups, of course; third-sector groups include Indigenous-led organizations, and Indigenous-led groups are also involved in networks to administer federal funding, for example. The same can be said for third-sector groups that are not Indigenous-led; they are considered to be third-sector actors but also are involved in networks to administer federal funding.
4 Not all actors are necessarily involved in homelessness governance in each case. The municipality is minimally involved in Calgary, the province is minimally involved in Ontario, and Indigenous actors are minimally involved in Montreal. But in each case, I looked at the actions of these actors or of groups representing them.
5 In this book, I generally use people first language (person who is or who has experienced homelessness), but in some cases I use identity first language especially when that is the language used by people interviewed. There are debates regarding these terms, and it is increasingly common to talk of people who are unhoused and underhoused. For a thoughtful discussion on people versus identity first language, see Withers 2021 and Prince 2009.
6 Thank you to Nadège Compaoré, Martha Balaguera and Phil Henderson for conversations about this and for contributions to this section.
7 Indigenous actors in Montreal can apply for funding to the designated community, or interface directly with the federal government for Indigenous Community NHI/HPS funding.

2 Homelessness

1 Colonialism does not just affect Indigenous individuals (Maynard 2017; Owusu-Bempah 2021). Colonialism is considered specifically, in this book, with respect to Indigenous homelessness as defined by Jesse Thistle, but future work should more centrally consider how colonialism contributes to the experience of homelessness among non-Indigenous individuals as well. Thank you also to Riley Yesno for conversations about this.

2 La fédération européenne des associations nationales travaillant avec les sans-abri.

3 *Salubre.*

4 Tellingly, he did not want his name on the definition, because it involved the contribution and knowledge of so many others (Winter 2017).

5 "Homelessness is the situation of an individual who does not have a permanent address or residence; the living situation of an individual or family who does not have stable, permanent, appropriate housing or the immediate prospect, means and ability of acquiring it. It is often the result of what are known as systematic or societal barriers, including a lack of affordable and appropriate housing, the individual/household's financial, mental, cognitive, behavioural, or physical challenges and/or racism and discrimination" (ESDC 2019b).

6 Turner, Albanese, and Pakeman propose a series of indicators to track progress toward absolute and functional zero, noting the importance of "interventions across levels of society rather than restricting these to the individual or the homelessness-prevention system" (26). This has since been used to track progress in efforts to fight homelessness in Canada. Officials in Medicine Hat had claimed for several years to have ended homelessness; the CAEH used this measure of ending homelessness to certify independently that Medicine Hat achieved functional zero (*As It Happens* 2015; CAEH 2021).

7 Gaetz is a long-time supporter of Housing First, using the COH platform to conduct and share extensive research on the practice, particularly as it relates to youth (Gaetz 2014).

8 This is consistent with Erin Dej's recent book, *A Complex Exile* (2020), in which she highlights the importance of inclusion and integration, as well as housing, in the fight against homelessness.

9 These studies are limited to people using emergency shelters of course, and do not include people sleeping outside, an important limitation that should be considered when unpacking what these results say about the overall homeless population.

10 85 per cent of shelter users were homeless temporarily, 14 per cent were home-less episodically, and 2 per cent were experiencing chronic homelessness.
11 Meaning three hot meals and a bed.
12 This history is reviewed more fully in chapters 3 and 4
13 Histories of the involvement of BC, Alberta, Ontario, and Quebec are re-viewed more thoroughly in chapters 5, 6, 7, and 8 respectively.
14 BC and Quebec were the only two provinces to continue funding housing
15 Canadian Confederation was in 1867.
16 To the extent that information about gender exists, it has historically been binary and has only considered male and female. More recent attempts to measure and track homelessness include non-binary gender identities as well.
17 The highest occupancy rate was 94.6 per cent in 2009, a likely result of the financial crisis that resulted in an increase in homelessness across the country (Falvo 2020).
18 Because homelessness is so hard on a person's physical and mental health, many studies and government reports consider people over the age of fifty to be seniors when it comes to homelessness.

3 Governance Matters

1 The production of social protection can be understood as a policy, program, or service response to a social risk. For example, social assistance would be social protection against the risk of income insecurity (if it is entirely inade-quate at protecting against poverty); provinces administer social assistance and are thus responsible for the production of this type of protection.
2 The constitution was amended in 1941, 1951, and 1964 to give the federal government responsibility for unemployment insurance, pensions, and survivor and disability benefits respectively (see Banting 1990).
3 A term often attributed to Patrick Johnston (see Menzies 2010), the Sixties Scoop refers to the decade (1960) when Indigenous children were removed by child welfare from their homes and placed in non-Indigenous homes.
4 BC and Quebec were the only two provinces that did not cut funding for social housing.
5 Third-sector actors in this work are considered to be analogous to what Rachel Laforest calls "voluntary associations" and identifies as "a rich array of organizations, institutions, and associations including charities, cooperatives, interest groups, community organizations, health and social services providers, social clubs, self-help and mutual aid groups, religious groups and research-oriented organizations" (Laforest 2011b, 14).
6 For the years 2006–10, I used 2006 population data; from 2011–15, I used 2011 population data, and so on.

7 Police are a dominant presence in the lives of people who are unhoused, experience homelessness, and live in poverty. This is particularly the case for Black and Indigenous people (Cole 2020; Maynard 2017; Owusu-Bempah et al. 2014; Owusu-Bempah 2017, 2021; Walia et al. 2020). Over the course of this research, I interviewed a number of police officers across the country, usually those involved in units or areas of patrol that put them in regular contact with people who are unhoused. In many locales, police are involved in the development of responses to homelessness, including on task forces and boards of directors, and liaise with elected officials through formal and informal channels. They are also clearly involved in implementing responses to homelessness. In the pages that follow, however, I do not consider them as distinct actors. The framework I have adopted is informed by critical political economy approaches to the study of the welfare state – its architecture and governance as well as how it produces social protection (Esping-Andersen 1990; Jenson 2013). States, markets, families, and community groups are all primary producers of social protection. To the extent that police were interviewed during my research, it was in the context of developing and implementing policy responses in relation to these primary producers of social protection. (For more on the role of policing in responses to homelessness and the consequences of criminalizing homelessness, see Bellot 2010; Bellot and Sylvestre 2017; Berti 2010; Boyd, Fast, and Small 2016; Cheng et al. 2013; Chesnay, Bellot, and Sylvestre 2013; Dej 2020; Goldman-Hasbun et al. 2019; Kouyoumdjian et al. 2019; O'Grady, Gaetz, and Buccieri 2013; and Sylvestre 2019.)

8 When citing these interviews, I do so anonymously. To do as much as I can to protect the anonymity of research participants, I use they/them pronouns when referring to specific interviews.

4 Federal Government

1 This process is reviewed more thoroughly in the Montreal chapter.
2 There are disagreements among service providers, advocates, scholars, and people experiencing homelessness regarding this particular methodology – most notably, that it recruits vulnerable people to participate and then gives only half of them the treatment. Another way of testing the effectiveness of a particular policy intervention is a pilot project designed without a control group. Ontario started one such project to study a guaranteed minimum income, but it was cancelled by the Ford government.
3 Funding decreased to $119 million per year (from $134.8 million), though government officials insisted this wasn't a substantial cut: "This is the result of administrative savings absorbed by ESDC. Communities will continue to receive the same amount of funding for programs to prevent and reduce homelessness as they did previously" (ESDC 2013).

4 Seven "allied" networks also work with the CAEH. They include a newly formed Advisory Council of People with Lived Experience, the Ontario Alliance to End Homelessness, and the National Alliance to End Rural and Remote Homelessness, as well as networks dedicated to the right to housing and the right to health. Together, these networks work with community groups and policy-makers in the fight against homelessness.

5 Plans to end homelessness were introduced in Alberta prior to the CAEH's national efforts; indeed, these Alberta plans influenced the CAEH as it developed A Plan Not a Dream.

6 Specifically, it included calls for the government to build 300,000 permanently affordable and supportive housing units, to increase investments in homelessness programs specifically, and to create a national guaranteed income that is not exclusive or penalizing (should people choose to work, for example), as well as calls for a separate Indigenous homelessness strategy.

7 According to the Canadian Mortgage and Housing Corporation, people are considered in core housing need if they are spending more than 30 per cent of their income on rent.

8 I was at the 2014 conference and attended the protest.

5 Vancouver

1 In 1975, 65 per cent of units were for families earning less than $13,000 per year (or $57,500 in 2017) and 35 per cent were for families earning between $13,000 and $20,000 per year (or between $57,500 and $88,500 in 2017).

2 The BC Liberals are in general to the right on the political spectrum and are not affiliated with the more centrist federal Liberal Party.

3 The Liberals would later claim credit for these new units (see BC Housing 2014a), but they only reluctantly agreed to build them in the first place in 2002.

4 In 2002–3, 1,386 units of social housing were created through the Provincial Housing Program: 305 for seniors requiring supports, 368 for the homeless or at risk, and 713 for low-income seniors and families.

5 The government committed to creating 3,500 supportive living spaces for seniors by 2006. Of these, 1,500 were new builds, 1,000 were existing social housing units converted into supportive spaces, and 1,000 involved rent supplements for private-market housing. So it is important to note that during this period, the province dipped into the existing stock to convert some existing units into supportive housing for seniors, effectively subtracting from the affordable housing stock available to low-income British Columbians.

6 The task force never produced a final report, but it widely said to have led to the creation of BC's 2006 housing policy, Housing Matters (BC Ministry of Health 2017).

7 The MOU agreements continued until at least 2020 and resulted in the creation of thousands of units of supportive and transitional housing across

the province for people experiencing chronic homelessness who also require social and health supports.

8 The province has also sold social housing stock, in some cases to generate
funds to build housing, as was the case with the Little Mountain development (see Chudnovsky and Shuto 2016; see also Pablo 2009).

9 Important gains were made with respect to emergency shelter and housing
for people exiting homelessness (rising from 3,556 units in 2006 to 11,600 in
2014, including an increase from 2,296 people housed to 8,085 housed), transitional supportive and assisted-living housing (going from 7,078 units in 2006
to 18,839 in 2014), and rent supplements (going from 14,020 in 2006 to 28,163
in 2014). Furthermore, the number of independent units of social housing
rose from 34,773 in 2006 to 41,183 in 2014 (BC Housing 2006a, 2014a).

10 Clark's close relationship with developers is well-documented, including a
donation of $400,000 from developer Peter Wall and his nephew (Hoekstra
2017).

11 Modular housing can be built rapidly and comparatively inexpensively.

12 Vancouver Area Network of Drug Users.

13 The original agreement was for 2000–5; it was extended to 2010, the year
Vancouver hosted the Olympics.

14 Huge challenges remain. Since the COVID-19 shutdowns began, overdose
deaths have reached devastating levels never before seen in BC. This has
led many to demand government involvement in ensuring a safe supply
(Baker 2021). In 2020, the BC Coroners Service reported that 1,716 people
in BC alone had died of an overdose (Nagy and Jones 2021).

15 Federal/provincial housing agreements negotiated in 2001, reviewed above.

16 Officials in the City of Vancouver recognize that they are on unceded territories of the xʷməθkʷəy̓əm (Musqueam), Sḵwx̱wú7mesh (Squamish), and
Səl̓ílwitulh (Tsleil-Waututh) Nations (Meiszner 2014).

17 Much of this process was guided by Vancouver Coastal Health's Mental
Health and Addictions Supportive Housing Framework in 2007. The framework identified the need for an additional 2,200 units of supportive housing, including 450 new units in as many as fifteen new buildings. The same
framework assessed city-owned land to identify areas where housing could
be developed. Some of the sites identified required that existing social housing be demolished; thus, new units were created but old units were lost.
That said, the quality of the new housing was higher than it had been.

18 I was a volunteer at First United in 2009.

19 Other municipalities in BC have had the same power since 1988 (BC Ministry of Forests and Range Housing Department 2005).

20 This differs from density bonusing, which is an exchange of increased density for these amenities; inclusionary zoning does not require the city to
give anything in return.

21 Developers contribute substantially to the right-of-centre Non-Partisan Association (NPA), with donations in the past reaching nearly $1 million (there are
no donation limits in local elections in Vancouver; see Howell 2014). While
community groups do not have this kind of cash flow, their allies in the main
unions in Vancouver have been strong financial supporters of Vision Vancouver (Howell 2014); the BC division of CUPE, for example, gave Vision a
donation of $152,000 in 2014 (Y. Cole 2014). (Vision Vancouver received dona-
tions from developers as well, and this became increasingly problematic for
the party, which had promised and failed to end street homelessness. However, the donations were nowhere near on the same scale as for the NPA; see
Howell 2014; Y.Cole 2014.) The province has since passed campaign finance
reforms, so these large donations are no longer possible. Current Mayor Kennedy Stewart disclosed his donation records, which indicated that he raised
more than $100,000 from just over 1,000 individual donations to his cam-
paign, the largest of which was from himself ($2,400) (Stewart 2018).
22 Most notably, the alliance that grew between Mayor Phil Owen, a Conservative, and the Vancouver Area Network of Drug Users and other progressive local forces, resulting in the opening of Vancouver's safe injection site.
23 The city adopted this same approach with its 2005 Homelessness Action
Plan, indicating coordination between different sectors and levels of
governance.
24 A plan for homelessness in London, Ontario, proposes an Indigenized
Housing First model (Atlohsa Family Healing Services 2020; see also Distasio et al. 2019).

6 Calgary

1 The development of Calgary's plan is reviewed thoroughly below.
2 These numbers can be contested as being at the very upper end of the
spectrum (Goering et al. 2014).
3 Though province-wide counts did not exist prior to 2016, this shows an
increase in the number of people experiencing homelessness from 2016,
when 5,367 people were identified as experiencing homelessness (Three-
Hive Consulting 2017).
4 Mangano had already been invited to Red Deer. Calgary actors say they
"captured him along the way and got him to give a talk in Calgary" (personal interview 2014).
5 Following a change in leadership at the Drop-In Centre, ideational disagreements between these two groups have largely disappeared. The
Drop-In Centre is now an ally of the CHF.
6 Reflecting on the origins of the 2008 plan, an impact report published
in 2018 notes the importance of ideas and also acknowledges how

disagreements at the beginning made implementation a challenge: "A critical mass of leaders, commitment, and passion was galvanized in 2008 at the start of Calgary's 10 Year Plan, but across the years people moved away, fatigue emerged, and commitment faltered at times. Further, it would be disingenuous to assert that everyone bought into the details of Calgary's 10 Year Plan when it launched. There were early adopters, mid and late adopters, and at various times, outright resisters" (Turner, Ballance, and Sinclair 2018, 80).

7 By way of comparison, Vancouver's population grew from 514,008 in 1996 to 631,486 in 2016, Toronto's population grew from 2,385,421 in 1996 to 2,731,571 in 2016, and Montreal's population grew from 1,775,778 in 1996 to 1,942,014 in 2016.

7 Toronto

1 There was also an important question of accountability. The 2009 Auditor General's Report notes that the province was unable to account for more than $300 million of transferred funding from the federal government for housing (Auditor General of Ontario 2009).

2 These were the consolidated homelessness prevention program; the emergency energy fund; emergency hostels; domiciliary hostels; and the rent bank (Ministry of Municipal Affairs and Housing 2010).

3 The city is the Community Entity and is therefore responsible for distributing funding.

4 Lastman originally asked Barbara Hall to chair the committee. Hall was a former City of Toronto mayor and had run against Lastman for mayor of Metropolitan Toronto in 1997. In a letter to Lastman in late 1997, Hall declined the offer: "Without significant participation from senior levels of government, the ability of municipalities to implement long-term, permanent solutions to homelessness is seriously limited. I do not wish to Chair this Task Force if it simply creates another report left to gather dust on a shelf." She continued: "As you informed me this morning you have met with Provincial Government officials who will not commit any resources to this effort. Without this essential component I must, with regret, decline your offer" (Hall 1997).

5 As explained in the film *Shelter from the Storm*, the original plan proposed by the activists was to move people living in the Tent City encampment to a temporary location owned by the city, but this plan did not work out.

6 The City of Toronto also has the power to enter into density bonusing agreements, though this is not often used to increase housing affordability. As outlined in Section 37 of the Planning Act, municipalities in Ontario can allow developers to surpass normal height and density by-laws in exchange for community benefits. Richard Drdla explains that these community

benefits are comparatively small in Toronto: "The value of the community benefits provided is assessed only against the added density or height, and not against the entire development" (Drdla 2014). This significant detail limits the extent to which this power can be leveraged into affordable or supportive housing. Another important detail is that city councillors have significant input into the community benefit that is obtained; the process is not negotiated by city staff, as is the case in Vancouver (Moore 2013). Affordable housing is desperately needed, yet it is hidden, and its direct benefit to the community (and to a councillor seeking credit and re-election) is also hidden. Studies have found that only around 9 per cent of the amenities acquired through density bonusing agreements in Toronto are housing (compared to 48 per cent in Vancouver) (Clayton and Schwartz 2015).

7 Under the latest provincial legislation, however, municipalities can only enforce inclusionary zoning near transit ("Protected Major Transit Station Areas") – in other words, city-wide inclusionary zoning in Toronto is not possible (City of Toronto 2020). By 2021, the City of Toronto was considering details regarding implementation, including a proposal to require between 3 and 10 per cent of a development's floor area to be affordable housing, defined as 80 per cent of market rent for 99 years.

8 OCAP organizers and members declined to be interviewed for this project, noting a preference for direct action. OCAP-allied individuals were interviewed, and to the extent OCAP is considered an actor in homelessness governance, I rely on their accounts, primary documents, as well as the book *Fight to Win: Inside Poor People's Organizing* by A.J. Withers (2021).

9 In full, the declaration and TDRC founding document reads: "We call on all levels of government to declare homelessness a national disaster requiring emergency humanitarian relief. We urge that they immediately develop and implement a National Homelessness Relief and Prevention Strategy using disaster relief funds both to provide the homeless with immediate health protection and housing and to prevent further homelessness. Canada has signed the International Covenant on Economic, Social and Cultural Rights guaranteeing everyone's right to '"an adequate standard of living ... including adequate food, clothing and housing.' Homeless people have no decent standard of living; our governments are violating these Human Rights. Despite Canada's reputation for providing relief to people made temporarily homeless by natural disasters, our governments are unwilling to help the scores of thousands of people in Canada condemned to homelessness. Morally, economically, socially, and legally, we cannot allow homelessness to become 'normal' in Canadian life. Inaction betrays many thousands of us to a miserable existence and harms our society for years to come" (TDRC 1998).

10 For an interesting discussion of the need for advocates and activists to be grateful, see Withers (2021), 168–70.

8 Montreal

1 The distinction between the two is important, and will be explained below.
2 For example, Quebec was the first province in the country to pass a "law against poverty," which strove to bring down levels of poverty in Quebec, particularly among children. In an impressive process of community engagement, non-governmental actors wrote draft legislation, adopted it in a symbolic people's parliament, and applied pressure to elected officials to adopt the law formally. In 2002, members of all political parties in Quebec's National Assembly formally adopted the law against poverty; in 2004, a plan to fight poverty was adopted (Noël 2002, 2005).
3 1,200 for low-income households, 500 for the elderly losing their autonomy, and 120 for people with special needs (including women fleeing violence, homeless people, and people with disabilities).
4 To the surprise of many advocates at the time, upon being elected in 2003 the right-leaning Parti libéral du Québec (PLQ) fully supported and at times even increased funding for housing. Indeed, in 2007 PLQ Premier Jean Charest committed to nearly doubling the units built through AccèsLogis, to 3,000 per year (FRAPRU 2015).
5 Philippe Couillard's successor Liberal government maintained funding, though the number of funded units of housing dropped to 1,500 per year. This is somewhat surprising in light of criticisms by Vaillancourt and colleagues (2016) and others, who accused Couillard of being obsessed with austerity and searching for any excuse to cut social spending.
6 The health system has since been reorganized. The HPS is now administered by regional social service centres that go by their acronym CIUSSS (Centre intégré universitaire de santé et de services sociaux).
7 CPHPS members include service providers, city officials, Service Canada officials, and agency officials.
8 The Comité liaison en itinérance has existed in Montreal since the 1990s. It was created to fulfil the mandate of participating in the policy-making process. It has a broader mandate than the CPHPS and exists to help the City of Montreal address the issue of homelessness in various ways – for example, by developing its own plans (notably the 2010–13 plan and Montreal's 2015–20 regional plan). It is comprised of community members, Indigenous-led service providers, institutions that work with the homeless population (such as child protective services and hospitals) and officials from the city, the agency, and the federal government.
9 The membership of the regional committee is diverse. It includes bureaucrats from the city and the agency, as well as community members and a representative of the health and social services sector (there is no federal representative on this committee).

10 The commission also recommended the creation of social housing and improved access to it, especially for people at risk of losing their housing, as well as increased and stable funding for service providers.

11 It is led by the Minister for Social Services but also involves the Ministers for Public Security, Education, Employment, Immigration, Health and Social Services, Justice, Municipal Affairs, and Aboriginal Affairs.

12 Réseau d'aide aux personnes seules et itinérantes de Montréal and the Réseau SOLIDARITÉ itinérance du Québec, respectively.

13 A second *Portrait of Homelessness* was set to be released in 2020 (but has not been released at the time of writing).

14 "D'entreprendre une nouvelle étape."

15 More commonly referred to (in English and French) by their acronym, CIUSS, which stands for centres intégrés universitaires de santé et de services sociaux.

16 One senior official with the City of Montreal pondered why the private sector is much more involved in homelessness governance in Calgary than in Montreal: "We don't have the same tradition of philanthropy here in Quebec. I think Quebec is less rich, we don't have the same kind of big business-people; it's more recent in Quebec history that we have a business class that has the means to do that kind of thing" (personal interview 2014).

17 Private-sector representatives are also often involved on the boards of individual shelters or social services, as is the case in many other cities (see Arsenault 2016)

18 I was the lead researcher for the homeless count, and researched for the MMFIM's plan as well.

19 An important reason for the lower cost of this plan compared to other plans is that it does not contain provisions to build housing, but rather relies on rent supplements; recall that private-sector housing is more available and more affordable in Montreal than in other cities.

20 The MMFIM's objective was to create two more plans, which would focus on transitional homelessness and prevention, though at the time of writing it has only produced one plan on chronic homelessness.

21 "Une richesse."

22 There are exceptions, of course, notably the fact that housing is a municipal responsibility in Ontario and has been since the 1990s. But this specific example was not mentioned in these conversations.

23 Accueil Bonneau; la Maison du Père and la Mission Bon Accueil.

24 This internal coordination is significant and merits further study (and perhaps comparison with Alberta, where under the Interagency Council on Homelessness there was internal coordination within the province as well).

Conclusion

1 Paradis identifies a third approach, service provision, but notes that the service provision approach is not concerned with addressing root causes of homelessness, so it is not included here in terms of approaches to advocacy.
2 For a different perspective on engaging with government, and especially the idea that advocates should express gratitude, see Withers 2021, 168–70.
3 I will also discuss the CHF as a private-sector actor below, given its origins and the strong influence of private-sector actors.
4 Systemic racism manifests in a host of other ways that are not directly related to governance, including over-policing, underfunding of Indigenous services and education, a lack of access to health care, etc.
5 People living in encampments point out that there are safety concerns with other government-supported forms of housing as well. For example, a woman with a disability was placed on the fifteenth floor of a building. She insisted that this was a fire hazard and requested that she be moved to the ground floor, but was not (Jewell 2021).

Bibliography

Abele, Frances, and Michael J. Prince. 2006. "Four Pathways to Aboriginal Self-Government in Canada." *American Review of Canadian Studies* 36(4): 568–95. https://doi.org/10.1080/02722010609481408.

Abramovich, Alex, and Maura Lawless. 2016. "Taking Pride in Creating Authentic Spaces for LGBTQ2S Homeless Youth." *HuffPost Canada.* https://www.huffingtonpost.ca/alex-ilona-abramovich/lgbtq2s-homeless-youth_b_10659100.html (October 13, 2020).

Abramovich, Alex, and Jama Shelton, eds. 2017. *Where Am I Going to Go? Intersectional Approaches to Ending LGBTQ2S Youth Homelessness in Canada and the US.* Toronto: Canadian Observatory on Homelessness Press.

Alberta Finance. 2009. "Budget 2009 Fiscal Plan." Edmonton, Alberta.

Alberta Housing Corporation. 1982. *Annual Report 1981–1982.* Edmonton: Government of Alberta.

Alberta Interagency Council on Homelessness. 2014. *A Progress Report on Housing and Homelessness in Alberta.* Edmonton: Government of Alberta.

– 2015. *2014/15 Progress Report on Housing and Homelessness in Alberta.* Edmonton: Government of Alberta.

Alberta Ministry of Municipal Affairs. 1992. *Annual Report 1991–1992.* Edmonton: Government of Alberta.

Alberta Secretariat for Action On Homelessness. 2008. *A Plan for Alberta.* Edmonton: Government of Alberta.

Alberta Seniors. 2002. *Annual Report 2001–2002.* Edmonton: Government of Alberta.

Alberta Seniors and Housing. 2017. *Making Life Better: Alberta's Provincial Affordable Housing Strategy.* Edmonton: Government of Alberta.

Alcantara, Christopher. 2018. *A Quiet Evolution: The Emergence of Indigenous-Local Intergovernmental Partnerships in Canada.* Toronto: University of Toronto Press.

Alini, Erica. 2017. "New Data Shows How Much It Costs to Rent a 2-Bedroom Unit across Canada." *Global News.*

Andrew, Caroline. 2003. "Municipal Restructuring, Urban Services, and the Potential for the Creation of Transformative Political Spaces." In *Changing Canada: Political Economy as Transformation*, edited by Leah Vosko and Wallace Clement. Montreal and Kingston: McGill-Queen's University Press.

APTN Nation to Nation. 2018. "Lack of funding piling up on the dreams of First Nations children: Blackstock." *APTN News*. https://www.aptnnews.ca /nation-to-nation/lack-funding-piling-dreams-first-nations-children-blackstock.

Arsenault, Gabriel. 2016. *The Social Investment State and the Social Economy: The Political Origins of Quebec's New Social Model.* PhD diss., University of Toronto.

– 2018. *L'économie Sociale Au Québec: Une Perspective Politique.* Québec: Presses de l'Université du Québec. https://www.leslibraires.ca/livres/l-economie -sociale-au-quebec-une-gabriel-arsenault-9782760549449.html.

ASCHH (Aboriginal Standing Committee on Housing and Homelessess). 2012. *Plan to End Aboriginal Homelessness in Calgary.* Calgary.

Aston, Mark. 2015. "Building Community Partnerships to End Homelessness." In Montreal.

– 2015. "Re: EX 9.6 George Street Revitalization Report to Council." 30 October.

Atlohsa Family Healing Services. 2020. *Giwetashkad Indigenous Homelessness Strategic Plan 2020–2023.* London.

Aubry, Tim, Susan Farrell, Stephen Hwang, and Melissa Calhoun. 2013. "Identifying the Patterns of Emergency Shelter Stays of Single Individuals in Canadian Cities of Different Sizes." *Housing Studies* 28(6): 910–27. https://doi.org/10.1080/02673037.2013.773585.

Auditor General of Ontario. 2009. *2009 Annual Report.* Toronto.

– 2017. *2017 Annual Report.* Toronto.

Australian Bureau of Statistics. 2012. "Homelessness Statistics." *A Statistical Definition of Homelessness, 2012.* http://www.abs.gov.au/ausstats/abs@.nsf /Latestproducts/4922.0Main%20Features22012?opendocument &tabname=Summary&prodno=4922.0&issue=2012&num=&view=.

Babich, Kristina, and Daniel Béland. 2009. "Policy Change and the Politics of Ideas: The Emergence of the Canada/Quebec Pension Plans." *Canadian Review of Sociology* 46(3): 253–71. https://doi.org/10.1111 /j.1755-618x.2009.01214.1.

Baker, Rafferty. 2021. "Safe Drug Supply Program Still Not Reaching Enough People in B.C., Say Advocates." *CBC News.* https://www.cbc.ca/news /canada/british-columbia/bc-safe-supply-drug-prescription-one -year-1.5964963.

Banting, Keith. 1987. *The Welfare State and Canadian Federalism.* Montreal and Kingston: McGill-Queen's University Press.

– 1990. "Social Housing in a Divided State: Federalism and Public Housing in Canada." In *Housing the Homeless and Poor: New Partnerships among the Private, Public, and Third Sectors*, edited by George Fallis and Alex Murray, 115–63. Toronto: University of Toronto Press.

– 2005. "Canada: Nation Building in a Federal Welfare State." In *Federalism and the Welfare State: New World and European Experiences*, edited by Herbert Obinger, Stephan Leibfreid, and Francis Castles, 87–137. Cambridge: Cambridge University Press.

– 2006. "Is a Federal Welfare State a Contradiction in Terms?" In *Democracy and Devolution*, edited by Scott Greer, 44–66. London: Palgrave Macmillan.

– 2012. "The Three Federalisms Revisited: Social Policy and Intergovernmental Decision-Making." In *Canadian Federalism: Performance, Effectiveness, and Legitimacy*, edited by Herman Bakvis and Grace Skogstad, 141–64. Toronto: Oxford University Press.

– 2020. "Three Federalisms and Change and Social Policy." In *Canadian Federalism: Performance, Effectiveness, and Legitimacy*, 4th ed., edited by Herman Bakvis and Grace Skogstad, 292–309. Toronto: University of Toronto Press.

Banting, Keith, and John Myles, eds. 2013. *Inequality and the Fading of Redistributive Politics*. Vancouver: UBC Press.

Banting, Keith, and Debra Thompson. 2021. "The Puzzling Persistence of Racial Inequality in Canada." *Canadian Journal of Political Science/Revue canadienne de science politique*: 1–22.

Barnabé, Manon. 2015. *Agir Ensemble, Créer Des Solutions Durables: Plan d'action Intersectoriel En Itinérance de La Région de Montréal (2015–2020)*. Montréal: Centre intégré universitaire de santé et de services sociaux du Centre-Sud-de-l'Île-de-Montréal.

Barnes, Trevor, and Thomas Hutton. 2009. "Situating the New Economy: Contingencies of Regeneration and Dislocation in Vancouver's Inner City." *Urban Studies* 46(5–6): 1247–69. http://doi.org/10.1177/0042098009103863.

Barrett, Jessica. 2014. "City Ponders Developers' Fund to Tackle Housing Shortage." *Calgary Herald*, 9 June. http://www.calgaryherald.com/business/City+ponders+developers+fund+tackle+housing+shortage/9922988/story.html.

BC Housing. 1980. *Annual Report 1979–1980*. Victoria.

– 1986. *Annual Report 1985–1986*. Victoria.

– 1994a. *British Columbia Management Commission Annual Report 1993–1994*. Victoria.

– 1994b. *Homes BC*. Victoria.

– 1997. *Annual Report 1996–1997*. Victoria.

– 2002. *Annual Report 2001–2002*. Victoria.

– 2003. *Annual Report 2002–2003*. Victoria.

– 2006a. *Annual Report 2005–2006*. Victoria.

– 2006b. *Housing Matters: A Housing Strategy for British Columbia*. Victoria.

– 2014a. "*BC Housing Annual Report 2013–14*." Victoria.

– 2014b. *Housing Matters: British Columbia's Housing Strategy*. Victoria.

– 2018. "Federal Agreements." *BCHousing.org*. https://www.bchousing.org/about/federal-agreements.

BC Ministry of Finance. 2005. *Budget and Fiscal Plan 2005/06-2006/07*. Victoria.

BC Ministry of Forests and Range Housing Department. 2005. *Market Housing Affordability*. Victoria.

BC Ministry of Health. 2017. *BC's Mental Health and Substance Use Strategy 2017–2020*. Victoria.

BCNPHA and Matt Thomson. 2017. *2017 Homeless Count in Metro Vancouver, Final Report*. Burnaby.

Beach, Derek, and Rasmus Petersen. 2013. *Process-Tracing Methods: Foundations and Guidelines*. Ann Arbor: University of Michigan Press.

Beattie, Sara, and Hope Hutchins. 2014. *Shelters for Abused Women in Canada 2014*. Ottawa: Statistics Canada.

Bédard, Mary-Anne. 2015. "Building Community Partnerships to End Homelessness." Conference to End Homelessness in Canada, Montreal.

Begin, Patricia, Lyne Casavant, Nancy Miller Chenier, and Jean Depuis. 1999. "Homelessness." Library of Parliament.

Béland, Daniel. 2005. "Ideas and Social Policy: An Institutionalist Perspective." *Social Policy and Administration* 39(1): 1–18. http://doi.org/10.1111/j.1467-9515.2005.00421.x.

– 2006. "The Politics of Social Learning: Finance, Institutions, and Pension Reform in the United States and Canada." *Governance* 19(4): 559–83. https://doi-org.myaccess.library.utoronto.ca/10.1111/j.1468-0491.2006.00340.x.

– 2019. *How Ideas and Institutions Shape the Politics of Public Policy*. Cambridge: Cambridge University Press.

Béland, Daniel, and Robert Cox. 2010. "Introduction." In *Ideas and Politics in Social Science Research*, edited by Daniel Béland and Robert Cox. Oxford: Oxford University Press.

Béland, Daniel, and Robert Henry Cox. 2016. "Ideas as Coalition Magnets: Coalition Building, Policy Entrepreneurs, and Power Relations." *Journal of European Public Policy* 23(3): 428–45. https://doi.org/10.1080/13501763.2015.1115533.

Béland, Daniel, and Pierre-Marc Daigneault, eds. 2015. *Welfare Reform in Canada*. Toronto: University of Toronto Press.

Béland, Daniel, and Alex Waddan. 2014. "Policy Change in Flat Pensions: Comparing Canada and the UK." *Canadian Public Administration* 57(3): 383–400. https://doi.org/10.1111/capa.12076.

– 2015. "Breaking Down Ideas and Institutions: The Politics of Tax Policy in the USA and the UK." *Policy Studies* 36(2): 176–95. https://doi.org/10.1080/01442872.2014.1000845.

Bellot, Céline. 2010. "Les Jeunes de La Rue." *Revue Criminologie* 43(1): 3–248.

Bellot, Céline, and Marie-Eve Sylvestre. 2017. "La Judiciarisation de l'itinérance à Montréal: Les Dérives Sécuritaires de La Gestion Pénale de La Pauvreté." *Revue générale de droit* 47: 11–44. http://doi.org/10.7202/1040516ar.

Bendaoud, Maroine. 2016. *L'État Providence Soutient Qui et Comment? Le Logement Des Ménages à Revenu Modeste Dans Trois Provinces Canadiennes, 1975–2015*. Montréal: Université de Montréal.

Benjaminsen, Lars, and Stefan Bastholm Andrade. 2014. "Testing a Typology of Homelessness across Welfare Regimes: Shelter Use in Denmark and the USA." *Housing Studies* 30: 858–76. https://doi.org/10.1080/02673037.2014.982517.

Benjaminsen, Lars, Evelyn Dyb, and Eoin O'Sullivan. 2009. "The Governance of Homelessness in Liberal and Social Democratic Welfare Regimes: National Strategies and Models of Intervention." *European Journal of Homelessness* 3: 23–51.

Berg, Bruce L. 2011. *Qualitative Research Methods for the Social Sciences*, 8th ed. Boston: Pearson.

Berti, Mario. 2010. "Handcuffed Access: Homelessness and the Justice System." *Urban Geography* 31(6): 825–41. https://doi.org/10.2747/0272-3638.31.6.825.

Bingley, Matthew. 2021. "Toronto Officials, Police under Fire for Tactics Used to Clear Homeless Encampments." *Global News*. https://globalnews.ca/news/8052972/lamport-stadium-park-encampment-toronto-police.

Blackstock, Cindy. 2015. "Social Movements and the Law: Addressing Engrained Government-Based Racial Discrimination against Indigenous Children." *Australian Indigenous Law Review* 19(1): 6–19.

Blint-Welsh, Tyler. 2019. "Federal Data Show Nearly 80,000 Homeless in New York City." *Wall Street Journal*, 24 October. https://www.wsj.com/articles/federal-data-show-nearly-80-000-homeless-in-new-york-city-11571922000.

Boesveldt, Nienke. 2015. *Planet Homeless: Governance Arrangements in Amsterdam, Copehagen, and Glasgow*. The Hague: Eleven International.

Bonnefont, Anne, and Pierre Gaudreau. 2016. "Le Triste 2e Anniversaire de La Politique En Itinérance." *Le Huffington Post*, 26 February. http://quebec.huffingtonpost.ca/anne-bonnefont/2e-anniversaire-de-la-politique-en-itinerance_b_9331250.html.

Bourque, Gilles. 2000. *Le Modèle Québécois de Développement*. Quebec City: Presses de l'Université du Québec.

Boychuk, Gerard. 1998. *Patchworks of Purpose: The Development of Provincial Social Assistance Regimes in Canada*. Montreal and Kingston: McGill-Queen's University Press.

Boychuk, Gerard. 2008. *National Health Insurance in the United States and Canada: Race, Territory, and the Roots of Difference*. Washington, DC: Georgetown University Press.

Boyd, Jade, Danya Fast, and William Small. 2016. "Pathways to Criminalization for Street-Involved Youth Who Use Illicit Substances." *Critical Public Health* 26(5): 530–41. https://doi.org/10.1080/09581596.2015.1110564.

Bradford, Neil. 2005. *Place-Based Public Policy: Towards a New Urban and Community Agenda for Canada*. Ottawa: Canadian Policy Research Networks.

– 2014. "The Federal Communities Agenda: Metagovernance for Place-Based Policy in Canada." In *Canada in Cities: The Politics and Policy of Federal–Local Governance*, edited by Katherine Graham and Caroline Andrew. Montreal and Kingston: McGill-Queen's University Press.

– 2018. *A National Urban Policy for Canada? The Implicit Federal Agenda*. Montreal: Institute for Research on Public Policy.

Bramwell, Allison, and David Wolfe. 2014. "Dimensions of Governance in the Megacity: Scale, Scope, and Coalitions in Toronto." In *Governing Urban Economies: Innovation and Inclusion in Canadian City Regions*, edited by Neil Bradford and Allison Bramwell. Toronto: University of Toronto Press.

Bula, Francis. 2010. "A Complicated Kindness." *Vancouver Magazine*.

Burns, Victoria F., Tamara Sussman, and Valérie Bourgeois-Guérin. 2018. "Later-Life Homelessness as Disenfranchised Grief." *Canadian Journal on Aging / La Revue Canadienne Du Vieillissement* 37(2): 171–84. https://doi.org/10.1017/s0714980818000090.

Burrows, Bob. 2010. *Hope Lives Here: A History of Vancouver's First United Church*. Madeira Park: Harbour.

CAEH (Canadian Alliance to End Homelessness). 2012. *A Plan, Not a Dream: How to End Homelessness in 10 Years*. Calgary.

– 2018a. "CAEH Receives Federal Funding for 20,000 Homes Campaign." Calgary.

– 2018b. "Why Real-Time Data Is the Foundation for Ending Homelessness." https://caeh.ca/real-time-data.

– 2020a. "Built for Zero Canada: Beginning the End of Homelessness in Canada." *Built for Zero Canada*. Calgary, Canada, CAEH.

– 2020b. "Canadian Alliance to End Homelessness Statement of Solidarity with Black Lives Matter." https://caeh.ca/black-lives-matter.

– 2020c. "Vision & Mission." Calgary, CAEH. https://caeh.ca/vision-mission/.

– 2020d. "We Can End Homelessness in Canada, Once and for All." Calgary, CAEH. https://caeh.ca/caeh-launches-recovery-for-all/

– 2021a. "Honouring Truth and Reconciliation Day on September 30." https://caeh.ca/truth-reconciliation-day.

– 2021b. "Medicine Hat Achieves Functional Zero Chronic Homelessness." *Blog News*. https://caeh.ca/medicine-hat-functional-zero/.

Calgary Drop-In. 2007. "Homeless Not Jobless." Calgary, AB.

Calgary Homeless Foundation. 2008. *Calgary's 10 Year Plan to End Homelessness, 2008–2018*.

– 2011. *Calgary's 10 Year Plan to End Homelessness 2008–2018, January 2011 Update*.

– 2015. *Calgary's Updated Plan to End Homelessness: People First in Housing First*.

– 2018. *Spring 2018 Point-in-Time Count Report.*
Calgary Neighbourhoods. 2004. *"The City of Calgary Homelessness Strategy."* Calgary.
Campbell, John. 2004. *Institutional Change and Globalization.* Princeton: Princeton University Press.
Campbell, Larry, Neil Boyd, and Lori Culbert. 2009. *A Thousand Dreams.* Vancouver: Greystone Books.
Canadian Council on Social Development. 1987. *Homelessness in Canada.* Ottawa.
Canadian Homelessness Research Network (CHRN). 2012. *"Canadian Definition of Homelessness."* Toronto: Canadian Observatory on Homelessness Press.
Canadian Intergovernmental Conference Secretariat. 2018. "Federal–Provincial–Territorial Meeting of Ministers Responsible for Housing." Ottawa.
CBC News. 2005. "Vancouver's Ex-Coroner Mayor Calls It Quits." *CBC News,* 30 June. https://www.cbc.ca/news/canada/vancouver-s-ex-coroner -mayor-calls-it-quits-1.564351.
– 2011a. "Women's Groups Outraged over Sexual Assault Comments." 2 March. https://www.cbc.ca/news/canada/british-columbia/women-s-groups -outraged-over-sexual-assault-comments-1.1000451.
– 2011b. "Metro Vancouver Homeless Count Finds Fewer Outside." 24 May. http://www.cbc.ca/1.1103549.
– 2013a. "5 Memorable Ralph Klein Moments." 29 March. http://www.cbc .ca/news/canada/calgary/5-memorable-ralph-klein-moments-1.1347249.
– 2013b. "Ralph Klein's Remarkable Political Life."29 March. http://www .cbc.ca/1.1330371.
– 2014. "Coderre Unveils Plan to Fight Homelessness." 26 September. http:// www.cbc.ca/news/canada/montreal/coderre-unveils-plan-to-fight -homelessness-1.2778618.
– 2015. "Medicine Hat Becomes the First City in Canada to Eliminate Homelessness." *As It Happens.* http://www.cbc.ca/radio/asithappens /as-it-happens-thursday-edition-1.3074402/medicine-hat-becomes-the-first -city-in-canada-to-eliminate-homelessness-1.3074742.
– 2019a. "Alberta Government Cuts $3.2M in Funding to Calgary Homeless Foundation." 15 August. https://www.cbc.ca/news/canada/calgary /calgary-homeless-foundation-cuts-budget-province-1.5247983.
– 2019b. "Vancouver Mayor Addresses Downtown Eastside Residents' Concerns." 9 September. https://www.cbc.ca/news/canada/british -columbia/vancouver-mayor-kennedy-stewart-concerns-downtown -eastside-livestream-1.5275091.
– 2020. "Vancouver Releases Strategy to Move Homeless People Out of Strathcona Park." 14 December. https://www.cbc.ca/news/canada/british -columbia/vancouver-strathcona-park-homeless-camp-strategy-1.5840332.

Chan, Kenneth. 2020. "Squamish Nation to Build 95 Affordable Rental Homes at North Vancouver Reserve | Urbanized." *Vancouver Urbanized*. https://dailyhive.com/vancouver/squamish-nation-capilano-reserve-north-vancouver-affordable-housing.

Cheng, Tessa, et al. 2013. "Transitions into and out of Homelessness among Street-Involved Youth in a Canadian Setting." *Health and Place* 23: 122–27. https://doi.org/10.1016/j.healthplace.2013.06.003. Medline: 3758414.

Chesnay, Catherine T., Céline Bellot, and Marie-Ève Sylvestre. 2013. "Taming Disorderly People One Ticket at a Time: The Penalization of Homelessness in Ontario and British Columbia." *Canadian Journal of Criminology and Criminal Justice* 55(2): 161–85. http://doi.org/10.3138/cjccj.2011-E-46.

CHF (Calgary Homeless Foundation). 2004. *The Calgary Community Plan 2004–2008*. Calgary.

– 2008. *Calgary's 10 Year Plan to End Homelessness, 2008–2018*. Calgary.

– 2011. *Calgary's 10 Year Plan to End Homelessness 2008–2018, January 2011 Update*. Calgary.

– 2012. "Winter 2012 Point-in-Time Count Report." Calgary.

– 2015. "*Calgary's Updated Plan to End Homelessness: People First in Housing First*." Calgary.

– 2018. *Two Decades of Time and Community Impact*. Calgary.

– 2019. *Calgary's Homelessness Community Plan*. Calgary.

Choudhry, Sujit, Lorne Mitchell Sossin, and Jean-François Gaudreault-DesBiens, eds. 2006. *Dilemmas of Solidarity: Rethinking Redistribution in the Canadian Federation*. Toronto: University of Toronto Press.

Christensen, Julia. 2017. *No Home in a Homeland – Indigenous Peoples and Homelessness in the Canadian North*. Vancouver: UBC Press. https://www.ubcpress.ca/no-home-in-a-homeland.

Christopher, Ben. 2012. "Addicted City: How Vancouver's War on Drugs Began." *Megaphone Magazine*, February. http://www.megaphonemagazine.com/magazine/353/addicted-city-how-vancouver-s-war-on-drugs-began.

CHRN (Canadian Homelessness Research Network). 2012. *Canadian Definition of Homelessness*. Toronto: Canadian Observatory on Homelessness Press.

Chudnovsky, David, and Linda Shuto. 2016. "The Sad Housing Lessons of Little Mountain." *The Tyee*. http://thetyee.ca/Opinion/2016/09/12/Little-Mountain-Sad-Housing-Lessons.

City Clerk. 2002. *Status of the Federal Affordable Housing Program*. Toronto: City of Toronto.

City of Calgary. 2002. *City of Calgary Corporate Affordable Housing Strategy*. Calgary.

– 2008. "Fast Facts #02." 25 July. https://www.homelesshub.ca/sites/default/files/attachments/dgrne2pl.pdf.

– 2016. *Foundations for Home: Calgary's Corporate Affordable Housing Strategy 2016–2025*. Calgary.

City of Toronto. 2007. *What Housing First Means for People: Results of Streets to Homes 2007 Post-Occupancy Research*. Toronto.
– 2013. "2013 Street Needs Assessment Results." Toronto.
– 2017. "CD 19.6: Proposed New Engagement and Planning Process for Emergency Shelters." 26–28 April.
– 2018. "2018 Street Needs Assessment Results."
– 2020. "Inclusionary Zoning Draft Official Plan Amendment and Zoning By-Law Amendment." Toronto.
City of Toronto and TAEH. 2018. "Toronto Housing and Homelessness Service Planning Forum Terms of Reference – Draft to Forum Meeting." Toronto.
City of Vancouver. 2005a. *A Housing Plan for the Downtown Eastside*. Vancouver.
– 2005b. *Homeless Action Plan*. Vancouver.
– 2006. *Project Civil City*. Vancouver.
– 2007. *Regular Council Meeting Minutes*. Vancouver.
– 2011. "Vancouver's Housing and Homelessness Strategy 2012–2021: A Home for Everyone." Vancouver.
Clark, Christy. 2015. "Letter to His Worship Gregor Robertson." Vancouver: City of Vancouver.
Clayton, Frank, and Geoff Schwartz. 2015. "Is Inclusionary Zoning a Needed Tool for Providing Affordable Housing in the Greater Golden Horseshoe?" Toronto: Centre for Urban Research and Land Development.
CMHC (Canada Mortgage and Housing Corporation). 2002. "Canada and Alberta Sign Affordable Housing Agreement" [press release]. Toronto: Centre for Urban Research and Land Development.
– 2010. *Rental Market Report: Calgary CMA*. Ottawa.
– 2011. *National AHI Funding Table*. Ottawa.
– 2020. *Canada to Rapidly Create Affordable Housing and Support the Homeless*. Toronto.
Cole, Desmond. 2020. *The Skin We're In*. Toronto: Penguin Books Canada.
Cole, Yolande. 2014. "Vision Vancouver Discloses More than $2 Million in Campaign Donations." *Georgia Straight*, 6 November. http://www.straight.com/news/766276/vision-vancouver-discloses-more-2-million-campaign-donations.
Comité de liaison en itinérance de Montréal. 2007. *Projet de plan d'action intersectoriel en itinérance*. Montreal.
Comité des sans-abri. 1987. "Vers une politique municipale pour les sans-abris." Montreal.
Commission de la santé et des services sociaux. 2009. *Itinérance: Agissons Ensemble*. Quebec City.
Commission permanente du conseil municipal sur le développement culturel et la qualité du milieu de vie. 2008. "Étude publique sur l'itinérance: Des visages multiples, des responsabilités partagées." Montréal.

Community and Neighbourhood Services, Policy and Planning Division. 2006. *Results of the 2006 Count of Homeless Persons in Calgary: Enumerated in Emergency and Transitional Facilities, by Service Agencies, and On the Streets.* Calgary.

Community Services. 2004. *Homelessness Strategy (Policy).* Calgary.

Connolly, Michael. 2001. *Shelter from the Storm.* DVD.

Conteh, Charles. 2013. *Policy Governance in Multi-Level Systems.* Montreal and Kingston: McGill-Queen's University Press.

Corntassel, Jeff. 2012. "Re-Envisioning Resurgence: Indigenous Pathways to Decolonization and Sustainable Self-Determination." *Decolonization: Indigeneity, Education, and Society* 1(1).

Coulthard, Glen Sean. 2014. *Red Skin, White Masks: Rejecting the Colonial Politics of Recognition.* Minneapolis: University of Minnesota Press.

Crowe, Cathy. 2007. "Bush's 'Homeless Czar' Tours Canada." *Straight Goods News.* Summer 2007. http://tdrc.net/index.php?page=35---spring-2007.

– 2011. "Action for Affordable Housing: Moving Housing Rights Forward in Our City, Our Province, Our Country." Presented at the Advocacy Centre for Tenants Ontario, Toronto, 25 February.

– 2018. "Faulkner Inquest Proceedings Avoid the 'H' Word." *rabble.ca*, June. https://rabble.ca/blogs/bloggers/cathy-crowes-blog/2018/06/faulkner-inquest-proceedings-avoid-h-word.

– 2019. *A Knapsack Full of Dreams: Memoirs of a Street Nurse.* Cananda: Friesen Press.

Dabbs, Frank. 2006. "Ralph Klein's Real Legacy." *The Tyee*, 8 September. http://thetyee.ca/Views/2006/09/08/RalphKlein.

Davies, Libby. 2019. *Outside In: A Political Memoir.* Toronto: Between the Lines.

Dawson, Tina. 2021. "How Can Cities Address the Challenge of Homeless Encampments?". 4 August. https://canurb.org/citytalk-news/how-can-cities-address-the-challenge-of-encampments.

Dej, Erin. 2020. *A Complex Exile.* Vancouver: UBC Press.

Dembicki, Geoff. 2017. "Christy Clark Isn't Being Honest about the Housing Crisis." *The Tyee*, 5 May. https://thetyee.ca/Opinion/2017/05/05/Clark-Not-Honest-About-Housing-Crisis.

Denzin, Norman. 1978. *The Research Act: A Theoretical Introduction to Socio20/12/2021 11:32:00logical Methods.* New York: McGraw-Hill.

Denzin, Norman, and Yvonna Lincoln. 2005. *The SAGE Handbook of Qualitative Research*, 3rd ed. Los Angeles: SAGE.

dev. 2011. "Profile: Judy Graves." *Vancouver Magazine*, 2 December. https://www.vanmag.com/profile-judy-graves.

Dimoff, Anna. 2018. "Metro Vancouver Residents Demand Transparency over Modular Housing Tenants They Fear Could Pose a Risk." *CBC News*, 5 February. https://www.cbc.ca/news/canada/british-columbia/modular-housing-opposition-vancouver-1.4521454.

Dingman, Shane. 2021. "Toronto's Affordable Rental Plans Take the Long View." *Globe and Mail*, 21 July. https://www.theglobeandmail.com/real -estate/article-torontos-affordable-rental-plans-take-the-long-view.

Distasio, Jino, Sarah Zell, Scott McCullough, and Betty Edel. 2019. *Localized Approaches to Ending Homelessness: Indigenizing Housing First*. Winnipeg: Institute of Urban Studies, University of Winnipeg.

Djuric, Mickey. 2021. "How Cowessess First Nation's Historic Child Welfare Agreement with Canada and Saskatchewan Works." *CBC*, 9 July. https:// www.cbc.ca/news/canada/saskatchewan/how-cowessess-first-nation -child-welfare-agreement-works-1.6095470.

Doberstein, Carey. 2016. *Building a Collaborative Advantage: Network Governance and Homelessness Policy-Making in Canada*. Vancouver: UBC Press.

Doberstein, Carey, and Jasmine Reimer. 2016. "Interagency Councils on Homelessness: Case Studies from the United States and Alberta." In *Exploring Effective Systems Responses to Homelessness*, edited by Naomi Nichols and Carey Doberstein. Toronto: Homeless Hub Press.

Drdla, Richard. 2014. "Ontario Legislation." *Inclusionary Housing Canada*. http://inclusionaryhousing.ca.

Encampment Support Network. 2001. "We Are Not the Virus." Apple Podcast. 1 September.

ESDC (Employment and Social Development Canada). 2013. "Homelessness Partnering Strategy: Myth vs Reality." Ottawa.

– 2014. *Summative Evaluation of the Homelessness Partnering Strategy: Final Report*. Ottawa.

– 2017. *The National Shelter Study 2005–2014: Emergency Shelter Use in Canada*. Ottawa.

– 2019a. *2018 Shelter Capacity Report*. Ottawa.

– 2019b. "Reaching Home: Canada's Homelessness Strategy Launch." Ottawa. https://www.canada.ca/en/employment-social-development/news /2019/04/reaching-home-canadas-homelessness-strategy-launch.html.

– 2020. "About Reaching Home; Canada's Homelessness Strategy." Ottawa.

Esping-Andersen, Gøsta. 1990. *The Three Worlds of Welfare Capitalism*. Princeton: Princeton University Press.

Fallis, George, and Alex L. Murray. 1990. *Housing the Homeless and Poor: New Partnerships among the Private, Public, and Third Sectors*. Toronto: University of Toronto Press.

Falvo, Nick. 2010. "Toronto's Streets to Homes Program." In *Finding Home: Policy Options for Addressing Homelessness in Canada*, edited by David Hulchanski et al. Toronto: Cities Centre, University of Toronto.

– 2017. "Thesis by Dr Maroine Bendaoud: Social Housing in British Columbia, Alberta, and Quebec." *CHF Research Blog*. 25 April. https:// www.calgaryhomeless.com/thesis-dr-maroine-bendaoud-social-housing -british-columbia-alberta-quebec-nick-falvo.

– 2020 (25 September). "Homelessness Could Rise with Economic Downturn." Montreal: IRPP.

Farha, Leilani. 2021. "How Can Cities Address the Challenge of Homeless Encampments?" Presented at the virtual webinar. https://canurb.org/citytalk-news/how-can-cities-address-the-challenge-of-encampments.

Farha, Leilani, and Kaitlin Schwan. 2020. "A National Protocol for Homeless Encampments in Canada: A Human Rights Approach." Toronto: Canadian Observatory on Homelessness.

FEANTSA. 2011. "ETHOS Typology on Homelessness and Housing Exclusion." http://www.feantsa.org/spip.php?article120.

Feng, Patrick, Ben Li, and Cooper Langford. 2014. "300 People Who Make a Difference: Associative Governance in Calgary." In *Governing Urban Economies: Innovation and Inclusion in Canadian City Regions*, edited by Neil Bradford and Allison Bramwell. Toronto: University of Toronto Press.

FRAPRU. 2015. "Historique." www.frapru.qc.ca/a-propos/historique.

– 2018. "Des Logements Sociaux Maintenant: Il Faut Investir Dans AccèsLogis!" Front d'action populaire en réaménagement urbain." https://www.frapru.qc.ca

– 2019. "Manifestation aux bureaux de François Legault: Le FRAPRU réclame un 'vrai changement' en matière de logement!" *Front d'action populaire en réaménagement urbain*. 7 February. https://www.frapru.qc.ca/manifestation-7fev2019/

Fujii, Lee Ann. 2017. Interview in Social *Science Research: A Relational Approach.* New York: Routledge.

Gaetz, Stephen. 2010. "The Struggle to End Homelessness in Canada: How We Created the Crisis, and How We Can End It." *Open Health Services and Policy Journal* 3: 21–6.

– 2014. *Coming of Age: Reimagining the Response to Youth Homelessness in Canada.* Toronto: Canadian Observatory on Homelessness. http://homelesshub.ca/comingofage.

Gaetz, Stephen, and Erin Dej. 2017. *A New Direction: A Framework for Homelessness Prevention.* Toronto: Canadian Observatory on Homelessness Press.

Gaetz, Stephen, Erin Dej, Tim Richter, and Melanie Redman. 2016. *The State of Homelessness in Canada 2016.* Toronto: Canadian Observatory on Homelessness Press.

Gaetz, Stephen, Tanya Gulliver, and Tim Richter. 2014. *The State of Homelessness in Canada 2014.* Toronto: Homeless Hub Press.

Gale, Star. 2015. "*Ask Them – Involving the Homeless in Their Own Future.*" Montreal: Mouvement pour mettre fin à l'itinérance à Montréal.

George, Alexander L., and Andrew Bennett. 2005. *Case Studies and Theory Development in the Social Sciences.* Cambridge, MA: MIT Press.

German, Beric. 2008. "Toronto Adopts Bush Homeless Czar's Plan: Another View of 'Streets to Homes' Programs." *Cathy Crowe Newsletter*. Summer 2008. https://tdrc.net/index.php?page=48---summer-2008-newsletter.

Goering, Paula, et al. 2014. *National Final Report: Cross-Site At Home / Chez Soi Project*. Calgary: Mental Health Commission of Canada.

Golden, Anne, William Currie, Elizabeth Greaves, and E. John Latimer. 1999. *Taking Responsibility for Homelessness: An Action Plan for Toronto*. Toronto: City of Toronto.

Goldman-Hasbun, Julia, et al. 2019. "Homelessness and Incarceration Associated with Relapse into Stimulant and Opioid Use among Youth Who Are Street-Involved in Vancouver, Canada." *Drug and Alcohol Review* 38(4): 428–34. https://doi.org/10.1111%2Fdar.12921.

Good, Kristin. 2009. *Municipalities and Multiculturalism: The Politics of Immigration in Toronto and Vancouver*. Toronto: University of Toronto Press.

Goodhand, Margo. 2017. *Runaway Wives and Rogue Feminists: The Origins of the Women's Shelter Movement in Canada*. Halifax: Fernwood.

Gouvernement du Québec. 2014. "Ensemble, Pour Éviter La Rue et En Sortir, Politique Nationale de Lutte à l'itinérance." https://www.msss.gouv.qc.ca/itinerance.

Government of Alberta. 2015. "*Supporting Healthy and Successful Transitions to Adulthood: A Plan to Prevent and Reduce Youth Homelessness*." Edmonton.

– 2020. "*Affordable Housing Review Panel*." https://www.alberta.ca/affordable-housing-review-panel.aspx.

Government of British Columbia. 2001. *Annual Report 2001–2002: A New Era Update*. Victoria.

Government of Ontario. 2008. *Breaking the Cycle: Ontario's Poverty Reduction Strategy*. http://www.children.gov.on.ca/htdocs/English/breakingthecycle/strategy/strategy.aspx.

Graefe, Peter. 2018. "State Rescaling, Institutionalized State–Citizen Relationships, and Canadian Health Policy." *Studies in Political Economy* 99(2): 175–93. https://doi.org/10.1080/07078552.2018.1492204.

Graham, Katherine A., Susan D. Phillips, and Allan M. Maslove. 1998. *Urban Governance in Canada: Representation, Resources, and Restructuring*. Toronto: Harcourt Brace Canada.

Graves, Judy. 2017. "Judy Graves: I Came out of Retirement to Run with OneCity Because I Know the Housing Crisis Has a Solution." *Georgia Straight*, 12 October. https://www.straight.com/news/980741/judy-graves-i-came-out-retirement-run-onecity-because-i-know-housing-crisis-has-solution.

Gregg, Allan. 2006. "The True West, Strong and Free: What Will Canada's Richest Province Do with Its New-Found Power?" *The Walrus*, 12 September. http://thewalrus.ca/the-true-west-strong-and-free.

Grenier, Amanda, et al. 2016. "Homelessness among Older People: Assessing Strategies and Frameworks Across Canada." *Canadian Review of Social Policy /Revue canadienne de politique sociale* 74: 1–39. https://crsp.journals.yorku.ca/index.php/crsp/article/view/39889.

Hacker, Jacob S. 2004. "Privatizing Risk without Privatizing the Welfare State: The Hidden Politics of Social Policy Retrenchment in the United States." *American Political Science Review* 98(2): 243–60. http://isps.yale.edu /research/publications/isps04-007#.U2bl661dUeM.

Hacker, Jacob S., and Paul Pierson. 2010. *Winner-Take-All Politics: How Washington Made the Rich Richer – and Turned Its Back on the Middle Class.* New York: Simon and Schuster.

Haddow, Rodney. 2015. *Comparing Quebec and Ontario: Political Economy and Public Policy at the Turn of the Millennium.* Toronto: University of Toronto Press.

Hall, Barbara. 1997. Letter to Mayor Lastman. 25 November.

Hanna, Kevin S., and Margaret Walton-Roberts. 2004. "Quality of Place and the Rescaling of Urban Governance: The Case of Toronto." *Journal of Canadian Studies* 38(3): 37–67. http://doi.org/10.3138/jcs.38.3.37.

Hargroup Research and Consulting. 2004. *Deliberative Dialogue on Who Should Pay to Shelter to Homeless – Executive Summary.* Calgary: Hargroup Research and Consulting.

Hay, Colin. 2011. "Ideas and the Construction of Interests." In *Ideas and Politics in Social Science Research,* edited by Daniel Béland and Robert Cox. New York: Oxford University Press.

Henley, Jon. 2019. "'It's a Miracle': Helsinki's Radical Solution to Homelessness." *The Guardian,* 3 June. https://www.theguardian.com/ cities/2019/jun/03/its-a-miracle-helsinkis-radical-solution-to-homelessness.

Heineck, Kira. 2018. "Investing in Housing to End Homelessness." Toronto: Budget Committee.

Hoekstra, Gordon. 2017. "Most Top-10 Liberal Donors in Construction Industry." *Times Colonist,* 28 January. https://www.timescolonist.com/bc-news /most-top-10-bc-liberal-donors-in-construction-industry-4645405.

Horak, Martin. 2012a. "Conclusion: Understanding Multilevel Governance in Canada's Cities." In *Sites of Governance: Multilevel Governance and Policy Making in Canada's Big Cities,* edited by Martin Horak and Robert Young, 339–70. Montreal and Kingston: McGill-Queen's University Press.

– 2012b. "Multilevel Governance in Toronto: Success and Failure in Canada's Largest City." In *Sites of Governance: Multilevel Governance and Policy Making in Canada's Big Cities,* edited by Martin Horak and Robert Young, 228–62. Montreal and Kingston: McGill-Queen's University Press.

Horak, Martin, and Robert Young, eds. 2012. *Sites of Governance: Multilevel Governance and Policy Making in Canada's Big Cities.* Montreal and Kingston: McGill-Queen's University Press.

Housing and Urban Affairs. 2010. *Annual Report 2009–2010.* Edmonton: Government of Alberta.

Howell, Mike. 2014. "Vision, NPA Running Multi-Million Dollar Campaigns." *Vancouver Courier,* 7 November. http://www.vancourier.com/vancouver-votes /election-news/vision-npa-running-multi-million-dollar-campaigns-1.1529557.

HRDC (Human Resources Development Canada). 2003. *Evaluation of the National Homelessness Initiative: Implementation and Early Outcomes of the HRDC-Based Components.* Ottawa.

– 2008. *Summative Evaluation of the National Homelessness Initiative: Final Report.* Ottawa.

– 2009. *Evaluation of the Homelessness Partnering Strategy.* Ottawa. http://www.hrsdc.gc.ca/eng/publications/evaluations/social_development/2009/july.shtml.

Hudson, Carol-Anne, and Peter Graefe. 2012. "The Toronto Origins of Ontario's 2008 Poverty Reduction Strategy: Mobilizing Multiple Channels of Influence for Progressive Social Policy Change." *Canadian Review of Social Policy / Revue canadienne de politique sociale* 65–6: 1–15.

Hughes, James. 2012. "Homelessness: Closing the Gap Between Capacity and Performance." Toronto: Mowat Centre for Policy Innovation.

– 2015. *Early Intervention: How Canada's Social Programs Can Work Better, Save Lives, and Often Save Money.* Toronto: James Lorimer.

Hughes, James, ed. 2018. *Beyond Shelters: Solutions to Homelessness in Canada from the Front Lines.* Toronto: James Lorimer.

Hulchanski, David. 2002. "Housing Policy for Tomorrow's Cities." Toronto: Canadian Policy Research Network.

– 2009. *Homelessness in Canada: Past, Present, Future.* Canada: Canadian Policy Research Network.

Hulchanski, J. David, et al., eds. 2009. *Finding Home: Policy Options for Addressing Homelessness in Canada.* Toronto: The Homeless Hub.

Hume, Mark. 2006. "Sullivan Takes Hard Line on City Homelessness." *Globe and Mail*, 28 November. http://www.theglobeandmail.com/news/national/sullivan-takes-hard-line-on-city-homelessness/article18178470.

Isin, F. 1998. "Governing Toronto without Government: Liberalism and Neoliberalism." *Studies in Political Economy* 56: 169–91. https://doi.org/10.1080/19187033.1998.11675296.

Jacobs, Alan. 2014. "Process Tracing the Effects of Ideas." In *Process Tracing: From Metaphor to Analytic Tool*, edited by Andrew Bennett and Jeffrey Checkel, 41–72. Cambridge: Cambridge University Press.

Jacobs, Jane. 1961. *The Death and Life of Great American Cities.* New York: Vintage Books.

Jago, Robert. 2021. "On Her Last Day, My Mother Wore a Shirt with the Words She So Believed. Every Child Matters." *Canada's National Observer*, 30 September.

Jarrett, Holly. 2016. *Nothing about Us without Us: Lived Experience Leadership from across the Country: Call for Inclusion in the Design of Canada's National Housing Strategy.* Toronto: The Homeless Hub.

Jenson, Jane. 2004. *Canada's New Social Risks: Directions for a New Social Architecture.* Ottawa: Canadian Policy Research Networks.

– 2010. "Diffusing Ideas for after Neoliberalism: The Social Investment Perspective in Europe and Latin America." *Global Social Policy* 10(1): 59–84. https://doi.org/10.1177%2F1468018109354813.

– 2013. "Historical Transformation of Canada's Social Architecture: Institutions, Instruments, and Ideas." In *Inequality and the Fading of Redistributive Politics*, edited by Keith Banting and John Myles. Vancouver: UBC Press.

Jewell, Jennifer. 2021. "How Can Cities Address the Challenge of Homeless Encampments?" Presented at the virtual webinar. https://canurb.org /citytalk-news/how-can-cities-address-the-challenge-of-encampments.

Johnson, Rhiannon. 2019. "Navigating the Toronto Housing Crisis as an Indigenous Person." *CBC News.* https://www.cbc.ca/news/indigenous /urban-housing-rental-market-toronto-1.5029653.

Jones, Allison. 2014. "Ontario Blames Ottawa for Falling Short of Province's Child-Poverty Goal." *Globe and Mail*, 3 September. http://www.theglobeandmail .com/news/politics/ontario-blames-ottawa-for-falling-short-of-provinces-child -poverty-goal/article20333768.

Kading, Terry, and Christopher Walmsley. 2018. "Homelessness in Small Cities: The Abdication of Federal Responsibility." In *Small Cities, Big Issues: Reconceiving Community in a Neoliberal Era*, edited by Christopher Walmsley and Terry Kading. Edmonton: Athabasca University Press.

Kauppi, Carol, Bill O'Grady, Rebecca Schiff, and Fay Martin. 2017. *Homelessness and Hidden Homelessness in Rural and Northern Ontario*. Guelph: Rural Ontario Institute.

Klein, Seth, and Lorraine Copas. 2010. *Unpacking the Housing Numbers: How Much New Social Housing in BC Building?* Vancouver: Canada: Canadian Centre for Policy Alternatives.

Klein, Seth, and Andrea Long. 2003. *A Bad Time to Be Poor: An Analysis of British Columbia's New Welfare Policies*. Vancouver: Canadian Centre for Policy Alternatives.

Klodawsky, Fran, and Leonore Evans. 2014. "Homelessness on the Federal Agenda: Progressive Architecture but No Solution in Sight." In *Canada in Cities: The Politics and Policy of Federal-Local Governance*, edited by Katherine Graham and Caroline Andrew. Montreal and Kingston: McGill-Queen's University Press.

Kopec, Anna. 2022. "The Politics of Homelessness: Poverty, Policy, and Participation." PhD thesis, University of Toronto.

Kouyoumdjian, Fiona G., et al. 2019. "Interactions between Police and Persons Who Experience Homelessness and Mental Illness in Toronto, Canada: Findings from a Prospective Study." *Canadian Journal of Psychiatry* 64(10): 718–25. https://doi.org/10.1177/0706743719861386.

Ladner, Kiera. 2003. "Treaty Federalism: An Indigenous Vision of Canadian Federalisms." In *New Trends in Canadian Federalism*, edited by Miriam Smith and François Rocher. Peterborough: Broadview Press.

– 2005. "Up the Creek: Fishing for a New Constitutional Order." *Canadian Journal of Political Science* 38(4): 923–53.

Lafferty, Catherine (Katłįà). 2020. "Potlatch Broken Up by Police 100 Years Ago Remembered by 'Namagis Chief." *APTN News*, 29 December 2020.

Laforest, Rachel. 2011a. "L'étude Du Tiers Secteur Au Québec: Comment Saisir La Spécificité Québécoise?" *Politique et Sociétés* 30(1): 43–55. https://doi.org/10.7202/1006058ar.

– 2011b. *Voluntary Sector Organizations and the State: Building New Relations.* Vancouver: UBC Press.

Larocque, Florence. 2011. "Regards comparatifs sur a Stsratégie québécoise de lutte contre la pauvreté et l'exclusion sociale: un poids significatif, ses choix partiellement distinctifs." *Politique et Sociétés* 30(1): 117–37. https://doi.org/10.7202/1006062ar.

Larocque, Florence, and Alain Noël. 2014. "The Politics of Poverty in the European Union: How States Respond to the Open Method of Coordination on Social Inclusion." *Policy and Politics* 42(3): 333–50.

Latimer, Eric, François Bordeleau, and Christian Méthot. 2018. *Housing Needs and Preferences of Indigenous People Using Community Resources in Montreal.* Montreal: Montreal Urban Aboriginal Strategy Network.

Latimer, Eric, James Macgregor, Christian Méthot, and Alison Smith. 2015. *Dénombrement des personnes en situation d'itinérance à Montréal le 24 mars 2015.* Montreal: City of Montreal.

Layton, Jack. 2008. *Homelessness: How to End the National Crisis.* Toronto: Penguin Books Canada.

Lecours, André, and Daniel Béland. 2010. "Federalism and Fiscal Policy: The Politics of Equalization in Canada." *Publius: The Journal of Federalism* 40(4): 569–96.

Lee, David, and Michael McGuire. 2017. "Intergovernmental Alignment, Program Effectiveness, and US Homelessness Policy." *Publius: The Journal of Federalism* 47(4): 622–47. http://doi.org/10.1093/publius/pjx044.

Lee, Jeff. 2006. "Cost of Civility Just Went Up: Contingency Fund Tapped for Extra Cash to Pay for Commissioner's Office." *Vancouver Sun*, 19 December. http://global.factiva.com/redir/default.aspx?P=sa&an=VNCS000020061219e2cj0001i&cat=a&ep=ASE.

Leo, Christopher. 2006. "Deep Federalism: Respecting Community Difference in National Policy." *Canadian Journal of Political Science / Revue canadienne de science politique* 39(3): 481–506. http://doi.org/10.1017/S0008423906060240.

Leo, Christopher, and Martine August. 2006. "National Policy and Community Initiative: Mismanaging Homelessness in a Slow Growth City." *Canadian Journal of Urban Research* 15: 1–21.

– 2009. "The Multilevel Governance of Immigration and Settlement: Making Deep Federalism Work." *Canadian Journal of Political Science / Revue*

canadienne de science politique 42(2): 491–510. http://doi.org/10.1017
/S0008423909090337.

Leung, Cheryl S., et al. 2008. "Homelessness and the Response to Emerging
Infectious Disease Outbreaks: Lessons from SARS." *Journal of Urban Health*
85(3): 402–10. https://doi.org/10.1007%2Fs11524-008-9270-2.

Lucas, Jack, and Alison Smith. 2019. "Multilevel Policy from the Municipal
Perspective: A Pan-Canadian Survey." *Canadian Public Administration* 62(2):
270–93.

Lupick, Travis. 2017a. *Fighting for Space: How a Group of Drug Users Transformed
One City's Struggle with Addiction*. Vancouver: Arsenal Pulp Press.

– 2017b. "How the Vancouver Area Network of Drug Users Fought City Hall
– and Won." *Ricochet*, 4 December. https://ricochet.media/en/2054.

– 2018. "Former B.C. Premier Christy Clark Booked as Featured Speaker by
the Ontario Real Estate Association." *Georgia Straight*, 20 January. https://
www.straight.com/news/1022166/former-bc-premier-christy-clark
-booked-featured-speaker-ontario-real-estate-association.

Mah, Julie. 2009. "Can Inclusionary Zoning Help Address the Shortage of
Affordable Housing in Toronto?" Ottawa: Canadian Policy Research Networks.

Mahon, Rianne. 2007. "Challenging National Regimes from Below." *Politics
and Gender* 3: 55–78.

Mahoney, James, and Dietrich Rueschemeyer. 2003. "Comparative Historical
Analysis: Achievements and Agendas." In *Comparative Historical Analysis in
the Social Sciences*, edited by James Mahoney and Dietrich Rueschemeyer.
Cambridge: Cambridge University Press.

Mahoney, Jill. 2001. "Klein Stays to 'Fight This Devil.'" *Globe and Mail*,
19 December. https://www.theglobeandmail.com/news/national/klein
-stays-to-fight-this-devil/article25452024.

Managing Director of Social Development. 2008. *Streetohome Vancouver:
Administrative Report*. Vancouver.

Mason, Gary. 2014. "Amid Calgary's Prosperity, Mayor Nenshi Senses
Housing Crisis." *Globe and Mail*, 28 March. http://www.theglobeandmail
.com/news/politics/amid-calgarys-prosperity-mayor-nenshi
-senses-housing-crisis/article17714161.

– 2020. "Opinion: If Canada Can't Address Its Homelessness Crisis in a
Deadly Pandemic, Then When?" *The Globe and Mail*, 12 December. https://
www.theglobeandmail.com/opinion/article-if-canada-cant-address
-its-homelessness-crisis-in-a-deadly-pandemic.

Maynard, Robyn. 2017. *Policing Black Lives: State Violence in Canada from Slavery
to the Present*. Halifax: Fernwood.

McBride, Stephen. 2019. "From Keynesianism to Neoliberalism: The State in a
Global Context." In *Change and Continuity: Canadian Political Economy in the
New Millennium*, edited by Mark Thomas, Leah Vosko, Carlo Fanelli, and
Olena Lyubchenko. Montreal and Kingston: McGill-Queen's University Press.

McElroy, Justin. 2019. "One Year In, Kennedy Stewart Is As Much Vancouver's Lobbyist-in-Chief As He Is Mayor." *CBC News*. https://www.cbc.ca/news /canada/british-columbia/kennedy-stewart-mayor-interview-one -year-2019-1.5338711.

McKeen, Wendy, and Ann Porter. 2003. "Politics and Transformation: Welfare State Restructuring in Canada." In *Changing Canada: Political Economy as Transformation*, edited by Leah Vosko and Wallace Clement. Montreal and Kingston: McGill-Queen's University Press.

Meiszner, Peter. 2014. "City of Vancouver Formally Declares City Is on Unceded Aboriginal Territory." *Global News*, 25 June.

Meralli, Farrah. 2017. "B.C. Liberals, NDP Spar over Donation from Billionaire Developer." *CBC News*, 26 April. https://www.cbc.ca/news/canada /british-columbia/liberals-ndp-spar-over-developer-donation-1.4086926.

Michener, Jamila, Mallory SoRelle, and Chloe Thurston. 2022. "From the Margins to the Center: A Bottom-up Approach to the Study of Welfare State Scholarship." *Perspectives on Politics* 20(1): 154–69.

Miller, Byron, and Alan Smart. 2012. "Ascending the Main Stage?: Calgary in the Multilevel Governance Drama." In *Sites of Governance: Multilevel Governance and Policy Making in Canada's Big Cities*, edited by Martin Horak and Robert Young, 26–52. Montreal and Kingston: McGill-Queen's University Press.

Ministère de la Main-d'ouevre et de la Sécurité du revenu. 1988. "Les sans-abri au Québec." Quebec City.

Ministry of Municipal Affairs and Housing. 2010. "Building Foundations: Building Futures: Ontario's Long-Term Affordable Housing Strategy." Toronto.

MMFIM. 2015. "Ending Homelessness in Montreal – Part 1: Ending Chronic and Cyclical Homelessness." Montreal.

Montréal. 2021. *Initiative pour la création rapide de logements: La ville de Montréal annonce la construction de 19 nouveaux logements à but non lucratif pour les clientèles vulnérables*. Ville de Montréal.

Moore, Aaron. 2013. *Trading Density for Benefits: Toronto and Vancouver Compared*. Toronto: Institute on Municipal Finance and Governance.

MSSS (Ministère de la Santé et des Services sociaux). 1998. "La Politique de La Santé et Du Bien-Être." Quebec City.

– 2009. *Pour leur redonner … Plan d'action interministériel en itinérance 2010–2013*. Quebec City.

– 2014. *L'itinérance Au Québec: Premier portrait*. Quebec City.

Nagy, Melanie, and Alexandra Mae Jones. 2021. "B.C.'s Overdose Crisis Killed 1,716 People Last Year, More Than Ever Before: Coroner's Service." *CTV News*, 11 February. https://www.ctvnews.ca/health/b-c-s-overdose -crisis-killed-1-716-people-last-year-more-than-ever-before-coroner-s -service-1.5306085.

National Inquiry into Missing and Murdered Indigenous Women and Girls. 2019. *A Legal Analysis of Genocide*. Supplementary Report. Ottawa.

Newman-Bremang, Kathleen, and Nadia Ebrahim. 2021. "6 Women on the Reality of Renting While Black in Canada." https://www.refinery29.com /en-ca/2021/03/9367732/racism-while-renting-canada.

Noël, Alain. 1999. "Is Decentralization Conservative? Federalism and the Contemporary Debate on the Canadian Welfare State." In *Stretching the Federation: The Art of the State in Canada*, edited by Robert Young, 195–219. Montreal and Kingston: McGill-Queen's University Press. https://papyrus .bib.umontreal.ca/xmlui/handle/1866/12386.

– 2000. *"Without Quebec: Collaborative Federalism with a Footnote?"* Montreal: Institute for Research on Public Policy.

– 2001. *Power and Purpose in Intergovernmental Relations.* Montreal: Institute for Research on Public Policy. http://encore.uleth.ca/iii/encore_leth /record/C__Rb1466935__SNo%C3%ABl,%20Alain__Orightresult;jsessionid =62D896FE4F30AF5CB65A7C698FE42886?lang=eng&suite=leth.

– 2002. "Une loi contre la pauvreté: La nouvelle approche québécoise de lutte contre la pauvreté et l'exclusion sociale." *Lien social et politiques* 48: 101–14. http://doi.org/10.7202/007895ar.

– 2005. "Lutte contre la pauvreté ou lutte contre les pauvres?" In *L'annuaire du Québec 2005*, edited by Michel Venne, 504–13. Montreal: Fides.

– 2009. "Balance and Imbalance in the Division of Financial Resources." In *Contemporary Canadian Federalism: Foundations, Traditions, Institutions*, edited by Alain-G Gagnon. Toronto: University of Toronto Press.

– 2010. "Quebec." In *The Oxford Handbook of Canadian Politics*, edited by John C. Courtney and David E. Smith, 92–110. Oxford: Oxford University Press.

– 2015. "Québec: The Ambivalent Politics of Social Solidarity." In *Welfare Reform in Canada*, edited by Daniel Béland and Pierre-Marc Daigneault, 127–42. Toronto: University of Toronto Press.

O'Grady, Bill, Stephen Gaetz, and Kristy Buccieri. 2013. "Tickets ... and More Tickets: A Case Study of the Enforcement of the Ontario Safe Streets Act." *Canadian Public Policy/Analyse de Politiques* 39(4): 541–58. http://doi.org /10.3138/CPP.39.4.541.

Ontario Ministry of Municipal Affairs and Housing. 2010. *Building Foundations: Building Futures: Ontario's Long-Term Affordable Housing Strategy.* Toronto.

Ontario Non-Profit Housing Association. 2011. *Timeline: A History of Social Housing in Ontario.* Toronto: Ontario Non-Profit Housing Assocation.

Ontario PC. 1995. "The Common Sense Revolution: Common Sense. For a Chance."

Owusu-Bempah, Akwasi. 2017. "Race and Policing in Historical Context: Dehumanization and the Policing of Black People in the 21st Century." *Theoretical Criminology* 21(1): 23–34. http://doi.org/10.1177/1362480616677493.

– 2021. "Understanding the Impact of Racism, Colonialism, and Poverty on Canada's Criminal Justice System." Maytree Foundation, 21 July.

https://maytree.com/publications/understanding-the-impact-of-racism
-colonialism-and-poverty-on-canadas-criminal-justice-system.

Owusu-Bempah, Akwasi, et al. 2014. "Years of Life Lost to Incarceration: Inequities between Aboriginal and Non-Aboriginal Canadians." *BMC Public Health* 14(1): 585. https://doi.org/10.1186%2F1471-2458-14-585.

Oxford, Dion. 2018. "Homes, Jobs, and Friends." In *Beyond Shelters: Solutions to Homelessness in Canada from the Front Lines*, edited by James Hughes, 112–27. Toronto: James Lorimer.

Pablo, Carlito. 2009. "Little Mountain Housing Project Moves Closer to Demolition." *Georgia Straight*, 3 June. http://www.straight.com/article -227898/housing-project-moves-closer-demolition.

Pagliaro, Jennifer. 2017. "City on Hook for $1.6 Billion to Fix Crumbling Public Housing | The Star." *The Toronto Star*, 28 September. https://www .thestar.com/news/city_hall/2017/09/28/city-on-hook-for-16-billion-to -fix-crumbling-public-housing.html.

Palier, Bruno. 2005. "Ambiguous Agreement, Cumulative Change: French Social Policy in the 1990s." In *Beyond Continuity: Institutional Change in Advanced Political Economies*, edited by Wolfgang Streeck and Kathleen Thelen, 127–44. Oxford: Oxford University Press.

Papillon, Martin. 2009. "Adapting Federalism: Indigenous Multilevel Governance in Canada and the United States." *Publius: The Journal of Federalism* 42: 289–312. http://doi.org/10.2307/41441083.

Paquet, Mireille, and Robert Schertzer. 2020. "COVID-19 as a Complex Intergovernmental Problem." *Canadian Journal of Political Science / Revue canadienne de science politique* 53(2): 343–47. https://doi.org/10.1017 %2FS0008423920000281.

Paradis, Emily. 2014. "Can Activists and Managers Work Together to End Homelessness?" Toronto: The Homeless Hub.

– 2016. "Outliers Within: Claiming Discursive Space at National Homelessness Conferences in Canada." *Social Inclusion* 4(4): 97–107. http:// doi.org/10.17645/si.v4i4.670.

Paré, Isabelle. 2015. "Montréal réclame les pleins pouvoirs pour agir sur la situation du logement." *Le Devoir*, 15 September. http://www .ledevoir.com/politique/montreal/450106/logement-social-montreal -reclame-les-pleins-pouvoirs-pour-agir-sur-la-situation-du-logement (11 March 2016).

Patton, Michael Quinn. 2002. *Qualitative Research and Evaluation Methods*, 3rd ed. Oxford: SAGE.

Paulsen, Monte. 2006. "The Tyee – Mayor Sullivan's Big Ambitions." *The Tyee*, 21 December. http://thetyee.ca/News/2006/12/21/CivilCity.

– 2007. "Dobell Homeless Plan Stalled." *The Tyee*, 5 June. http://thetyee.ca /News/2007/06/05/DobellHomelessPlan.

– 2008a. "Robertson Puts HEAT on Vancouver Homelessness." *The Tyee*,
9 December. http://thetyee.ca/Blogs/TheHook/Housing/2008/12/09
/RobertsonHEAT.

– 2008b. "Vision Promotes 'Housing First,' NPA Proposes Pre-Fab Homes."
The Tyee, 10 November. http://thetyee.ca/Blogs/TheHook
/Housing/2008/11/10/MayoralHomelessPlans.

Pearce, Matthew. 2018. "Agent of Social Integration." In *Beyond Shelters:
Solutions to Homelessness in Canada from the Front Lines*, edited by James
Hughes, 81–99. Toronto: Lorimer.

Perras, Floyd. 2004. "Re: Comments on Proposed City Homelessness
Strategy." Submission to city cconsultations, Calgary.

Peters, Evelyn, ed. 2012. *Urban Aboriginal Policy Making in Canadian
Municipalities*. Montreal and Kingston: McGill-Queen's University Press.
https://www.mqup.ca/urban-aboriginal-policy-making-in-canadian
-municipalities-products-9780773539488.php.

Piat, Myra, et al. 2015. "Pathways into Homelessness: Understanding
How Both Individual and Structural Factors Contribute to and Sustain
Homelessness in Canada." *Urban Studies* 52(13): 2366–82. http://doi.org
/10.1177/0042098014548138.

Plante, Caroline. 2016. "Montreal Gets Metropolis Status, with More Building
and Property Powers." *The Gazette* (Montreal), 8 December. http://
montrealgazette.com/news/local-news/montreal-gets-metropolis
-status-with-more-building-and-property-powers.

PMO (Pime Minister's Office). 2020. "New Rapid Housing Initiative to Create
up to 3,000 New Homes for Canadians" (press release), 27 October. https://
pm.gc.ca/en/news/news-releases/2020/10/27/new-rapid-housing
-initiative-create-3000-new-homes-canadians.

Policy and Planning Social Research Unit. 2004. "Biennial Count of Homeless
Persons in Calgary: Enumerated in Emergency and Transitional Facilities,
by Service Agencies, and On the Streets." Calgary.

Pomeroy, Steve, and Nick Falvo. 2013. "Housing Policy in Canada under the
Harper Regime." In *How Ottawa Spends 2013–2014*, edited by Christopher Stoney
and G. Bruce Doern. Montreal and Kingston: McGill-Queen's University Press.

Preston, Valerie, et al. 2009. "Immigrants and Homelessness: At Risk in
Canada's Outer Suburbs." *The Canadian Geographer / Le Géographe canadien*
53(3): 288–304. http://doi.org/10.1111/j.1541-0064.2009.00264.x.

Prince, Michael J. 2009. *Absent Citizens: Disability Politics and Policy in Canada*.
Toronto: University of Toronto Press.

– 2015. "Shelter and the Street: Housing, Homelessness, and Social Assistance
in the Canadian Provinces." In *Welfare Reform in Canada*, edited by Daniel
Béland and Pierre-Marc Daigneault. Toronto: University of Toronto Press.

Province of British Columbia. 2019. *TogetherBC: British Columbia's Poverty
Reduction Strategy*. Victoria.

Qaqqaq, Mumilaaq. 2021. *Sick of Waiting: A Report on Nunavut's Housing Crisis.*

Queen, Lisa. 2010. "Linda's Walk Remembers Homeless Woman Who Died in Gas Station." *Toronto.com*, 28 July. https://www.toronto.com/news-story/54275 -linda-s-walk-remembers-homeless-woman-who-died-in-gas-station.

Rabinovitch, Hannah, Bernadette Pauly, and Jinhui Zhao. 2016. "Assessing Emergency Shelter Patterns to Inform Community Solutions to Homelessness." *Housing Studies* 31(8): 984–97. https://doi.org/10.1080 /02673037.2016.1165801.

Ranasinghe, Prashan. 2017. *Helter-Shelter: Security, Legality, and an Ethic of Care in an Emergency Shelter.* Toronto: University of Toronto Press.

RAPSIM (Réseau de'aide aux personnes seules et itinérantes de Montréal). 2009. *Pour une politique plus qu'un plan d'action en itinérance.* Montreal. http://www.rapsim.org/102/Politiqueeeneitinerance.montreal.

– 2012. *L'itinérance: Une histoire et des actions pour en sortir.*

– 2013a. "Budget Fédéral 2013 – Le RSIQ dénonce l'orientation en itinérance." Montreal.

– 2013b. *Campagne du RSIQ: Mobilisons-nous pour le maintien de la SPLI communautaire et généraliste au Québec!* Montreal.

– 2013c. *Financement fédéral – les groupes en itinerance tirent la sonnette d'alarme!* Montreal.

– 2014. "Position du RAPSIM sur le mouvement pour mettre fin à l'itinérance (MMFIM)." Montreal.

– 2016. *L'itinérance à Montréal: Au-delà des chiffres.* Montreal.

– 2019a. "LE RAPSIM." *Historique: Quelques jalons d'histoire.* http://rapsim .org/le-rapsim.

– 2019b. "LE RAPSIM." *Actions gouvernementales.* http://rapsim.org/le-rapsim.

– 2019c. *Plan d'action 2019–2020.* Montreal.

Refresh Steering Committee. 2019. "Enough for All 2.0." Calgary.

Régie régionale de la santé et des services sociaux de Montréal. 2003. "Plan communautaire: Régie régionale de la santé et des services sociaux de Montréal." Montreal: FOHM.

Rice, James, and Michael Prince. 2013. *Changing Politics of Canadian Social Policy*, 2nd ed. Toronto: University of Toronto Press.

Richter, Tim. 2020. "Recovery for All Campaign Strategy Session." Presented at Calgary Homeless Foundation. https://www.youtube.com/watch?v =XYTbMqStRWo

– 2021. "Recovery for All Final Strategy Session." Presented at the Calgary Homeless Foundation. https://www.youtube.com/watch?v =ZEE0kG9qb7I&t=132s.

Roberts, Terry. 2004. "Re: Proposed City of Calgary Homelessness Strategy." Toronto: The Homeless Hub.

Robertson, Gregor. 2008a. "Inauguration Address." https://vancouver.ca /files/cov/Mayor-Gregor-Robertson-2008-inaugural-speech.pdf.

– 2008b. "Robertson Promises Mental Health Advocate, More Rental Housing." *The Tyee*, 22 October. http://thetyee.ca/Blogs/TheHook/Housing /2008/10/22/gregor-robertson-homelessness-debate.

– 2015. "Letter to the Honourable Christy Clark."

Robichaud, Olivier. 2018. "Divorce entre organismes voués à l'itinérance." *HuffPost Québec*, 12 April. https://quebec.huffingtonpost.ca/2018/04/12/mesentante -sur-les-priorites-entre-organismes-voues-a-litinerance_a_23410087.

Rocher, François. 2009. "The Quebec–Canada Dynamic or the Negation of the Ideal of Federalism." In *Contemporary Canadian Federalism: Foundations, Traditions, Institutions*, edited by Alain-G. Gagnon, 81–130. Toronto: University of Toronto Press.

Rocher, François, and Patrick Fafard. 2013. "Is There a Political Culture of Federalism in Canada? Charting an Unexplored Territory." In *The Global Promise of Federalism*, edited by Grace Skogstad, David Cameron, Martin Papillon, and Keith Banting, 43–68. Toronto: University of Toronto Press.

Rook, John. 2004. "Re: Proposed City of Calgary Homelessness Plan." Calgary: City of Calgary.

– 2018. "A New Model of Care." In *Beyond Shelters: Solutions to Homelessness in Canada from the Front Lines*, edited by James Hughes, 161–76. Toronto: James Lorimer.

Rose, Albert. 1980. *Canadian Housing Policies (1935–1980)*. Oxford: Butterworths.

Saint-Arnaud, Pierre. 2015a. "L'entente Canada-Québec sur l'itinérance confirme les priorités fédérales." *Le Devoir*, 21 March. https://www .ledevoir.com/politique/canada/435151/l-entente-canada-quebec-sur-l -itinerance-confirme-les-priorites-federales

– 2015b. "Lutte contre l'itinérance: Québec a cédé aux exigences d'Ottawa." *La Presse*, 15 March. http://www.lapresse.ca/actualites/national/201503/15/01-4852332-lutte-contre-litinerance-quebec-a-cede-aux-exigences-dottawa.php.

Schiff, Jeannette Waegemakers, Rebecca Schiff, and Alina Turner. 2016. "Rural Homelessness in Western Canada: Lessons Learned from Diverse Communities." *Social Inclusion* 4(4): 73–85. http://doi.org/10.17645/si.v4i4.633.

Schiff, Jeannette Waegemakers, and Alina Turner. 2014. *Housing First in Rural Canada: Rural Homelessness and Housing First Feasibility across 22 Canadian Communities*. Toronto: The Homeless Hub.

Scott, Marian. 2019. "Proposed Bylaw Aims to Fix Affordable Housing Dilemma in Montreal." *The Gazette* (Montreal), 12 June. https:// montrealgazette.com/news/local-news/city-presents-housing-bylaw.

– 2020. "Plante Makes Passionate Plea as City Council Debates Social Housing Bylaw." *The Gazette* (M ontreal), 17 November. https://montrealgazette .com/news/local-news/montreal-passes-housing-plan.

Scott, Susan. 2012. *The Beginning of the End: The Story of the Calgary Homeless Foundation*. Calgary: Calgary Homeless Foundation.

Severs, Sandra, and Ric Matthews. 2011. "Criticism of Low-Barrier Shelter 'Superficial': First United." *The Tyee*, 16 December. http://thetyee.ca /Opinion/2011/12/16/First-United-Shelter.

Shapcott, Michael. 2001. *The Ontario Alternative Budget 2001*. Toronto: Canadian Centre for Policy Alternatives.

– 2007. *Ten Things You Should Know about Housing and Homelessness*. Toronto: Wellesley Institute.

– 2011. "Affidavit of Michael Shapcott." Ontario Superior Court of Justice.

Sheffield, Lin. 2009. "Homeless Shelters a Magnet for Mayhem in False Creek North." *Vancouver Sun*, 22 June. http://www.vancouversun.com/news /Homeless+shelters+magnet+mayhem+False+Creek+North/1818177 /story.html.

Shelter, Support Housing, and Administration. 2014. *Housing Stability Service Planning Framework*. Toronto: City of Toronto.

– 2018. *Toronto 2018 Budget*. Toronto.

Simpson, Leanne Betasamosake. 2021. *As We Have Always Done: Indigenous Freedom through Radical Resistance*. Minneapolis: University of Minnesota Press.

Singh, Sandra. 2021. "Alternatives to Homeless Count amid COVID-19 Pandemic." 8 February. City of Vancouver.

Skogstad, Grace. 2003. "Who Governs? Who Should Govern? Political Authority and Legitimacy in the Twenty-First Century." *Canadian Journal of Political Science / Revue canadienne de science politique* 36(5): 955–73. http://doi.org/10.1017/S0008423903778925.

Smart, Amy. 2019. "Vancouver Mayor Blames Ottawa for Continued Growth of Homelessness in City." *CTVNews*, 12 June.

Smith, Alison. 2015. "Can We Compare Homelessness across the Atlantic?" *European Journal of Homelessness* 9(2): 111–36.

Smith, Alison, and Anna Kopec. 2021. "Mapping Research on Homelessness in Canada." Paper presented at the Annual Conference of the Canadian Political Science Association, 4 June, Ottawa.

Smith, Alison, and Zachary Spicer. 2018. "The Local Autonomy of Canada's Largest Cities." *Urban Affairs Review* 54(5): 931–61. http://doi.org/10.1177 /1078087416684380.

Société d'habitation du Québec. 1992. *La société d'habitation du Québec: Une histoire en trois mouvements*. Quebec City: Gouvernement du Québec.

– 1997. *L'action gouvernementale en habitation: Orientation et plan d'action*. Quebec City: Gouvernement du Québec.

– 2017. *L'habitation à cœur depuis 50 ans 1967 à 2017*. Quebec City: Gouvernement du Québec.

SPARC BC. 2005. "On Our Streets and in Our Shelters ... Results of the 2005 Greater Vancouver Homeless Count." Vancouver.

– 2011. *Knowledge for Action: Hidden Homelessness in Prince George, Kamloops, Kelowna, Nelson, and Nanaimo.* Vancouver: Social Planning and Research Council of BC.

Springer, Amira. 2021. *"Living in Colour: Racialized Housing Discrimination in Canada."* Toronto: The Homeless Hub.

Star Editorial Board. 2018. "Ontario Badly Botches Affordable Housing Policy." *Toronto Star*, 26 January. https://www.thestar.com/opinion/editorials /2018/01/26/ontario-badly-botches-affordable-housing-policy.html.

Statistics Canada. 2001. "Population and Dwelling Counts, for Canada and Census Subdivisions (Municipalities) with 5,000-plus Population, 2001 and 1996 Censuses." Ottawa.

– 2016. *Population and Dwelling Count Highlight Tables, 2016 Census.* Ottawa.

Stewart, Kennedy. 2018. "Kennedy Stewart Releases Latest Campaign Donations Disclosure." 21 June. https://www.kennedystewart.ca/kennedy _stewart_releases_latest_campaign_donations_disclosure.

Streetohome Foundation. 2008. *Streetohome Vancouver.* Vancouver: City of Vancouver.

– 2010. "A High Price to Pay: Community Action on Homelessness." Vancouver.

Stueck, Wendy. 2011. "A Night at Downtown Eastside's 'Ghetto Mansion.'" *Globe and Mail*, 7 December. https://www.theglobeandmail.com/news /british-columbia/a-night-at-downtown-eastsides-ghetto-mansion /article4085572.

Suttor, Gregory. 2016. *Still Renovating: A History of Canadian Social Housing Policy.* Montreal and Kingston: McGill-Queen's University Press.

Sylvestre, Marie-Eve. 2019. *Red Zones: Criminal Law and the Territorial Governance of Marginalized People.* Cambridge: Cambridge University Press.

Taylor, Juanita. 2020. "Northern First Nation Sees New Housing Strategy as a Way to 'Take Back Sovereignty.'" *CBC Radio News*, 28 November. https://www.cbc .ca/radio/thehouse/yellowknives-dene-first-nation-housing-1.5818157.

TDRC (Toronto Disaster Relief Committee). 1998. "National Disaster Declaration." *TDRC Online.*

The Guardian. 2019. "Los Angeles Homeless Population Hits 36,000 in Dramatic Rise," 4 June. http://www.theguardian.com/us-news/2019/jun /04/los-angeles-homeless-population-city-county.

THHSPF. 2018. "Toronto Housing and Homelessness Service Planning Forum." Presented at the Toronto.

Thistle, Jesse. 2017. *Indigenous Definition of Homelessness.* Toronto: Canadian Observatory on Homelessness Press.

– 2019. *From the Ashes: My Story of Being Métis, Homeless, and Finding My Way.* Toronto: Simon and Schuster.

Thompson, Debra. 2016. *The Schematic State: Race, Transnationalism, and the Politics of the Census.* New York: Cambridge University Press.

ThreeHive Consulting. 2017. "2016 Alberta Point-in-Time Count of Homelessness." Prepared for 7 Cities on Housing and Homelessness. Calgary: Seven Cities on Housing and Homelessness.

Torgersen, Ulf. 1987. "Housing: The Wobbly Pillar under the Welfare State." *Scandinavian Housing and Planning Research* 4(1): 116–26. https://doi.org/10.1080/02815737 1987.10801428.

Toronto Board of Trade. 2000. "Building Solutions to Homelessness: A Business Perspective on Homelessness and Toronto's Housing Crisis." Toronto.

Trampusch, Christine, and Bruno Palier. 2016. "Between X and Y: How Process Tracing Contributes to Opening the Black Box of Causality." *New Political Economy* 21(5): 437–54. https://doi.org/10.1080/13563467.2015.1134465.

TRC (Truth and Reconciliation Commission of Canada). 2015. *Honouring the Truth, Reconciling for the Future.* Ottawa.

Trocmé, Nico, Della Knoke, and Cindy Blackstock. 2004. "Pathways to the Overrepresentation of Aboriginal Children in Canada's Child Welfare System." *Social Service Review* 78(4): 577–600.

Tsemberis, Sam, and Vicky Stergiopoulos. 2014. "How the Federal Government Plans to End Homelessness." *Toronto Star*, 30 April. https://www.thestar.com/opinion/commentary/2013/04/30/how_the_federal _government_plans_to_end_homelessness.html.

Turner, Alina. 2015. *2014 Alberta Point-in-Time Homeless Count: Provincial Report.* Calgary: Seven Cities on Housing and Homelessness.

Turner, Alina, Tom Albanese, and Kyle Pakeman. 2017. "Discerning 'Functional and Absolute Zero': Defining and Measuring an End to Homelessness." Calgary: School of Public Policy.

Turner, Alina, Victoria Ballance, and Joel Sinclair. 2018. *Our Living Legacy: Calgary's 10 Year Plan to End Homelessness Collective Impact Report.* Canada: The Homeless Hub.

Turner Strategies. 2018. *2018 Alberta Point-in-Time Homeless Count: Technical Report.* Calgary: 7 Cities on Housing and Homelessness.

Vaillancourt, Yves, and Marie-Noëlle Ducharme. 2001. "Social Housing – a Key Component of Social Policies in Transformation: The Quebec Experience." Toronto: Maytree Foundation.

Vaillancourt, Yves, Marie-Noëlle Ducharme, François Aubry, and Stéphane Grenier. 2016. *AccèsLogic Québec (1997–2015): Les Hauts et Les Bas de La Con-Construction d'une Politique Publique.* Quebec City: Centre de recherche sur les innovations sociales.

Vancouver Sun. 2008. "Homeless Man Dies from Accidental Burns," 5 February. http://www.canada.com/vancouversun/news/story .html?id=67557a46-a821-4a90-bfb6-fa30391fab81&k=58603.

Ville de Montréal. 2008a. *Commission du conseil municipal sur Le développement culturel et la qualité du milieu de vie.* Montreal.

– 2008b. "Montréal's Inclusionary Housing Strategy: A Progress Report."
– 2009. *Agir résolument pour contrer l'itinérance.* Montreal.
– 2014. *Parce que la rue es tune impasse: Plan d'action Montréalais en itinérance 2014–2017.* Montreal.
– 2018. "Parce que la rue a différents visages: Plan d'action montréalais en itinérance 2018–2020." City of Montreal.
Voth, Daniel. 2020. "'Descendants of the Original Lords of the Soil': Indignation, Disobedience, and Women Who Jig on Sundays." *Native American and Indigenous Studies* 7(2): 87–113.
Walia, Harsha, et al. 2020. "Immediate Municipal and Provincial Ban on Police Street Checks."
Wallner, Jennifer. 2010. "Beyond National Standards: Reconciling Tension between Federalism and the Welfare State." *Publius: The Journal of Federalism* 40(4): 646–71.
– 2014. *Learning to School: Federalism and Public Schooling in Canada.* Toronto: University of Toronto Press.
Webster, Andrew. 2007. *Sheltering Urban Aboriginal Homeless People: Assessment of Situation and Needs.* Ottawa: National Association of Friendship Centres.
Willison, Charley. 2021. *Ungoverned and Out of Sight: Public Health and the Political Crisis of Homelessness in the United States.* Oxford and New York: Oxford University Press.
Winter, Jesse. 2021. "Vancouver Works to Close Strathcona Park Tent Encampment." *Globe and Mail*, 255 April. https://www.theglobeandmail.com/canada/british-columbia/article-vancouver-works-to-close-strathcona-park-tent-encampment.
Wilson-Raybould, Jody. 2019. "Each of Us, in Our Own Way, Is a Hiligax̱te.'"
Withers, A.J. 2021. *Fight to Win: Inside Poor People's Organizing.* Toronto: Fernwood.
Wolfe, Jeanne M. 1998. "Canadian Housing Policy in the Nineties." *Housing Studies* 13(1): 121–34. https://doi.org/10.1080/02673039883524.
Yesno, Riley, and Xicotencatl Maher Lopez. 2020. "Four Case Studies of Land Back in Action." 10 September. *Briarpatch Magazine.*
Young, Robert. 2012. "Conclusion." In *Urban Aboriginal Policy Making in Canadian Municipalities*, edited by Evelyn J. Peters, 202–28. Montreal and Kingston: McGill-Queen's University Press. http://myaccess.library.utoronto.ca/login?url=http://books.scholarsportal.info/viewdoc.html?id=/ebooks/ebooks3/upress/2013-08-23/1/9780773587441.

Index

consultations, 167; history of, 175–6; and Mangano, 176–7; and NHI/HPS funding, 187–91; as powerful, 181; and private sector committee, 180; and province responsibility, 178; ten-year plan to end homelessness, 169, 172–3, 182–3, 184–8. *See also* private sector

Calls to Action (TRC), 191

Campbell, Gordon, 108, 109, 110, 132

Campbell, Larry, 119–20

Canada Health and Social Transfer (CHST), 53–4

Canadian Alliance to End Homelessness (CAEH): overview, 77–8, 94–102, 103–4; conferences, 74, 100–2, 218; and definition of homelessness, 31, 91; and MMFIM, 257; networks of, 310n4

Canadian Homelessness Research Network (CHRN), 28, 33, 67, 91

Canadian Lived Experience Leadership Network, 99–100

Canadian Observatory on Homelessness, 31

case overview, 7–14

Castellano, Marlene Brant, 41

causality, 64

chapter one overview, 25–6

Charest, Jean, 316n4

charities, 99

children: babies born in shelters, 47–8; child care, 56; homelessness as shocking, 3; homelessness in Calgary, 186; number in shelters, 45; poverty in Ontario, 199, 200; queer youth, 5; youth in Alberta, 162. *See also* residential "schools"

Chrétien, Jean, 79

Christiansen, Kathy, 181

chronic homelessness: and City of Vancouver, 34; defining,

27, 91, 139; vs. episodic and hidden, 239; federal impact on, 7; housing in Vancouver, 111; as increasing, 44–5, 309n17; intergovernment alignment and impact, 7; and MMFIM, 253–4, 317nn19–20; as new issue, 36; and PCC in Vancouver, 123–4; and RAPSIM, 254, 255; and typologies, 32, 34. *See also* Housing First

City of Calgary (government): overview, 193; Ad Hoc Committee on Homelessness, 173–4; affordable housing, 170–1; and CHF ten-year plan, 169, 172–3; Corporate Affordable Housing Strategy, 166–7; counts of homeless people, 12, 67, 164–6, 168–9, 183–4; engagement as minimal, 164; as involved, 164; and shelter funding, 166–9, 172

City of Montreal (government): overview, 262–3; affordable housing, 248; Comité de liaison en itinérance, 245–6, 316n8; counts of homeless people, 67, 74, 247, 249, 254, 259–60; guided by liaison committee, 11; inclusionary zoning, 248; increasing involvement, 246; learning from Toronto, 244; policy on homelessness, 243–5; and provincial relationship, 249–50; RHI, 243, 251; *Towards a Municipal Policy for the Homeless*, 244–5; 20-20-20 policy, 248

City of Toronto (government): overview, 13–14, 201–2; affordable housing, 1 97–8, 204, 315n7; co-governance, 202, 210–11; counts of homeless people, 67, 208;

Studies in Comparative Political Economy and Public Policy

Printed and bound by CPI Group (UK) Ltd, Croydon, CR0 4YY

16/04/2025

14658336-0003